INTERVENTION!

D1247939

Other books by JOHN S. D. EISENHOWER:

The Bitter Woods

Strictly Personal

Letters to Mamie (ed.)

Allies: Pearl Harbor to D-Day

So Far from God:
The United States War with Mexico

INTERVENTION!

****

The United States and
the Mexican Revolution
1913–1917

****

JOHN S. D. EISENHOWER

W · W · NORTON & COMPANY
New York   London

Copyright © 1993 by John S. D. Eisenhower

All rights reserved
Printed in the United States of America
First published as a Norton paperback 1995

The text of this book is composed in Trump Mediaeval
with the display set in Novarese.
Composition and manufacturing by The Haddon Craftsmen, Inc.
Book design and cartography by Jacques Chazaud.

Library of Congress Cataloging-in-Publication Data

Eisenhower, John S. D., 1922–
Intervention! : the United States and the Mexican Revolution,
1913–1917 / John S.D. Eisenhower.
p. cm.
Includes bibliographical references and index.
1. Mexico—History—Revolution, 1910–1920.   2. Mexico—Foreign
relations—United States.   3. United States—Foreign relations—Mexico.
4. Veracruz Llave (Mexico)—History—American occupation, 1914.
5. United States.   Army—History—Punitive Expedition, 1916.
I. Title.
F1234.E32   1993
972.08'16—dc20   93-12852

ISBN 0-393-31318-2

W. W. Norton & Company, Inc., 500 Fifth Avenue, New York, N.Y. 10110
W. W. Norton & Company Ltd., 10 Coptic Street, London WC1A 1PU

2 3 4 5 6 7 8 9 0

99.431

peterson

gift

5-26-99

To Joanne

CONTENTS

****

	List of Maps	*ix*
	Introduction	*xi*
	Prologue	*3*
1	Assassination	*7*
2	Uprising	*10*
3	"I Have Overthrown This Government"	*19*
4	Watchful Waiting	*30*
5	First Chief	*38*
6	The Return of Pancho Villa	*46*
7	Huerta Agonistes	*60*
8	The Benton Affair	*69*
9	The Tampico Incident	*79*
10	The Landing at Veracruz	*109*
11	The Clouds of War	*125*

12   The Fall of Victoriano Huerta   *139*

13   The Convention at Aguascalientes   *151*

14   Villa's and Zapata's Reign of Terror   *165*

15   Carranza by Default   *175*

16   Blood on the Border   *187*

17   Villa Raids Columbus   *217*

18   "You Will Promptly Organize . . ."   *228*

19   Pancho Villa's Narrow Escape   *241*

20   Colonia Dublán   *251*

21   Gunfight at Parral   *260*

22   To the Brink   *276*

23   Carrizal   *288*

24   Exit the United States   *301*

25   The Triumph of Obregón   *308*

     Epilogue   *321*

     APPENDIX A: Sequence of Events, Mexican Revolution
        1910–1917   *329*

     APPENDIX B: Visiting Points of Interest   *337*

     APPENDIX C: The Plan of Guadalupe   *343*

     NOTES   *345*

     BIBLIOGRAPHY   *373*

     ACKNOWLEDGMENTS   *379*

     INDEX   *381*

Photographs follow pages 82 and 192

LIST OF MAPS

****

Mexico City in 1913   *13*

The Rise of Pancho Villa, 1913   *49*

Veracruz, 1914   *112*

The Battle of Celaya, April 6–15, 1915   *178*

Full Circle. The Last Campaign of the Division of the North   *190*

Columbus, New Mexico, 1916   *220*

Route of the Punitive Expedition,
     March 1916–February 1917   *244*

Reconnaissance to Villa Ahumada via Carrizal, June 1916,
     and Battle of Carrizal, June 21, 1916   *296*

INTRODUCTION

****

Between 1910 and 1920, the Republic of Mexico underwent the great upheaval commonly known as the Mexican Revolution. The Revolution shook the nation to its roots, touching every citizen. During that decade, an estimated one million people died, victims of violence, devastation, and the disruption of Mexican society.

The Mexico that emerged from those years of revolution, however, had attained a new identity. The privileges of the wealthy, while still too great, had at least been reduced. Mexican soldiers, both Federal and revolutionary, had seen parts of Mexico far away from their homes, creating an increased feeling of the individual's relationship to the whole country. Mexico's new constitution, drawn up to consolidate revolutionary gains in 1917, proclaimed economic independence from those foreign powers that had freely exploited Mexico's resources in the past. For these reasons, the Revolution is universally considered the single most significant event in Mexico's history.

Though the Revolution was an internal Mexican affair, it was not always so viewed by the world's powers, especially by the United States, which shared two thousand miles of open border with Mexico. The industrial nations had great investments in Mexico, especially in mining, and other powers, primarily European, looked to the United

States to care for all their interests. The "Colossus of the North," in fact, had taken a proprietary interest in Mexico ever since it had attained independence from Spain in 1821.*

As the Mexican Revolution developed, the United States could not resist a temptation to meddle. Usually, the moves were diplomatic, but on at least two occasions President Woodrow Wilson intervened by force of arms. Either of those interventions could have caused war between the two countries, and quite possibly Mexico would have declared war had it not been so helpless. But though war was avoided, the American interventions were still unfortunate. They contributed nothing to the welfare of either country and left a legacy of resentment in the hearts of the Mexicans. This book addresses such questions as why those interventions were ordered, how they were conducted, and how they were brought to an end.

As of 1910, the Republic of Mexico was in reality a dictatorship, ruled arbitrarily since 1877 by General José de la Cruz Porfirio Díaz. Díaz had attained prominence as a successful commander under the national hero Benito Juárez, and he exploited his well-earned laurels to attain the presidency of Mexico. Díaz remained in power almost continuously for those thirty-three years.

The Díaz regime was beneficial to Mexico at first. A strong and decisive leader, Díaz provided Mexican society some much longed-for stability. Furthermore, he greatly strengthened Mexico's infrastructure—roads, industry, and public works—by making use of the best technical brains available, intellectuals and planners who came to be known as *científicos*. Under Díaz, this clique masterminded the so-called Mexican Miracle.

But through the thirty-three years of Díaz rule, both the president and his *científicos* became progressively more authoritarian and separated from the people they were meant to serve. As their ambitious public works required capital, they catered more and more to the interests of the rich and powerful, especially to the foreigners, who had such capital to provide. In so doing, they enriched their wealthy allies at the expense of the Mexican poor. The term *científicos* therefore lost its original favorable connotation and grew synonymous in the popular mind with oppression.

---

*The Mexicans like to date their independence from 1810, when a priest, Father Hidalgo y Costilla, proclaimed it. However, the Spanish crushed all rebellions until 1821. The United States sent a minister to Mexico City in 1825.

The dictatorship of Porfirio Díaz appeared invulnerable as late as 1910. In that year, the dignified old dictator hosted an elaborate state celebration marking the completion of a century of Mexican independence. The elite of the world attended his parades and galas. Díaz himself was toasted in lavish tributes.

Nevertheless, the Díaz regime had lost the support of the people, and the army, the source of its power, had grown soft. As a result, the whole structure collapsed with amazing ease only a year after the centennial celebration, the fall engineered by the one man who dared to oppose him: Francisco I. Madero. In late May 1911, Díaz boarded a ship bound for Spain, where he survived for a few, mournful years.

Madero, the thirty-seven-year-old leader of the revolution against Díaz, rode triumphantly into Mexico City on June 7, 1911, and in the autumn of that year was legally elected president. The Mexican Revolution had thus far been an unquestioned success. It had overthrown Díaz at minimum cost of lives and property.

President Madero, however, severely disappointed the people of Mexico. Though it would have been difficult for anyone to meet the high expectations of the peasants who had supported his revolt, he soon demonstrated that he lacked the drive to make even a good effort. Furthermore, he came under attack for nepotism, deemed excessive even in a country where such practice was common. What brought Madero down, however, was his almost mystical naïveté. He not only spared the lives of his political rivals; he left many in positions of power. His enemies rewarded his compassion with contempt rather than with gratitude. Madero was overthrown and murdered within thirteen months of assuming office.

The leader of the counterrevolution that deposed Madero in February 1913 was a friend and supporter of Porfirio Díaz named Victoriano Huerta. Huerta had been one of Madero's generals, despite his close affiliation with Díaz, and as a regular officer commanded the loyalty of much of the army. Most members of the foreign community in Mexico were willing to accept Huerta as the new Mexican dictator, and he might have survived in office save for his fatal mistake of murdering Madero a couple of nights after assuming power. Though he had been ineffective as a president, Madero was not hated; he attained a stature in death that he had never attained in life.

To add to Huerta's discomfiture, Madero's grisly murder was given great play in the press. So Madero's former followers, now infuriated, rebelled once more. Other chronic rebels joined in.

Mexico at that time was a nation of city-states, partly because of its mountainous terrain and partly because of its lack of a transportation system. As a result, the rebellions against Huerta were partly local in character, a mere asserting of power among the various warlords.* But three uprisings grew to national importance. One was the movement begun by Venustiano Carranza, governor of Coahuila. The second was launched in Chihuahua by Francisco ("Pancho") Villa, a former bandit who had held Madero in almost filial affection. The third was that of Emiliano Zapata, in the state of Morelos, just south of Mexico City.

At this time, the American public began to take a real interest in the Mexican situation. American investments, inviolate in the Díaz years, had not been deemed at risk by Díaz's overthrow. But the midnight murder of President Madero provided a piece of melodrama lacking in the Mexican scene for decades, and Americans were intrigued by the immediate reaction of the Mexicans. And one of the rebels, Pancho Villa, caught the imagination of certain segments of the American press, who were duped into thinking of him as a sort of Robin Hood, a selfless friend of the poor.

But the real impetus behind American involvement in Mexico came from the new occupant of the White House. Whereas President William Howard Taft had maintained a "hands off" policy in Mexican affairs, the newly inaugurated Woodrow Wilson was shocked by Huerta's manner of gaining power and therefore refused to recognize him as Mexico's president. At that point, the United States became involved.

At first, in 1913, Wilson and Secretary of State William Jennings Bryan confined their anti-Huerta efforts to marshaling moral pressure to force Huerta to resign. That approach proved ineffective, however, and in 1914 they used a flimsy pretext to justify more direct involvement. President Wilson sent the U.S. Atlantic Fleet to occupy Mexico's main seaport, Veracruz.

By the middle of 1914, Huerta had lost his hold on power in Mexico. The occupation of Veracruz contributed to his downfall, but only peripherally. The real cause was the series of military successes achieved by the forces of Carranza, Villa, and Zapata. In July, Huerta sailed from Mexico, like Díaz before him. And, as in the case of Díaz,

---

*Meanwhile, the more militant revolutionists had taken the field—Francisco Villa, the Herrera brothers, and Rosalío Hernández in Chihuahua, and Manuel Chao, Tomás Urbina, the Arrieta brothers, Calixto Contreras, and Orestes Pereyra in Durango. There were scattered uprisings in Sinaloa, Tepic, Colima, San Luis Potosí, Tamaulipas, Michoacán, and Guerrero. William Weber Johnson, *Heroic Mexico* (New York, 1968), p. 152.

the vice president took over power until elections could be arranged. Soon Mexico City was occupied by troops under Carranza's able general, Alvaro Obregón.

That moment, in mid-1914, saw Mexico's greatest tragedy. Venustiano Carranza and Pancho Villa, both difficult men, broke off relations with each other. Despite the efforts of a group of victorious generals to bring the leaders together, the revolutionaries who had defeated Huerta were soon fighting among themselves.

The year 1915 brought a bloody resolution to the rivalry. General Obregón, still Carranza's military commander, defeated Villa's Division of the North in four major battles, and by January of 1916 Villa had been toppled from the heights. Once Mexico's foremost military commander, Villa was reduced to the status of a bandit, which he had been in his youth.

In early 1916, Villa raided the New Mexico town of Columbus, partly out of a need for supplies and possibly to take revenge on an American government that had overtly helped his enemies bring about his downfall. This invasion of U.S. soil inflamed American public opinion. President Wilson succumbed reluctantly to the demand for action and sent the "Punitive Expedition" into Mexico to capture Villa.

The Punitive Expedition was an ill-conceived idea from the start. It had almost no chance of capturing Villa and nearly brought about war. General John J. Pershing, commander of the Punitive Expedition, was ordered to withdraw across the border between Mexico and the United States in early 1917, after spending nearly eleven months in the field. Two months later, the United States declared war against the kaiser's imperial Germany.

Under the new Mexican constitution drawn up in early 1917, Venustiano Carranza began a four-year term as president. Again, however, Mexico's leader misused his power. Carranza was ousted and murdered. When Alvaro Obregón was inaugurated president, in late 1920, the large-scale violence ended, and the Mexican Revolution was complete.

I am often asked why I selected the Mexican Revolution as a subject on which to spend a period of years. One can never explain such decisions fully; one can offer only partial explanations.

For one thing, I have always felt a personal association with this episode in American history. When General Pershing was sent into

Mexico in early 1916, nearly the entire U.S. Army was mobilized along the Mexican border. My father, a new second lieutenant of infantry, was sent to Fort Sam Houston, Texas, where he met his future wife, my mother, who was wintering in nearby San Antonio. Though my father was not sent into Mexico as a member of the Punitive Expedition, the prospects of his immediate departure gave an excuse for an early wedding, much to the discomfiture of my appearance-conscious Victorian grandparents. Villa, or at least the pursuit of Villa, was always a conversation piece in the Eisenhower household.

I was later attracted to writing about Mexico when I came to appreciate the importance of Mexican-American relations. No other subject of comparable importance, in my opinion, has been so neglected and so misunderstood. Therefore, when I finished writing an account of the U.S.–Mexican War of 1846–48 (*So Far from God*, 1989), I decided to investigate the American incursions of 1914 (Veracruz) and 1916 (Punitive Expedition) as logical sequels to what I had already written.

There are, of course, some similarities between these two periods in our history, though they are separated by about seventy years. One difference, however, I found striking. The U.S. march from Veracruz to Mexico City in 1847 was engineered by an avowed disciple of American expansionism, President James K. Polk. But the Veracruz occupation and the Punitive Expedition were ordered by a man truly dedicated to peace, President Woodrow Wilson. This seeming irony—of an idealistic liberal acting the jingo—so intrigued me that I considered trying my hand at an in-depth study of Wilson. I soon realized the impracticability of such a project, for many reasons.

At the same time, though, I came to understand that the U.S. interventions, no matter how misguided, had been brought about largely by the chaotic situation then existing in Mexico. Most accounts of that situation are not simple enough to be understood by the general reader. I therefore decided to study the conditions existing in Mexico during 1914 and 1916, in an effort to justify, or at least explain, American actions.

It might be well to say a word about some of the main characters that appear on these pages, since virtually all of them, especially the Mexicans, are unknown to the American reading public. Personalities, always a strong influence on the course of events, played a critical role in the outcome of the Mexican Revolution. The break that occurred between Carranza and Villa in late 1914—and that cost Mexico so dearly—might well have been averted. Different personalities might have done better. Other examples abound: the ambitions of Huerta and the split between Carranza and Obregón in 1919, to name only two.

By all odds, the most colorful of the revolutionary figures was General Francisco ("Pancho") Villa, a man of penetrating intelligence who, had he possessed any degree of self-restraint, might have become one of Mexico's greatest leaders. For all his grave flaws, this nearly illiterate man developed into a first-class fighting general. For a few months, in late 1914 and early 1915, Villa and his powerful Division of the North seemed invincible. But Villa never learned to control his passions and appetites. His principal biographer remarked, "Villa . . . had more of a jaguar about him than a man. A jaguar tamed, for the moment, for our [the revolutionaries'] work, or for what we believed was our work; a jaguar whose back we stroked with trembling hand, fearful that at any moment a paw might strike out at us."

A rival to Villa as Mexico's most successful military leader—and eventually Villa's nemesis—was Alvaro Obregón, a civilian-soldier from Sonora. Though late in coming on the scene—he took no part in Madero's overthrow of Porfirio Díaz—Obregón owed much of his prominence to his political acumen and organizational ability. The practical Obregón gradually became aware of his differences with Carranza but at the same time recognized Carranza's worth to the Revolution as a political leader. He therefore remained loyal to Carranza (by and large) throughout the period of U.S. involvement in Mexico. As a man considered trustworthy as well as capable, Obregón played an increasingly important role in all things military and political during the Revolution.

The most important figure of the Mexican Revolution, however, was the self-styled "First Chief" of the Constitutionalist movement, Venustiano Carranza. Either Villa or Obregón could have served as the Revolution's single military chief, but Carranza held the movement together, particularly when it came to maintaining Mexico's dignity before the outside world.

Such a judgment is far from welcome to the American reader, since Carranza's nature—pompous, ambitious, devious, and cold—holds little appeal. Yet Carranza triumphed over his rivals because of his political acuity, which led to his policy of unswerving hostility to the United States, an immensely popular stand in Mexico.

Generally, Carranza preferred to let others do his fighting for him, but he could show both physical and moral courage when the situation demanded. When necessary, he could undergo physical hardships in taking the field, even though his advanced age (fifty-five years) might have excused him had he chosen to see primarily to his own physical comfort. Ironically, Carranza's finest moment was his last, when he and his few remaining followers were being set upon by assassins. At that moment, he urged his friends to leave him behind and save themselves.

Next to Pancho Villa's, the Mexican name most familiar to Americans is that of Emiliano Zapata. In many ways, Zapata resembled Villa: they were both recognized by their admirers as the "true revolutionaries," the real "friends of the poor." Like Villa, Zapata was an Indian, with no Spanish in his ancestry. And like Villa, he was practically illiterate. But there the similarities end. Of all the revolutionaries, Zapata had the most clear-cut objective: to restore to the poor farmers of Morelos the lands stolen from them by the rich under the umbrella of the Díaz regime. He had no ambitions for himself on a national scale.

Zapata's single-minded devotion to the ideal of justice to the poor of Morelos did, however, limit his effectiveness in battling with Díaz, Huerta, Madero, and, later, Carranza. Neither he nor his men had any stomach for fighting outside of their own state. The main forces in all the critical fighting were therefore those controlled by either Villa or Carranza.

Of the Americans who participated in the Punitive Expedition, the two best remembered are Brigadier General John J. Pershing and Lieutenant George S. Patton, Jr. But this is Pershing's story. The young Patton served only as one of Pershing's aides-de-camp, and though a couple of his exploits provide revealing and entertaining sidelights, Patton exerted no real influence on the events covered in this book.

Pershing is a different matter. His performance during the eleven months of the Punitive Expedition reveals him to be anything but the stereotype the world saw in the years of his subsequent fame.

During the American participation in World War I, which began only two months after the withdrawal of the Punitive Expedition, the world applauded a stiff, formal man, immaculately turned out, strong, and dignified. But since Pershing was reticent by nature—and since his role in command of the American Expeditionary Force did not call for great communication skills—he appeared as a remote marble statue to those not close to him. The general we see sleeping in a small tent on a windswept hill in Chihuahua, however, is very human. Although always dignified, even during the hardships of the Punitive Expedition, Pershing proved he was not made of marble.

The Pershing of 1916 was above all determined. As time went on, he became more and more frustrated by the enormous obstacles he faced, but he never whimpered. No records ever show Black Jack Pershing complaining about the difficulty of his mission. He is seen complaining only when not permitted to go all out to accomplish it.

It is possible that the rigors of the Punitive Expedition provided something of a tonic for the grief-stricken Pershing, who had recently lost his wife and three of his four children in a tragic fire. Hardship and challenge seemed to focus his mind and to alleviate his grief. He therefore threw himself into his present task with a vengeance, appearing almost to relish living under conditions that approached deprivation.

Perhaps Pershing can be faulted for driving so deep into southern Chihuahua in pursuit of Villa. But he was merely acting within his orders. The instructions he received from Washington on March 10, 1916, set no limits on the depth of his penetration. He was admonished only to avoid entering population centers. It lay within the purview of the powers in Washington to specify a line south of which he could not go. And that they utterly failed to do.

The four-year U.S. intervention in Mexico breaks down into roughly three periods: (a) that of President Woodrow Wilson's efforts to force General Huerta to resign as provisional president of Mexico; (b) that of the so-called War of the Winners between Carranza and Villa, which began with Huerta's resignation; and (c) that initiated by the U.S. recognition of Carranza as "de facto" president of Mexico in August of 1915, after which the United States, though in a state of hostility with Villa, was still unable to reach a satisfactory understanding with the enigmatic Carranza.

Only the first of these periods was covered extensively by both American and Mexican newspapers and memoirs. Up until August of 1914, European developments had not yet directed American attention across the Atlantic, and for most of that time the United States maintained a functioning embassy in Mexico City. However, the internecine warfare between Carranza and Villa during the next year caused little stir in the United States, and news of it was relegated to the back pages of American newspapers.

Pershing's Punitive Expedition, prompted by trouble along the border, soon followed. The events involving his men were of great concern to Americans but of little concern to Mexicans, except for the fact that Yankee invaders were on their soil. So American accounts abound, while few details about the expedition come from Mexican sources. This book therefore contains three separate stories, each told from a different viewpoint.

Excellent secondary sources exist on the subject of the Mexican Revolution, but two primary accounts, one Mexican and one American, are of exceptional value. The first of these is *The Eagle and the Serpent*, written by an irreverent young Mexican intellectual, Martín Luis Guzmán. It represents a personal account of his experience as a revolutionary between 1913 and 1915. Guzmán operated in high circles and was switched from position to position, possibly because he refused to accept responsibility for any important post. This exceptional observer provides unconventional insights into the characters of such Mexican leaders as Carranza, Obregón, Gutiérrez, and especially Pancho Villa—none of whom he admired very much.

Guzmán also wrote a second book, *The Memoirs of Pancho Villa*, which could easily pass for Villa's true memoirs. Its many details suggest that Guzmán must have had access to extensive documentation and perhaps to Villa himself. Unfortunately, both of Guzmán's books end in mid-1915, when Villa was still in command of the Division of the North and his fortunes were only beginning to wane.

On the American side, a mass of detailed material pertaining to Pershing's Punitive Expedition was collected by Major (later Colonel) Frank Tompkins, a central participant. Tompkins's book, *Chasing Villa*, includes an extensive compendium of official orders, official reports, and newspaper articles, interwoven with a generous dose of his own views and prejudices.

Today's reader is likely to find Tompkins's bluster amusing, perhaps offensive; but so thorough is Tompkins's research that other books—even Herbert Molloy Mason's splendid account, *The Great Pursuit* (1970)—draw on it very heavily. We are fortunate that Tompkins collected the documents, which speak for themselves.

Any American who studies the Mexican Revolution must develop a deep admiration for the long-suffering Mexican people, especially the poor. William Weber Johnson recognized the admirable qualities of the Mexican underclasses by naming his monumental account of the Mexican Revolution *Heroic Mexico.* Johnson explained his reasons by citing a dictionary definition of the word "heroic":

> "adj . . . as having or involving recourse to boldness, daring, or extreme measures. *Heroic surgery saved his life . . .*"

The Mexican nation has lived up to that definition and more. The price that the Mexican people paid to overthrow the reactionary Díaz regime and to give themselves at least a chance for a better future is inestimable. But the Mexicans were willing to pay it.

History goes on, and regardless of where one may place the culmination of the Revolution, that moment could never be construed as the end of Mexico's serious problems. But relations between Mexico and the United States have been improving steadily. Certainly, the United States has had neither cause nor inclination to repeat the interventions of the years 1914 and 1916.

The Mexicans have long memories. They have not forgotten the role that the United States once played in their internal affairs. However, we can hope that in time they can come to relegate those events to the category of bygones or at least to view them with some objectivity.

INTERVENTION!

INTERVENTIONS

****

Prologue

In early May 1911, an unknown photographer at Bustillos, a hacienda in northern Mexico, recorded the meeting of a remarkable group of men. Francisco I. Madero, Jr., leader of the Mexican forces rebelling against the dictator Porfirio Díaz, had called a conference of leaders. They gathered at his headquarters, a few miles south of the border town of Juárez.

The governors of all five of Mexico's northwestern states—Chihuahua, Sonora, Coahuila, Aguascalientes, and San Luis Potosí*—had responded to Madero's invitation, a surprising turnout considering that Madero held no official status in Mexico. That such realistic and hardheaded politicians would travel hundreds of miles to meet with a private citizen provides convincing evidence of Mexican resentment against the regime of President Porfirio Díaz. Díaz had ruled Mexico for over thirty years, ever more oppressively. As was traditional in Mexican politics, the rebellion had begun in the north, far from Mexico City.

The meeting at Bustillos, though little noticed elsewhere, in-

---

*Respectively, Abraham González, José María Maytorena, Venustiano Carranza, Alberto Fuentes, and Vazquez Gómez.

cluded at least three men whose names would become household words. One, of course, was Madero himself. Another was Venustiano Carranza, then governor of Coahuila, who as "First Chief" later unmercifully tweaked the nose of Uncle Sam, the Giant of the North. The third was Francisco ("Pancho") Villa, destined to be the target of a major U.S. incursion into Mexico in 1916.

In that set of self-assured men, Madero himself seemed out of place. He was only thirty-seven years old, small of stature (five foot two, about a hundred pounds), gentle in personality, and colorless in manner. But Madero had earned his position of leadership by his sheer courage. At a time when people all over Mexico were becoming resigned to the prospect of another presidential term for Porfirio Díaz, Madero alone had dared to oppose the dictator openly. He had run against Díaz in the election held in July 1910, been imprisoned by Díaz before the election, jumped bail, and fled to San Antonio, Texas.

On November 20, 1910, a day still commemorated in Mexico, Madero had returned to his homeland not as a politician but as an armed revolutionary. Since nobody else on the Mexican scene was willing to accept such personal risk, the little aristocrat had become the rallying point for all who opposed another four years of Porfirio Díaz.

Apart from the five governors, the conferees at the Bustillo conference also included three soldiers, on whose military skills the short-term future of the Revolution depended. The most important of these men at that time was Pascual Orozco, a onetime muleteer who had shown a flair for military command. As Madero's chief commander, Orozco had gained enough stature to earn a seat in the front row of the photograph, where he glowered uncomfortably, the outsider among the governors.

Of lesser importance in that gathering was the thirty-three-year-old Pancho Villa, a former bandit who had gained such prestige in his chosen line of work as to be recruited to Madero's cause by no less a personage than the governor of Chihuahua, Abraham González. Villa's éclat as a ferocious bandit-general, lothario, and military genius still lay ahead of him as he slouched unobtrusively in the back row.

The third soldier was Giuseppe Garibaldi, a soldier of fortune and grandson of the Italian liberator, a man whose romantic venture in Mexico was about to peter out because his heart was not in it.

The pictured group also included two of Madero's relatives: his father, Francisco Madero, Sr., and one of his brothers, Gustavo. The modest, one-eyed, pince-nezed Gustavo was without doubt Madero's most capable and loyal assistant. In any dealing—financial, political, whatever—Gustavo Madero would be his brother's point man. But the idealistic Madero would too often turn a deaf ear to his realistic brother's advice.

The photograph of the 1911 Bustillos meeting depicts most of the future central figures of the Mexican Revolution. Two (Madero and Carranza) were future presidents; one (Villa) was later the most powerful warlord. At least seven of the conferees would die violent deaths in the Revolution's course.* And the subsequent rivalry between two of Madero's lieutenants, Carranza and Villa, would condemn the Mexican people to years of unnecessary death and destruction.

Two prominent future revolutionaries are missing from this historic photograph. Emilio Zapata, the single-minded agrarian reformer of Morelos, was at the time fighting Díaz far to the south. And Alvaro Obregón, another future president of Mexico, was sitting out this early phase of the Revolution at his home in Sonora—much to his later embarrassment.

Only a few days after this photo was taken, the group began to splinter. Villa and Orozco, in almost open defiance of Madero's orders to refrain from violence, launched an attack on the important border town of Juárez. Juárez fell, triggering the collapse of Díaz. But the triumph was short-lived. Enraged by Madero's compassion for the Federal commander at Juárez, Villa and Orozco left Madero's service. Villa retired temporarily to civilian life; Orozco, disappointed by Madero's unwillingness to appoint him minister of war or governor of Chihuahua, rebelled against his former chief throughout the following year, 1912.

President Díaz fled Mexico in early June 1911, a little over a month after this meeting. Madero occupied Mexico City but postponed assuming the presidency until his formal election in November 1911, the outcome of which was never in doubt.

Had the Mexican Revolution ended with the election of Fran-

---

*The future presidents Madero and Carranza; the Chihuahua governor Abraham González; Gustavo Madero; Generals Orozco, Villa, and Lucio Blanco.

cisco Madero, this overthrow of a decadent dictatorship would have been a mere footnote to history. Unfortunately, his election marked only the beginning of a long and bloody tragedy.

During the summer of 1911, as the Díaz regime was collapsing in Mexico City, the United States was taking an unprecedented step. On orders from President William Howard Taft, the U.S. Army began concentrating its various independent regiments into a "Maneuver Division," training in anticipation of a possible incursion into Mexico. With the success of the Madero revolution, the alarm in the United States subsided, and components of the Maneuver Division were sent back to their permanent stations. But for the first time in decades, the U.S. Army had been made aware of troubles brewing on the southern side of the Rio Grande.

1

****

Assassination

Ricardo Romero was feeling decidedly uneasy. It was late in the evening of Saturday, February 22, 1913, and the nineteen-year-old chauffeur reflected ruefully that he would ordinarily have been out dancing. Instead, he was sitting in his limousine, parked in a courtyard of the gigantic National Palace of Mexico City. It was a forbidding place, a small, spooky enclosure amid three balconied stories of offices. Near his parking place was the door of the palace "intendancy," the office of the palace superintendent.

Romero had reason to be fearful, for death was in the air. During the past ten days, the streets of downtown Mexico City had been ravaged by artillery shells and machine-gun bullets. Many people had been killed, most of them innocent civilians. Admittedly, the firing had ceased a couple of days earlier, when Don Francisco I. Madero, Jr., had been ousted from the presidency of Mexico by a rebellious group of army officers. Romero feared that he, like so many others, would also become a victim in the aftermath.

As Romero thought back to the events of the past few hours, he was puzzled. Late that afternoon, his employer had put him and his Proto limousine at the disposal of a grim-faced businessman who called himself Cecilio Ocón. Ocón had remained silent as the two had shuttled between the palace and the home of General Félix Díaz, nephew of the deposed dictator. Romero had driven Ocón back and forth three times, sensing all the while that something sinister was afoot. He fervently wished he were somewhere else.

As Romero looked around the palace courtyard, he became aware that he was not alone. Two other cars were also parked there. One was the familiar limousine he had often seen carrying the president of Mexico around the streets. It stood alone, without a driver. The other vehicle was a touring car, driven by a young man about his own age. Romero approached the other driver and learned that his name was Ricardo Hernández. Both boys were utterly bewildered.

Shortly before midnight, the door of the intendancy opened, and a small man wearing a black felt hat and a military cloak stumbled out into the darkness. He was soon followed by another, both men obviously prisoners of a group of soldiers. The first man headed toward the presidential limousine, but an officer quickly motioned him toward Romero's car. Once the small man had been shoved into the rear, Romero could recognize him as the deposed Mexican president, Francisco Madero. The officer, who Romero later learned was Major Francisco Cárdenas, climbed into the backseat with Madero. Two others also got in. Cárdenas then ordered Romero to drive to the Lecumberri penitentiary, about a mile away.

The trip to Lecumberri took only a few minutes, as traffic was exceedingly light. When the two limousines pulled up at the front entrance, Cárdenas ordered Romero to stop. Romero could hear President Madero start to open the car's rear door and Cárdenas stop him. Cárdenas himself then got out of the vehicle, strode to the front door of the prison, picked up a guide, and returned. The guide stepped on the running board and directed Romero along the north wall toward the rear of the building. The second car, driven by Hernández, followed. Both stopped again, near a small door.

Cárdenas got out first. Then, turning to his prisoner, he shouted, "Get out, you prick!" As Madero climbed out of the car, Cárdenas jerked a pistol from his belt and shot him in the back of the head. The former president crumpled to the ground without a sound. Within a few instants, the prisoner in the second car met the same fate. The young Mexicans fell back and cowered in the shadows, expecting to be shot because of what they had witnessed.

But Cárdenas ignored the boys. He and several soldiers were now emptying their guns into the backseats of both cars, apparently attempting to make it appear that they had been caught in an ambush. Even in his terror, Romero noticed that the assassins were careful to avoid damaging the engines or the driving mechanisms.

The assassins then tugged at the limp bodies of the two victims and finally managed to stuff them into the backseat of Romero's bullet-riddled car. Cárdenas then ordered Romero to drive back to the front door of the Lecumberri penitentiary. There several men dumped the corpses out on the ground. Soon three or four other unidentified corpses were placed beside them. The conspirators made fun of the bodies with coarse jokes.

The next morning, Sunday, February 23, Mexican embassies around the world received a message from the Foreign Ministry:

> Last evening, while Señores Francisco I. Madero and [former Vice President] José María Pino Suárez were being taken from the National Palace to the Penitentiary . . . , two groups of armed men attempted to release the prisoners and twice attacked the escort. There was a fight in which five persons, among them Señores Madero and Pino Suárez, lost their lives.

Nobody knows for sure who ordered these murders. But Major Cárdenas and his assistant, a corporal, were both promoted to the rank of general shortly thereafter.

2

****

Uprising

President Francisco I. Madero, Jr.,
had been in office only some fifteen months before he and his vice
president, José María Pino Suárez, were deposed and murdered. Their
fates were perhaps inevitable, late or soon.

In mid-1911, Madero had triumphantly ridden his white horse
into Mexico City, cheered by enthusiastic and boisterous crowds as
their liberator, the man who had freed them from the oppressor Díaz.
His first act at his moment of victory showed ill-considered idealism:
he allowed Porfirio Díaz's vice president, Francisco León de la Barra,
to remain in office and finish out Díaz's unexpired term. Madero's
election in December was assured, and his demonstration of respect
for democratic institutions established his liberal credentials. Nevertheless, his gesture was a mistake; it allowed de la Barra to undermine
him in the intervening few months.

Madero's difficulties would have been insurmountable in any
case. No human, not even an inspiring leader and strong executive,
could have solved Mexico's problems as readily as the multitudes had
expected. And Madero turned out to be neither a leader nor an executive.

Madero, in fact, had never been the sort of revolutionary the masses longed for. He possessed little magnetic appeal in public. Balding, slight, and ascetic, with a weak, faltering voice, he had no power over a crowd. A man of drive and energy might have overcome those physical weaknesses, but Madero lacked the revolutionary fervor necessary to establish a viable revolutionary regime; he lacked even an understanding of the people.

Born into the ruling class, from a family of great wealth, Madero had been educated in France. He once admitted, "I belong by birth to the privileged class . . . neither I nor any member of my family have cause for complaint against General Díaz." Granted, Madero had been sincere in his sympathy for the downtrodden, and he meant to keep his promises of land reform, secularization of education, and freeing of the press. But he had shown no fire in his belly in pushing his reform program. Thus Emiliano Zapata, the tough southerner who was serious about real land reform, never ceased fighting against Mexico City when Madero replaced Díaz.

Madero could have survived the persistent hostility of Zapata, but he repeated the error he had committed with de la Barra by continually failing to reward his friends and get rid of his enemies. His government remained permeated with *cientfficos*, men left over from the Díaz regime who had never transferred their loyalties to him. As a result, most of Madero's original supporters had either retired from public life or rebelled against him by early 1913.

The most serious uprising against the Madero regime was staged by his former military chief, Pascual Orozco, in 1912. Lacking any loyal military following, Madero was forced to call on an avowed friend of Porfirio Díaz, General Victoriano Huerta. Huerta, a capable professional soldier, succeeded in destroying Orozco's army and driving its leader once more into exile in the United States. The upshot of the successful campaign, however, was that the crafty Huerta greatly enhanced his own personal prestige—at the expense of Madero's.

Even as the ranks of his friends dwindled and those of his enemies swelled, Madero still appeared to trust everyone around him. He was said to be a mystic (as well as a teetotaler and vegetarian), an idea advanced by some to explain his unrealistic self-confidence. His brother, adviser, and troubleshooter, Gustavo Madero, once said, "In a family of clever men, the only fool was President." But Gustavo was loyal to his brother, and through his one good eye he could detect the perils in Madero's situation. He tried repeatedly to alert his brother to the impending dangers, but the little president paid no heed.

The plot that eventually overthrew President Madero was headed by a four-man cabal consisting of General Manuel Mondragón, General Félix Díaz, General Bernardo Reyes, and Cecilio Ocón, the man who later arranged Madero's murder. It had been hatching for several months, its original target date set at mid-March 1913. However, the conspirators became aware that knowledge of their intentions was spreading, and when they learned of Gustavo Madero's suspicions, they decided to act quickly, over a month earlier than they had planned. The revolt therefore came as a complete surprise.

During the early hours of Sunday, February 9, 1913, an alert forest guard at the Chapultepec Castle was jolted from his sleep by the noise of a column of troops marching eastward into Mexico City. The guard could not confirm whether this unusual troop movement was authorized, but he suspected that it was not. And since the column seemed to be headed toward the National Palace, the guard jumped in a car and drove the two and a half miles to confer with the palace superintendent, retired Admiral Adolfo Bassó. Bassó believed the report; like everyone else, he knew that unrest was simmering. But Bassó could not be sure. He therefore proceeded to the home of Gustavo Madero, on nearby Calle Londres, to give him the news. Madero, convinced that this was what he had been waiting for, set out for the palace with Bassó and his driver.

The guard's report was accurate, and his suspicions were borne out. The troops he had spotted were part of the garrison stationed at Tacubaya, a military post about four miles to the southwest, under Mondragón's direct command. But Mondragón was not headed for the National Palace, at least not right away; two of his fellow conspirators, Díaz and Reyes, were in prison, so his first task was to liberate them before going any further. After that was accomplished, the four could lead their columns toward the National Palace, which they expected to occupy without resistance.

Reyes and Díaz had rebelled against Madero before, and by law—and by the dictates of good sense—Madero should have executed them for treason. But since they were both gentlemen—General Reyes was a former governor of Neuvo León, and Félix Díaz was Porfirio's nephew—Madero had reduced their sentences, even directing that the venerable old Reyes be held in the comfortable minimum-security prison of Santiago Tlatelolco. Félix Díaz, the plump and vain nephew of the recent dictator, had been incarcerated, also comfortably, in the modern Lecumberri penitentiary.

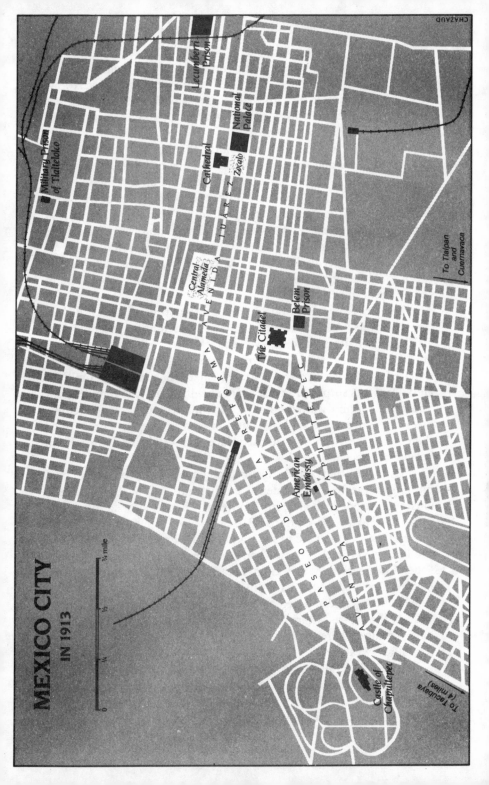

Despite Madero's generosity, however, Reyes and Díaz had showed no gratitude. Indeed, they had begun plotting his overthrow as soon as they were able to make contact with each other. Their agents, given free rein by Madero's indifferent guards, carried messages back and forth across the city.

Mondragón was supremely confident that he could easily liberate Reyes and Díaz and take the National Palace. Since he expected Adolfo Bassó to offer no resistance, he counted on a detachment of young cadets from the National Military School at Tlalpan, who were preceding them, to be in control before his columns even arrived there. But the distances between the prisons and the palace were great—several miles—so Mondragón split his force, sending one detachment of cavalry under General Gregorio Ruiz to free Reyes at the Santiago Tlatelolco while he, with the main body, released Díaz at the Lecumberri penitentiary.

The Díaz-Reyes rebellion started off smoothly, though it had its comic aspects. At Santiago Tlatelolco, Ruiz found General Reyes waiting in full dress uniform, even though it was still dark. Reyes was quickly freed and astride his favorite horse, riding at the head of two hundred cavalry toward the National Palace. But at the Lecumberri, Félix Díaz was surprised in the act of shaving. So while Mondragón's impatient column waited outside, Díaz meticulously completed his preening. Once Díaz appeared, he joined Mondragón. The two led their troops westward toward the palace, but well behind the column headed by Reyes.

The word that Adolfo Bassó brought to Gustavo Madero that morning triggered the president's brother into action. It was useless, Gustavo reasoned, to alert his brother at Chapultepec; so instead he went straight to the National Palace, where by supreme efforts he induced the palace guard to switch its loyalty from the conspirators to the legal government. Bassó then summoned the commander of the Federal garrison of Mexico City, a fearless old soldier named General Lauro ("Remington") Villar. Villar quickly dispersed the frightened cadets and organized a defense, emplacing his machine guns on the walls of the palace, where they could fire into the Plaza de la Constitución (Zócalo). There the flat concrete provided an ideal killing ground for Villar's weapons.

When General Bernardo Reyes arrived at the palace late in the morning, he was astonished to encounter a hostile force waiting for him. This new situation made him pause a moment. Then, perhaps trying a bluff, he sent General Ruiz ahead to demand the surrender of the palace. Villar, in personal command, intended nothing of the kind. Instead, he contemptuously seized the reins of Ruiz's horse and demanded that Ruiz surrender as a traitor. The fat, inept Ruiz dismounted and complied. A firefight then broke out. General Reyes spurred his horse forward into a hail of the defenders' bullets and fell dead in the saddle. The rebel column retreated in confusion.

All comic aspects of the rebellion were now over, as rebels and loyalists alike settled down exchanging fire. Though the marksmanship was erratic, the volume was heavy. Over three hundred bodies littered the Zócalo ten minutes after the action began. Most of the victims were rebels, but among them also lay shoppers, vendors, and members of families on their way to mass.

Mondragón and Díaz arrived at the Zócalo soon after Reyes's fall. Shocked by the scene of carnage and possessing no alternative scheme in case of failure to seize the palace, they fell back through the streets of the city to the southwest, wondering what to do next. After retreating about a mile, they were saved from abject failure by some informer who advised Mondragón that the Ciudadela (Citadel) was only lightly held. They had no difficulty brushing aside the few defenders of the old fortress, so they occupied it. Finding ammunition and supplies, they settled into the Citadel with their eighteen hundred remaining troops. In the confusion, they occupied several blocks of the city around the building. Félix Díaz was now the leader of a rebellion that had already run out of steam.

Back at Chapultepec Castle, the president's residence, Gustavo Madero gave his brother an optimistic report. He had remained at the National Palace long enough to witness Reyes's death and Díaz's frustration, and those developments left him certain that the uprising had petered out. Four thousand Federal troops in or around Mexico City should have no trouble reducing eighteen hundred rebels holding out in the relatively vulnerable Citadel, cut off from resupply. This incident, Gustavo believed, was just another of the periodic failed coups.

President Madero agreed. As soon as Gustavo returned with his optimistic tidings, Madero decided that the time had come to show himself to the people. He mounted a fine Arabian horse, descended the pathway from Chapultepec onto the Paseo de la Reforma, and headed for the palace. Amid a festive atmosphere, he rode bareheaded up the wide, tree-lined parkway, accompanied by an honor guard of loyal cadets, surrounded on all sides by a wildly cheering populace. The presidential party traversed three miles in the bright sun between stately homes of the Avenida de la Reforma to the Avenida Juárez without incident.

Down the Avenida Juárez Madero's party went, all still relatively quiet. As the procession passed the Central Alameda and approached the Palace of Fine Arts, however, the procession slowed up. The heretofore occasional sniper shots had become more frequent and too accurate for Madero to ignore any longer. When a bystander fell dead a few feet away, the president finally agreed to take refuge in the nearby Daguerre photo shop. There the presidential party would wait for the firing to subside.

At that moment, fate turned against the little president. While still in the photo laboratory, he received a message that old Remington Villar had been seriously wounded in the renewed fighting at the palace. At about that time, as Madero was considering whom to put in Villar's place, General Victoriano Huerta, on an inactive military status, appeared. The general offered to assume command of Federal forces in the city, including the palace. Madero paused.

President Madero, though usually a trusting soul, had great misgivings about placing Huerta in Villar's position. He had recently relieved Huerta from active duty for misconduct—cruelty, hard drinking, and light fingers in handling government funds. Huerta had pretended to accept his demotion with grace, but in private he was furious.* Known as a disgruntled general, Huerta had recently been approached by the chief conspirator, General Mondragón, to join the cabal. Huerta's refusal had not been prompted by loyalty to Madero; he simply would not accept a subordinate position in any undertaking. Madero, while knowing none of this, still feared Huerta.

Nevertheless, Huerta was professionally competent, as he had proved during the 1912 Orozco rebellion. Furthermore, Huerta still swore fealty to his president in the most elaborate of terms. So Madero placed him in command of the forces protecting the palace, intending to replace him at the earliest possible moment. It was a bad move: "The whole Madero clan fell at that shot [Villar's wounding]."

Huerta took over his new duties high-handedly. Once Madero

*"Huerta was very, very angry, and like an Indian he swore revenge on Madero. I marveled at the incredible innocence of Mr. Madero, who seemed to think he could play fast and loose with men like this." Rosa E. King, *Tempest Over Mexico* (Boston, 1935), p. 87.

was safely in the National Palace, Huerta sent for General Ruiz, who had surrendered to old Villar that morning in the Zócalo. Huerta ignored the pleas of Ruiz and ordered him shot without a trial. Despite Ruiz's admission of treason, executing a brother officer and an old friend was shocking, especially since Huerta had done so without having asked authority from the president. Perhaps Ruiz knew too much. Perhaps Huerta was testing Madero. In any case, the little president did nothing to interfere.

Madero, by now extremely uneasy, left Mexico City by car that same afternoon and headed for Cuernavaca, seventy-five miles away, there to contemplate his next move. At Mrs. Rosa King's famed Bella Vista Hotel, Madero sent for General Felipe Angeles, the officer with whom he had recently replaced Huerta. Madero needed a loyal officer in Mexico City, so he ordered the respected Angeles to return to the capital with him.

But Madero picked the wrong man to conduct a power struggle against Huerta; the gentlemanly Angeles was totally incapable of shouting down a bully. Thus, when Madero and Angeles arrived back in Mexico City, they both knuckled under to the positive and dynamic Huerta, who simply refused to turn over command of the forces besieging the Citadel. As the "senior military officer on the spot," Huerta assigned a docile Angeles to a secondary sector of the city, and Madero, still putty in Huerta's hands, made no protest.

Mexico City was quiet on Monday, February 10. But on Tuesday, two days after the rebellion had begun, the worst fears of the people became a reality. On that morning, Victoriano Huerta launched a series of costly and futile attacks on rebel positions around the Citadel. After losing about five hundred men, Huerta suspended the infantry attacks and pounded the Citadel and its environs with artillery. The Federal pieces with which he was conducting his bombardment were located in the Zócalo. Rebel guns around the Citadel answered. Though the hostile batteries were situated only about a mile apart, observation of the effects was impossible in the close streets. Therefore, the fire became haphazard, ineffective on both sides. The palace sustained only two random artillery hits in the course of the entire day; the Citadel, just one.

While the Palace and Citadel were escaping almost unscathed, the part of the city that lay between the two positions was pounded unmercifully. Shells crashed among the crowded houses, and machine-gun fire raked the streets. Electrical service disappeared. Fresh food became scarce. Burial crews were unable to cope with the ever-increasing piles of bodies. Citizens tried incinerating some of the corpses, but many simply putrefied. Mobs of prisoners escaped from the local prisons and joined in the looting, spreading panic among the usually comfortable foreign colony. The number of casualties eventually reached five thousand. This was a new experience for the inhabitants of Mexico's capital, especially the foreigners. For years, they had lived in peace under the reign of Porfirio Díaz; his departure in 1911 had come while the guns of the rebels were far away; no devastation had afflicted Mexico City. But Mexico City was now in the line of fire.

And yet, despite the horrors in the streets of Mexico City, the rebels in the Citadel somehow remained well supplied with all they needed, including ample quantities of beer and champagne.

Somewhere along the line, Victoriana Huerta had decided to join the rebels—on his own terms, of course, for he now had Díaz and his troops bottled up in the Citadel. Perhaps Huerta came to an understanding early, because on Tuesday morning, just as the infantry attacks began, he and Díaz were seen entering the home of a mutual friend together.

Be that as it may, Huerta's actions spoke loudly. In the course of five days, hundreds of veteran rurales, "hard core Maderistas," paid with their lives for Huerta's treachery. Huerta singled out these troops for suicidal attacks against the crossfires of the Díaz machine guns. Huerta, a capable soldier, knew exactly what he was doing.

But Huerta was not the only enemy Madero had. The American ambassador, Henry Lane Wilson, stood right along with him.

3

****

"I Have Overthrown This Government"

At the spacious American embassy, just northwest of the Citadel of Mexico City, Ambassador Henry Lane Wilson was in an agitated state. During the years of the Porfirio Díaz regime, Mexico City had been a peaceful place, insulated from the upheavals that periodically shook the Mexican countryside, but that snug, safe world was now being shattered. Wilson felt responsible for the safety of Americans and other foreigners in the city. He was to confront his responsibilities with commendable energy but with such a lack of discretion as to cause untold embarrassment to his country.

Lane Wilson, age fifty-six, was a compulsive, hard-drinking man who had been appointed to his present position by President William H. Taft two years earlier. Wilson was not a career Foreign Service officer, but he had attained some experience in diplomacy during two previous ministerial posts, first to Chile and later to Belgium. He enjoyed influential connections in high political places; his late brother, John Lockwood Wilson, had been a U.S. senator and the powerful owner of the *Seattle Post Intelligencer*. Lane Wilson himself was associated with railroad and mining interests, particularly the Guggenheim American Smelting and Refining Company. In Mexico

City, he surrounded himself with a group of businessmen, lawyers, and publishers called the Society of Friends of the American Ambassador. That society pretended to represent the American community in advising Wilson, but it tended more to keep him reminded of their special interests.

Lane Wilson's compulsiveness drove him to become overly concerned with internal Mexican politics, matters considered outside of an ambassador's purview. In his messages to Washington, Wilson had in the past voiced mild complaints about even the friendly Porfirio Díaz, but those complaints were trivial compared with those he levied against Francisco Madero. Wilson's antipathy toward Madero was long-standing, personal, and reciprocated in kind. From the outset of their relationship, Madero had refused to tolerate Wilson's bullying attitude. As a result, Wilson described Madero in official messages as "a dreamer, more of a mountebank than a messiah . . . a disorganized brain." By early 1913, a fed-up Madero had secretly asked President-elect Woodrow Wilson to recall the ambassador as soon as possible after Wilson took office, in March 1913.

When fighting broke out in Mexico City on February 9, 1913, Ambassador Wilson acted promptly. That same afternoon, he invited his diplomatic colleagues to the American embassy to discuss how to deal with the danger in the streets. This he did in his capacity as the "dean of the diplomatic corps," a position that other nations accorded to the American ambassador by the habit of sending only "ministers" rather than "ambassadors" to head their missions to Mexico. At the same time, tacitly in exchange, the international community looked to the United States to provide all the local missions whatever security the nearby Colossus of the North could manage.

Wilson's responsibilities were admittedly daunting. There were 25,000 foreigners residing in Mexico City, 5,000 of them Americans. Their physical danger was acute, because most of their offices and homes were located in and around the fashionable area in the center city, between the National Palace and the Citadel, where the fighting was taking place. Their safety could be best assured if Wilson could persuade the Mexicans on both sides of the fighting to cease fire, and to that end the diplomats granted Wilson virtual carte blanche to act in their behalf. Armed with that authority, Wilson arranged to meet with Madero's foreign minister, Pedro Lascuráin, later that same afternoon.

Wilson's conference with Lascuráin that first Sunday held little prospect of accomplishing anything, for Lascuráin, exercising no control over the rebels in the Citadel, could give no "assurances" regarding the safety of foreigners. Wilson therefore presented similar demands to a representative of Félix Díaz who called late in the day at the embassy.

Wilson's bias in favor of Díaz over Madero was clear from the outset. When he reported the two meetings to the State Department that evening, he grossly exaggerated the extent of the support the rebels were receiving from the people of the city. "Large but perfectly ordered crowds," he reported, were "crying 'Viva Díaz!' and 'Death to Madero!' That assertion flew in the face of reports from local American consular agents, who saw much less support for Díaz. American newspaper reporters supported the consuls against Wilson; they claimed that the situation was just the reverse of what Wilson reported.

During the lull in the fighting that occurred during the day of February 10, Lane Wilson was busy trying to bolster his bargaining power with the Mexican government. He resorted to a familiar weapon, the threat of American intervention. In two messages to Washington, he recommended that war vessels be sent to Mexican ports, specifying that the ships be "of sufficient size to produce an impression." These U.S. naval deployments could obviously not directly affect events in Mexico City, two hundred miles inland from the coast, but the threat of intervention could heighten pressures on an already beleaguered Mexican government.

Wilson received some but not all of what he wanted from his superiors. Washington responded that same afternoon by sending warships to Veracruz, Tampico, Acapulco, and Mazatlán; but the State Department partly defused the move by warning that the ships were being sent solely for the purposes of "observation and report[ing]." Sending them, the announcement specified, represented no change in policy, "no bias . . . as to which side should attain ascendancy." Secretary Philander Knox had no intention of placing those ships under the supervision of Henry Lane Wilson.

When the fighting resumed on Tuesday, February 11, the real devastation of the city began. No place was safe, not even the American embassy. "Firing all day long was heavy and indiscriminate," Wilson wrote later. "Shells exploded in many of the houses, and quantities of bullets penetrated the rear of the embassy building." It was dangerous for members of the embassy to try to communicate with the palace or with other diplomats. Americans and foreigners took refuge under Wilson's roof. Their numbers eventually swelled to 175.

Under the circumstances, Wilson decided to see Madero in person. On Wednesday, February 12, he asked the Austrian and Spanish ministers to accompany him through the crowds and "singing bullets" to call on President Madero. When they met, Madero refused to be cowed by Wilson's protests. For one thing, he pointed out, it was Díaz, not he, who was rebelling. Furthermore, he met Wilson's complaints about danger to Americans by offering a secure villa in Tacubaya to serve temporarily as the American embassy. Wilson refused, claiming that he could not perform his embassy's mission from a place four miles outside of Mexico City.

Wilson then went to the attack. President William H. Taft, he told Madero, was "greatly concerned" about developments in Mexico City. The American warships steaming toward Mexican ports, he added meaningfully, were carrying three thousand marines. Wilson was overplaying Taft's concern—of which he had no knowledge—but he seemed to relish the shock effect his words had on Madero.

Two days later, on Friday, February 14, the Mexican government showed signs of splintering. Foreign Minister Pedro Lascuráin called personally on Wilson at the American embassy and disclosed that even some in Madero's own cabinet were thinking that Madero should resign as president. Though Wilson was undoubtedly pleased, he was shrewd enough to attribute the first mention of that idea to Lascuráin, not himself.

Up to this time, Ambassador Wilson had made no contact with General Huerta, for he had never considered Huerta to be a major figure in the current Mexican crisis. Wilson's view of things was altered that Friday afternoon when a Huerta representative dropped by the American embassy claiming that he "carried a message from the General [Huerta]." It might be possible, the man said, that Huerta and Díaz could come to an understanding, *if the Ambassador thinks it would be a good idea.* Though advised not to see the man, Wilson received him in his office. No record was made of the meeting, but when Wilson went to the palace with the German minister the next day, he sought out Huerta, not Madero.

Wilson and the German minister, Admiral Paul von Hintze, were frustrated in their attempt to see Huerta alone when Madero intercepted them and sent for Huerta. When the four sat down together, Madero quickly granted Wilson's request for a twelve-hour cease-fire the next day but then administered a shock. He produced a message he had just sent directly to President Taft demanding to know if Taft actually intended to land American troops on Mexican soil.

That development was sobering enough, but Wilson was in for more. On his return to the embassy, he learned that Madero had sent a second message through the Mexican embassy at Washington, complaining about his own interference in Mexico's internal affairs. In a shrill protest to Washington, Wilson claimed that his actions had been misunderstood. He also dropped all pretense of impartiality between Madero and the rebels, who were still supposedly being headed by Félix Díaz.

Two days later, President Madero received an answer from President Taft. The United States, Taft wrote, had no intention of intervening in Mexico. Elated, Madero made Taft's message known to everyone in the Mexican government.

Despite his mystical courage, time was running out for Madero. His military officers were leaving his side in favor of the Díaz rebels. Yet, through it all, he remained unable to face up to the overpowering personality of General Huerta.

Huerta was playing his cards skillfully, pretending to consult the president on every change of plan and to curse the slowness of the army's movements. He continued to promise an all-out attack on the rebel-held Citadel, which could end the rebellion. He did have a telling argument for waiting until the moment when he had overwhelming force. Both sides in this battle were members of the Mexican regular army, and they were reluctant to kill each other simply because they belonged to two factions. Huerta also claimed that he might not be able to enforce orders considered repugnant by soldiers under his command. It was better to keep Díaz bottled up in the Citadel, where he could do no harm, than to initiate premature action. The preoccupied president did not interfere.

As in other instances, Gustavo Madero could see through Huerta's deceptions but could not convince his brother of the urgency of the situation. On the same day that Taft's message of reassurance reached Francisco Madero, Gustavo reported to his brother that Huerta's troops had allowed eighteen resupply carts to enter the Citadel in broad daylight. For the first time, the president sent for Huerta and demanded an explanation.

At first, Huerta denied Gustavo's accusation. But he soon changed his tactic and admitted that he had allowed the resupply. He had done so, he claimed, to avoid forcing the Díaz troops to plunder the city for food. Risking a bit of humor, he added, "Perhaps they should be supplied with wine and women also." Then, as Madero stood pondering, Huerta put his arms around the little president and assured him, "You are secure in the arms of General Huerta."

The next night, Gustavo Madero tried once more to bring Huerta's deceit into the open. At about midnight, he found Huerta half drunk in the palace command post, so he disarmed the general and marched him down the halls at gunpoint. Before the president, Gustavo recited a formidable list of questionable actions to support his accusation of Huerta's treachery. But again Huerta proved master of the situation. He protested the charges, reminding Madero of his loyal services during the Pascual Orozco uprising the year before. As for his meeting with Díaz a few days earlier—one of Gustavo's main points—that was just "an affair of skirts," an assignation. He promised to make an all-out attack on the Citadel the next afternoon. Once more, Madero accepted Huerta's pledges of loyalty.

That afternoon, nine days after the beginning of the Díaz rebellion, Ambassador Wilson met personally with Huerta for the first time alone. At 4:00 P.M. the ambassador reported to Washington that President Madero would be removed from office very soon.

Tuesday, February 18, appeared to bring a rise in President Madero's fortunes. Huerta had promised to assault the Citadel, and Madero even enjoyed a moment of triumph when he showed several hostile senators the reassuring message from President Taft. And despite the confrontation of the night before, Victoriano Huerta appeared to hold no grudge. The general had even invited Gustavo Madero to a sumptuous luncheon at the Hotel Gambrinus.

Early that afternoon, Madero sat down to preside over a meeting of his cabinet, secure in the knowledge that the palace was being guarded by General Aureliano Blanquet's powerful (4,000 men), newly arrived Twenty-ninth Battalion. After all, Blanquet was loyal; only a day earlier, he had so declared himself. Never mind that Huerta had removed Madero's loyal palace guards; all was well.

At 1:30 P.M., Madero's cabinet meeting was interrupted by an intruder. An officer of the Twenty-ninth, Colonel Jiménez Riveroll, burst into the Cabinet Room and strode straight up to the president. An unforeseen danger had arisen, he announced; a new rebel force was descending upon the city, and the president must accompany him to safety.

Madero, annoyed at the interruption, refused to budge. At that moment, a crowd of soldiers burst into the room, firing at random. Several of Madero's cabinet members fired back. Riveroll fell dead— shot by Madero himself, Huerta later claimed—and two of Madero's aides, one of them his cousin, were also killed. The invading soldiers, now leaderless, paused in confusion. Madero, believing the invaders to be renegades, then walked right through them, admonishing them to be calm. He opened the window and shouted to the troops in the Zócalo below: "It's all right; I'll be with you in a moment!"

Madero then led his cabinet members down the steps into the palace courtyard. Seeing Blanquet, resplendent in black uniform and gold braid, Madero started to speak. Blanquet, pistol in hand, interrupted him. "You are my prisoner," he said.

Madero was finished. He and his vice president, José María Pino Suárez, were herded off to be incarcerated comfortably in the intendency of the palace. There they found General Felipe Angeles, also a prisoner. Angeles had been arrested for insubordination; he had refused to obey Huerta's order to cease firing on Díaz's garrison in the Citadel. The three prisoners would spend four days in draped and mirrored rooms, receiving visitors and wondering where the Madero administration had gone wrong.

Across the city, Gustavo Madero was enjoying the luncheon at the Gambrinus restaurant with General Huerta. Huerta, he concluded, must have been chastised by his own actions the night before. Huerta was going out of his way to be jovial. When Gustavo asked what Huerta would take to drink, Huerta did not call for his usual brandy. Instead, he said, "I'll take the Citadel."

So unwary was the usually suspicious Gustavo that he willingly lent Huerta his pistol to carry along when the general excused himself to step out of the room. As soon as Gustavo was disarmed, however, a squad of soldiers stepped in and took him prisoner. He was locked in a closet for the time being.

That evening, as Madero, Pino Suárez, and Angeles were languishing in the palace intendancy, Ambassador Wilson hosted a reception at the American embassy, attended by both Huerta and Díaz. As Díaz entered the room, Wilson greeted him with a ringing toast: "Long live Félix Díaz, the leader of Mexico!"

The event was far from a purely social affair. Díaz had complaints against Huerta that he wished to air in front of the ambassador. The complaints were serious: in arresting Madero, Huerta had "temporarily" taken over the reins of government. That action, Díaz insisted, exceeded the understanding the two had previously reached. Furthermore, Díaz demanded that Huerta give him custody of the two Maderos, Pino Suárez, and Adolfo Bassó, all of whom were in Huerta's hands. Wilson assumed the role of mediator, sitting off in a corner with the two conspirators as they searched for ways to devise a new agreement.

Finally the three arrived at a formula. Huerta would serve temporarily as "provisional president," but Díaz would name the cabinet. As soon as possible, Huerta should call for a general election, in which he pledged to support Díaz for the presidency. As to the prisoners in his hands, Huerta agreed to turn over only Gustavo Madero and Bassó; he needed President Madero and Vice President Pino Suárez for his own purposes.

Victoriano Huerta headed straight back to the palace when he left the American embassy that evening. Immediately on his arrival, he sent for Madero and Pino Suárez. When they reached his office, he presented them with a grim choice—exile or death. To make the exile alternative more believable—and more palatable—Huerta promised to submit their resignations to disinterested members of the diplomatic community, after which diplomatic representatives of Japan and Chile would accompany them and their families to Veracruz. Having no real choice in the matter, both Madero and Pino Suárez signed resignations and turned them over to Huerta.

Victoriano Huerta, however, had no intention of abiding by his promise. Once he had the resignations in his hands, he submitted them straightaway to the Chamber of Deputies, which he had called into emergency session. Foreign Minister Lascuráin, next in line of succession, was inaugurated provisional president of Mexico. Lascuráin then appointed Huerta minister of government, next in line, after which Lascuráin resigned the provisional presidency. Forty-five minutes later, the Chamber of Deputies accepted his resignation in turn. Huerta was inaugurated provisional president on the spot.

Provisional President Huerta then sent a cheerful message to Washington: "I have the honor to inform you that I have overthrown this government. The armed forces support me and from now on peace and prosperity will reign." Everything had been carried off legally, in accordance with the letter of the Mexican constitution.

Gustavo Madero, still held prisoner at the Gambrinus restaurant, was now of no further use to either Huerta or Díaz. His desperate situation was exacerbated by the fact that the Díaz group regarded Gustavo with a special fear and loathing. It was Gustavo who had always suspected their loyalty and whose pryings had forced the rebels to launch their plot prematurely. So Gustavo Madero could expect no mercy.

He received none. At about midnight, in accordance with the Huerta-Díaz agreement, Gustavo was taken in a car from the restaurant to the Citadel. When he arrived, he saw Adolfo Bassó, the former palace superintendent, also in custody. General Mondragón, long since eclipsed as a major conspirator but still working under Díaz, immediately decreed the death sentence for both.

Gustavo was not permitted to die with dignity. Instead, he was shoved out the door of the Citadel into the park, where a drunken mob of about a hundred people swarmed over him, beating his face and tearing his clothing. Gustavo tried vainly to hold them off, at the same time pleading for his life in the names of his wife and children. The mobs jeered; a soldier gouged out Gustavo's one good eye with a bayonet; a badly aimed bullet tore away his jaw.

The blinded Gustavo Madero made no more sounds; he merely covered his face with his hands and tried to turn away. But it was of no use. As the crowd mocked him as a coward, Gustavo fell about thirty feet from the base of the great statue of the patriot José María Morelos. There he was repeatedly shot, stabbed, and finally torn apart. Someone made off with his glass eye as a souvenir; almost nothing else of Gustavo's body was ever found.

Adolfo Bassó met his doom in a more humane fashion: he was placed before a firing squad and permitted to shout the order for his own execution.

General Huerta had achieved his end; he was now provisional president. But he still faced the thorny problem of how to dispose of former President Madero and former Vice President Pino Suárez. Should they be executed, as many feared they would be? Or should he honor his agreement and permit them to leave the country? Huerta hesitated.

From the outset, Huerta realized that formal execution of the two prisoners was out of the question. World opinion would not stand for such an outrage. Messages urging clemency were pouring in, some of them through the American embassy. Included among those so pleading were the ministers of Cuba and Japan, the Masonic Lodge of Mexico City, even members of the Texas legislature. Huerta once again turned to Ambassador Wilson for guidance.

When Wilson visited Huerta in the National Palace, he showed little concern for the fate of Madero and Pino Suárez. Huerta asked whether he should "send the ex-President out of the country or place him in a lunatic asylum," and Wilson answered noncommittally that Huerta should "do that which was best for the peace of the country."

On his return to the embassy from his meeting with Huerta, Wilson found Madero's wife, Sara, waiting to plead that he intercede to save her husband's life. Wilson was unsympathetic. "That is a responsibility that I do not care to undertake," he declared. At the end, however, Wilson gave Señora Madero grudging assurances that her husband would suffer no bodily harm.

Wilson now turned his full attention to securing U.S. recognition of the Huerta government. His urgings were rebuffed, however. Washington seemed to be primarily concerned for the safety of Madero. Secretary Knox warned Wilson, "General Huerta's consulting you as to the treatment of Madero gives you a certain responsibility in the matter," adding that cruel treatment of Madero would "injure the reputation of Mexican civilization." Knox hoped to hear that Madero was being treated in "a manner consistent with peace and humanity."

On the evening of February 22, Ambassador Henry Lane Wilson, ignoring the devastation of Mexico City, went through with the usual reception observing the anniversary of George Washington's birth. Huerta attended. During the evening, Wilson and Huerta were noticed conferring seriously in the anteroom, with Wilson doing most of the talking.

At that same time, Madero, Pino Suárez, and Felipe Angeles were sitting despondently in the intendancy of the National Palace. They had heard of Gustavo's brutal death, and when Madero's mother came to visit, the grief-stricken ex-president assumed responsibility for his brother Gustavo's fate. On his knees, he begged his mother's forgiveness.

On the whole, however, Madero harbored no regrets. "My dear Suárez," he mused to his colleague. "In going over my life I can truly find little I would change. Is that the sign of vanity? I hope not."

Pino Suárez was not so sanguine: "What did we do wrong? What was our crime? Why has God deserted us this way?"

Madero always saw the bright side. "We'll be all right. We'll go to Cuba, or England, or even Japan. Their ministers are with Huerta right now. It's just a matter of where or when. We've been exiled before."

At about midnight, Major Cárdenas abruptly entered the room. Madero and Pino Suárez were to be taken to the Lecumberri penitentiary for "greater comfort," he said. But they were allowed no time to gather their personal effects.

Outside, in the dark courtyard, the drivers Ricardo Romero and Ricardo Hernández were waiting by their limousines.

4

##########

Watchful Waiting

As soon as Victoriano Huerta was inaugurated provisional president of Mexico, U.S. Ambassador Henry L. Wilson stepped up his pressure on the U.S. government to recognize the new regime. Without approval from home, he assembled the Mexico City diplomatic corps and extracted from its members an agreement that "recognition was imperative in order to allow [the new government] to impose its authority and establish order." He apparently hoped that the expressed consensus would influence Washington to act. The State Department, however, refused to be railroaded into giving Wilson the endorsement he sought. Though Secretary Knox was "disposed" to regard the provisional government as legally established, his main concern was the safety of Madero and Pino Suárez; recognition could wait.

Wilson also took the murders of Madero and Pino Suárez in stride. Apparently underestimating the reaction of the people in the United States, he blandly notified the State Department on February 24 that he had accepted the government's version of the affair. He considered the murder a "closed incident" and seemed to believe that his own judgment would satisfy the U.S. government and the American public.

But few agreed with Wilson's assertion that what had happened in Mexico City was a "closed incident." Protests rumbled in the northern Mexican states of Sonora, Chihuahua, and Coahuila as soon as Huerta seized office, even before Madero and Pino Suárez were murdered. In Coahuila, Governor Venustiano Carranza refused to recognize the new Huerta regime and quickly secured emergency powers from the legislature to raise troops in order to "sustain constitutional order." Soon Carranza went even further and rather presumptuously adopted the posture of "independent spokesman" for all of Mexico. Five days later, he fled the state capital, Saltillo, and took refuge in a small mountain village where he was relatively safe from Federal forces.

Dramatic events also occurred in both Sonora and Chihuahua, though the opposition to Huerta in those states was less clear-cut. In Chihuahua, Consul Edwards predicted "a real war." In Sonora, the situation was so uncertain that the governor, José María Maytorena, decided to leave for Tucson, Arizona, for "reasons of health." But Ambassador Wilson seemed unmoved by these reports. On March 1, 1913, he informed Washington that Carranza had submitted "unconditionally" to Huerta—a complete fabrication.

When the State Department began noticing the contradictions between Wilson's reports and those of the consuls, the ambassador tried to defend himself. "Our consuls in the field," he wrote, "have inadvertently been sympathizing with local activities against the [Mexican] federal government . . . and should be instructed to work for submission to the federal authorities."

President Taft's hesitation in recognizing Huerta's regime was not based on any great moral revulsion for either the coup or the murders; both he and Secretary of State Knox were inclined to recognize any regime that seemed securely in power. But both believed that the current uncertainty might afford the opportunity to exercise some leverage in certain disputes between Mexico and the United States.* Recognition could be used as a bargaining chip in such matters, and it was deemed advantageous to keep Huerta feeling insecure and beholden to Ambassador Wilson. That line of reasoning was all well and good, but other countries had recognized the Huerta regime almost immediately. American hesitancy placed Lane Wilson, Huerta's best friend, in a humiliating position.

*One example was the small but annoying matter of the Chamizal territory dispute, between El Paso, Texas, and the Mexican town of Juárez, across the Rio Grande.

On Tuesday, March 4, Woodrow Wilson was inaugurated as the twenty-eighth president of the United States. Although the Democratic party was inaugurating one of its own for the first time in twenty years, a spirit of good will between incoming and outgoing administrations dominated the event. The nation was enjoying prosperity, and President William Howard Taft, the "good loser" in his defeat at the polls, was personally popular. The 1912 presidential election did not represent a political upheaval. Wilson's popular vote was only 6,286,214, whereas the combined tallies of the Republican Taft and the Progressive-Republican Theodore Roosevelt were 7,699,942. So Wilson was wise in referring to his inauguration day as one of "dedication," not one of victory.

Nevertheless, Woodrow Wilson was entering the White House with a purpose. As a former professor of political science (later president) at Princeton University, he considered himself uniquely equipped to improve the state of all society in the United States. So focused was Wilson on domestic affairs that his inaugural address mentioned nothing of foreign affairs and omitted any reference to his attitude toward Mexico, Japan, and even Europe. This omission was conscious. A few days before his inauguration, the president-elect remarked to an old Princeton friend, "It would be an irony of fate if my administration had to deal with foreign affairs."

Wilson's selection of William Jennings Bryan as secretary of state appeared to be a political gesture, because Bryan lacked expertise in foreign matters. But the appointment had its merits. Bryan was willing to set his former leadership of the Democratic party aside and serve the new president loyally. And though they came from different backgrounds, the two men approached foreign affairs in much the same way. Both were moralists, who thought of foreign policy in terms of the "eternal verities rather than in terms of the expedient, missionaries, evangelists, confident that they comprehended the peace and well-being of other countries better than the leaders of those countries themselves." And Wilson tended to act the professor in dealing with countries to the south. "I am going to teach the South American Republics to elect good men!" he once declared to a British interviewer.

Not surprisingly, Wilson and Bryan took a view of Huerta different from that held by Taft and Knox. Wilson and Bryan did not consider a coup d'état a natural occurrence, especially not when compounded by brutal murders; they judged Huerta largely by the way he had seized the presidency of Mexico. So Wilson, perfectly confident of his right to do so, called on Huerta to step aside as president and hold a general election. On March 11, after only a week in office, President Wilson issued his "Declaration of Policy in Regard to Latin America": "Cooperation is only possible when supported at every turn by the orderly process of just government based upon law, not upon arbitrary or irregular force. . . . We can have no sympathy with those who seek to seize the power of government to advance their own personal interests or ambition." That statement set the tone for Wilson's vendetta against Huerta, a vendetta that would persist throughout Huerta's tenure of office.

When Victoriano Huerta had predicted "peace and prosperity" under his administration, he was riding a wave of euphoria rather than expressing his sober judgment. Nevertheless, Huerta had little reason to expect the virulence of the reaction to the crimes he was committing.

Even in his most sanguine moments, Huerta undoubtedly expected to face some resistance. Emiliano Zapata was certain to resist his rule in Morelos, and defiance of Mexico City was nothing new in the northern states. But Huerta could normally have coped with these troubles; what he had failed to anticipate was the power of Francisco Madero's ghost. Madero, Huerta reasoned, had been an unpopular president, and the country should be glad to be rid of him. And men of influence in the United States had for years befriended Porfirio Díaz, Huerta's mentor. Historically, much of American opinion had always favored friendly dictators such as himself.

In person, Huerta was no ogre, though he has often been so portrayed. Admittedly, he was a heavy drinker, suspicious, and cruel, but he also possessed some good qualities. He was loyal to the soldiers under his command, and in person he was unpretentious. He maintained a relatively simple life-style, living in a moderate home on the Calle Alfonso Herrera rather than in the presidential palace of Chapultepec. He was a shrewd poker player on the international scene, and false pride did not turn his judgment. Consistent with his Aztec Indian heritage, Huerta accepted setbacks. When the object of President Wilson's condescension, he reacted only with a shrug. And Huerta was physically courageous; the barber who shaved him daily was the brother of a man he had executed before a firing squad.

Huerta's regime seemed to start auspiciously. The terror of the Ten Tragic Days was over, and the people felt a sense of relief. They could now walk the streets without fear of instant death from stray bullets or misaimed artillery rounds. And those who had chafed under the ineptitude of Francisco Madero were elated. The army was, of course, glad to have one of its own back in power; bankers offered loans to the new regime. The church not only lent Huerta money; the authorities also arranged a Te Deum mass in the cathedral to celebrate the country's "pacification." And the coup was noted abroad. The German kaiser, always sympathetic to the "strong man," sent Huerta a message calling him "a brave soldier who would save his country with the sword of honor."

But support from the wealthy element in Mexico City could not, in itself, maintain a regime over a long period of time, and Huerta's administration had many grave weaknesses. The most glaring, perhaps, was the miserable quality of the men whom Huerta (actually Díaz) had appointed to positions of responsibility. One of the most notorious was Enrique Cepeda, the dissolute governor of the Federal District, who instituted a pogrom against all former Madero supporters, regardless of their stature in the community. One of Cepeda's first acts was to execute General Gabriel Hernández, a popular twenty-four-year-old Maderista leader. Cepeda, drunk, had ordered Hernández dragged out of prison in the middle of the night and shot without formality. Cepeda was soon removed from office, but not before he had caused untold damage to Huerta's standing with the people.

Huerta's political hierarchy now began to fall apart. Félix Díaz, for one, had not forgotten the "Pact of the Embassy," agreed under the eye of Ambassador Wilson. It committed Huerta to relinquish his office, hold a presidential election in April 1913, and support Díaz in that election. When Huerta deferred the election until October without consulting Díaz, the latter protested. Then, fearing for his life, he renounced his candidacy and accepted the post of special ambassador to Japan.

Others also deserted Huerta. Minister of War Manuel Mondragón, one of the original conspirators against Madero, was actually a Díaz follower, not a Huertista. When Díaz knuckled under, therefore, Mondragón became embittered and resigned his post. He left for the United States emitting a volley of curses at Díaz. (He did not dare to mention Huerta by name.)

As a result of this erosion in his government, Huerta came to rely more and more on his cronies. The most prominent of these was General Aureliano Blanquet, who became minister of war in place of Mondragón. Those officials who had not been loyal members of

Huerta's inner circle were gradually removed. Administrative ability was no noticeable criterion in the selection of their replacements.

As his civilian administration fell apart, Huerta took on the trappings of a military dictator. He ordered a general mobilization so thorough that by the end of 1913 his theoretical force had reached the astonishing level of 200,000 troops. Such a troop strength meant, of course, that most of his soldiers were unwilling conscripts, many of them inducted by rather creative methods. One writer described a typical scene: "After the bullfight on Sunday seven hundred unfortunates were seized, doubtless never to see their families again. . . . At a big fire a few days ago nearly a thousand were taken, many women among them, who are put to work in the powder-mills. . . . [The people] scarcely dare to go out after dark. Posting a letter may mean, literally, going to the cannon's mouth."

In common with anyone depending on an army for survival in power, Huerta took steps to ensure the loyalty of the officers and men. He lavished military decorations and promotions on them. He promoted the military's mystique by creating a new super rank, "general of the army," on three officers: Porfirio Díaz, Blanquet, and himself. His mainstay, of course, was the regular establishment, so he was particularly careful to maintain its dignity, assigning such dirty details as executions to the rurales, or constabulary. But in addition to his regulars, rurales, and conscripts, Huerta also militarized the civilian population, requiring factory workers and shopkeepers to participate in military drill on Sundays. The mobilization of Mexico in 1913–14 has been called "unprecedented in the nation's history."

As 1913 wore on, civilian dissatisfaction with the Huerta government was reflected by growing opposition in the Mexican Congress. In mid-September, the discontent came to a head when a respected senator, Belisario Domínguez, attacked Huerta openly. In a speech which he was forbidden from presenting, Domínguez labeled Huerta's promise of peace "spurious," called attention to Huerta's declining prestige abroad, bewailed the depreciation of the Mexican currency, and condemned the gagging of the press. Domínguez called for an upheaval. "The fatherland," he exhorted, "demands that you cast out the shame of having as its first magistrate a traitor and assassin."

The text of Domínguez's speech was circulated surreptitiously among the members of Congress and reached the press. So, predictably, he was doomed. Two weeks after the text became public, four policemen appeared at the Domínguez doorstep, dragged the senator out of bed, drove him to a cemetery at Coyoacán, and shot and buried him. Congress in particular and the Mexican people in general grew thoroughly alarmed.

In Washington, President Woodrow Wilson viewed the degenerating Mexican scene with horror but also with perplexity. On the one hand, he was determined not to recognize Huerta as provisional president of Mexico; on the other, his options for taking action were limited. Powerful interests in the United States, intent on preserving economic and political stability in Mexico, called for tolerance of the Huerta regime. In early May 1913, a spokesman representing a group of large American corporations* came to the White House with a compromise plan. It called on the State Department to recognize Huerta's temporary regime provided that Huerta would promise to hold a presidential election before the last day of October 1913—in which Huerta would not be a candidate. In addition to granting recognition, the United States would also prevail upon Governor Carranza to suspend his growing revolt in the northern states.

Wilson was at first intrigued by this new proposal, but he soon backed off. It was premature, he believed. He was not yet aware of the worst aspects of the Huerta administration, and his trusted adviser Colonel Edward House could find no fault with Huerta other than his method in grabbing power. Before taking any action, Wilson thus decided to check further into the true state of affairs in Mexico.

But where should the president turn in order to obtain advice? Henry L. Wilson, though still U.S. ambassador, was discredited in Washington and was destined soon to be removed. So the president decided to send a friend, William Bayard Hale, to make a survey. Hale, a forty-four-year-old journalist and onetime clergyman, had written Wilson's "official" campaign biography, a hagiography that had contributed markedly to Wilson's election as president in 1912. Whatever his faults, Hale was Wilson's own man, whom the president could trust.

Hale departed for Mexico City in May and with astonishing rapidity concluded that the Huerta regime was doomed. He went so far as to predict that Huerta's continuance in power could eventually call

---

*The Southern Pacific Railway; Phelps, Dodge and Company; the Greene Canea Copper Company; and Edward L. Doheny's Mexican Petroleum Company.

for U.S. intervention in Mexico. Wilson took Hale's conclusions to heart and on June 14 made a "public declaration of policy," which once more called on Huerta to step aside as a presidential candidate in the October elections. Shortly after issuing this statement, the president called Ambassador Lane Wilson back to Washington. The ambassador never returned to Mexico.

Though apparently satisfied with Hale's reports, President Wilson nevertheless decided to send a second emissary, John Lind, a former governor of Minnesota and a friend of Bryan's. Unlike Hale, who had only unofficial status, Lind was sent as a representative, though without the status of an ambassador. Huerta saw quickly that Wilson was trying to send an agent without recognizing his government with an ambassadorial title. So Huerta rebuffed Lind's request for an appointment and ordered him out of Mexico City.

Lind retreated to Veracruz, where he sulked for some months and plotted Huerta's overthrow.* Meanwhile, Victoriano Huerta began to drum up anti-American feeling in Mexico City.

President Wilson reacted mildly to Huerta's rejection of Lind, probably aware that he himself had handled the matter ineptly. So on August 27 he announced a new policy, that of "watchful waiting."

The term "watchful waiting" included *(a)* neutrality between Huerta and the rebels in the hinterlands of Mexico and *(b)* the establishment of an arms embargo against both sides, government and revolutionary. The concept was well received. The people of Mexico had viewed with alarm the volumes of arms being sold across the Rio Grande by American merchants. The favorable reception brought on a period of calm in relations between the two countries.

All in all, Huerta had not been seriously threatened by the actions of the United States, annoyed though he may have been. His regime was in danger not from outside of Mexico but from the inside, where the successes scored by the warlords of the north were rapidly eroding the territory under his control.

---

*One elaborate scheme for a U.S. occupation of Mexico City, drawn up with Marine Major Smedley Butler, was actually sent to the U.S. Army War College for study.

5

****

First Chief

Victoriano Huerta never controlled all of Mexico, not even at the moment he seized power from President Madero. Even Madero's orders had been strictly obeyed only in the settled regions. In a mountainous country, where villages were connected only by narrow dirt roads, local warlords had long diluted the power of the central government. The Mexico of 1913 has often been compared to ancient Greece, a nation of city-states.

In "normal" times, most of these warlords remained fairly quiet, running local affairs as they saw fit but rendering lip service to the authority of Mexico City. The beginning of the Madero presidency was one of those quiet times. Soon, however, a disappointed Emiliano Zapata had resumed his rebellious activities, and Madero had also been forced to face the Orozco, Reyes, and Díaz rebellions during 1912. Those three uprisings had been quelled, but the seeds of revolt remained.

Madero's removal and assassination ignited new revolts. The state of Durango was one of the hotbeds. There three groups—led by Manuel Chao, Tomás Urbina, and the Arrieta brothers—defied the central government, and Huerta could do nothing about it. Scattered uprisings occurred in seven other states.*

---

*Sinaloa, Tepic, Colima, San Luis Potosí, Tamaulipas, Michoacán, and Guerrero. See William Weber Johnson, *Heroic Mexico* (New York, 1968), p. 152.

The greatest threat to any unpopular regime had always come from the northern states of Sonora, Chihuahua, and Coahuila. This northern tier was separated from central Mexico by formidable obstacles—deserts and mountains. Furthermore, they bordered on the United States, a source of supplies and independent ideas. Nearly all effective revolutions had begun in the Sonora-Chihuahua region, including those of Madero against Díaz and later of Orozco against Madero. Zapata, though operating within a few miles of Mexico City, was poorly organized, and his objectives were limited to reform in Morelos; therefore, the major upheavals against Mexico City nearly always came from the north.

In early 1913, the outrage against Huerta, though widespread, was neither unanimous nor at first coordinated. In Sonora, Governor José María Maytorena found the political situation too explosive, so he took a vacation in Tucson, Arizona, for his health. In Chihuahua, Governor Abraham González quickly came out against Huerta and was brutally murdered by Federal soldiers. And even Coahuila's governor, Venustiano Carranza, exhibited a great deal of ambivalence and vacillation before he took a firm stand.

At this point, concessions by Huerta toward the northern states might have saved his hold on the whole northern region. Instead, he made implacable enemies of all the local chiefs, mainly of Governor Carranza.

Carranza, the man destined to lead the political opposition against Victoriano Huerta, was an enigmatic figure. He was, like Madero, a comfortable Coahuila landowner, not the type of man likely to become the leader of a revolutionary movement. The stereotype of the revolutionary was that of a young, tough Indian, driven to drastic action because he had everything to gain and nothing to lose by following the cause. Carranza, by contrast, was fifty-four years of age, calculating, and conservative. In person, he played the role of the patriarch. His movements were slow and ponderous, accentuated by his great height and his large potbelly. Because of his weak eyes he wore blue-tinted sunglasses, and he had the disconcerting habit of stroking his white beard when in thought. He enjoyed luxurious living and kept his emotions to himself.

And yet Carranza had qualities that fitted him admirably for the role of political front. He was viewed as "civilized," educated, but practical, unburdened by unrealistic ideals or humanitarian concerns.

He was above all a purposeful man, who thoroughly understood the nature of revolution. Once, in exasperation over Madero's kindness to former Díaz supporters, Carranza admonished the president, "Revolutions must be implacable if they are to triumph. . . . The revolution which compromises commits suicide!"

Carranza was shrewd enough to recognize the immense value of maintaining a civilian status. Though he had been called secretary of war in Madero's revolutionary establishment—and though he allowed himself to be called "general" when that title worked to his advantage—Carranza disliked and mistrusted all military men. He would always, no matter the circumstance, be viewed in the public mind as the governor of Coahuila.

Though Carranza participated in the Madero revolution, he had never been a devoted Madero loyalist. His political mentor was actually General Bernardo Reyes, the future rebel, who at that time was governor of the neighboring state of Nuevo León. When Reyes fell out with Porfirio Díaz, however, Carranza deemed that his political prospects were eclipsed, and he looked to Francisco I. Madero. Though Carranza had previously considered Madero to be "of no political significance," he joined Madero during the latter's temporary exile in San Antonio, Texas. Madero appointed him provisional governor of Coahuila and later, for a short time, minister of war. Upon the fall of Díaz in June 1911, Madero again appointed Carranza provisional governor of Coahuila. Carranza was elected governor in his own right in December, when Madero was elected president.

The relationship between Madero and Carranza was always tentative, however, partly because of Carranza's sensitive political ear, which was always to the ground. Thus, when the Madero regime teetered in 1912, Carranza considered a rebellion of his own. He invited the governors of Chihuahua, Sonora, San Luis Potosí, and Aguascalientes to a conference at Saltillo, during which he gave the impression that he planned to take action against Madero—which he never did.

By early February 1913, Carranza had reconciled himself to Madero—or had at least become concerned about a possible coup by Porfirio Díaz's nephew, Félix Díaz. In any case, Carranza was one of those who communicated with Gustavo Madero, warning him of the Reyes-Díaz threat. Later, after the beginning of the Ten Tragic Days, Carranza sent a message to Madero in which he offered him a safe refuge under his own protection in Saltillo.

With his acute consciousness of Madero's vulnerability, Carranza was mentally prepared for the president's downfall. He quickly denounced Huerta's coup and requested authority from the state legislature to raise an armed force. Nevertheless, aware that his own position was isolated, he took pains to avoid committing himself irrevocably. On February 21, the day before Madero's murder, Carranza sent two emissaries to Huerta with a conciliatory message. He had changed his mind, he said, and was now convinced that Huerta's assumption of power had "followed constitutional norms." Carranza declared himself "willing to conform to the new administration." Huerta, however, showed no interest in negotiating with a state governor on an equal basis, and the next day Federal troops began moving into Coahuila to restore order. That rebuff, along with Madero's murder the next day, brought an end to Carranza's attempt to curry Huerta's favor.

Venustiano Carranza was nothing if not flexible. On being rebuffed by Huerta, he immediately assumed the role of "independent spokesman for Mexico." Misinformed by Henry Lane Wilson through the local consul that President Taft had recognized Huerta's presidency, Carranza took it upon himself to issue a public letter to Taft: "The Mexican nation condemns the villainous *coup d'état* which deprived Mexico of her constitutional rulers by cowardly assassination. . . . I am certain that both the government of Your Excellency as well as that of your successor will not accept the spurious government which Huerta is attempting to establish."

Carranza was now at war with Huerta. However, he lacked sufficient military forces to resist a Federal occupation of Coahuila. So on February 27, the day after his message of protest to President Taft, Carranza left Saltillo with a small retinue and headed for the town of Arteaga, in the hills. There, though only a few miles from Saltillo, he felt relatively safe from surprise attack.

Up to this time, Carranza's objective had been limited. He saw himself only as the governor of Coahuila, in which capacity he was trying to form an anti-Huerta bloc with the governors of the two other northern Mexican states. When word came of Governor Maytorena's flight from Sonora and of the death of Governor González in Chihuahua, Carranza realized that he had been placed in a position of unique influence—provided that he could avoid a fate similar to that of González. Carranza therefore decided to pull up stakes once more. He dropped back to Piedras Negras, a small town on the Rio Grande as far from Saltillo as possible within the borders of Coahuila. Once convinced that Federal forces were content to occupy Saltillo, he edged part of the way back and established a provisional capital at Monclova. Monclova remained Carranza's headquarters for the rest of his three months in Coahuila.

In late March 1913, Carranza had amassed sufficient military force that he risked a dramatic attack on Saltillo. It was a mistake; the defenders were too strong. After fifty-five hours of costly fighting, Carranza gave up the effort and fell back toward Monclova. At that time, whether because of that defeat or in spite of it, Carranza's fertile mind gave birth to his next move. He would declare himself leader of all the opposition against Huerta in Mexico. So when he reached a hospitable hacienda named Guadalupe, Carranza decided to compose a "plan."

Carranza spent a long, sleepless night on March 25, thinking. By the next morning, he knew what he wanted. He called his secretary and dictated his "Plan of Guadalupe." The provisions of the document were very general; they simply set forth the organization of his rebel government, which he chose to call "Constitutionalist." His newly organized Constitutionalist party nominated him, Venustiano Carranza, as the leader of revolutionary Mexico. But since the constitution of 1857 forbade a president from succeeding himself, Carranza avoided using any such term as "provisional president." Instead, he called himself the "First Chief of the Constitutionalist Army." Thus was the Constitutionalist party born.

The Plan of Guadalupe, drawn up by Carranza and for Carranza, required ratification by other rebel leaders in order to give it status. The self-styled First Chief therefore invited the representatives of the dissident factions in other northern states to join him in a meeting at Monclova. Only two states, Chihuahua and Sonora, sent delegates, and even with that limited group Carranza had problems in selling his plan. Even Carranza's own followers were reluctant to support a "plan" that did nothing more than castigate Huerta's methods and propose Carranza as a substitute leader of Mexico.

Fortunately for Carranza's cause, the Chihuahua representative, Interim Governor Ignacio Pesqueira, was not a man of sufficient stature to rival him. Moreover, Pesqueira hated the absent Maytorena so heartily that he gladly acknowledged Maytorena's chief rival, Carranza, as the supreme authority. After three days of debate, therefore, the delegates half-heartedly accepted the plan and recognized Carranza's vague political leadership in those geographical areas controlled by the newly named Constitutionalists.

First Chief Carranza remained at Monclova for over three months, from late March to early July 1913. The Federal commander, General Joaquín Maass, allowed him to do so. To Maass, Carranza represented no threat. Finally, however, Maass bestirred himself and mounted a force, so Carranza prudently retreated. He retraced his steps up to Piedras Negras but then gave way to pressure and left Coahuila. His destination was Sonora, where the political situation seemed to favor the Constitutionalists. On his departure from Coahuila, Carranza left the loyal General Pablo González to represent his remaining interests.

At this point, Carranza demonstrated his political sensitivity. Instead of traveling to Sonora in comfort aboard an American train, he rode on horseback. He headed southwestward to the Laguna district in Durango to meet the leaders of two large local families that had joined his cause, the Arrietas and the Herreras. These clans were about to attack the important city of Torreón, and Carranza wanted to be seen as a participant in this action. The attack failed miserably, but Carranza's efforts to cement his relationships with the troops were highly successful:

> For a short-sighted, corpulent, middle-aged *político*—to his critics, then and now, "mediocrity incarnate" . . . —this was a sort of achievement, which probably helped establish Carranza's shaky reputation and authority. Though a civilian and a *político* . . . he was at least prepared to show himself, in boots and leggings, sombrero and khaki jacket, to the troops in the field; to trek across country, discarding frock-coat, wing collar, and all the other accoutrements of the respectable bourgeois.

Once the attack was abandoned, Carranza led his contingent of a hundred men across the Sierra Madre to his temporary capital in Sonora, the town of Nogales, on the U.S. border.

Carranza's transfer of his capital from Coahuila to Nogales proved to be wise. Sonora provided an ideal base where he and his followers could organize and equip troops, relatively safe from Huerta in Mexico City. It was, moreover, conveniently located next to the United States, the principal source of easy supply for his army. In Sonora, Carranza also discovered a new military chief of remarkable potential, a man named Alvaro Obregón.

Obregón, at thirty-five, possessed attributes that Carranza found congenial. He came from the gentry, of Spanish descent, though from a family impoverished by the early death of his father. Only casually educated in the formal sense, Obregón was schooled in the practical world as a successful local politician. His military career began only in 1912, when he joined the Sonora National Guard to fight against Pascual Orozco. He was cited for personal valor and leadership during that campaign.

Nevertheless, Obregón at least professed that he was not a military man at heart. Like Carranza, he distrusted professional soldiers. As an agnostic and socialist, he was emotionally at odds with both the professional military caste and the Catholic church. He was no dedicated Maderista, though he and Carranza paid lip service to the martyred president. On the whole, therefore, Obregón had no problem in maintaining a posture of loyalty to Carranza, at least for the time being. In their respective roles—Carranza the politician and Obregón the civilian soldier—the two would make an effective team.

Another newcomer to Carranza's entourage was more ambivalent. Martín Luis Guzmán, a highly educated, enthusiastic, idealistic young man, joined Carranza at Nogales with high hopes of making an intellectual contribution to the Revolution. Guzmán had no desire to be a soldier; he had, in fact, sworn to his soldier father that he would never serve in the military. But though determined to make his contribution in the political arena, Guzmán was also unfit to be a courtier, particularly in the retinue of the vain Carranza. He was, however, a superb recorder of events. His book on the Mexican Revolution, *The Eagle and the Serpent*, has become recognized as a classic.

When Guzmán joined Carranza, he was appalled by the quality of the people who surrounded the First Chief. Intrigue and "the lowest kind of sycophancy," he wrote, placed in the front rank the "talebearers, the bootlickers, and the panderers." Guzmán saw no hope that Carranza would ever make changes in the quality of his staff; he was too old and stubborn for that! Carranza would always respond to "flattery rather than acts, to servility rather than ability."

The fault, Guzmán concluded, lay in Carranza himself, "whose mind was totally devoid of greatness, not free from essential paltriness. His calculating coldness, which the incense bearers called the

gift of a great statesman, was useful to him in measuring the pica-
yune, not the great. . . ."

Guzmán's uncomfortable situation on Carranza's staff was rec-
tified, in a way, by an incident that he may have brought on sub-
consciously. Guzmán became impatient at a dinner one evening by
Carranza's "arbitrary and shallow observations." He therefore contra-
dicted the First Chief in front of all the entourage. Carranza treated
the outburst with benign condescension, but Guzmán realized that
his own future with Carranza was finished.

The First Chief voiced no objection when Martín Luis Guzmán
asked to leave Nogales in order to join the new star on the revolutionary horizon, General Francisco ("Pancho") Villa.

6

****

The Return of
Pancho Villa

Late in the night of March 23,
1913, a lone horseman plunged into the Rio Grande at a point near
El Paso, Texas, his mount breasting chest-deep waters to carry him
over to the Mexican side. Once across, the horse and rider galloped
through a line of trees to a large clearing. Satisfied that no Huertista
troops lurked in the area, the horseman returned to the riverbank,
stood up in his stirrups, and waved his hat. Eight other mounted men,
waiting on the Texas side of the river, then spurred their mounts and
came across. In a few moments, they splashed up on the bank. Francisco ("Pancho") Villa had returned from exile to Mexican soil, sworn
to avenge the death of Francisco I. Madero.

There was nothing quixotic about Villa's invading Chihuahua
with a force of only nine men. The state of Chihuahua was his
adopted home, and he was sure that the people of the region would
join him. He had good reason to believe so. Born in the adjacent state
of Durango, he had spent sixteen years as a bandit. During that time,
there grew among the people the legend that he was a Mexican Robin
Hood, a gallant who robbed only the wealthy and shared at least some
of the proceeds with the poor. His reputation was enhanced by stories
of his impoverished youth on a prosperous hacienda, of his heroism in

avenging his sister's virtue by shooting the landlord's son who had molested her, and of his years as a fugitive from an oppressive legal system. These tales, true or not, gave Villa a rapport with the poor people of Chihuahua that lasted throughout his lifetime.

Villa had other reasons for expecting the people of Chihuahua to rally to his movement. The strong anti-Huertista sentiment in the region also permeated the Federal troops, many of them local conscripts. Villa had many friends among the Federal military, whose comrade he had been during the previous year when he commanded the Federal cavalry under Huerta in the campaign against Orozco. The discontented Federal troops would provide a rich source of potential recruits for the army Villa intended to build.

Villa's optimism was quickly justified. By late morning, only hours after crossing the river into Mexico, Villa's band of nine men had grown to twenty. The band kept increasing through the day as Villa's party rode on. From them, Villa learned for the first time of Abraham González's cruel death at the hands of Huertista soldiers. González was the man Villa revered most, after Madero, and Villa's thirst for revenge intensified.

Villa's first destination was his home in San Andrés, a hamlet about sixty miles west of Chihuahua City, where he intended to remain among friends while he built his power base. To reach San Andrés, he and his men rode through sparsely settled country, avoiding centers of Federal strength, collecting men and horses along the way. After seven days of riding, he arrived home for a brief reunion with his wife, Luz Corral.* He did not tarry long; soon he left to begin building his fighting force.

Villa had spent three months in El Paso before returning to Mexico. Sentenced to death by Huerta for insubordination nine months earlier, he had escaped the firing squad only by a last-minute reprieve from Madero himself. He was incarcerated for four months in the Santiago Tlatelolco prison, in Mexico City, during which time he learned to sign his name. He refused to join the uprising of his fellow prisoner General Bernardo Reyes, but he said nothing about Reyes's plans. He escaped at Christmastime, making his way across the Rio Grande to safety. In El Paso, Villa did not stay in hiding; as a famous

*María Corral, nicknamed Luz. Though Villa "married" many women in his travels, it was she who stayed by him and survived him.

though not completely welcome figure in El Paso, he lived openly, received visitors, and made public statements—all the while planning for the day of his return to Mexico.

During these months, Villa thought much about the way he would organize his future army. Though admired throughout Mexico for his prowess as a cavalry commander, Villa knew that he had much to learn about the other military arms. He had listened carefully when General Reyes expounded on his theories of military operations. Villa resolved that his army should include not only cavalry but infantry and artillery as well.

Now, in Chihuahua, Villa sought out an old comrade, Colonel Fidel Avila, to help him organize his army. He easily persuaded Avila to desert Huerta's service and join him. Avila knew about infantry operations, and Villa planned to use him as a trainer. Together the two recruited about eight hundred men, and Villa placed Avila in charge of his "military academy," which he located at Satevó, near San Andrés. Meanwhile, Villa led a small band of men out to do what damage they could to the Federals.

Pancho Villa loved to play cops-and-robbers, and the freedom he now enjoyed with his band of partisans allowed him to create a little mischief. On the day he left Avila at Satevó, Villa trotted over to nearby Santa Isabel and there sent a taunting telegram to the governor of Chihuahua, in Chihuahua City: "Knowing the government you represent was preparing to extradite me, I have saved you the trouble. I am now in Mexico ready to make war upon you."

While in the telegraph office, Villa's quick eye spied another telegram on the operator's desk. It revealed that a train carrying a consignment of government silver was due to arrive. A delighted Pancho Villa led his men to nearby Chavaría to intercept it. On the train, they found 122 large silver bars in a secret compartment. Before leaving with the silver, Villa toyed with its terrified custodian and then, annoyed by the man's abject terror, shot him in the face and hung the corpse on a pole for all the people to see.

At that point, Villa suffered a setback. When he tried to take his stolen silver back to San Andrés, he discovered that not everybody in town was on his side. The mayor had set up an ambush, intending to finish him off. Villa and most of his men escaped the trap and managed to bury the silver in the hills, but the episode convinced Villa that his original plan of organizing an army in his own territory was too perilous.

Villa decided to move to the northwestern border of Chihuahua.

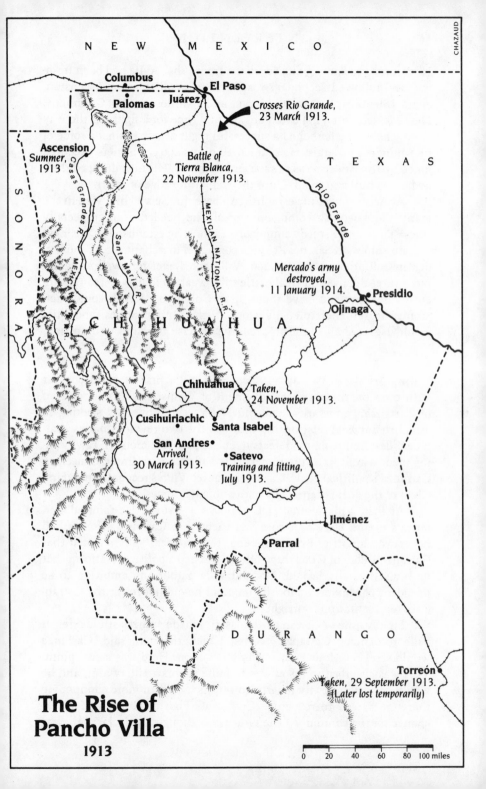

CHAZAUD

NEW MEXICO

Columbus

El Paso

Palomas

Juárez

Crosses Rio Grande,
23 March 1913.

TEXAS

Ascension
Summer,
1913

Battle of
Tierra Blanca,
22 November 1913.

Rio Grande

SONORA

CHIHUAHUA

Mercado's army
destroyed,
11 January 1914.

Presidio

Ojinaga

Chihuahua

Taken,
24 November 1913.

Cusihuiriachic

Santa Isabel

San Andres
Arrived,
30 March 1913.

Satevo
Training and fitting,
July 1913.

Jiménez

Parral

DURANGO

Torreón

Taken, 29 September 1913.
(Later lost temporarily)

The Rise of
Pancho Villa
1913

0 20 40 60 80 100 miles

He returned to Satevó, picked up the troops that Avila had been training, and followed secondary roads to the small town of Ascensión,
about 150 miles southwest of Juárez and 80 miles south of Columbus,
New Mexico. But Villa could always find time for a fight; on the way
to Ascensión, he launched a successful night attack against a force of
four hundred Federals. He ordered all of his sixty prisoners executed
(lined up three deep so as to save ammunition). His men dumped their
bodies—a hundred in all—into the well at the edge of town.

At Ascensión, Villa established a base that served him well in the
many campaigns to come. First of all, he needed arms, especially
rifles. To ensure a steady supply of weapons, he established a business
relationship with Samuel Ravel, a congenial merchant across the border at Columbus, New Mexico. Villa and Ravel followed a regular
procedure; Villa would steal cattle from wealthy landowners in northern Chihuahua and drive them up to Columbus. Ravel would then
arrange to sell the stolen livestock in the United States, and Villa
would use his share of the proceeds to purchase arms and ammunition.

During his six-week stay at Ascención, Villa first came in contact
with the Constitutionalist movement of Venustiano Carranza. Two
of Carranza's emissaries rode into Villa's camp one day seeking to
establish a formal relationship between the two revolutionaries. Carranza, despite his many defeats over the past few months, saw nothing inconsistent in trying to persuade Villa to subordinate himself to
Carranza's political goals. Carranza wanted Villa's recognition as First
Chief of the anti-Huertista Constitutionalist forces.

At first, Villa scoffed at Carranza's overtures. He taunted Carranza's errand boys by reminding them that Carranza's forces had
never won a battle. But in the end, the practical Villa realized that
Carranza's Plan of Guadalupe offered Mexico a political platform that
he himself totally lacked. Nor did Villa harbor any ambition to be
president of Mexico. So for the moment he did not reject the Carrancista representations outright.

Finally, one of Carranza's emissaries made an irresistible offer. If
Villa recognized Carranza as First Chief, the man said, Carranza
would send him four French 75-mm cannon. Here was a real plum!
Villa was absorbed in his efforts to build up his artillery arm, and he
would go to almost any lengths to get his hands on more cannon. He
therefore agreed to recognize Carranza's Plan of Guadalupe in exchange for the cannon. At the same time, though, he declared that he

would not tolerate any meddling in his sphere of action. "If I need generals," he told the Carrancistas, "I will appoint them myself."

Villa was careful, in framing his request for the artillery pieces, to direct the message to the governor of Sonora, Don José María Maytorena, not to Carranza himself.

Toward the end of the summer of 1913, Pancho Villa decided that his army was ready to begin a serious campaign. He therefore marched his seven hundred men southward toward San Andrés, picking up other guerrilla forces along the way. They arrived at San Andrés on August 26, to find a superior Federal force of thirteen hundred men waiting for them. Their commander, General Félix Terrazas,* was expecting Villa to attack with the same sort of light cavalry assault that had earned him fame in the past. But Terrazas was in for a surprise; Villa now fielded a balanced, well-disciplined force of infantry, cavalry, and artillery.

The outcome of the battle was never in doubt. Early in the fighting, Villa's men captured two French 75-mm guns and turned them about, pouring round after round into Terrazas's attacking troops. The Federals soon fled, leaving a hundred dead behind them. Terrazas himself escaped to the south by train, and Villa then systematically shot the prisoners he had taken—236 in all. This time, Villa set a new record for economy of ammunition. He lined his victims up in four ranks, so that one bullet could take four lives. The amount of spoils Villa took at San Andrés was astounding: seven railroad trains, over four hundred rifles, and 20,000 cartridges.

Word of Villa's victory at San Andrés spread like wildfire across Chihuahua. Enthusiastic recruits poured in to join him, and Villa's efficient cadre integrated them quickly into the overall force. Independent guerrilla units also flocked to his banner.

Villa's new army was no parade ground unit, to be sure. It was truly the army of the poor, made up largely of Indians, of peoples suppressed from time immemorial first by the Aztec, then by the Spanish, and most lately by the wealthy haciendados. Motivated by a

*The Terrazas family was the wealthiest in Chihuahua, its members always among the state's leaders. Generally, as landowners, they opposed the Revolution, supporting Orozco in his 1912 counterrevolution. They especially hated Villa, as he habitually stole their cattle for sale in the United States. Nevertheless, the members of the family were not always united. Silvestre Terrazas, for example, supported the Revolution, sometimes acting as Villa's chief staff officer.

common cause, Villa's troops cheerfully sustained severe hardships.
They were good-humored and boisterous men who, with their female
companions (soldaderas), traveled miles on end atop Villa's freight
trains while their horses, mules, and cattle rode inside. Their con-
sumption of marijuana and pulque was formidable, and their main
entertainments were gambling, cockfighting, and sexual promiscuity.
These informal warriors did not see themselves as noble crusaders;
rather, they wryly compared their army to a gigantic cockroach, as
celebrated in their battle song, "La Cucaracha":

> La cucaracha, la cucaracha
> Ya no puede caminar;
> Porque no tiene, porque se falta
> Marijuana por fumar!*

But it was a great error, as many of Villa's enemies learned, to
underestimate these troops because of their lack of military panoply.
When it came to a fight, they were formidable, inspired by loyalty to
Villa and by hatred of their former oppressors. That shared hatred
held Villa's army together through thick and thin.

Villa himself felt that hatred; his whole campaign against Huerta
was driven by it. He vented his greatest fury on those who he surmised had betrayed him, because his simple creed demanded personal
loyalty above nearly all else. He hated Huerta not so much because
Huerta was a killer—killing was common—but because he had betrayed Francisco Madero.

For that reason, the name of the consummate turncoat Pascual
Orozco stood at the top of Villa's list of targets, right below that of
Huerta himself. Orozco had returned to Mexico again and been accepted as one of Huerta's principal field commanders. As one of
Villa's biographers described Villa's attitude, "There was but one policy cruel enough and durable enough to match the treachery of those
two Judases [Huerta and Orozco]: Extinction. . . . Had he had his way,
the bodies of Pascual Orozco and Victoriano Huerta would have been
smeared with human excrement and staked out in the sun to feed the
ants and the buzzards."

Throughout his strange career, Pacual Orozco retained a special
body of troops known as *colorados*, or "red-flaggers." These men were

---

*"The cockroach, the cockroach! He cannot travel. Because he lacks, because
he needs, marijuana to smoke."

universally feared for their wanton cruelty, and at one time they made the error of executing some of Villa's men without justification. The *colorados* therefore became Villa's special target. Since Villa always sought qualified recruits, he often spared the lives of Federal prisoners, integrating them into his own forces. But he treated Orozco's *colorados* differently: he hanged every one he could get his hands on.

Villa's personal staff was augmented in September of 1913 by the arrival of a man named Rodolfo Fierro. The strikingly handsome Fierro, formerly a railroad man, had already earned a wide reputation as a killer. To him, killing was not a painful necessity but a pleasure. He was noted for his enthusiastic and creative ways of eliminating enemy prisoners. When Fierro first arrived, he and Villa eyed each other with some suspicion. After a bit of exploration, however, they became friends. Fierro soon grew so devoted to Villa that he assumed the role of bodyguard, watching over his chief with a possessiveness that both amused and frightened witnesses. It was a rare occasion when Villa was seen without his right-hand man, Rodolfo Fierro.

Villa never forgot his days as a bandit, when a price was affixed to his head. As a result, he never trusted anyone. He never ate a bite of food unless someone else had sampled it first. To guard against being shot or stabbed in the middle of the night, he always slept away from camp. In his comings and goings, he invariably left in one direction and returned from another. A bandit Villa had been and a bandit he would remain, no matter how accomplished his military exploits and no matter how impressive his titles.

It seems strange that a man like Pancho Villa could be seen in certain quarters of the American press as a noble, romantic figure. But so he was, and Villa eagerly exploited that view of his personality. The error, of course, lay in the eyes of the observers. The fact that Villa lived outside the law, always on his own terms, appealed to those who were disaffected by contemporary society. Some saw him as representing their own view of the world. Others hoped that he could be made useful to their own interests. Those people likened Villa to a social reformer, contrasting him with his political superior, Carranza, whom they pictured as a tool of the reactionaries. Villa's appeal to the mass of the people was genuine. "No rival *caudillo*," wrote one Mexican supporter, "won the hearts of a greater army of believers [than Villa]. Although the better part of the *gente decente* judged Villa criminal, the poor idealized him as their 'avenging angel.' . . ."

The American correspondents whom Villa attracted were mostly those of a radical bent. The best-known were Ambrose Bierce and John Reed. At the time, the seventy-one-year-old Bierce was already famous. Like Villa, Bierce offered a study in contrasts. Wounded and cited for bravery at Kennesaw Mountain during the Civil War, Bierce later became a journalist by trade but a creative writer by instinct. Though employed as a correspondent for the Hearst newspaper chain, he held journalism in contempt throughout his life and vented his rage against a society that forced him to write ordinary newspaper prose in order to make a living. When the burned-out Bierce left the United States to join Villa, he wrote a friend, "Goodbye. If you hear of my being stood up against a Mexican stone wall and shot to rags please know that I think it a pretty good way to depart this life. It beats old age, disease, or falling down the cellar stairs. To be a Gringo in Mexico—ah, that is euthanasia!"

Bierce joined Villa as one of a group of American correspondents seeking colorful stories. They also had a pecuniary interest: Villa had looted much treasure and could therefore afford to pay journalists well for writing favorable stories about him. Bierce enjoyed a privileged position in this group, staying with Villa as a personal guest and using his considerable charm and abilities as a raconteur to play up to Villa's love of laughter and fun. Bierce was one of Villa's great favorites.

In contrast, John Reed was an unknown before he came to Mexico. But the future apologist for Soviet communism sent dispatches from Mexico that earned him public attention. Reed's book *Insurgent Mexico* contains vivid descriptions of high literary quality. Unlike Bierce, Reed seemed to believe in Villa's cause, though he refused to stay with him full-time. Instead, Reed traveled throughout the revolutionary territory and wrote colorful studies about other figures as well.

Men like Bierce and Reed—and young adventurers like the future actor Tom Mix—made Villa's name a household word, and Villa a hero, in the United States.

Villa was now ready to seize control over the rest of Chihuahua. His eventual goal was Mexico City, but the consolidation of Chihuahua would provide him with a base from which to launch later operations. In order to control the state, Villa first needed to seize the capital, Chihuahua City, and to gain control of the north–south railroad. Controlling the railroad would facilitate taking Chihuahua, so that objective governed Villa's planning.

The main line of the Mexican National Railroad ran about 250 miles from Juárez, on the Rio Grande, southward to Torreón, over the Durango border. A secondary line, known as the Mexican Northwest Railroad, also joined Juárez and Chihuahua, but its track ran in a wide arc to the west, serving a series of small communities such as the American-owned Cusi Mining Company, at Cusihuiriáchic. The important branch was the National Railroad; the Mexican Northwest Railroad would never have been built except for the American mining interests.

From his base at San Andrés, Villa could attack any of the key cities he wished—Juárez, Chihuahua, or Torreón—and he eventually decided to take Torreón first, as its capture would shield him against any Federal reinforcements that Huerta might send from Mexico City. With Torreón in his hands, Villa would be safe to move at will along the length of the railroad in Chihuahua.

Villa and his men arrived near Torreón on September 29, 1913. Since a whole Federal division held the city, Villa was facing a major operation. To make absolutely sure he had uncontested control over the attacking force, therefore, Villa called for an election among the commanders of the six semi-independent brigades that composed it. It was a wise gesture. Some of the brigades were nearly as large as his own, and their commanders were men of consequence. Two of them, Maclovio Herrera and Aguirre Benavides, came from prominent families, and one, Tomás Urbina, was an old compadre.

Villa's election to command this force was a foregone conclusion, but the assembled brigade commanders were pleased to be consulted. They decided to call themselves the Division of the North, the name by which Villa's army was henceforth known.

The Division of the North won an easy victory at Torreón, and the results might have been even more decisive had Villa exploited the Federals' weak position. The Federal commander had deployed his troops bestride the Nazas River, and Villa missed the opportunity to destroy it one piece at a time. Instead, he sent part of his army against each Federal force, splitting his own army also. But the zeal of Villa's men made up for any flaws in his tactics. At the end of the battle, five hundred Federals lay dead on the field, half the original force. Villa picked up two cannon, 600 rifles, 150,000 cartridges, and 360 grenades. Afterward Villa shot all the Federal prisoners he had taken except some artillerymen he considered of potential future use to him. Under the circumstances, these terrified men were glad to sign up with Villa. One of Villa's future biographers, Elias Torrés, was among them.

Villa entered Torreón in early October amid pomp and brass bands. He established his headquarters in the Hotel Salvador and remained a whole month, savoring his success. While there, he took a fancy to a young beauty named Juana Torres and immediately "married" her. Villa's original wife, María ("Luz") Corral, was waiting back at San Andrés; but Villa was unconcerned about such trivialities as bigamy. He was the law wherever he went. Who was to stop him from the many "marriages" he enjoyed during his career? Certainly no power in Mexico!

Villa's month at Torreón, while enjoyable, was also busy. As a magistrate for the first time, he showed much concern for the people. He provided surgical supplies to the local hospitals and distributed food to the city's poor. He procured money to supply his army by levying taxes on local businessmen. Then, in early November 1913, he embarked on his campaign to take Chihuahua City.

Villa's campaign against Chihuahua City showed him at his best—imaginative, daring, insolent to his enemies. But it began with a setback. Overruling his staff, Villa launched an all-out attack on Chihuahua, even though the garrison was alert and well armed. The defenses were strong, and Villa's troops, short of ammunition, were repulsed. But the Federal forces refused to leave their fortifications, so both sides settled into a siege. The Federal commander, General Salvador Mercado, wired to Mexico City that Villa had been "defeated and dispersed."

At nightfall, November 13, Pancho Villa broke the deadlock at Chihuahua by reverting to his old role of the quick-moving guerrilla. Leaving his supplies, his infantry, and his artillery behind, he slipped around Chihuahua with two thousand cavalry, headed north toward Juárez. So effective was his covering force that nobody in the city suspected what was afoot.

Good fortune continued to smile on Villa's undertaking. On the first afternoon of his sweep around Chihuahua, he ambushed an unguarded coal train and at the same time discovered that he had captured a telegrapher. Soon the telegrapher, a gun at his head, was wiring to Juárez: "Derailed. No line to Chihuahua. Everything burned by revolutionaries. Send second engine and orders."

In a few minutes came a reply: "No engines. Find tools. Advise and await orders when back on rails." Then, later: "Back in to Juárez. Wire at each station."

Within two hours, Villa's men had dumped the coal from the train and boarded it. The train then backed up toward Juárez. At each telegraph station, Villa's captive telegrapher called in for confirmation of his orders to continue. Villa's train arrived in Juárez at midnight, November 14.

Nobody suspected the ruse. Villa's cavalry, believed to be in central Chihuahua, took full possession of Juárez within two hours. Villa's feat broke the spirit of the Federal forces in the north of Mexico.

While occupying Juárez, Villa began to realize that Venustiano Carranza, still at Nogales, was becoming jealous of his own successes. On the morning after the capture of Juárez, Villa sent Carranza a proud message announcing that the place "is at your disposal." Carranza wired back his congratulations but did nothing more. He hedged on Villa's request for reinforcements, reneged on his promise to send money, and also, Villa suspected, began planting disaffection in Villa's army.

Villa soon had his most serious suspicions confirmed. On November 20, the third anniversary of Madero's return to Mexico, Carranza showed no interest in observing the now traditional rites. In fact, he deliberately ignored the date.

The trivial incident was important to Villa. He had deferred to Carranza in the belief that Carranza, like him, was fighting Huerta to avenge Madero. Villa now realized that Carranza was opposing Huerta only to promote his own interests.

In Chihuahua City, General Salvador Mercado flew into a panic when he learned of Villa's coup at Juárez. His own neck was now in the noose; Huerta had taken stern disciplinary action against the luckless Federal commander who had been routed by Villa the previous month at Torreón. Mercado, described by the columnist John Reed as "a fat, worried, undecided little man," was incapable of taking the field himself, and he did not trust his deputy, Pascual Orozco. In desperation, therefore, Mercado sent an Orozquista general, José Inés Salazar, with a force of about seven thousand men, to retake Juárez and destroy Villa. Most of Salazar's troops were tough *colorados*, more effective than the regular Federals, but their commander was not as tough as his men. Salazar marched his force up to a place called Tierra Blanca, about twenty-five miles south of Juárez. There he stopped and dug in. The initiative had passed to Villa by default.

When Villa learned of Salazar's approach, he moved out of Juárez without delay. He had no desire to be bottled up in there, and he was always concerned about maintaining good relations with his American friends. He would be blamed for any Federal artillery shells that might fall in the streets of El Paso. Villa marched his army, now grown to fifty-five hundred men, out to Tierra Blanca. Salazar, apparently still immobilized, was waiting. It was the night of November 22.

The Federals entered this battle with all the material advantages. The two forces were about equal in numbers, but Salazar's army possessed superior artillery—Villa had only two field guns—as well as an abundance of machine guns and ammunition. Lacking resources, Villa was forced to remain on the defensive during the first day of the battle while Federal artillery raked his lines. At one point, Federal cavalry threatened Villa's left flank, forcing him to stretch his defensive position and depriving him of any spare troops to hold in reserve. Because of their shortage of small-arms ammunition, the Villistas had to lie low, accepting casualties without replying to Salazar's machine guns. At the end of the day, Villa's situation looked grim.

In that predicament, Villa decided to frighten the Federals with an attack. Before dawn on November 24, Villa assaulted Salazar's trenches, forcing some of the Federals back toward their trains. Then a group of three hundred Villista cavalry hit Salazar's left flank. Determined troops could have stopped this cavalry charge easily, but Salazar's Federals lacked the heart. Their line began to waver.

At that critical moment, a violent explosion shook the ground in the Federal rear. The intrepid Rodolfo Fierro, sent by Villa to blow up the railroad tracks leading down to Chihuahua, had added a bit of flair; he had loaded a locomotive with explosives and turned it loose. The impact in the Federal rear was too much. Salazar's army broke in panic, leaving the field to Villa. At the cost of three hundred casualties, Villa had gained eight guns, four locomotives, and many small arms. The action had cost the Federals one thousand casualties. Villa later considered Tierra Blanca his most spectacular victory.

Salvador Mercado, back in Chihuahua, saw the hopelessness of his situation. So despite the pleas of the local people, he abandoned them to Villa's mercy. He took his army out on foot and horseback over the 120 desolate miles to Ojinaga, a town northeast of Chihuahua on the Rio Grande. If pressed, Mercado could cross the Rio Grande and take refuge in Presidio, Texas. There he would at least be safe from Huerta's wrath.

Villa entered Chihuahua on Mercado's heels, and he immediately set himself up as governor. To the great relief of the worried shopkeepers, he indulged in no looting or mass executions; instead, he established an administration that, though autocratic, turned out to be fair and efficient. While he was organizing his government, Villa tried to delegate the task of destroying Mercado to a subordinate commander. That expedition, however, failed.

Once again, Villa took to the field himself. Mercado and Orozco, at Ojinaga, with only thirty-five hundred men, were no match for him, especially since the two Federal leaders made no effort to cooperate with each other.* Villa attacked so violently that resistance lasted only one hour before Mercado and Orozco were fleeing to safety across the Rio Grande.

The internment of Mercado's five thousand refugees, including camp followers, constituted a major problem for the U.S. Army. Presidio, Texas, was only an isolated village, nearly as far from Juárez as it was from Chihuahua. The Americans were now obligated to feed these refugees, house them, and transport them over miles of desert to the refugee cage at Fort Bliss. Brigadier General John J. Pershing, commander at Bliss, was on hand at Presidio to supervise the move. So Villa stayed at Ojinaga long enough for a short but friendly visit with Pershing. Villa then returned to Chihuahua. It was now early January 1914.

Nine months earlier, Pancho Villa had reentered Mexico with a band of only eight men. His Division of the North now numbered in the thousands. Pancho Villa was the undisputed master of the state of Chihuahua.

---

*"I wanted to interview General Mercado . . . and sent a polite request. The note was intercepted by General Orozco, who sent back the following reply: 'Esteemed and honored sir: If you set foot inside of Ojinaga, I will stand you sideways against a wall, and with my own hand take great pleasure in shooting furrows in your back. Pascual Orozco.'" John Reed, *Insurgent Mexico* (1914; reprint, New York, 1969), p. 2.

7

****

Huerta Agonistes

When President Woodrow Wilson announced his new policy of "watchful waiting" in late August 1913, the tensions between Mexico and the United States temporarily eased. But the honeymoon lasted for only six weeks. It came to an end in early October, when Victoriano Huerta moved dramatically to assume dictatorial power in Mexico City.

The Mexican Congress had returned from its recess the previous month in a belligerent mood, eager to launch an investigation of Senator Belisario Domínguez's murder and upset over Constitutionalist military successes in the north, the most spectacular of which was Pancho Villa's capture of Torreón on October 1. The series of disasters suffered by the Federal army was seen as an indication of low morale, casting serious doubt on the general's ability even to defend Mexico City, much less to govern the whole country. But while the members of Congress were fulminating, Huerta was meeting with Minister of War Aureliano Blanquet and Minister of Government* Manuel Garza Aldape to draw up a list of those

---

*The minister of government, Mexico's secretary of the interior, was responsible for interior security, including the suppression of subversion.

members of Congress to be arrested as hostile to the Huerta regime.

The blow fell on October 10. General Blanquet's old reliable Twenty-ninth Battalion surrounded the Congress while it was in session, sealing all the doors. A representative of President Huerta strode inside the building and delivered Huerta's demand that Congress cease investigating the Domínguez murder. The members of Congress saw this ultimatum as an attempt to infringe their rights, and many began to leave the floor. Blanquet's men thereupon arrested over a hundred members and took them off to the penitentiary. Some were quickly released, but most were charged and retained. Huerta immediately declared that congressional elections would be held concurrently with the presidential election, still scheduled for late October.

Up to this time, Huerta had remained noncommittal about his political intentions, but he now "drafted" himself to run as a presidential candidate, abandoning all pretense of observing the forms of the constitution of 1857. His arbitrary actions have been dubbed "Huerta's second coup."

On the surface, Huerta's second coup caused little excitement among the people in Mexico City. Nor did it arouse the European nations. The new British minister, Sir Lionel Carden, presented his credentials to Huerta the day after the episode. But in Washington the story was different. Woodrow Wilson and William J. Bryan were now confronted with the stark reality that Victoriano Huerta intended to retain presidential power indefinitely and by any means at his disposal.

Huerta went through the motions of conducting a presidential election on October 26, but he need not have bothered, for the sham did not even present a plausible front. Understandably, few men desired to be elected to the Mexican Congress under the conditions of the time, and Huerta lacked even weak opponents, straw men, to oppose him in the campaign for president. Félix Díaz, the only politician who showed the slightest interest, had avoided taking his post as minister to Japan the previous summer in order to run, but now he found the situation changed so drastically that he was afraid to move outside Veracruz. His followers, too, were afraid to conduct any kind of real campaign on his behalf. Thus the Huerta-Blanquet ticket won the election by an overwhelming majority but with such a low voter participation (5 percent in Juárez) that even Huerta acceded when the courts declared the exercise null and void. Huerta therefore set a new election for July 1914, and Díaz prudently fled the country once again.

The nullified election gave Victoriano Huerta a pretext for continuing as president for at least nine more months. And no matter how transparent that pretext was, his control of the army assured his retention of power in those areas still under Federal control. But the clouds were gathering on the horizon as the rebel armies steadily tightened their grip in the north of Mexico and began to move southward. In Chihuahua, Pancho Villa had temporarily abandoned Torreón as part of his all-out campaign to seize Chihuahua City and Juárez, which he would accomplish by the end of 1913. In Sonora, Carranza's Constitutionalists were ready to begin a parallel campaign under Obregón as soon as they worked out some political complications.

The complications in Sonora, however, were sticky for Carranza. They centered on the future role of Governor José María Maytorena, whose improved "health" had allowed him to return from Arizona to Hermosillo, the state capital. Not everyone in Sonora was sympathetic to Maytorena's wish to resume his duties as governor, especially not the local military establishment, headed by Obregón. But Maytorena was still legally governor, and before deposing him the colonels referred the matter to First Chief Carranza. Carranza favored Maytorena as a fellow patrician, so Obregón and his followers deftly switched sides. Maytorena was officially reinstated.

In northeastern Mexico, Constitutionalist fortunes were bogging down, in part because of Carranza's pettifoggery in removing from command the only general who had ever given him a victory. The general was Lucio Blanco, a dashing cavalryman. In August 1913, Blanco had successfully seized the border town of Matamoros and had taken it upon himself to make a reality of Carranza's pious statements about land reform. Blanco seized Los Borregos, the hacienda of Félix Díaz, and in a flood of pomp and fanfare arbitrarily divided Díaz's property among the local peasants.

Carranza was justifiably annoyed by Blanco's action. His complaint was not the issue of how rapidly (if ever) he intended to break up the great haciendas; he resented Blanco's usurping the role of his civilian superior. When Carranza relieved Blanco of his command, Blanco, to his credit, complied with Carranza's dictum—Carranza had no way of enforcing it—and reported to Nogales for reassignment.

The result was that Blanco's arena of action was added to that of

Pablo González, a Carranza loyalist who seemed unable ever to win a battle. So with the incompetent González commanding all the Constitutionalist forces in the northeast, the danger to Huerta from that direction was at least temporarily eliminated.

In the southern state of Morelos, the warlord Zapata simply held his ground. He had never recognized Carranza's Plan of Guadalupe, and he continued to reject Carranza's authority as First Chief of those fighting against Huerta. In November 1913, Zapata showed further disdain for Carranza by sending a representative to make contact with Pancho Villa, the only man Zapata respected as a "true revolutionary." Carranza chose to ignore Zapata's rebuff, but he and Zapata did not communicate, much less coordinate their efforts against Huerta. The result was that Zapata would always be working alone, his threat to Huerta at least somewhat diminished.

The U.S. government remained relatively ignorant of the stresses that existed among the Constitutionalists in their efforts to dislodge Huerta. Newspaper accounts of Constitutionalist successes gave hope to Wilson, Bryan, and the public in general that drastic measures on the part of the United States might not be necessary to remove Huerta (an objective that seems to have been totally accepted); Mexico might solve its own problems without American intervention. As the *New York Times* expressed it in November, "Every report of a rebel victory in Mexico raises the hope here that the days of General Huerta's power are numbered. The hope seems to rest more than ever on the belief that he will be ousted by the Mexican rebels without foreign assistance."

Content for the moment to hope for a Constitutionalist victory in Mexico, President Woodrow Wilson now turned his wrath from Huerta to the European powers, particularly Britain. Those powers, he claimed, had "perpetuated" Huerta in power by recognizing him as provisional president when he seized power. In Wilson's view, the European powers had accorded Huerta a measure of respectability that contributed to his survival.

Wilson therefore felt constrained to respond to Huerta's second coup moderately. He limited his protest to a harmless diplomatic note accusing Huerta of bad faith, in the meantime withholding U.S. recognition of the upcoming election in advance. Two days before the election, Wilson sent a note to the nations that had first recognized Huerta—fourteen in all—asking them also to withhold recognition of the election results, regardless of the outcome.

So much for Wilson's attitude before the results of Huerta's spurious reelection became known. When Wilson learned of Huerta's defiance—or so Wilson saw it—he became incensed. Sitting down at his typewriter, he hammered out the draft of a message to the European powers that accused them of keeping Huerta in power "without regard to the wishes . . . of the United States" and possibly necessitating "domination and force." He pointed a special finger at Britain, blaming the arrival of the new British minister, Sir Lionel Carden, for Huerta's "rehabilitation."

Since Bryan was expected to send Wilson's draft over his own signature, the secretary dutifully followed the lines Wilson had sent him, but for good measure he added an accusation of his own. The European powers, he wrote, had been allowing their citizens to assist Huerta in exchange for commercial concessions, particularly Mexican oil.

Fortunately for relations between the United States and Britain, the Wilson/Bryan draft went to John Bassett Moore, who, as counsel of the White House, was asked to check it for legalities. Moore, according to his own account, found no adverse legal implications in the draft, but he was alarmed by the substance. He wrote a note to the president pointing out that it had "never been considered necessary for foreign powers to ask our consent to the recognition of an American government." He added that the U.S. position was weak in that Wilson and Bryan themselves had been conducting informal diplomatic relations with the Huerta regime for months.

President Wilson quickly recognized that Moore had a point. He watered down the language in the "circular note" he sent to the European powers two weeks later. And in late February, the British, choosing the friendship of the United States over Mexican oil, withdrew their recognition of the Huerta regime. The disagreements between Britain and the United States over Mexican policy had passed or at least been glossed over.

Wilson now settled down to draw up a long-term plan to rid Mexico of Huerta, a task he considered to be completely within the purview of the United States, even to the point of declaring war in order to do so. He revealed some of his ideas to his close adviser Colonel Edward House, in a conversation at the White House in late October 1913.

The kind of war that Wilson visualized would not necessarily entail invading Mexico; his purpose was only "to keep the powers from interfering and entirely out of the situation." A declaration of war would, however, give the United States the right under international law to blockade Mexico's ports, "thereby cutting off all revenue from the Mexican Government which will have a tendency to break down Huerta's resistance."

But Wilson's plan included another possibility, that of "throwing a line [of troops] across the southern part of Mexico, and perhaps another line just south of the Northern States." This seemed to contradict the notion of a war "without invading Mexico." He was willing to make such an American action subject to the consent of First Chief Venustiano Carranza. If Carranza granted permission, American troops would remain "neutral." They would be in Mexico "only to protect the lives and property of foreign citizens," not to "contend against either the Constitutionalists or Federals unless some overt action was made by one or the other."

As House listened, he observed that the president was "alert and unafraid." He was willing to take great risks. He admitted, for example, that a blockade of Mexican ports by six battleships might create such resentment among the European powers that they would form some sort of coalition against the United States. But Wilson nevertheless seemed "ready to throw our gauntlet into the arena and declare that all [foreign] hands must be kept off excepting our own."

Wilson decided, however, that before taking such a radical step, he must learn more about Carranza, whose movement he regarded as the true continuation of the Madero regime and the representative of the Mexican people. To sound out Carranza's views on his plan of action, he called once more on his friend William Bayard Hale. Hale left Washington in mid-November 1913 for Carranza's headquarters at Nogales, on the Sonora—Arizona border, there to hold a personal meeting with the First Chief.

The conference was a disaster. Wilson's plans to send American troops into Mexican territory and his demand that Carranza step down and call new elections enraged Carranza. He would oppose any U.S. troops sent into Mexican territory, he declared, and he had no need for U.S. advice and support. He was conducting a "thoroughgoing" revolution, he declared, and would not participate in any election conducted under the auspices of Huerta's "facsimile government." All he wanted, Carranza said, was U.S. recognition, accompanied by the right to buy arms across the border.

Having finished his tirade, Carranza announced that he must leave Nogales for two days in order to meet an official obligation elsewhere. After Carranza's departure, an incensed Hale went straight to the press and made no effort to sugarcoat what had happened: "You know, the world is full of all kinds of people. Some of them are not only impossible, but highly improbable. Please understand that I am not speaking of the gentlemen across the border who are with such admirable skill preventing their friends from helping them." So saying, Hale left Nogales for Washington. The American press exulted that he had "called Carranza's bluff."

Wilson's brief courtship of Carranza thus ended with the immediate reinstitution of the U.S. arms embargo against Carranza. Wilson and Bryan were now at odds with both Huerta and Carranza. Only the emerging Francisco Villa, in Chihuahua, remained a mystery.

In early October 1913, the ocean liner *Espagne* pulled into Veracruz harbor. The first passenger down the gangplank was the glamorous Edith Coues O'Shaughnessy, who had been vacationing with her mother in Europe. Edith O'Shaughnessy's husband, Nelson, a staff member of the American embassy, had been elevated to the position of chargé d'affaires when Ambassador Henry Lane Wilson was recalled in July. This was a heady promotion. Mexico City was gaining considerable attention in the United States, and Nelson O'Shaughnessy would now be the principal personal link between Washington and Victoriano Huerta. He certainly looked the part of a diplomat, adding dignity to his thirty-eight years by immaculate dress, English-style handlebar mustaches, and an appropriately statesmanlike stoop in his carriage.

The prospect of this new life as the wife of the de facto U.S. ambassador was exciting for Edith O'Shaughnessy also. She would soon be moving their belongings into the embassy, which would provide a household full of servants and plenty of room for their seven-year-old son, Elim, to run around in. And though the lavish O'Shaughnessy life-style had run them into debt in the past, prices were low enough that they could afford to live and entertain well in Mexico City.

Despite her surface frills, Edith O'Shaughnessy was a practical person, aware of her diplomatic responsibilities. She would become popular among the high-ranking officers of the Mexican government and the diplomatic corps for her beauty but also for her warmth and friendliness. She had a kind heart and a genuine empathy for all the Mexicans, rich and poor alike. More important to history, she was perceptive and articulate. Although her aristocratic prejudices some-times cause her published letters to be sniffed at, no historical ac-counts of the time ignore these documents completely.

When Edith O'Shaughnessy was introduced to President Huerta, she was uncertain how she felt about him. She was aware, of course, of his disregard for human life (his own included), but she was soon won over by his considerable charm. With very little basis for judg-ment, she concluded that Huerta, strong and astute, might eventually bring peace to Mexico "if the United States were not on his back." Huerta quickly sensed potential allies in the two O'Shaughnessys, and he courted them. At every official gathering, the Mexican presi-dent arranged to have Mrs. O'Shaughnessy sit beside him. Señora Huerta, when present, was equally considerate. When Huerta learned that the O'Shaughnessys were planning a trip to Veracruz, he sent them on his own train, with guards to ensure their safety.

Soon Huerta felt free to use Edith O'Shaughnessy as an unofficial messenger to the Americans: "If our great and important neighbor to the north chooses to withhold her friendship," he said to her one day, "we can but deplore it—and try to perform our task without her." Huerta was not idly musing.

President Wilson's adviser on Mexican affairs, Governor John Lind, had been at Veracruz ever since the previous August, still flood-ing the State Department with his views of the Mexican situation, as he saw it from that remote location. Edith O'Shaughnessy met Lind when she arrived in October, and she liked him. She detected "some-thing magnetic, something disarming of criticism, in his clear, straight gaze, blue Viking eye, his kindly smile, and his tall, spare figure." But as Lind sulked at Veracruz, he became more and more convinced that the "strongest possible moves" must be taken against Huerta, and as his antagonism toward Huerta grew, so did Edith O'Shaughnessy's hostility toward him.

The break came in November 1913, when Edith O'Shaughnessy learned of the prospective meeting between William B. Hale and Car-ranza at Nogales. Lind added to her horror when he told her that Wilson hoped to lift the arms embargo against the Constitutionalists. "Oh, Mr. Lind!" she cried. "You can't mean that! It would be opening a pandora box of troubles here." But Lind did mean it, and she blamed him for President Wilson's actions. Their friendship came to an abrupt end.

President Wilson retained the arms embargo against the Consti-tutionalists for three months following Hale's rebuff by Carranza at

Nogales. On February 1, 1914, however, Wilson's animosity toward Huerta triumphed over his pique at Carranza, and he lifted it. Carranza and Villa could now legally buy arms from the United States. The slap at Huerta was the most serious measure that Wilson had yet resorted to.

Edith O'Shaughnessy was "dazed and aghast." She predicted that this act would "definitely prolong this terrible civil war and swell the tide of the blood of the men and women, 'and the *children*'. . . . A generation of rich and poor alike will be at the mercy of the hordes that will fight, and eat, and pillage, and rape their way through the country." She added ominously, "There is sure to be violent anti-American demonstrations, especially in out-of-the-way places."

Huerta took the news of Wilson's action calmly, Edith O'Shaughnessy reported. At a reception shortly afterward, Huerta had given her "some flowers and all the good things on the table, and in return [she] gave him a red carnation for his buttonhole."

Edith O'Shaughnessy's view of American foreign policy toward Mexico in early 1914, though colored by Huerta's flattery, was shared by nearly all Americans living and doing business in Mexico. But that view counted for little, because it was not President Wilson's view.

8

****

The Benton Affair

Pancho Villa's tenure as warlord of
Chihuahua, from November 1913 to the following March, was in
many ways the high point of his tempestuous career. He was now the
undisputed master of his home state, and as a leader of the Mexican
Revolution he had come to rival even Carranza. Indeed, Villa was
considered to be Carranza's coequal in foreign and domestic circles
alike.

The city of Chihuahua was Pancho Villa's adopted hometown.
Only a few blocks west of Plaza Hidalgo, on which stood the Governor's Palace and the Cathedral, was the comfortable home that he and
Luz Corral had occupied intermittently for years. To that house, Governor Abraham González, hat in hand, had come to ask the prosperous outlaw to join the cause of Madero back in 1910. Villa returned
there a year later, on Madero's request, to spy on Pascual Orozco as
Orozco was planning his 1912 rebellion.

Villa had little time to enjoy these congenial surroundings, however, for he was intent on building up the Division of the North for
further military operations against Victoriano Huerta. Villa's efforts
were given a gigantic boost when General Felipe Angeles arrived to
serve as Villa's chief of artillery.

Angeles, the gentlemanly soldier once referred to as the "master technician of war," had come close to death along with President Madero and Vice President Pino Suárez the previous February. Huerta spared Angeles's life when Angeles agreed to accept a foreign assignment in France. Unwilling to serve under Huerta, Angeles left France and made his way to join Carranza at Nogales. Carranza's headquarters, however, was no place for a man with a mind of his own. So Angeles bided his time, performing empty duties as titular minister of war to the best of his abilities. At the same time, he watched admiringly as Villa cleared Chihuahua of Federal forces.

Angeles came to the Division of the North at Villa's request, one of the few such requests that Carranza willingly approved. Perhaps the presence of Angeles at Nogales annoyed Carranza, because his personal prestige diverted some of the spotlight from the First Chief.* In any case, Carranza conferred the meaningless title of "deputy minister of war" on Angeles and sent him on his way.

Villa was out to meet Angeles when the general arrived at the Chihuahua train station. A band played, and an honor guard stood at attention. Villa, sparing nothing, was humble in his welcome: "Señor General," Villa said, "we need your services on the battlefield. Chance alone has made me a soldier, and your professional knowledge will help us."

Angeles was even more complimentary. "Señor General," he replied, "I can teach you nothing because you have nothing to learn. Battles like Tierra Blanca would be a credit to any professional soldier. I am happy to place myself under your orders." It was a happy beginning to an odd but spectacularly successful association.

The presence of Felipe Angeles in Villa's command introduced a measure of military conventionality to the casual habits of the Divi-

---

*One time we were sitting around the table after dinner. . . . Carranza began to pontificate, as usual, and finally set up, as an indisputable fact, the superiority of an improvised and an enthusiastic army over a scientifically organized one. . . . Angeles waited and then, gently, . . . but most energetically . . . , rose to the defense of the art of warfare as something that can be learned and taught. . . . But Carranza . . . interrupted his Minister of War brusquely with this bald statement, closing the matter:
"In life, General, especially in leading and governing men, the only thing that is necessary or useful is goodwill."
Angeles took a sip from his coffee cup and did not utter another syllable.

MARTÍN LUIS GUZMÁN,
The Eagle and the Serpent (New York, 1930), pp. 55–56.

sion of the North. Though a modest man in person, he was nonetheless a graduate of the Mexican Military Academy, and he liked panoply. He therefore took it upon himself to see that Villa received honors commensurate with both his accomplishments and his responsibilities. Villa, torn between his dual roles as division commander and as the "friend of the poor," resisted playing the role of garrison general. But Angeles persisted in organizing a ceremony honoring Villa for his battlefield heroism, and Villa assented, mostly out of respect for Angeles.

The decoration ceremony took place at the Governor's Palace in Chihuahua City. Thousands of Villa's supporters were massed in the plaza, eager to honor their leader. Four regimental bands played stirring music. The ceremonial room, according to the reporter John Reed, was festooned with "great luster chandeliers, crimson portières, gaudy American wallpaper, and a throne for the governor." The throne was "a gilded chair with lion's claws for arms, placed on a dais under a canopy of crimson velvet. . . ." The officers of the artillery wore gilt-braided hats and smart blue uniforms faced with black velvet and gold. At their sides, they carried flashing new sabers. A double line of well-turned-out artillerymen stood at present arms.

When the big moment arrived, the crowd burst out, "Here he comes! Viva Villa, the friend of the poor!" Thousands of hats flew into the air as the band in the courtyard struck up the Mexican national anthem.

Down the steps came Villa, dressed in a plain khaki uniform with several buttons missing. He was unshaven, hatless, his hair disheveled. He walked slightly humped over, with his hands in his pockets. As he lumbered between the two rigid lines of soldiers, he seemed embarrassed, nodding every now and then to a compadre he recognized. At the foot of the staircase, he was met by Governor Manuel Chao and Secretary of State Sylvestre Terrazas, both resplendent in full dress uniforms. The three then walked together into the throne room. Villa shook the arms of the throne to test them before sitting down.

The ceremony was formal. Señor Bauche Alcalde did the honors, posturing "like Cicero denouncing Catiline," according to Reed. Bauche Alcalde intoned the citations for six separate acts of personal bravery in "florid detail." Angeles then rose impressively and pronounced, "The army adores you! We will follow you wherever you lead! You can be what you desire in Mexico!" Three other speeches followed, all lavish in their praise. Villa was hailed as "the Friend of the Poor," "the Invincible General," "the Inspirer of Courage and Patriotism," "the Hope of the Indian Republic."

Through all this, Villa sat slouched, his eyes scanning the room. Once or twice he yawned, "like a schoolboy in church." When a colonel came forward to present him with the small cardboard box that contained the decoration, Chao nudged Villa. Villa stood up amid thunderous cheers. He seized the box and peered at its contents, scratching his head. "This is a hell of a little thing to give a man for all that heroism you are talking about!" he said.

As thousands waited for a word from him, Villa addressed them softly: "There is no word to speak. All I can say is my heart is all to you." Then he sat down and spat on the floor.

Villa's time in Chihuahua was marred by one tragic incident, which seemed trivial to Villa at the time. It was the murder of William S. Benton, euphemistically known as the Benton affair. More than any other single event, the Benton affair gave the outside world a glimpse of the type of killer their romantic hero Pancho Villa really was.

William Benton was a prosperous but controversial landholder whose ranch, Los Remedios, was one of the largest in Chihuahua. Hardly a nonentity, Benton was, in fact, a remarkable man. He had left his home in Scotland at the age of twenty-two, and sometime around 1892 he began prospecting for gold in Durango. He did well at that activity; he settled down and married a wealthy Mexican girl. After a few years, he bought a fine ranch for a reasonable price and set himself up in the cattle business. A hard worker and ruthless manager, Benton developed Los Remedios into a going concern within the space of only five years. By the time the revolt against Díaz began in 1911, the ranch itself was estimated to be worth some million pesos and the cattle and horses a like amount.

Since Benton's prosperity had been aided by the Díaz regime's generous policies toward landowners, he was unsympathetic to the Mexican Revolution. His philosophical distaste was brought to a boiling rage by the unapologetic way in which rustlers stole his cattle in the lofty name of "the cause." To prevent these thefts, Benton built a fence around Los Remedios, despite the protests from the inhabitants of the nearby village of Santa María de Cuevas. He called on the local rurales for protection.

Under Díaz, Madero, and Huerta, the local authorities in Chihuahua, especially the powerful Terrazas family, had supported

Benton by fining anyone who trespassed on Benton's property. But when Villa took over administration of the state in late 1913, support ceased. Los Remedios became one of the favorite sources of the cattle Villa needed to steal for his business transactions in the United States. Villa, in fact, regarded the Terrazas family as his personal enemies, and since Benton was a foreigner allied with the Terrazas, he ordered Benton's ranch confiscated and Benton banished from Mexico.

Benton was not one to take such arbitrary actions passively, so in early February 1914 he decided to confront Villa, even though it meant traveling all the way to Juárez, where Villa was busy obtaining munitions and equipment across the border in El Paso. Though warned against such a venture, Benton remarked dramatically that he "feared no one." Furthermore, he was confident that, as a British subject, he should be inviolable in all respects, particularly since he did not meddle in local political matters.

Benton had little difficulty in finding Villa. In the company of an adventurous American he had met in a local bar, Benton was soon at Villa's headquarters on the Calle de Comercio. As the two men pushed their way in, Villa's guards gave them little thought. They were accustomed to Villa's policy of treating all gringos, even ill-mannered ones, with unusual courtesy.

Inside the headquarters building, Benton left his American companion sitting on a bench in the hall while he burst into the room. He found Villa instructing an El Paso financial agent to give a thousand pesos to a woman and an eight-year-old girl, the family of a recently killed Villista captain. In an adjoining room, the alert Rodolfo Fierro was having his boots shined.

At the age of forty-five, Benton cut a forceful figure. Though only of medium size, he was athletic and erect, noted for his military bearing. He strode up to the desk with authority. He fixed a fierce blue eye on Villa and shouted, "I have come to get my land back."

"I cannot return your land," Villa answered with surprising mildness. "But since you are English and I wish to avoid international incidents, I intend to pay you what it is worth, or what you paid for it, after which you will stay out of Mexico."

What happened next is not clear, but by Villa's account Benton answered, "I will not sell at any price, and I will not let a bandit like you rob me!" So saying, Benton drew his pistol. But before Benton could fire, Villa and a couple of guards were upon him. Villa ordered the Scotsman hauled away and turned back to the business at hand.

In due time, Villa got around to considering what to do with Benton. He consulted with Fierro, whose immediate response was to execute him on the spot. Villa hesitated for a moment because of Benton's nationality, but he soon ordered him taken down to Samalayuca, away from Juárez, and shot. By midnight, a handcuffed Benton had been shoved into a caboose, and a lone railroad engine took him and his executioners to the south. Benton still expected to be freed; this was all a trick.

Benton remained cool even after the execution party reached Samalayuca. He watched defiantly as Fierro and his party discussed one location after another as a proper place for burial. Soon the party found a satisfactory site, and Fierro asked Benton, "Is that all right with you, mister?" Benton merely shrugged. He lit up a cigarette and tossed a casual quip to the gravediggers, "Listen, amigo, make a deeper hole. The coyotes will get me out of this one."

Soon all was ready. But as Benton faced the firing squad, Fierro stole up behind and hit him over the head with a shovel. Benton toppled over and was shoved into the grave—whether dead or not nobody knows. The gravediggers covered him up.

Benton's execution did not mark the end of the affair; in fact, it marked only the beginning. Shortly after the Scotsman's disappearance, his Mexican wife, with the American consul George Carothers, appeared at Villa's headquarters. Maxima Benton knew that her husband had come through the door of that house earlier, and she feared that his impetuosity might have caused him trouble. Villa was annoyed at the aide who allowed these people to reach him, but he played for time. He told Mrs. Benton that he had not seen her husband. He then went through the motions of making a search everywhere in Juárez, through the streets and into gambling halls. Villa even admonished the mayor to be on the lookout.

Villa had far more to contend with than just a frantic wife and an American consul, for Benton was a man of many friends. Villa's capture of an important British subject immediately became common knowledge. Word reached Carranza, who sent a telegram ordering Villa to release Benton.

By Friday, February 20, 1914, American citizens in El Paso were proclaiming that Benton had been murdered. Simplifying the matter a bit, they claimed he had been slain only because he had protested against the confiscation of his property, which had been repeatedly looted. They mentioned nothing about his drawing a gun.

The Texans seemed to be intent on making a major issue of Benton's fate. The incident, the newspapers said, was "but another crime to be added to the hundreds against all foreigners living in Mexico . . . for no reason other than on account of their nationality."

That accusation was of course unfair; Benton's British status was the only reason why the Mexicans had tolerated his argumentative nature as long as they had; he was not being persecuted because he was a foreigner. Still, the important thing was not the truth but what people believed to be the truth.

Governments and the press took up the issue. The *New York Times*, in blazing headlines, predicted that Benton's killing might "force the hand of the Wilson administration" against Villa, not against Huerta. Wilson's policy of "watchful waiting" was decried as "vacillating and weak." And Huerta, making use of Villa's "exposure as a criminal," was asking all nations to cease sending the Constitutionalists more arms. The American consul in Juárez brought Villa a message from Secretary of State Bryan describing the matter as a "serious affair."

Villa now knew that he could no longer feign ignorance of Benton's death, so he admitted to the consul, "Benton tried to kill me and paid for it with his life." He also insisted that Benton had been duly tried by the revolutionary army and wrote a letter to the *New York Times*, published on February 21:

> CHIHUAHUA, Mexico. A court-martial sentenced Benton to death with complete justification, due to his crimes in having made an attempt on my life, as I am able to prove.
>
> FRANCISCO VILLA, General in Chief

In Nogales, First Chief Venustiano Carranza was becoming infuriated with the whole episode. He cared nothing about Benton or even about British animosity; it aroused his ire that foreign governments were dealing directly with Villa, his theoretical subordinate, not with him. Carranza was also irritated by the continued British recognition of the Huerta government, a circumstance that forced His Majesty's government to depend on the United States to represent British interests with Carranza. Carranza demanded that the British, not the United States, deal with him. Unwittingly, Carranza was therefore easing Villa's position by insisting that questions regarding Benton "be addressed to me as First Chief of the Revolution."

In Chihuahua, the correspondent John Reed received instructions from the *Metropolitan* magazine to look into the Benton affair from Carranza's viewpoint. Messages and press releases were one thing, but Reed's editors wanted more than that. So Reed headed for Nogales to find Carranza in person. He took the train to El Paso, then across New Mexico and Arizona, entering Nogales from the American side.

When Reed arrived at Carranza's headquarters in Nogales, he learned that he was expected. He could see, however, that securing an audience was going to be difficult. Carranza's cabinet members were all on hand, but the authority to grant appointments lay in the hands of the secretary of foreign relations, Isidro Fabela. Fabela, Reed sensed, relished his own petty power. Worse, he lived in awe of the First Chief.

Carranza, Fabela told Reed, had agreed to receive him. However, the First Chief would not answer direct questions from members of the press. Reed would therefore have to submit his questions in writing and wait a day or so for a written answer.

Reed protested, but as he had no choice, he drew up a list of twenty-five questions. Fabela immediately deleted a number of them for fear that they might "offend" Carranza. Under protest, Reed deleted the questions and recopied the list. Fabela, satisfied, set the next morning for the interview—on the condition that Reed promise to ask no questions. When presented to the First Chief, he was to say simply, "How do you do," and leave promptly.

The next morning, Reed and another American correspondent arrived at the municipal palace in ample time for the interview. After being kept waiting for an hour, they were finally admitted into Carranza's office.

As they entered, Reed was struck by the darkness. Then, as his eyes adjusted, he was able to make out an unmade bed in a corner and a small table, covered with papers, on the other side of the room. Another table held a tray with the remains of breakfast. In another corner stood a table with a tin bucket of ice cooling two or three bottles of wine. Reed's eye finally came to the large bulk of the First Chief, seated in a big chair, clad in khaki and wearing dark glasses. Carranza sat motionless, with hands on the arms of the chair. He did not seem to be working—he did not seem to be doing anything.

Finally, Carranza stood up to greet his guests, a towering, distant figure. His smile was vacant and expressionless, and Reed believed that he did not look well. As they shook hands, Fabela announced, "These gentlemen have come to greet you on behalf of the great newspapers which they represent. This gentleman (without indicating which) says that he desires to present his respectful wishes for your success." Carranza bowed slightly and said, "Allow me to assure the gentlemen of my grateful acceptance of their best wishes." The interview was officially over.

An impulse swept over Reed: he must say at least something before leaving! So in his fluent Spanish he blurted out, "Señor Don Venustiano, my paper is your friend and the friend of the Constitutionalists!"

Carranza started. Then he spoke:

To the United States I say the Benton case is none of your business. Benton was a British subject. I will answer to the delegates of Great Britain when they come with representations of their government. Why should they not come to me? England now has an Ambassador in Mexico City, who accepts invitations to dinner from Huerta, takes off his hat to him, and shakes hands with him!

When Madero was murdered, the foreign powers flocked to the spot like vultures to the dead, and fawned upon the murderer because they had a few subjects in the Republic who were petty tradesmen doing a dirty little business.

. . . England, the bully of the world, finds herself unable to deal with us unless she humiliates herself by sending a representative to the Constitutionalists; so she tried to use the United States as a cat's paw. More shame to the United States . . . !

Through all this tirade, a distraught Fabela seemed frantic to bring the interview to a close. First he attempted to interrupt Carranza with words of the gentlemen's gratitude for the interview. Then he tried to change the subject to the forthcoming advance on Torreón. But Carranza was not yet through; instead, he took a step forward, shouting:

I tell you that, if the United States intervenes in Mexico upon this petty excuse, intervention . . . will provoke a war which, besides its own consequences, will deepen a profound hatred between the United States and the whole of Latin America . . . !

Then, as suddenly as he had begun, Carranza stopped and turned away. Fabela hastily ushered the two Americans out, warning Reed not to publish what he had witnessed.

Reed retained a strange impression from the encounter. He felt not that he had witnessed the thundering voice of an aroused Mexico but that he had seen only a "slightly senile old man, tired and irritated."

Venustiano Carranza could protest, but the British were not, at that point, prepared to withdraw recognition from Huerta (though they did so soon thereafter). The United States, through consuls and representatives in Mexican cities, tried to learn more about Benton's fate, but Villa was finished talking. Neither the British government nor Benton's widow ever received complete information.

A final, macabre incident closed the episode. Under the pressure of newspapers and governments, Villa agreed at last to surrender Benton's body for examination by an international commission. Before the investigation began, however, Villa needed to prepare the corpse. He feared that the commission would discover the lack of bullet holes.

Villa therefore ordered Benton's body dug up and shot. To a doctor who warned that an autopsy would reveal that Benton had been dead long before he was shot, Villa issued a simple threat: "Señor, you will perform the autopsy and find that [Benton] was shot and then given a blow on the head as an act of mercy. And if there is a second autopsy, it must confirm the first one."

Carranza, however, spared the world the ordeal of further investigation. The conduct of an investigation in Chihuahua would represent a violation of Mexico's sovereignty, he declared. So Villa happily forbade his followers ever again to mention the name of William S. Benton.

9

****

The Tampico Incident

Throughout the first fourteen months of the Huerta regime, the U.S. government had been diplomatically correct in all dealings with Mexico. Admittedly, Ambassador Henry Lane Wilson had overstepped his bounds during the Ten Tragic Days of February 1913, but his actions had never been sanctioned in Washington, and the manner of his removal reflected Washington disapproval. And President Woodrow Wilson, though incredibly presumptuous in trying to foist his own ideas on the Mexican government, had never been guilty of overt interference. Even his periodic imposition and removal of arms embargoes against one or the other of the Mexican groups had been technically within Wilson's rights—and ineffective.

Up to the spring of 1914, American lives and American commercial interests did not seem threatened by any of the factions fighting in Mexico. All the revolutionaries, even Pancho Villa, had been careful to protect the citizens and property of their powerful neighbor across the Rio Grande. That situation came to an end at Tampico, a Mexican Gulf port in the northeastern Mexican state of Tamaulipas. There the interests of the Huertistas, the revolutionaries, and the Americans clashed for the first time.

The danger signal sounded in late March 1914, when the Constitutionalists of the northeast under the command of Pablo González
began laying siege to the federally controlled Tampico. Taking that
port, next to Veracruz the most important in Mexico, would represent
the first step in their drive to control the entire Gulf coastline. Tampico would serve as a base from which to launch an attack toward
Veracruz, three hundred miles down the coast. Veracruz was the ultimate objective of the revolutionaries, at this time still out of reach.

Historically, Tampico played a secondary role to Veracruz, being
farther from Mexico City. Nevertheless, Tampico's importance had
grown dramatically since the early 1900s, when great oil resources
were discovered nearby and when the world was just beginning to
convert from coal to oil as a source of energy. By 1914 Tampico's
population had reached thirty thousand, and its foreign colony,
mostly Americans, ranked second in size only to that of Mexico City
itself. Railroads linked Tampico to Monterrey by way of Victoria in
the north, and to San Luis Potosí in the west. Pipelines from nearby
oil fields led into the city, where the crude was refined. The American
Standard Oil Corporation was one of the major concerns concentrated
around Tampico.*

As General Pablo González moved his Constitutionalist forces
toward Tampico, the commander of the Federal garrison, General
Ignacio Morelos Zaragoza, realized that his position was precarious.
The town of Tampico itself was indefensible, for it sat on low ground
to the north of the Pánuco River, nine miles from its mouth. Ideally,
Morelos Zaragoza should have defended the heights to the north and
west of Tampico, but he had only two thousand troops, including
national guardsmen. Defending along the ridges would spread his
troops too thin. He therefore kept his entire force bottled up in the
city, depending on the firepower of his gunboat *Veracruz* to discourage the Constitutionalists from leaving their dug-in positions in the
hills. Against Pancho Villa, such a tactic would have been suicide;
against Pablo González, it had a reasonable chance.

---

*"As we continued up the river," wrote the reporter Jack London, "more and
more terminals and tank farms lined both banks. . . . This was the Coronal terminal,
and that was the Aguila on both sides, and adjoining were the huge solid buildings of
Standard Oil. There was the National Petroleum, there the Waters-Pierce, the Gulf
Coast, the Mexican Petroleum, the Texas, the International Oil, the East Coast
oil—and thereat I ceased taking account of the companies." London, "Our Adventures at Tampico," *Collier's,* 27 June 1914.

Any fighting in or around Tampico would place foreign lives and property at great risk. The protection of American and foreign lives therefore became the preoccupation of Admiral Henry Thomas Mayo, the dynamic fifty-seven-year-old commander of the Fifth Division, U.S. Navy. Mayo commanded the strongest naval force at Tampico— two battleships and two cruisers—so other nations looked to him for protection. The German *Dresden* and the British *Hermione* were also present in the Tampico harbor, but their firepower was small compared with that of Mayo's battlewagons.

Mayo's task was difficult and complex. The sandbar at the mouth of the Pánuco River prevented him from taking his battleships upstream. Furthermore, the foreigners whose lives he was there to protect were difficult people to deal with. Mayo therefore determined to keep in close personal touch with events in Tampico. He made the gunboat *Dolphin* his flagship and lived aboard her on the river, inside the sandbar. He kept in contact with the battleship *Connecticut*, his usual flagship, by courier service.

Mayo had no radios powerful enough to reach the United States, even by relay. So in order to communicate with Washington, he had to go through the communications net of Rear Admiral Frank F. Fletcher, his counterpart at Veracruz. Mayo and Fletcher, coequal commanders, were on excellent terms. However, despite Fletcher's cooperation, Mayo's communications with Washington were slow, to say the least.

On March 26, General González's Constitutionalists seized a small town only about one mile up the Pánuco River from Tampico. The lives of the foreigners in Tampico were therefore placed in great jeopardy. Not only was the danger of gunfire serious; even more frightening was the possibility that exploding shells would ignite oil fires among the refineries. Nevertheless, many Americans in Tampico ignored Admiral Mayo's pleas and warnings; they even refused to allow their women and children to be evacuated. The psychology of "it can't happen here" was too strong, and Mayo had no authority to give orders to American civilians.

By the end of the first week of April the Constitutionalist rebels had penetrated into the outskirts of Tampico, and the lines between them and the Federals stabilized temporarily at the Iturbide Bridge, located at the northern boundary of the city. On the next day, many of the foreign civilians, now thoroughly frightened, consented to be evacuated to the cruisers and subsequently to the battleships—only to be returned to Tampico because of a storm approaching from the Gulf. The heavy weather put a damper on military action in Tampico, but the situation remained tense.

On the cool, gray Thursday morning of April 9 a whaleboat from the USS *Dolphin*, commanded by Assistant Paymaster Charles C. Copp, headed up the Pánuco River with a crew of eight sailors. It was a routine errand. Copp and his men were bound for a warehouse about ten miles up the river. The German proprietor had offered to sell some gasoline to propel Admiral Mayo's launch. Copp caught a tow from a passing launch and just before noon arrived at his destination. The men prepared to load up the gasoline.

The river at Tampico was a scene of confusion. Smoke poured from burning oil tanks, and Federal gunboats on the Pánuco River were lobbing shells over the city into rebel lines. Nevertheless, the port was officially open to U.S. naval forces. Since the Americans did not expect to be molested, none of the sailors with Copp were armed.

Unbeknownst to the Americans, the part of the river where the warehouse was located had been declared by the Federals to be a forbidden zone, as it was only a few hundred yards below the critical Iturbide Bridge. Being concerned only with his loading, Copp failed to notice the Mexican patrol boat that was chugging down from the bridge and signaling to a squad of Mexican troops onshore. To Copp's surprise, Mexican sailors and troops converged on the whaleboat from the land and the river.

The Mexicans spoke no English, and Copp spoke no Spanish. But by gestures, the Mexican officer made it clear that the Americans were to drop their work, leave the whaleboat, and come with him. Two of the sailors, still in the whaleboat, ignored the order until they found themselves staring down the muzzles of Mexican rifles. Upon a nod from Copp, they also disembarked, and a Mexican officer marched all nine Americans a few blocks up the Calle Altamira to the Mexican regimental headquarters.

The German merchant, who witnessed the incident, returned hastily to the Fiscal Wharf, where the *Dolphin* was moored. Admiral Mayo dispatched an emissary toward Tampico to demand the bluejackets' release.

At the Mexican headquarters, Colonel Ramón Hinojosa, the regimental commander, was aghast at what his men had done. Even

General Porfirio Díaz
President of Mexico (1876–1911).
(Library of Congress)

Meeting of Francisco I. Madero, Jr., with rebel leaders, at Bustillos, Chihuahua, May 1911. Seated, *left to right,* are Governors Venustiano Carranza (Coahuila) and Vasquez Gómez (San Luis Potosí); Madero; Governors Abraham González (Chihuahua), José María Maytorena (Sonora), and Alberto Fuentes (Aguascalientes); General Pascual Orozco.

Standing, *left to right,* **are Colonel Francisco ("Pancho") Villa; Gustavo Madero, Francisco I. Madero, Sr., Colonel Giuseppe Garibaldi; unknown; General Lucio Blanco; unknowns.** (Courtesy Fort Bliss Museum, Fort Bliss, Texas)

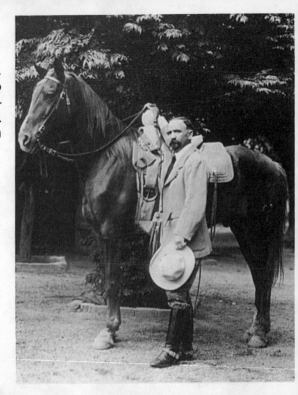

**Francisco I. Madero, Jr.,
president of Mexico
(December 1911–
February 1913).**
(Library of Congress)

Félix Díaz
(Library of Congress)

Incoming President Woodrow Wilson and outgoing President William Howard Taft at Wilson's inauguration, March 4, 1913. (Library of Congress)

Opposite page (bottom, right): **General Victoriano Huerta, provisional president of Mexico (February 1913–July 1914).** (National Archives)

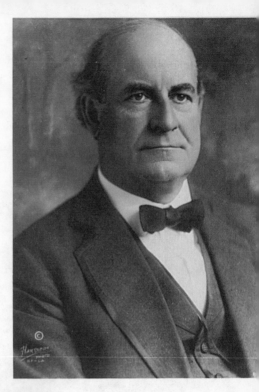

William Jennings Bryan, secretary of state (March 1913–June 1915). (Library of Congress)

Henry Lane Wilson, U.S. ambassador to Mexico, in the embassy library, Mexico City, 1913. (Library of Congress)

First Chief Venustiano Carranza. Later president of Mexico (1917–20)
(Aultman Collection, El Paso Public Library)

General Felipe Angeles.
(Aultman Collection, El Paso Public Library)

Villa and his staff, late 1913. On Villa's right is Rodolfo Fierro, the "Butcher." On his left are Generals Toribio Ortega and Juan Medina, his chief of staff. (National Archives)

General Emiliano Zapata. This photograph of Zapata is the only one that has attained wide circulation. It shows the "peasant general" the way he chose to be portrayed, as a prosperous Mexican charro. (National Archives)

Federal artillery during the Mexican Revolution. The number of infantry guards may suggest the inability of this small piece to protect itself. (Courtesy Fort Bliss Museum, Fort Bliss, Texas)

Mexican rurales, members of the Guardia Rural, described by Atkin as a "Mexican version of the Mounties." Mrs. Alice Moats called them bandits but "the world's most picturesque policemen." (National Archives)

A Federal conscript says good-bye to his wife and child.
(Bazar de Fotografía Casasola, Mexico)

Villistas on the move. The railroad was by all odds the best way of moving troops and supplies. The Villistas habitually carried the horses inside the boxcars, while the men, with their families, rode on top. (National Archives)

"Adobe Wall"—the standard and often-used method of executing condemned men. Photographs of such executions, unfortunately, are far from rare. (National Archives)

Rear Admiral Henry T. Mayo, commanding U.S. Naval Forces at Tampico, 1914. (Naval Institute, Annapolis)

Rear Admiral Frank Fletcher, commanding U.S. Naval Forces at Veracruz, 1914.

Brigadier General Frederick Funston, commanding the Fifth Infantry brigade, Veracruz, 1914. (Library of Congress)

Admiral Frank Fletcher's bluejackets firing from a defensive position during the fighting in Veracruz on April 21 or 22, 1914.
(National Archives)

Federal officers during the Mexican Revolution.
(University of Texas at Austin)

Yaqui Indians fought under both Pancho Villa and Alvaro Obregón. They usually wore conventional military garb for fighting. An intrepid newspaper photographer is with them in this photo. (Aultman Collection, El Paso Public Library)

Soldaderas. Most of the women played nurturing roles, caring for the men and protecting the children when necessary. (Bazar de Fotografía Casasola, Mexico)

Sometimes women took up arms themselves. Soldadera on horseback. (Aultman Collection, El Paso Public Library)

before Mayo's messenger arrived, Hinojosa was explaining the error to Copp. The Federals were expecting a rebel attack, he said, and the recent actions at the bridge had put the troops in a state of tension. Hinojosa insisted that the Americans had no business in that area, but he released them almost at once. On being freed and reaching the dock, Copp reboarded the whaleboat and returned to the *Dolphin*, where Mayo was waiting impatiently.

There the Tampico incident should have ended. General Morelos Zaragoza immediately arrested Colonel Hinojosa for negligence and sent a word of verbal apology to Admiral Mayo. Morelos Zaragoza considered the affair over.

The Tampico incident, however, was far from over; it was just beginning. Admiral Mayo considered Morelos Zaragoza's oral apology totally insufficient to atone for the indignity done to the American flag.

Mayo was one of the U.S. Navy's outstanding officers, the commander of the Atlantic Fleet in World War I. But April 9, 1914, was not his best day. He reprimanded Assistant Paymaster Copp for surrendering the whaleboat and then sent an officer, formally attired in dress uniform, with a stern message to General Morelos Zaragoza. Taking men from a boat flying the American flag, the message began, was a "hostile act, not to be excused," even by ignorance. In retribution for this act, Mayo levied a draconian penance:

> ... I must require that you send me, by suitable members of your staff, formal disavowal of and apology for the act, together with the assurance that the officer responsible for it will receive severe punishment. Also that you publicly hoist the American flag in a prominent position on shore and salute it with twenty-one guns, which salute will be duly returned by this ship.

Mayo gave Morelos Zaragoza until 6:00 P.M., April 10, twenty-four hours, to reply.

That afternoon, Mayo sent Admiral Fletcher a brief message describing in general terms what he had done. Fletcher, a bystander in the affair, transmitted Mayo's message to Washington without comment. It was received by the Navy Department early on Friday, April 10, twenty-four hours after the incident. But as the weekend was just beginning, nobody in authority was on hand to process it. The Navy Department forwarded the message, again without comment, to the State Department that afternoon at five.

In Mexico City, U.S. Chargé Nelson O'Shaughnessy learned of the Tampico incident from one of his friends in the Mexican Foreign Office on Friday morning, April 10. The Mexican official had received word through local reports and, like O'Shaughnessy, was inclined to discount the importance of the incident.

The information that O'Shaughnessy received from U.S. sources was a terse message from Admiral Fletcher. O'Shaughnessy, a canny diplomat, soon sensed that the incident was serious, even a potential cause for war. He therefore left the American embassy and set out on one of his frantic wild-goose chases, to which he was becoming accustomed, to find President Victoriano Huerta. O'Shaughnessy found nobody at the National Palace; it was Easter weekend. A junior official advised him that the president was taking a siesta and was not to be awakened. A suspicious O'Shaughnessy, however, drove off to check out Huerta's favorite bars and other haunts. Still unable to locate Huerta, he returned to the palace just in time; Huerta was about to leave. Huerta invited O'Shaughnessy to accompany him and a Mexican foreign service officer in his car. O'Shaughnessy accepted quickly.

Huerta's first reaction, on hearing O'Shaughnessy's version of the Tampico incident, was to dismiss it with a wave: he would simply apologize. However, as O'Shaughnessy went on describing Admiral Mayo's demands of General Morelos Zaragoza, Huerta balked. The demand for a formal salute as well as an apology was too much. At that point, the foreign service officer in the front of the car put in his contribution: it would be derogatory to the national honor to render the salute. Huerta stiffened. The first effort to defuse the situation had failed.

Huerta apparently had second thoughts, however, for at 6:00 P.M., he sent a seemingly conciliatory note to O'Shaughnessy, now back at the American embassy. "An investigation," Huerta's note stated, "will be made to establish the responsibility of Colonel Hinojosa," adding, "The Government of Mexico deplores what has occurred." The case was one of "a mistake of subordinate officials." General Zaragoza had placed Colonel Hinojosa under arrest, and he promised

30219000078261

strong punishment should the investigation "develop greater responsibility on the part of Colonel Hinojosa."

After O'Shaughnessy transmitted Huerta's message to the State Department, he handed a copy of it to the press. The next morning, the *New York Times* interpreted Huerta's statement as an apology, calling the matter "serious but not critical, an apparent misunderstanding." The *Times* added, however, that Mayo's demands were generally regarded in Mexican circles as "outrageous." It predicted that the affair would go no further, "unless the United States is looking for an excuse to start trouble."

The incident could have concluded again at this point. Back at Tampico, Admiral Mayo extended the deadline for the Mexican salute and awaited further orders.

The Tampico incident was now a diplomatic matter, no longer a military one. In Washington, however, Secretary of State William Jennings Bryan reacted strangely when he received Mayo's message on April 10. Though an avowed pacifist, Bryan seemed to sense nothing untoward in Mayo's saber-rattling. He consulted briefly with Navy Secretary Josephus Daniels and then transmitted Mayo's message to the White House with the notation "I do not see that Mayo could have done otherwise." And to the press he said, "I am inclined to believe that Admiral Mayo, who after all has the matter in his own hands, will regard the apology as sufficient."

At the White House, President Woodrow Wilson was preoccupied. He was taking his ailing wife, Ellen Axson Wilson, for a long Easter weekend at White Sulphur Springs, West Virginia, for a family gathering. Mrs. Wilson had been in declining health for some time, although the seriousness of her kidney disorder was not generally admitted. The outing, Wilson hoped, would do her good.

At White Sulphur Springs, Wilson passed a leisurely weekend. He played his usual Saturday round of golf, and on Sunday he accompanied his daughters and others at religious services in the little hotel chapel. The president then spent an entire hour inspecting the old registers of the White Sulphur Springs hotel. That afternoon he took Mrs. Wilson for a buckboard drive with two of their daughters, Margaret and Jessie, with Jessie's husband, Francis B. Sayre. Wilson was determined to avoid showing any concern over the Tampico matter in front of the press or his family.

Despite his public protests that he had "no interest in the [Tampico] situation,'' Wilson was secretly worried. He had received Mayo's report while engaged in his Saturday golf game. His first reaction was sober: "I have known for months that some such thing could happen—it was inevitable, in fact." But his real feelings were less detached. All through Sunday, he later told Daniels, he was "oppressed with the thought that he might be the cause of the loss of lives of many young men." Nevertheless, he insisted in public that he had come to White Sulphur Springs to rest and that he would not discuss any official business.

On Tuesday, April 14, Wilson was back in Washington. At a cabinet meeting that morning, all the news was gloomy. Nelson O'Shaughnessy had forwarded the Mexican government's refusal to meet Mayo's demands since "carrying courtesy to that point would be equivalent to accepting the sovereignty of a foreign state to the derogation of national dignity and decorum." Huerta had told O'Shaughnessy that he, Huerta, feared serious anti-American outbreaks throughout the countryside should Mexico submit to "the humiliating terms of the United States."

Two other incidents, small ones, also aroused interest. At Veracruz, the U.S. consul, William W. Canada, reported that a mail orderly from the battleship *Minnesota*, though wearing uniform, had been arrested and jailed by a policeman at the orders of a Mexican soldier. In addition, an American diplomatic courier had been detained in Mexico City by a blundering Mexican censor. Neither of these incidents should have constituted crises. In the case of the mail orderly, the local political chief had released the American and had jailed the Mexican soldier; Admiral Fletcher had declared the matter to be "without significance." And in Mexico City, Nelson O'Shaughnessy had cleared up the matter of the delayed telegram "in two minutes." Nevertheless, Wilson's cabinet, especially Wilson himself, attached considerable significance to both matters.

By Tuesday evening, April 14, President Wilson had come to a drastic decision. He ordered the U.S. Atlantic Fleet, under the command of Vice Admiral Charles T. Badger, to sail from Norfolk to Tampico. Bryan notified O'Shaughnessy that seven battleships, two cruisers,* and the troopship *Hancock* were to depart without delay. The *Hancock* was carrying a regiment of marines.

---

*The battleships were the *Michigan, Louisiana, New Hampshire, South Carolina, Arkansas, Vermont,* and *New Jersey.* The cruisers were the *Tacoma* and *Nashville.*

On Wednesday morning, April 15, the press reported that support for the president's action was virtually unanimous in the Senate. "No senator," the *New York Times* crowed, "questioned the right of the United States to occupy Tampico or Vera Cruz . . . and all agreed that a firm course must be followed. . . ." Democratic members of the Senate, restive with Wilson's policy of "watchful waiting," were relieved to see some action taken. The Republicans were delighted. The redoubtable Republican senator William Borah, the "Lion of Idaho," admitted that ordering the fleet to Veracruz looked like intervention, but the idea did not offend him. "If the flag of the United States is ever run up in Mexico," Borah declared, "it will never come down. This is the beginning of the march of the United States to the Panama Canal!"

With such support from Congress, Wilson felt even more emboldened. Notified by O'Shaughnessy that Huerta was preparing to send a message to the Mexican Congress, Wilson decided to preempt him. On Saturday, April 18, Wilson officially declared that Huerta must accede to Mayo's demands by 6:00 P.M., Sunday, April 19. Assuming that Huerta would refuse, Wilson did not wait for the Sunday evening deadline to announce that he would address the Congress on Monday, April 20. After that announcement, Wilson played his Saturday round of golf at the Congressional Country Club and departed by train that evening for White Sulphur Springs.

President and Mrs. Wilson spent Sunday at White Sulphur driving and strolling. At the same time, the president was keeping in touch with a nearly frantic Secretary of State Bryan back in Washington. That Sunday evening, the Wilsons returned to Washington.

The Wilsons arrived back at the White House early Monday morning. Wilson began his schedule by consulting with Bryan and then met with his cabinet. By now, Wilson was showing signs of nervousness and fatigue. His secretary of agriculture later described him as "profoundly disturbed" over his "terrible responsibility." At one point, Wilson told the group, "If there are any of you who still believe in prayer, I wish you would think seriously over this matter between now and our next meeting."

The president thereupon left the cabinet meeting and met the press outside the door. In that moment his demeanor changed. The issue, he said cheerfully, was only between the U.S. government and "a person calling himself the Provisional President of Mexico." "In no conceivable circumstances," Wilson went on, "would we fight the people of Mexico."

At 2:00 P.M. that Monday, President Wilson received four influential members of Congress, two from each party, in the Executive Offices of the White House. By now, he had decided on the thrust of the statement he would make to Congress that afternoon, but he needed converts to his cause. The issue did not revolve around intervention as a matter of principle—that was universally supported—but views differed regarding the justification for taking such an action. Wilson's key target for persuasion was Senator Henry Cabot Lodge, the ranking Republican member of the Foreign Relations Committee. The Democrats in Congress could be counted on to support the president; it was the Republican side that needed convincing.

Lodge was a formidable man, a student of history and the author of several books on government, politically conservative. Philosophically, he was inclined to support Wilson's position, for he strongly believed in national unity during times of foreign crises and worried about the protection of American lives and property abroad. But Lodge protested when he read the text of the president's proposed statement, contending that Huerta's refusal to salute the American flag was a "weak and insufficient" excuse for taking action against Mexico. Lodge also disliked Wilson's specifying Huerta personally as the target for military action. Wilson should justify his request on the basis that the lives and property of American citizens in Mexico had to be protected, Lodge insisted.

At this point, Wilson took the four congressional leaders into his confidence. He had just received a message from William Canada, the U.S. consul in Veracruz, advising that a large cargo of arms, destined for Huerta, would soon arrive in that port aboard the German freighter *Ypiranga*. Huerta, Wilson declared to the senators, must never receive those arms; he planned to intercept the shipment.

However, Wilson did not wish to disclose this new development to Congress; he wanted congressional authorization for intervention, but he wanted it granted without revealing his secret reason for the haste. And Wilson considered "protection of Americans" as too broad a basis for requesting authority to act. Such a proclaimed objective, he said, would widen the issue and possibly lead to war.

Senator Lodge, like the others, was sobered by this latest news from Veracruz, but he continued to press his arguments. Risking war, he insisted, was a secondary issue, since the United States, if it seized Veracruz, would be committing an act of war by that very action. And Lodge threw in a new consideration, the attitude of Germany. By international law, the United States could not legally intercept a foreign ship (in this case German) unless a state of war existed between Mexico and the United States.

Lodge had other objections, but Wilson was finished. He handed each senator and congressman a copy of his proposed resolution and left. He was due to speak at the Capitol in only a few minutes.

In his appearance before Congress at 3:00 P.M. on April 20, President Wilson ignored Lodge's objections and stuck to his original argument that "our quarrel was with Huerta, not the Mexican people." The United States, he said, was being "singled out . . . in retaliation for its refusal to recognize the pretensions of General Huerta to be regarded as the Constitutional President of the Republic of Mexico." He assured the Congress that "the present situation need have none of the grave complications of interference if we deal with it promptly, firmly, and wisely."

The weakness of his logic in depicting the United States as being "singled out" was emphasized when Wilson buttressed it with the trivial matters of the captured mail orderly back on April 10 and the short delay of the diplomatic message in Mexico City. Nevertheless, Wilson was an eloquent and persuasive speaker, and the standing ovation he received was sincere.

The speech was only halfway successful. After Wilson left for the White House, the House of Representatives passed his resolution overwhelmingly, but the Senate, led by Lodge, refused to be railroaded. Its Foreign Relations Committee unanimously rejected the idea of naming Huerta as the target of military action. Lodge then drew up a substitute resolution incorporating his own ideas.

The Democratic senators at first tended to join the Republicans in protesting against singling out Huerta as the target for intervention. But that afternoon a group of them were invited to the White House to visit the president, and they returned with their support for his position strengthened. Therefore, the Senate accepted only part of Lodge's resolution, and debate continued through the evening and into the next day.

Though President Wilson had refrained from mentioning the *Ypiranga* in his address to Congress, he had already decided that Veracruz, not Tampico, would be the target of any U.S. action. Accordingly, Secretary Daniels passed up the joint session of Congress, going instead straight to the Navy Department. Even while Wilson was speaking in Congress, Daniels sent an urgent message to Admiral Mayo. Mayo was to leave Tampico for Veracruz with all his vessels except the *Dolphin* and to be ready to land troops, if necessary, on his arrival.

Rear Admiral Frank F. Fletcher, at Veracruz, had not expected military action. His "Detached Squadron of the Atlantic Fleet" had been sent to Veracruz at the request of Ambassador Henry Lane Wilson during the Ten Tragic Days, and it had remained there during the intervening fourteen months. His duties had been peaceful. Veracruz was a friendly place, and aside from the task of interrogating émigrés leaving Mexico, his duties involved largely public relations. The small booklet he had just issued for the guidance of the officers and men of his command covered such matters as relations with the local Mexican citizens, policies for shore leave, and the entertainment of visitors aboard U.S. warships. It had outlined policies for tennis, swimming, boating, and fishing parties—even the season's schedule of boat races. Hardly a primer for immediate combat action.

All that was now changed. Fletcher faced a combat situation with a very small force. His flotilla included two battleships, the *Florida* and the *Utah*, which carried heavy firepower. But aside from them he had only the old gunboat *Prairie,* with a provisional marine battalion aboard. These limited resources would not provide much by way of a landing force. When Admiral Badger arrived with the Atlantic Fleet on April 22, the United States would have considerable strength, but events might not wait for Badger's arrival. So Fletcher knew that through April 21 at least, he would be on his own.

Still, a landing at Veracruz might not be necessary, and so long as Fletcher's mission was limited to preventing the *Ypiranga* from landing, he had little cause for concern. And that was all he had been warned to prepare for. At 11:00 P.M. of April 20, Fletcher thus notified Washington confidently, "Have sent USS *Utah* outside [the breakwater] to intercept and confer with *Ypiranga*."

At the Navy Department, however, Secretary Daniels was becoming frantic. Though President Wilson had appeared to ignore Senator Lodge's warnings about the seriousness of intercepting a foreign vessel in open water, Lodge's words had affected him and

Bryan—and Daniels. At midnight, therefore, Daniels sent Fletcher a message hedging on his previous instructions: "Use every possible persuasion to prevent the landing of arms and supplies by *Ypiranga*. If you cannot persuade ship not to land stores, endeavor to secure delay until Congress will act Tuesday evening."

During the next hour, Daniels hit on a possible solution to the problem. Perhaps an interception of the *Ypiranga* at sea could be abandoned in favor of seizing the cargo at the Veracruz customhouse after the ship had docked. In that way, the United States would be offending only Mexico, not Germany. At 1:00 A.M., Daniels sent Fletcher another warning order: "Be prepared on short notice to seize customs house at Vera Cruz. If offered resistance, use all force necessary to seize and hold city and vicinity." But that was only a warning. No decision had yet been reached.

Daniel's order sending Mayo to Veracruz never reached either Mayo or Fletcher. Thus Fletcher learned of it only when his radio operator intercepted a message sent from Daniels to Badger. Fletcher was confused. Here was a message instructing Mayo to prepare for a landing at Veracruz, and he, Fletcher, had not yet received any such orders. Since the Navy Department refused to clarify the matter, Fletcher and Mayo decided simply to consult each other. They concluded that Mayo should send Fletcher only the cruiser *San Francisco*, a ship in excess of Mayo's needs. Aside from making that transfer, they delayed doing anything else pending clarification from Washington.

In the early morning hours of Tuesday, April 21, Consul Clarence Miller, at Tampico, received a note from Admiral Mayo asking him to attend a conference aboard the *Dolphin*. When Miller arrived on Mayo's flagship, he found that the admiral had assembled his staff, the captains of his vessels, and his marine officers. The message that Secretary Daniels had sent nine hours earlier ordering him to Veracruz had finally arrived, superseding his informal agreement with Fletcher.

Every officer aboard the *Dolphin*, Miller later reported, was downcast, appalled at the prospect of depriving the American citizens in Tampico of naval protection. The Tampico incident had aroused so much anti-American feeling among the Mexicans in that seaport that Miller, like Mayo's officers, considered such a move "inconceivable." Mayo, "almost in tears," was demanding confirmation of Daniels's message.

Miller did the only thing he could. He returned to shore and sent a message to the secretary of state "earnestly and vigorously" protesting Mayo's orders for departure. Miller never received an answer.

As the Senate continued its debate throughout the night of April 20, Wilson conferred once more with Bryan, Daniels, Secretary of War Lindley M. Garrison, and the military chiefs of the army and the navy. He ordered that detailed plans for the occupation of Veracruz be drawn up, in case they should be needed. The meetings over, Wilson went to bed.

At 2:00 A.M., the White House telephone rang. When Wilson was awakened, Bryan and Daniels were on a three-way hookup. Consul William Canada, in Veracruz, had just received word that the *Ypiranga* had left Havana and would arrive at Veracruz the next morning. Three railroad trains were waiting at the dock to speed her cargo of arms to Huerta in Mexico City. Bryan recommended that the navy be directed to prevent the landing.

"What do you think, Daniels?" the president asked.

"The munitions should not be permitted to fall into Huerta's hands," Daniels replied. "I can wire Admiral Fletcher to prevent it and take the custom house. I think that should be done."

Wilson hesitated and, after a few more words, said, "There is no alternative but to land."

At 8:00 A.M., April 21, the radio operator aboard the battleship *Florida* brought Admiral Fletcher an emergency message from the Navy Department: "Seize custom house. Do not permit war supplies to be delivered to Huerta government or any other party."

10

****

The Landing at
Veracruz

When Admiral Frank F. Fletcher first received Secretary Daniels's order to seize the Veracruz customhouse, he was tempted to wait a day. It was early on April 21, 1914, and Admiral Charles J. Badger, with the bulk of the Atlantic Fleet, would arrive the next day. Daniels's order did not specify a time for the landing, and it occurred to Fletcher that the real objective was to prevent the arms aboard the *Ypiranga* from reaching Huerta's armies. If he could accomplish that end without landing, Fletcher might be able to argue that he had not violated his orders.

In accordance with his warning orders, Fletcher and his staff had organized a landing party of twelve hundred officers and men. Half of these men, however, were seamen with important duties aboard ship, so sending them ashore would affect the functioning of the crews on his vessels.

Fletcher estimated that this force of twelve hundred, if so used, would be opposed by some six hundred Mexican regulars, who could be quickly reinforced with two or three thousand other troops in the area. In addition, Fletcher had heard that the Mexican commander, General Gustavo Maass, had freed a large number of prisoners from the dungeons of Fort San Juan d'Ulloa, pressing at least some of them into service. Maass was capable of meeting a landing with strength; whether he would resist or accept a "peaceful" occupation of the customhouse was completely unknown.

Daniels's order, however, carried a note of immediacy, and any delay, no matter how well justified by local considerations, would probably not be understood in Washington. As Fletcher pondered his dilemma, a turn in the weather made his decision easy. At 10:00 A.M., "the breeze suddenly shifted to the north, increasing in force with all the appearances of an approaching 'norther' which would preclude the landing."

That was it! Old sea dog Fletcher decided to land his force at Veracruz immediately.

Fletcher was as well prepared as could be expected. He had thought the matter through and hoped to accomplish his task with a minimum of bloodshed and destruction—ideally with none. He had therefore ruled out supporting the landing with heavy naval gunfire. He could have destroyed the whole city in short order by employing the great twelve-inch guns of the battleships *Utah* and *Florida*, each of which carried ten of these monster weapons. But Fletcher sought to avoid wanton destruction by acting quickly and presenting the Mexicans with a fait accompli. By limiting his advance to the customhouse and treating the Mexican civilians with respect and consideration, he might be able to avoid a tragic fight.

The layout of the Veracruz harbor favored Fletcher's efforts. The space inside the breakwater was very limited; the end of Pier Four, Fletcher's projected landing point, was only five hundred yards across the water from the wall of the fortress San Juan d'Ulloa. The troop-ship *Prairie*, carrying the marine battalion, was lying at anchor only about three hundred yards off the end of the pier. This meant that the bluejackets and marines would be on the water, exposed to hostile fire, for only a limited time.

Reassuring the citizens of Veracruz about American intentions was also important; if the people were not frightened, Fletcher reasoned, their resistance might be minimized. During the previous days, therefore, he had kept the American consul, William Canada, well informed on everything that was happening. On Fletcher's request, Canada had notified General Maass that the Americans intended only to prevent the *Ypiranga* from unloading her cargo of arms at Veracruz; they would go no farther. Canada, of course, was already aware that tensions were building; for days, he had been flooded with foreign refugees from Mexico City. He had placed many of them aboard two chartered Mexican liners, the *Esperanza* and the *Mexico*. The *Mexico* was occupying a slip at Pier Four; the *Esperanza* was lying at anchor in the inner harbor.

In anticipation of Daniels's order, Fletcher was already waiting with the force commanders aboard the *Florida*. All had received their instructions: Captain W. R. Rush, the hard-driving captain of the *Florida*, would command the provisional naval brigade, and under Captain Rush the marine regiment would be led by Lieutenant Colonel W. C. ("Buck") Neville, USMC, a man with much experience in this kind of operation. The total landing force would come to 787 officers and men, made up of the seaman battalion from the *Florida* and the marines from the *Florida*, *Utah*, and *Prairie*. The seaman battalion from the *Utah* would remain aboard that ship awaiting developments; the *Ypiranga* was expected soon.

Until the order arrived, however, Fletcher had to be ready to go either way. So he held the *Utah*, commanded by Commander H. I. Cone, ready to (1) intercept the *Ypiranga* at sea or (2) send her seaman battalion to join the landing party. Fletcher also sent an officer to alert Admiral Sir C. G. F. M. Cradock, aboard the HMS *Essex*, and the captain of the Spanish ship *Carlos V*. Another officer paid a visit to the commander of the fortress of San Juan d'Ulloa. The Mexican commander was unperturbed. "Mexican honor would necessitate my returning fire in case I am fired upon," he said. Otherwise, he would take no part in any action that might occur.

At 9:45 A.M., Fletcher took a courageous step. On his own responsibility, he told Admiral Mayo to keep the *Connecticut*, *Dolphin*, *Des Moines*, *Solace*, and *Cyclops* at Tampico. Only the *Chester*, with her marine battalion, was to come under full speed to Veracruz.

At the American Consulate in Veracruz, William Canada had a ringside seat for the events of the day. His second-floor office afforded a close view of all the locations critical to Fletcher's plans: Pier Four, the main wharf, lay almost under his nose, just beyond the Terminal Hotel, on his immediate left. And down to the right, barely discernible at about four hundred yards, stood the customhouse and the customs warehouse, the ultimate objectives of the American landing. Below Canada's window, between the customs area and Pier Four, stood the Veracruz post office and the telegraph station. He sat in suspense—waiting.

At 10:15 A.M., Canada noted the liner *Mexico* pulling away from

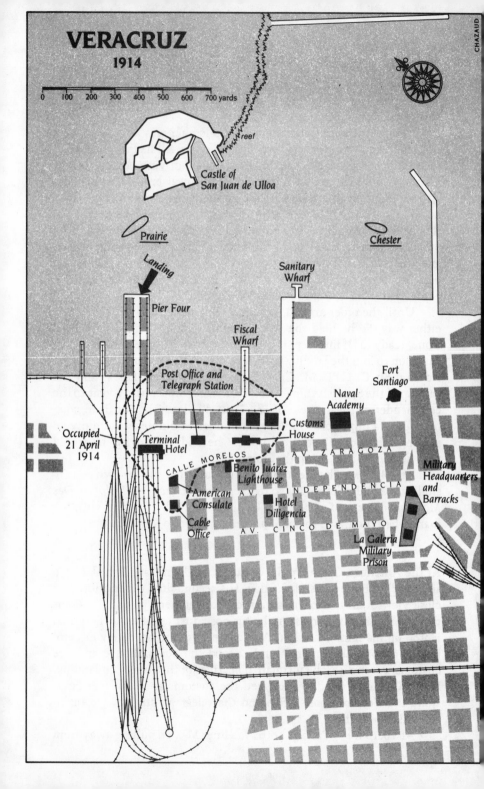

VERACRUZ
1914

CHAZAUD

0 100 200 300 400 500 600 700 yards

reef

Castle of
San Juan de Ulloa

Prairie

Chester

Landing

Pier Four

Sanitary
Wharf

Fiscal
Wharf

Post Office and
Telegraph Station

Fort
Santiago

Naval
Academy

Occupied
21 April
1914

Terminal
Hotel

Customs
House

CALLE MORELOS

A V. ZARAGOZA

Benito Juárez
Lighthouse

A V. INDEPENDENCIA

Military
Headquarters
and
Barracks

American
Consulate

Hotel
Diligencia

Cable
Office

A V. CINCO DE MAYO

La Galeria
Military
Prison

its berth at Pier Four with her load of American and foreign refugees. She had been ordered out by the Mexican authorities to provide room for the *Ypiranga.* At 11:00 A.M. the U.S. occupation of Veracruz began.

As Canada watched and made notes, American sailors and marines began clambering over the side of the *Prairie,* loading into whaleboats. He then saw tugboats, each towing several whaleboats, heading slowly across the water toward Pier Four. The same scene unfolded at the *Florida* and the *Utah,* outside the breakwater. Canada reached for a phone to call General Maass.

When Gustavo Maass came on the telephone, Canada read off his prepared list of things to say. The Americans intended to seize the customhouse, the telegraph office, and the railway yards but would go no farther, he read. They would not fire unless first fired upon. Finally, Canada urged Maass to "remain on hand and lend all the assistance in his power to keep order in the city." The American forces were "overwhelming," he claimed, and Admiral Fletcher trusted that no resistance would be offered.

Canada was surprised at General Maass's strong reaction. Despite the previous warnings Canada had given him, Maass cried out, "No! It cannot be!" The Mexican then slammed the phone down. Canada heard no more.

He fared no better in his attempts to secure cooperation from other Mexican officials. The collector of the port, like Maass, became highly agitated. He begged for time in which to warn his subordinates, to lock up the office, and to return home to his family. Canada then reached the chief of police, who declared that he would remain and help keep order—but then disappeared like the others.

His calls completed, Canada returned to his window view of the harbor. By now, a long string of landing boats headed unmolested toward Pier Four. At 11:30 A.M., Canada made a note that all the landing parties—sailors and marines—were ashore. They had brought with them some machine guns and a three-inch fieldpiece.

As each boat landed, the men hurried down the pier toward their objectives, and in a few minutes the Americans occupied the railroad terminal, the adjoining Terminal Hotel, and the cable office. Bluejackets soon stood guard outside the consulate. So far, all was going according to plan.

The Veracruz port area in 1914 was a little over half a mile in length. The waterfront street, on which the Terminal Hotel, the American

Consulate, the post office, and the customhouse stood, ran roughly north–south, with the railroad terminal and Pier Four on the north. This waterfront street was named Calle Morelos in the northern part and Avenida Zaragoza in the southern. One block west and running parallel to Morelos-Zaragoza ran the Avenida Independencia, and one block still farther west ran the Avenida Cinco de Mayo. On the south end of Cinco de Mayo, on the opposite end of town from Pier Four, stood the military headquarters, La Galera military prison, and a small secondary railway station.

General Gustavo Maass, in command at Veracruz, was an easy man for Americans to underestimate, for certain of his eccentricities seemed comical. As General Antonio López de Santa Anna impersonated the emperor Napoleon during the nineteenth century, so Maass seemed intent on emulating the German kaiser in 1914 by sporting "imperial" mustaches and plumed helmets. But despite his oddities, Maass was a patriotic Mexican determined to make the Americans pay for their aggression. He did not await orders from Huerta before taking action, and his response would frustrate American hopes for a peaceful occupation of the Veracruz waterfront.

The force with which Maass intended to defend Veracruz consisted of two "regiments" of regular infantry, the Eighteenth and Nineteenth, whose total strength came to about a thousand men—small by conventional standards but stronger than Admiral Fletcher had anticipated. In preparation for this kind of development, Maass had also organized and trained a second group, of over three hundred volunteers, who called themselves the "Society of Defenders of the Port of Veracruz." He had issued Mauser and Winchester rifles to the members of the society the day before the American landing.

The rumors that Fletcher had heard regarding Maass's releasing prisoners from Fort San Juan d'Ulloa turned out to be correct. These unfortunate wretches, freed from unbearable conditions, were not the kind of troops a commander might want to rely on, because most of them had originally been imprisoned for evading the military draft; but many were at least willing to act as guerrillas in support of the regulars in order to protect their city from the Yankees.

Immediately after his brief telephone conversation with Consul Canada, General Maass dashed across the street to the military barracks. There he encountered an officer of the Nineteenth Regiment and ordered him, with about a hundred regulars, to march up the Avenida

Independencia toward Pier Four. Since this street ran a block inland from the waterfront, it was protected from the threat of American naval gunfire. Maass also ordered the commander of the Eighteenth Regiment, General Luis Becerril, to arm what civilian volunteers he could find, including the inmates of the nearby La Galera prison. Soon motley crowds of citizens and prisoners were straggling up the Avenida Cinco de Mayo. Maass then sent a messenger to the nearby radio station to notify the minister of defense, General Aurelio Blanquet, back in Mexico City, what had happened.

Blanquet answered quickly, ordering Maass not to oppose the American occupation with his small force. He was to withdraw the Mexican troops to the small town of Tejería, about ten miles inland on the secondary railroad line, and there to await further developments.

Blanquet's orders, however, came too late. The troops and civilians that Maass had sent up the Avenida Independencia and the Avenida Cinco de Mayo could not be recalled.

At the other end of Veracruz, the American landing party, unaware of Maass's activities, began preparing to defend the waterfront installations it had occupied. At 11:50 A.M., April 21, Captain Rush reported to Fletcher that he had established his headquarters in the Terminal Hotel, with signalmen sending wigwag messages back to the fleet from the top of the building. On Rush's right, north of the city, Colonel Neville's marine battalion pushed five blocks inland from the railway terminal, effectively cutting Veracruz off from possible reinforcement at the northern end. Rush now occupied the railway terminal, Pier Four, the consulate, the customhouse, and the sanitary wharf on the south. All remained quiet at first. The Mexican citizens stood along the waterfront watching curiously. The American civilians still in the city gathered in the Terminal Hotel. These Americans had long been urging the United States to occupy Veracruz, and they cheered every move that Rush's men made.

At around 12:30 P.M., however, something changed. Merchants began closing their stores and children began hurrying home from school. Squads of Mexican soldiers appeared in the side streets that opened into the Avenida Independencia. The Mexican soldiers could be seen lying in firing position, though at first remaining quiet.

Then a shot rang out. It came from the direction of the railway yard. A navy signalman who had been flagging messages atop the

Terminal Hotel fell dead. Almost at once, other shots followed from other parts of the city: the plaza, the nearby Benito Juárez lighthouse tower, and the Plaza Constitución, a block south on Independencia. Captain Rush immediately ordered the bluejackets and marines to fire as necessary in self-defense.

A battle was on. Captain Rush signaled to Admiral Fletcher that "a thousand men with machine guns" had been reported in his vicinity and asked Fletcher to "hurry *Utah*'s troops." Fletcher responded. He signaled the *Utah*, "Send your battalion ashore; urgent; you may steam in closer." At 12:41 P.M., Rush reported the first American casualties.

The Americans went no deeper into the city that day. Even the positions they had taken were not secure; they soon discovered that they had bypassed pockets of resistance within the areas they now occupied. On the north, the marine regiment caught the brunt of the first heavy fire and was soon heavily engaged at the northern end of the city. Since this peaceable landing now promised to degenerate into a drawn-out battle, Admiral Fletcher transferred his flag from the distant battleship *Florida* to the close-in troopship *Prairie*, where he could personally direct land operations.

The fighting eventually quieted down for the landing party on the waterfront, but the ships' gunners still had work to do. The guns on the *Prairie* fired at some mounted Mexican cavalry that had been spotted in the sand hills west of the city. The *Florida*, out in the harbor, poured fire from its five-inch guns into the Benito Juárez lighthouse, silencing the snipers who had been picking off Americans along the Avenida Morelos.

Heroic acts were performed that day. Some of them went largely unsung, such as the dedication exhibited by the signalmen atop the Terminal Hotel. After the first shot of the day had killed the bluejacket sending messages, others stepped up to take his place. Three of the seven men assigned to the signal detachment were killed or wounded while wigwagging messages, but communications between Rush and Fletcher were never interrupted.

The most touted feat of heroism was performed by Chief Boatswain McCloy, the petty officer in charge of three picket boats unloading supplies at Pier Four. Early in the fighting, McCloy's detachment came under the fire of sharpshooters located in the Mexican Naval Academy building, down past the customhouse. On his own initiative, McCloy took his boat away from Pier Four and fired on the school building with his one-pounder guns. His small cannon did little damage, but the action drew retaliatory fire, and the puffs of smoke from the Mexican rifles gave away the snipers' positions. The *Prairie's* three-inch guns then fired over the heads of McCloy and his picket boats, silencing all the enemy fire from that section of the city. McCloy was wounded and one of his men was killed.

After the street fight had been under way for about an hour, a lookout aboard the *Utah* spotted smoke far out on the horizon; it was the *Ypiranga*. Immediately, Fletcher instructed Commander Cone to take the *Utah* out to meet her. When the battleship intercepted the *Ypiranga*, Cone found the German captain the soul of cooperation as he welcomed Cone aboard.

The courtesies finished, Cone advised the captain that Admiral Fletcher would permit the *Ypiranga* to enter the Veracruz inner harbor but would not allow her to leave with her cargo of arms on board. The German was not perturbed by this turn of events, and he produced his bill of lading for inspection. Cone was surprised to see that the shipment had originated not in Hamburg, as presumed, but in New York. Huerta's agents had purchased the arms directly from the Remington Company and routed them by way of Hamburg to mask their origin.

In the light of Admiral Fletcher's warning, the German captain decided to drop anchor outside the breakwater. There the *Ypiranga*, the trigger for the fighting at Veracruz, remained during the night of April 21–22.

During the early afternoon of April 21, Consul William Canada received an unexpected visitor. Admiral Fletcher's chief of staff, Captain H. M. Huse, had made his way through the sniper fire to solicit Canada's help. The firing in the streets of Veracruz must be brought to a stop, Huse said, and he asked Canada to try again to reach some Mexican officer who had the authority to order a cease-fire. If resistance continued, Huse added, Admiral Fletcher would consider stern measures. He would, though he hated to do so, destroy the city by shellfire.

Canada immediately sent a messenger under a flag of truce toward the center of the city. When the man failed to return after a reasonable time, Canada sent a second one, named Julio Franco. Franco proved to be more fortunate than the unnamed first messenger—at least he came back with his life—but he was also unsuccessful. On his return, Franco claimed that he had gone to the mayor's residence only to find it locked up. He then climbed to the roof of an adjacent house and dropped into the courtyard of the mayor's house. The mayor, barricaded in his bathroom, was in no mood to help. Franco also claimed that he had tried in vain to find the chief of police before returning to the American consulate.

In the meantime, General Maass had obeyed his superiors' orders to leave Veracruz, and nearly all the regular Mexican forces had left for Tejería by train during the afternoon. As they chugged out, Maass put out demolition parties to destroy the tracks behind them. From that time on, resistance in Veracruz came almost solely from the irregular elements of the streets.

Veracruz was relatively quiet by 4:00 P.M. Services such as the cable office's were functioning. Since cable was a far more efficient means of communication than relay radio, Admiral Fletcher used it to send a succinct message to Secretary of the Navy Josephus Daniels:

> In face of approaching norther landed marines and sailors from *Utah, Florida, Prairie* and seized customs house. Mexican forces did not oppose landing but opened fire with rifle and artillery after our seizure of the custom house. *Prairie* shelling Mexicans out of their positions. Desultory firing from housetops and streets. Mayo reported critical conditions at Tampico and directed him to remain there with *Connecticut, Dolphin, Des Moines, Solace, Cyclops. Ypiranga* arrived Vera Cruz two p.m. anchored in outer harbor and notified he would not be allowed to leave port with munitions of war on board. Holding custom house and section of city in vicinity of wharves and Consulate. Casualties two p.m. four dead twenty wounded.

In the early evening of that Tuesday, April 21, President Wilson sat down in the upstairs office of the White House with Secretaries Bryan, Daniels, and Garrison. Wilson feared trouble. A message had come in from Canada reporting that there had been firing around the Veracruz consulate, that the landing parties were now "simply defending themselves," and that Fletcher was contemplating bombardment of the city with his big naval guns.

This startling chain of events was not the scenario that Wilson had expected when giving the order to land early that morning. John Lind had assured him that the Mexicans would never resist, and others had backed him up. Occupation of Veracruz, they had all insisted, would be simply a "gesture." But during the meeting, Wilson learned the worst. An aide entered and gave him a slip of paper: "At this time reported four of our men killed, twenty wounded."

The next day, as Wilson faced the press, one reporter noticed "how preternaturally pale, almost parchmenty, Mr. Wilson looked when he stood up there and answered the questions of the newspapermen. The death of American sailors and marines owing to an order of his seemed to affect him like an ailment. He was positively shaken."

When dusk fell on Veracruz the night of April 21, organized resistance to the American landing subsided. The Mexican regulars had left the city hours earlier, and nearly all the citizens who had turned out to repel the invaders had returned to their homes. But the electric system was out, and the streets were dark. Groups of drunken and noisy men disturbed the quiet. Some of the thugs who had been released from prison fired their weapons into the air; others looted the stores; some took occasional shots at each other. None, however, seriously molested the Americans.

Fletcher's men took little heed of those disorders; they had much reorganizing to do after the day's fighting. The American dead and wounded had to be removed to the dock and then taken out to the aid station aboard the *Prairie*. Medical facilities were taxed by the unexpected number of wounded, so doctors from the British cruiser *Essex* and the Spanish cruiser *Carlos V* volunteered their services, earning Fletcher's gratitude. The men on shore needed resupply. During the night, the *Utah* and the *Florida* kept their searchlights trained on the waterfront to discourage any serious hostile action while whaleboats plied from ship to shore.

Early in the morning of April 22, Admiral Charles T. Badger, with the battleships *Arkansas*, *New Hampshire*, *South Carolina*, *Michigan*, and *New Jersey*, arrived in the outer harbor of Veracruz. At 2:45 A.M., Admiral Fletcher boarded the *Arkansas* to explain the tactical situation to Badger in person. Badger approved of Fletcher's handling of the landing and decided to leave Fletcher in command of the operation ashore. He placed his own contingents of seamen and marines at Fletcher's disposal, and those landing parties, numbering about three thousand men, debarked at 4:00 A.M. Upon landing, they moved out to their preassigned sectors of the city. Sniper fire began as soon as they stepped ashore.

Fletcher's forces had thus far taken only the waterfront and the railway yard, specific facilities located on the eastern and northern edges of Veracruz. Fletcher had planned to go no farther, but Mexican snipers located in the unoccupied areas of town persisted in shooting into his positions, endangering the lives of his men. Fletcher therefore decided to clear out every house in Veracruz. It was not a pleasant prospect—street fighting would inflict more casualties, both Mexican and American. But the decision was inevitable.

Before resuming his attack, however, Fletcher asked William Canada one last time to find some Mexican authority with whom to negotiate terms of truce. Canada tried but was unable to do so. Fletcher therefore sent word to Rush at 8:00 A.M.: "Advance at your discretion, and suppress this desultory firing, taking possession of the city and restore order, respecting as much as possible the hotels and other places where foreigners are lodged." Half an hour later, Rush informed Fletcher that the advance had begun. He asked that Mexican military positions in Veracruz be shelled by the American warships.

Clearing out the entire city of Veracruz entailed searching every one of its houses. Possibly to keep the sailors closer to the shore—and possibly because the marines had experience in city fighting—Rush first employed the two seaman regiments to clear a narrow strip, the two blocks adjacent to the waterfront. Then the first and third provisional marine regiments, using the Avenida Independencia as a line of departure, attacked westward to clear the rest of the city.

Local resistance turned out to be heavier than expected. Determined groups of Mexicans—some volunteer soldiers, some civilians—sniped from the flat-topped buildings. Neville's marines employed the techniques they had developed in such places as Honduras, Nicaragua, and Panama. They methodically hacked their way from house to house, blasting holes in successive walls to avoid the streets. After entering each building, they cleared out the top floor. Those were the same methods that the armies of Zachary Taylor and Winfield Scott had employed during the U.S. invasion of Mexico during the 1840s. The methods were effective; casualties among the marines were light.

The men of the second seaman regiment were not so fortunate. Their commander, the handsome and much admired Captain E. A. Anderson, captain of the battleship *New Hampshire*, had never fought on land even though his career had spanned thirty-two years. Overconfident, Anderson refused to send out scouts when his regiment turned in to the gigantic flat area between the New Lighthouse and the edge of town. He also felt it unnecessary for his men to spread out into skirmish line.

Suddenly, a heavy volley burst out from the Naval Academy building, four hundred yards away. Some forty Mexican naval cadets and citizens were shooting from behind barricades of mattresses and pillows that they had piled in the windows. Anderson's men could not pinpoint targets, and panic hit them. The bluejacket ranks temporarily disintegrated as the leading companies retreated headlong for safety. Anderson himself stood his ground with a few of his men around him.

As soon as the first shots rang out from the Naval Academy, however, the three-inch, four-inch, and five-inch batteries of the *Chester, Prairie,* and *San Francisco* opened fire as one. Resistance in the Naval Academy ceased, and Captain Anderson was soon able to reorganize his companies and resume his march. Some fifteen Mexican naval cadets had been killed; among the mortally wounded was Lieutenant José Azueta, the son of the prominent Mexican naval officer Commodore Manuel Azueta. The younger Azueta, one of the student leaders, was immediately made a hero. He would be "extolled," in Canada's words, "in the same category as the Chapultepec cadets who fought against the Americans in 1847."

Despite their determination to resist the Yankee invaders, the Mexicans in Veracruz were generally considerate of the American citizens who, remaining behind, had been caught in the crossfires of the streets. In the Hotel Diligencias, for example, the forty Americans, most of them women, were unharmed. These women voluntarily acted as nurses, caring for the Mexican wounded as they were dragged into the hotel.

But casualties were heavier on that second day of fighting than they had been on the first. Eventually, the total came to 17 Americans killed and 63 wounded.* A navy surgeon estimated the Mexican dead at 126 and the wounded at 195.

---

*The tragedy had its wryly amusing aspects. As the Medal of Honor had recently been authorized for issuance to officers as well as enlisted personnel, a total of fifty-five Medals of Honor were awarded, thirty-seven to officers and eighteen to enlisted men. All the members of the command team, from Fletcher, Anderson, and Rush to Major Smedley Butler, USMC, were awarded. None of the seventeen dead were included in the list of recipients. Butler later tried to return his medal but was given direct orders not only to keep it but to *wear* it. Lowell Thomas, *Old gimlet Eye* (New York, 1933), p. 180.

By 11:00 A.M., April 22, Fletcher's force controlled the whole city of Veracruz.

In Washington, President Wilson was shocked when he grasped what a catastrophe the occupation of Veracruz had turned out to be. Wilson continued to feel his own role deeply. "I cannot get it off my heart," he mused to his aide Joseph Tumulty. "It was right. Nothing else was possible, but I cannot forget that it was I who had to order these young men to their deaths."

Secretary Bryan had more-immediate concerns. He quickly concluded that Admiral Fletcher had exceeded the bounds of international law by intercepting the *Ypiranga* and denying her captain permission to depart with her cargo. So Bryan scurried over to the German embassy to pay a call on the ambassador, Count Johann H. von Bernstorff. Fletcher's action, Bryan said, had been the result of a "misunderstanding." Fletcher, he promised, would be instructed to apologize to the ship's captain. The matter of the *Ypiranga* was thus set aside for the moment.

But the military threat to U.S. forces in Veracruz was not yet over. Fletcher's brigade, not designed for sustained ground warfare, was at least perceived as being in a perilous situation, for General Maass, wrote a reporter in the *New York Times*, was concentrating a force of about sixteen thousand Mexican troops twenty miles west of Veracruz. Such a numerical superiority on the ground—about three to one—could make the brigade's very survival doubtful. Fletcher's force would be most vulnerable to night attack, when the big guns of the American battleships would be practically useless. The occupation of Veracruz was expected to last a while, and that required a larger ground force.

Wilson's cabinet was alarmed. The president's strategists reportedly urged him to call up as many as 400,000 reservists. He was not prepared to go that far, but he did approve sending an army occupation force of about 5,200 men to Veracruz, prepared for a long stay. Some reservists were called up, and popular songs fanned the flames of excitement:

> *Goodbye sister, goodbye sweetheart,*
> *Goodbye mother too;—*
> *Don't be grieving for I'm leaving*
> *'Neath the dear old red, white and blue.—*

Hark! I hear the bugles calling,
Kiss me, I must go; to my country I'll be true;
Think of me, I'll think of you, I'm off for Mexico.

On the night of April 19, the commander of the U.S. Fifth Infantry Brigade, located at Houston, Texas, received a phone call from headquarters, Second U.S. Infantry Division, in Texas City. The Fifth Brigade was to march to nearby Galveston, prepared for action at Veracruz. Tentage and trains were to be left behind; five days' rations were to accompany all troops; and each regiment was to take only a skeleton allowance of twenty-two mules. By April 24, the brigade, under Brigadier General Frederick Funston, was on the high seas.

Admiral Fletcher's task now was to tighten his hold on the city of Veracruz. To do so, he established strong outposts beyond the city limits to warn of any impending attack and to secure the water supply at El Tejar. To get the city functioning normally, he first had to evacuate all wounded civilians to the local hospitals and to clear the streets of dead. That clearance proved to be no easy task; the heat and workload made it impossible to bury all the corpses. Many had to be burned, right under the gaze of the public. To restore normal living, Canada requested all citizens to carry on regular business. At the same time, Fletcher himself called upon all municipal officials to resume their duties. The American authorities, he promised, would not interfere with local administration—provided that peace and order prevailed.

The response was mixed. The hotels and cafés opened immediately; the commercial houses, a little more slowly. The city officials, however, refused to remain at their posts. A draconian Mexican law of 1867, originally directed toward Mexicans who had served under the emperor Maximilian, was still in effect: it decreed severe punishment for any Mexican serving a foreign government. The local authorities would therefore have been afraid to cooperate with Fletcher, even had they desired to do so. That disappointment, plus the continuation of sporadic shooting, led Fletcher, on April 26, to issue a proclamation putting Veracruz under martial law.

Martial law required that the U.S. flag be flown over any territory under military administration, and that provision now applied to Veracruz. At 2:00 P.M., April 27, therefore, Fletcher's naval brigade formally raised the American flag over the headquarters at Veracruz.

The brigade paraded through the streets, the bands playing "The Star-Spangled Banner."

Tragic and unnecessary though the occupation of Veracruz was, any raising of Old Glory touches the heart of its soldiers. As Colonel John A. Lejeune, USMC, later recalled, "there was scarcely a dry eye among the Americans who participated in it or witnessed it. President Huerta had declined to hoist and salute the American flag, but we had forcibly seized his principal maritime city and had ourselves wiped out the indignity which had been put upon our country."

11

****

The Clouds of War

Shortly before midnight of Monday, April 27, 1914, the U.S. Army transports *Kilpatrick*, *Meade*, *Sumner*, and *McClellan* appeared outside the breakwaters at Veracruz. They were carrying the Fifth Infantry Brigade, commanded by Brigadier General Frederick Funston.

The feisty, redheaded Funston—just five feet five inches tall—had taken command of the brigade only four days earlier, as a result of the previous commander's poor health. The forty-nine-year-old Funston, a brigadier general for thirteen years, was considered to be the army's foremost field commander, just the man to cope with an uncertain situation in Veracruz.

Funston was the youngest brigadier in the army, a remarkable fact considering that he had not even entered active service until the outbreak of the Spanish-American War, in 1898. At that time, he raised a regiment of Kansas volunteers and came in as a volunteer colonel, probably expecting to return to civilian life when the war was over.

In the bloody Philippine Insurrection (1898–1901), Funston distinguished himself. In 1901, after the insurrection had dragged on for three years, Funston conceived, planned, and personally executed a daring and difficult mission designed to capture General Emilio Aguinaldo, the leader of the Philippine insurgents. Funston's scheme succeeded, and he was awarded the Congressional Medal of Honor. He was also commissioned as a brigadier general in the regular army, mentioned as a presidential candidate in 1904, and lauded by Theodore Roosevelt himself. At that time, Funston was thirty-six.

On the morning after his arrival at Veracruz, Funston went ashore to confer with Admiral Frank Fletcher about the changeover of the command from the navy to the army. Most matters were easily disposed of, since Funston agreed to take over the tactical positions already occupied by Fletcher's men. And Funston accepted Fletcher's choice of an American civilian, Robert J. Kerr, for appointment as mayor of the city, since Funston preferred to retain only the title of Commander, U.S. Forces Ashore. On one matter, however, the two men disagreed. Since Funston's brigade strength came to only about four thousand officers and men, he needed to retain Colonel John A. LeJeune's marine regiment with his brigade. Fletcher saw the validity of Funston's request and agreed that LeJeune should stay. But Fletcher could not bear to give up titular command of LeJeune's regiment, and he insisted that LeJeune continue to report directly to him, aboard ship. Funston refused to accede to that arrangment, and the matter was soon settled in Washington, in Funston's favor. The disagreement caused no ill will. LeJeune was temporarily attached to Funston and reported to him just as he would have reported to Fletcher.

Complete arrangements for the army's relief of the navy took three days, during which Funston's men waited aboard their crowded transports. On April 30, the two commands formed up on the Veracruz waterfront to formalize the changeover from one branch of service to the other.

The ceremony has been described as a "family affair," at which good will flowed freely. After the soldiers, sailors, and marines had passed in review, the cheering began. In the course of it, an army captain from the Twenty-eighth Infantry jumped up on a bench and led a cheer for the navy. The bluejackets responded with a cheer for the army. When the band played "Auld Lang Syne," the few Mexican spectators mistook that solemn refrain for the American national anthem, so they stood up and removed their hats. And as the naval brigade marched to the fiscal wharf, some of the girls from the red-light district recognized old acquaintances. A few rushed out and threw their arms around the embarrassed bluejackets. All the witnesses had a good laugh. The ceremony was an auspicious beginning.

Despite the exuberance in Veracruz, the political leaders in Washington were fretting. Wilson, Bryan, Daniels, and Garrison were becoming concerned about the long-range consequences of the Veracruz occupation. The United States had committed an act of war against Mexico—no doubt about that—but would a full war actually result? And if it came, would the United States be able to count on support from any of the civil factions fighting among themselves in Mexico?

To answer that knotty question, President Wilson needed to sound out the attitude of Venustiano Carranza once again. As early as the night of April 21, just after the landing, Secretary of State Bryan sent a message to George C. Carothers, the consul in Chihuahua, where Carranza was now located. Carothers was to approach Carranza and explain President Wilson's "position."

Carothers finally secured an audience with Carranza and made the familiar point that the Veracruz landing was simply "American redress for a specific indignity perpetrated by Huerta." At the same time, he again emphasized the friendship that Americans felt for the Mexican people. Carranza refused to respond orally to Carothers's presentation. Instead, he composed a long written reply that called the U.S. invasion a violation of Mexican sovereignty that threatened to "drag [Mexico] into an unequal war." He demanded that the United States immediately evacuate Veracruz and submit all complaints regarding the Tampico incident to Carranza, not to Huerta. After the United States had complied with these conditions, he wrote, the First Chief would consider the matter "in a spirit of elevated justice and conciliation."

On the same day, however, the *New York Times* carried a message that Carranza had previously sent to his representative in Paris: "It must be perfectly understood that in no case will we make common cause with Huerta, whom we consider an usurper, traitor, and assassin."

Pancho Villa received the news of the landings while at Torreón, which he had recently recaptured. He had accepted an invitation from his old friend General Hugh Scott to meet on the border between El Paso, Texas, and Juárez, Chihuahua. Villa recognized that he could use that conference to drive a wedge between Washington and Carranza. On the afternoon of Tuesday, April 22, Villa appeared in Juárez carrying in his baggage train a hundred woven wool rugs, which he intended as a gift for Scott.

Before he met Scott, however, Villa met the press. "Mexico has trouble enough of her own," Villa declared expansively, "without seeking a war with a foreign country, especially the United States." Smiling broadly for the photographers, he threw his arm around the shoulder of a bewildered George Carothers and exclaimed, "Why, all the European powers would laugh at us if we went to war with you. They would say, 'that little drunkard Huerta has drawn them into a tangle at last.' "

Villa then invited Carothers to join him for dinner in a public place. Between mouthfuls, he exclaimed that the Americans could "keep Veracruz and hold it so tight that not even water could get in to Huerta!" He and his men wished "only the closest and most friendly relations with our neighbors to the north."

Bryan and Wilson were delighted to receive this expression of approval from a powerful Mexican leader, whom they termed a "high minded and noble citizen of Mexico." Bryan wrote to Carothers and exulted that Villa showed "a comprehension of the whole situation that is greatly to his credit."

The reaction of nearly all the other Latin American republics, however, resembled Carranza's, not Villa's. A series of anti-American demonstrations immediately broke out in Uruguay, Chile, Costa Rica, Guatemala, and elsewhere. Word arrived that anti-American rioting had erupted in Lower California, and the monitor USS Cheyenne was dispatched from San Diego to protect Americans in that region.

In the United States, the bulk of the public reaction reflected dismay and a desire for peace. There were exceptions. A small group of Republican senators, led by Senator Lodge, attempted to push through Congress a bellicose resolution giving the president authority to intervene anywhere in Mexico. But most Americans agreed with Cyrus L. Sulzberger, a prominent businessman and Jewish leader, who asked, "Why must we back up the admiral? Who charged him with the responsibility of our international relations? The people of the United States elected Woodrow Wilson to attend to that job. . . . If the President must back up every admiral, there is no reason why we should not get into a war with every country having a seaport."

Opinion in Europe generally followed that in Latin America. Lon-

doners had always viewed Wilson's reaction to the Tampico incident
as ridiculous, and the London *Economist* expressed the general sentiment: "If war is to be made on points of punctilio raised by admirals
and generals, and if the Government of the United States is to set the
example for this return to mediaeval conditions it will be a bad day for
civilization."

Victoriano Huerta, of course, made the most of American discomfiture. He leaked word that he was preparing to demolish the railroad
between Veracruz and Mexico City as a safeguard against invasion,
and the world began to fear that the United States and Mexico were at
the brink of war. Newspapers in Mexico City reinforced that impression. "Federal bullets will no longer spill brothers' blood," the *Independiente* screamed, "but will perforate blond heads and white
breasts swollen with vanity and cowardice." Huerta's "official" statement was a bit more ambiguous: "In the port of Vera Cruz we are
sustaining with arms the national honor. The offense the Yankee
government is committing against a free people . . . will pass into
history—which will give to Mexico and to the government of the
United States the place each merits."

In the American embassy, in Mexico City, Edith O'Shaughnessy was
distraught. Since Huerta was breaking relations with the United
States, she and her husband, Nelson, would have to leave. She was
also frightened by the strident reaction of the Mexican press.

In the late afternoon of April 22, Edith O'Shaughnessy went
down the stairway to her private drawing room, there to receive the
streams of visitors coming to pay their sad farewells. After the guests
had departed, Edith sat down alone with the German minister, Admiral Paul von Hintze, conjecturing on what would happen next.

A detachment of Mexican soldiers came to the door of the embassy and demanded entry; let in by Edith O'Shaughnessy, they
quickly removed 250 rifles, two machine guns, and 85,000 rounds of
ammunition from the basement. Then, at about 7:30 P.M., a Mexican
officer appeared and announced that President Huerta was coming for
a visit. Von Hintze quickly disappeared, and Edith O'Shaughnessy
went down to the front door.

Huerta was dressed informally, in a gray sweater and soft hat, not
in his usual top hat. After he had climbed the steps to the geranium-

scented veranda, Edith O'Shaughnessy invited him to sit in the drawing room.

Following some awkward chitchat, Huerta got around to the reason for his visit. He hoped that the O'Shaughnessys would, despite
their imminent departure, honor their long-standing invitation to attend the wedding of his son Victor the next day. Edith O'Shaughnessy
readily agreed. She told herself that acceptance was "expedient," but
she wished to make one last gesture of friendship.

Nelson O'Shaughnessy soon returned home, and when told of
Huerta's removing all the arms from the basement, he was furious.
Huerta, however, paid no attention to his protests. He did, however,
offer to send the departing couple to Veracruz the next evening aboard
his personal train, with a full escort, including three officers of high
rank. "I would go myself," he said, "but I cannot leave. I hope to send
my son in my place. . . ."

As the three stood together for the last time, Huerta spoke quietly: "I hold no rancor toward the American people, nor toward *su
Excelencia el Señor Presidente* Wilson." After a pause, he added, "He
has not understood."

The next evening, April 23, Nelson and Edith O'Shaughnessy
were escorted with honors to Huerta's special train. Besides the
chargé and his wife, the train was carrying 150 prominent foreign
refugees. Huerta's nephew accompanied the O'Shaughnessys to the
train, and his chief of staff commanded the honor guard. Huerta's
kindly feelings toward Nelson and Edith seemed truly unaffected by
events in Veracruz.

But regardless of his affection for the O'Shaughnessys, Huerta
had no intention of continuing diplomatic relations with the United
States. From then on, Brazil would represent U.S. interests in Mexico
City. In response, President Wilson reinstituted the arms embargo
against all parties in Mexico, apparently unaware that the embargo
would affect only Carranza and Villa. The arms ban against Huerta,
after all, was what the Veracruz landing was all about.

On the international scene, the United States now stood alone, castigated on all sides for occupying the major seaport of a sovereign nation. In Spanish-speaking America, the feelings against the United
States were bitter; in many places, Americans found it unsafe to walk
the streets. To make matters worse, the Veracruz landing had so far
failed in its obvious purpose—to topple Huerta—and no success was

in sight. The episode appeared from all sides to be Yankee imperialism in its baldest form—and futile at that!

American diplomats were working behind the scenes, however, and on Saturday, April 25, their efforts bore fruit. The ambassadors from the three most powerful nations in Latin America—Argentina, Brazil, and Chile—called at the State Department with a request to see Secretary Bryan. The "ABC representatives," as they were soon called, offered to mediate the differences between the United States and Mexico. Bryan accepted the offer with alacrity, and Wilson, writing through Bryan, quickly confirmed the acceptance. Wilson expressed his relief in a letter to a friend: "I am hoping (I must admit a little against hope) for the best results of the mediation. We have been in a blind alley so long that I am longing for an exit."

To ensure congressional support for submitting to the mediation of the ABC countries, the president invited the usual four leaders of Congress to confer with him the same day that the offer was accepted. Senator Lodge approved in general but asked if the scope of the mediation was limited only to the Tampico incident and the occupation of Veracruz. "Certainly not!" the president answered. His note, he said, meant "settlement by general pacification of Mexico." That answer satisfied Lodge, but such a broad interpretation of the items to be settled spelled trouble ahead.

News of the proposed ABC mediation electrified the world, especially Latin America. This show of respect for the three Latin American countries caused a complete turnaround of attitudes in that region. Now an American in a South American city wrote, "The transformation was amazing; American flags were run up; the United States was cheered." He himself had been "seized and carried on the shoulders of a yelling, rejoicing mob, which had been ready to tear him in pieces a moment before."

In Mexico City, the regime of Victoriano Huerta had never been recognized by the ABC powers, so he saw no reason to give them any credence in mediating a dispute between Mexico and the United States. He finally accepted the mediation offer, though reportedly only under pressure from the British minister. But since President Wilson's concept of the meeting's agenda included a broad range of topics, including the fighting in Mexico, Wilson felt compelled to include First Chief Venustiano Carranza among the invitees.

Carranza responded even more negatively than Huerta. He would never, he announced, agree to an armistice with Huerta. The Constitutionalists would send a representative to the ABC conference, but *only* to discuss the differences between the United States and Huerta. The internal situation in Mexico was none of the United States's concern.

The ABC mediators and the two U.S. representatives* met at Niagara Falls, Canada, on May 20, 1914. From the outset, the conference encountered predictable difficulties in defining its scope. The ABC mediators, like Carranza, sought only to fashion enough of a compromise between the United States and Mexico to avoid a war. Still, Wilson remained adamant in calling for a discussion of the broader aims he had in mind. "No settlement," the president wrote, "could have any prospect of . . . proving acceptable to public opinion in the United States" that did not provide for the "entire elimination of General Huerta" and the setting up of a provisional government acceptable to all parties.

President Wilson's fixation on removing Huerta from power appears to have been the result of a peevish personal vendetta, motivated by resentment at Huerta's refusal to obey his dictates. That factor probably entered in, but Wilson also held strong convictions, which he revealed candidly in an interview with Samuel G. Blythe, from the *Saturday Evening Post*. When they met on the second floor of the White House, Blythe found Wilson elated; Huerta had just accepted the ABC mediation. When they sat down, the President defined his "ideal" as "an orderly and righteous government in Mexico." His passion, however, was "for the submerged 85 per cent of the people of the Republic who are now struggling for liberty."

Then, hitting the desk with a clenched fist, Wilson went on:

I challenge you to cite me an instance in all history where liberty was handed down from above. Liberty always is attained by the forces working below, underneath, by the great movements of the people. Every demand for the establishment of order in Mexico takes into consideration, not order for the benefit of the people of Mexico, the great mass of the population, but order for the benefit of the old-time régime, for the aristocrats, for the vested interests.

*Associate Supreme Court Justice Joseph Rucker Lamar and Frederick W. Lehmann, former solicitor general, represented the United States. The ABC representatives were Ramón S. Naón, of Argentina, D. da Gama, of Brazil, and Eduardo Suárez Mujica, of Chile.

The aristocrats wanted order, the old order, Wilson concluded, "but I say to you that the old order is dead." His mission, as he saw it, was "to aid in composing those differences so far as I may be able, that the new order, which will have its foundation on human liberty and human rights, shall prevail."

Unfortunately, Wilson overestimated the willingness of Latin Americans to follow his guidance. Even if his egalitarian objectives had been shared by the Latin American leaders—and they were not— his high-handed methods would have defeated him anyway. Apparently oblivious to the attitudes of the ABC representatives, he informed his representatives at Niagara Falls that he would have nothing to do with any sort of "provisional authority [in Mexico] which would be neutral [between Huerta and Carranza]." A new government must conform to Wilson's views. That meant the unconditional replacement of Huerta as president. Wilson assumed that a Constitutionalist victory over Huerta was inevitable. His main concern, he wrote through Bryan, was that the transfer of power be effected with minimum bloodshed.

President Wilson was undoubtedly correct in thinking that Huerta was on the way out. But his hope that Huerta's removal would bring peace to Mexico failed to take into account the rift widening between Carranza and Villa. Wilson still assumed that Carranza and Villa were parts of a single Constitutionalist movement.

It soon became apparent that Carranza did not appreciate Wilson's helpfulness, even though the president was backing Carranza's own cause. Carranza remained as adamant as Huerta in condemning the U.S. occupation of Veracruz. And as to arranging for a free election in Mexico, Carranza would never "be made a party to proceedings which place the election of a President of Mexico in the hands of the Washington government." He "would not accept as a gift anything which the Mediators would give, even though it was what [the Constitutionalists] were otherwise seeking. . . ." No provisional president appointed by the mediators would be satisfactory, "even if it was Carranza himself."

Consequently, the ABC mediation at Niagara Falls failed. A month's haggling produced nothing more than an innocuous agreement, reached in late June. It called for a provisional government "constituted by agreement of all parties involved in the civil war." Such a government, whatever its nature, was to be recognized by the

United States "as soon as constituted." Huerta was not mentioned by name, nor was the incident at Tampico. All the concessions in the agreement were made by the United States.

There the political impasse stood as June came to an end. The Americans had by then occupied Veracruz for over two months.

At Veracruz, General Frederick Funston felt restless and frustrated. He had just received a pointed order from the secretary of war forbidding him from pushing inland toward Mexico City. He was to remain in the positions he had inherited from the navy. Such passivity was contrary to Funston's nature and to his previous understanding. He had come to Veracruz expecting to fight, to advance on Mexico City as soon as he had whipped his reinforced brigade into readiness. He had assumed that war would be declared and that he would be the commander of an invasion force.

Funston set about to do battle with his superiors in Washington. He began a campaign to spread alarm in Washington. On May 2, he reported the existence of a threat, which turned out to be groundless, against the American pumping station at El Tejar. The next day, he passed on an unconfirmed report that five trains, loaded with an estimated eight thousand troops and numerous field guns, had been seen at Puebla on April 30.

Funston combined these reports and deduced from them that a serious threat faced his command: "If [the Mexicans] contemplate breaking [the] truce and taking the offensive, there will be some interesting times here." He had seven thousand men, but they were strung out in a long line of outposts. Funston advised that Admiral Fletcher had agreed to help him in case of attack, but Fletcher's providing a garrison for the city—which is what he promised—would take time. Funston did not anticipate the need for such a move.

Funston also protested recent orders that prohibited him from sending combat reconnaissance units out to find any Mexican forces near him. "If a disaster should result," he warned, "I must not be held responsible." The Mexicans, he explained, are "a people practically devoid of any sense of honor or fair dealing and who are smarting over their recent humiliation here."

Four days after sending his messages of alarm, Funston truly showed his hand. He had previously couched his desires to move inland in terms of maintaining his present position, but now he urged outright action: "Have just been informed [that] foreigners and citizens in Mexico City will unite in request that US troops occupy city to prevent massacre and pillage by Zapata. . . . Under such conditions [we] can go through in a day or two. . . . Merely give the order and leave the rest to us."

Actually, Funston was far from alone in advocating an advance on Mexico City. With him were Secretary of War Lindley M. Garrison, most of the American newspapers, many members of the Republican party, the Americans living in Mexico, and even the British government, for which the impact of the Benton killing was still fresh. One American offered some prescient advice to the adjutant general regarding the potential of air power:

> Bokchito Drug Co.
> Drugs, Chemicals, Patent Medicines
> Bokchito, Okla.
>
> April 24, 1914
>
> Dear Sir—In case of invasion of Mexico by the United
> States, it looks like it would be easy to drive the Mexicans
> from their impregnable positions by means of bombs and
> torpedoes from Air Ships. Yours Patriotic
>
> J. O. Jack

The most aggressive of the saber rattlers were the members of the American press who had converged on Veracruz expecting action. Among them were two adventurers, Jack London and Richard Harding Davis. London seemed interested in enjoying the visit—he even brought his wife. He therefore wrote patriotic but relatively factual articles. Davis, on the other hand, appeared intent on promoting hostilities for his own ends. Always one to picture American fighting men as sun-crowned heroes, Davis let his imagination run wild in describing how Mexicans must have viewed the invading American warriors: "Except in bronze on their monuments the [Mexicans] had never seen such supermen of such heroic aspect. . . . This morning they could have marched not only from the wharf to the plaza, but from the harbor to Mexico City." Heroic words indeed, but written more than a week after the Veracruz invasion and by a man who had not been there.

Davis did more than write sensational articles; his impatience caused Funston real difficulties. He once took off from Veracruz for Mexico City, reaching a place called Paso del Macho. There he and his companions were arrested and taken to General Maass, who amazingly allowed them to continue on. Davis was arrested once more in Mexico City, his life saved only by the intercession of the correspondent for the London *Times*. General Funston was not amused.

As the days dragged on, both the troops and the correspondents in Veracruz came to realize they were not going anywhere soon despite Funston's messages to Washington. The Americans now concentrated on administering the city, which meant cleaning it up enough to permit safe habitation by Americans and other foreigners.

Even here Funston had his problems with Washington. Only one day after assuming command from Admiral Fletcher, the general received a message from Secretary Garrison advising that Robert Kerr, the man Funston and Fletcher had appointed mayor of Veracruz, was unacceptable to serve in that capacity. Kerr, it turned out, was an active Republican and a vociferous critic of Wilson's foreign policy.

Funston fumed. Politics had nothing to do with the situation in Veracruz, he protested. He was merely "trying to secure the services of the best and most qualified Americans in Mexico," with about as much "regard for a man's politics as . . . about the color of his hair." He extolled the patriotism of the Americans willing to take civil positions in Veracruz.

Funston's protests were to no avail. Secretary Garrison directed that Funston himself administer Veracruz, so on May 2 Funston assumed the title "Military Governor of Vera Cruz."

Funston's functions as military governor included the collection of customs and taxes, and the maintenance of order. However, the need for establishing an acceptable system of sanitation was the most urgent matter on Funston's agenda. The name "Veracruz" had long been synonymous with filth and disease. The yellow fever season, which began in April every year, had made service at Veracruz more dangerous for American soldiers in the war with Mexico (1847–48) than had frontline duty with Winfield Scott's army. Funston went about rectifying the public health situation as if he were attacking an enemy position.

Instituting a sanitation system in Veracruz was an uphill battle, made harder because the people themselves had always accepted their high mortality from disease as something foreordained. One sign of their apathy was the condition of the New Market, where food for the city was brought in from the countryside to be sold. Since its construction some four years earlier, the New Market had never been cleaned. The urinals were used as repositories for cigarette butts and other trash. Animals wandered through the open markets at will. Food on display often attracted a thick black coat of flies. The tiled floors were cracked and barely visible beneath "a festering meringue of dried blood, fish scales, chicken feathers, entrails, putrid produce, and excrement." The odor was so strong that "it was almost unbearable for a white person to remain in the vicinity." All that had to be cleaned up.

Veneral disease also needed to be controlled. Funston did not try to forbid prostitution, but he had it strictly supervised. Mexican prostitutes were frequently examined; foreign prostitutes were deported. The problem of the prostitutes, however, defied complete solution.

In one case, a thirteen-year-old Mexican girl had run away from her home in nearby Orizaba to see the American army when it arrived in Veracruz. Described as "innocent and unsophisticated," she soon fell into prostitution to avoid starvation. She was treated twice for gonorrhea and twice for fever in the Women's Hospital. Finally, the American authorities arrested her and sent her home to Orizaba, but not before she was discovered to have syphilis and to be three months pregnant. Her case was dramatic enough to prompt the American authorities to ship other young, unattached women out of Veracruz before it was too late.

Funston's sanitary procedures were remarkably successful. The death rate from disease among the Mexicans dropped by 25 percent from that of the previous three months, even though the yellow fever season was just beginning. Yet Funston's reforms did not make a permanent impression on the Veracruz population. After the departure of the American troops, the relieved citizens reverted to their old ways as if the Yankees and their regulations had never been there.

By and large, the physical condition of the soldiers and marines in Veracruz remained good. Their health records, in fact, were even better than those for a corresponding command in the United States. But boredom and the summer heat combined to sap morale. Some men tried to break the routine by sneaking through the lines; some even headed for Mexico City. On May 10, Funston arrested a lieutenant for going to Mexico City without authority. And on June 20 a marine private escaped from a psychiatric ward and left camp with a rifle and ammunition.

The most bizarre and macabre case, however, was that of Private Samuel Parks, Twenty-eighth Infantry, who stole two valuable horses and rode into Mexican lines on the night of May 6. Witnesses later reported having seen the horses, but stories came in that Parks had been executed near General Maass's headquarters at Tejería.

Much later, the Associated Press representative in Mexico City sent Funston Parks's identification tag, which had been found with his "bloodstained clothing." Parks had been executed as a spy on May 7 by the local Mexican commander at Tejería. Funston requested the War Department to pressure the Mexicans to court-martial the officer for the action, but he obtained no satisfaction. In the last days of the American occupation, Funston received a few charred bones, supposedly those of the unfortunate soldier. Parks had been cremated.

The bored fighting men of Veracruz were always hoping for some change in their situation. If they were to see no combat action, perhaps Huerta would be killed or deposed, so the Americans could go home. That hope was encouraged by an increasing number of reports that one of the rebel leaders, either Zapata or Villa, would soon take Mexico City. Villa apparently expected to do so; he promised his men four days' looting when they took the city.

General Funston affirmed his men's hopes. The fall of Huerta, Funston advised Washington, was "close at hand."

12

****

The Fall of
Victoriano Huerta

As Pancho Villa returned from
Juárez to Torreón following his conference with General Scott, his
spirits were high. The Division of the North had enjoyed a whole
month in which to reorganize and resupply. The members of the
division, like Villa himself, were eager to push on to Zacatecas, a city
about three hundred miles to the south, on the main railroad line to
Mexico City. Everything seemed to be developing well.

The three Constitutionalist armies closing in on Huerta—
Villa's, Obregón's, and González's—were each about five hundred
miles from Querétaro, the main hub where the three rail routes converged. Villa was in the best position. Obregón, on Mexico's west
coast, was a little closer geographically, but he still had to cross the
rugged Sierra Madre. No such obstacles stood in Villa's way.

Pablo González, the third commander, lagged far behind the
other two. He had not yet taken Tampico and would therefore be
unable to move on Saltillo until mid-May. And between Saltillo and
San Luis Potosí, González would still have to cross the terrible desert
that had cost General Santa Anna so dearly on his way to Buena Vista
seventy years earlier. And the Napoleon of the West had marched
unopposed.

In early May 1914, Villa invited First Chief Venustiano Carranza to visit the Division of the North at Torreón. Villa suspected that Carranza's attitude toward him was not altogether friendly or generous. Carranza had given him little or no credit for the spectacular victories that had kept Carranza's movement alive. But that was a petty matter, Villa told himself. And Villa appreciated Carranza's mild reaction to his own support of the U.S. occupation of Veracruz, a move that Carranza opposed. So all in all, Villa was determined to show deference to Carranza's position.

During that visit, though, Carranza dealt a severe blow to Villa's ambitions. Exercising his authority as head of the Constitutionalist movement, Carranza now ordered Villa to suspend his projected advance south toward Zacatecas and to turn east toward Saltillo instead. Villa correctly interpreted Carranza's order as an effort to halt a triumphal Villa march toward Mexico City.

Though shocked and disappointed by Carranza's order, Villa eventually decided to comply with it. The forces fighting Huerta needed at least a titular political chief, he reasoned, and his defying Carranza's orders outright would break up the team. But in complying, Villa did things his own way. He turned his army east toward Saltillo without waiting for the promised help from the fumbling Pablo González, in whose territory Saltillo lay.

Seizing Saltillo turned out to be easy. Villa launched a massed charge against the Federal position at Paredón, north of Saltillo, and that in itself sufficed to break what will existed among the weary, ill-supplied, demoralized Federals. Still, even the weak Federal resistance caused deaths. Four Federal generals were killed, and one thousand troops surrendered. Villa took possession of Saltillo on May 20. Carranza could now return to his home state of Coahuila, from which he had fled to Sonora a year before.

Villa was feeling expansive after his easy victory, and during his brief stay at Saltillo, he comported himself with remarkable restraint. He forbade his men to loot Carranza's home capital, and he took time to become acquainted with González, whose troops had entered the city to take over after Villa had seized it. Actually, Villa liked González, though he recognized his limitations as a soldier. So generous was Villa's mood that he installed one of Carranza's fainthearted *perfumados*, Jesús Acuña, as provisional governor. Villa returned to Torreón content.

Villa's hopes that he could earn Carranza's respect and support by acts of loyalty were soon shattered, however. On his return to Torreón, Villa learned that the First Chief, in an interview, had referred to Madero (and Maderistas) with contempt. Carranza blamed "the shortcomings of Madero and Pino Suárez" for "the disaster of their administration." He promised to "seek new men, not stained with the responsibility of that disaster." He also predicted that the "hypocritical bandit Villa" would soon rebel against him.

Carranza's statement cut Villa deeply, but the words were overshadowed by Don Venustiano's next action: Carranza ordered Villa to cancel plans for attacking Zacatecas, assigning that mission instead to the local chieftains Pánfilo Natera and the Arrieta brothers (Domingo and Mariano). Villa felt that he had earned the right to take Zacatecas because of his record of uninterrupted victories.

Actually, Carranza may have had a reason for his decision other than his distrust of Villa. The Arrietas, members of an influential Durango family, had been attempting to take Zacatecas for some time.* And Natera had once captured Zacatecas, only to lose it again. Their efforts might not be hopeless.

But Villa considered Carranza's order to be an intolerable slight. He held Natera in low regard because of his failure to take Ojinaga the previous December, which failure had forced Villa to leave Chihuahua and assume personal command. The Arrietas seemed even worse: not only were they incompetent; they were openly hostile to Villa.

For the moment, however, Villa bided his time. He knew that Natera's force was weak, numbering only five thousand men, and that the Federal garrison was much larger. It was just possible, Villa conjectured, that the crafty Carranza was trying to discredit Natera as well as Villa himself. Even that desperate rationalization was soon discredited, though. On June 10, after Natera's predictable repulse at Zacatecas, Carranza sent orders for Villa to send him a number of reinforcements from the Division of the North. Villa refused mildly. The next day, Carranza made his order clear: "If you have not already done so, have no less than three thousand men and two batteries of cannon leave [for Natera's headquarters] at once."

On the morning of June 13, Villa requested a telegraphic conference with Carranza.

Carranza opened the conference on a supercilious note: "Good morning, Sr. General Villa, and what is the reason for the conference I have

---

*Carranza, it will be recalled, had gone out of his way to witness one of their attempts a year earlier, when he was traveling between the states of Coahuila and Sonora.

granted?" Villa tried to be reasonable by explaining that it would be five days before his troops could be ready to move to Natera's support. But then his restraint broke down. "Who sent the men on that job without the assurance of complete success?" he demanded. "Tell me, Señor, if I go to command the division, will it be under Arrieta or Natera, with them to take the credit?"

Carranza was the better man in debate, and he soon caused Villa, in a fit of temper, to play into Carranza's hands: "Señor, I resign command of this division. Tell me to whom to deliver it." Carranza accepted.

Villa's generals were shocked by news of his resignation. They notified Carranza that they refused to accept what had happened. In a lengthy exchange of telegrams, they defied Carranza's repeated demands that they name a general to replace Villa.

Finally, Villa's generals sent Carranza a message. They intended to continue the struggle under Villa, they insisted. And in case of doubt, they told Carranza, they had made their decision in Villa's absence. Villa had consented to continue in command only after they told him what they had done. To formalize their declaration, all the generals of the Division of the North signed it.*

Carranza was nothing if not resilient. He realized that he had no direct way of imposing his will on these tough men, so he resorted to bluff, assuming a posture of magnanimity. He offered to confer, provided that six of Villa's generals would report at Saltillo the next morning. That toploftiness finally angered even the diplomatic Felipe Angeles. He composed a message that ended in a thoroughly insubordinate tone: "we know well that . . . your purpose [is] to remove from the Revolutionary scene the men who can think without your orders, who do not flatter and praise you, or struggle for your aggrandizement but only for the rights of the people."

The die was cast. Villa, with the hearty concurrence of his generals, prepared to move out against Zacatecas despite the fury of the First Chief.

---

*Filipe Angeles, Tomás Urbina, Toribio Ortega, Maclovio Herrera, José Isabel Robles, Eugenio Aguirre Benavides, Raúl Madero, Martiniano Servín, Calixto Contreras, Severino Ceniceros, Mateo Almanza, Orestes Pereyra, Máximo García, and Manuel Madinabeitia. Martín Luis Guzmán, *The Memoirs of Pancho Villa* (Austin, 1975), p. 219.

The Battle of Zacatecas

Zacatecas, Pancho Villa's target, was important for many reasons. One was its position on the railroad line to Mexico City. Further, it had economic value because most of Mexico's coinage contained silver from the mine of nearby Casa Moneda. It also boasted elaborate churches and fine houses, squeezed into a steep north–south canyon. Its military value lay in its natural defenses. Zacatecas was the last stronghold available to the Federals before Mexico City.

Huerta, a good soldier, also appreciated the importance of Zacatecas. He had therefore moved into place a sizable garrison for its defense. A resounding Federal defeat there would amount to a coup de grace for Huerta's army, so he ordered that Zacatecas was to be held by Federal troops at all costs.

Villa was ready. His Division of the North was now a mature military organization. Villa no longer led his troops in reckless cavalry charges against the enemy; he now commanded his division in a conventional manner. For the Zacatecas campaign, therefore, he delegated the initial planning to two trusted subordinates, his old compadre Tomás Urbina and General Felipe Angeles. No two men could have been more dissimilar personally, but they worked together on the best of terms, with complementary strengths.

On June 16, General Urbina loaded all of Villa's infantry troops aboard railroad cars and began the long trip to Zacatecas. There Urbina would join up with other Constitutionalist forces under Pánfilo Natera, a man who, despite his shortcomings, was always quite willing to serve under Villa. Villa's artillery, under Angeles, would leave Torreón for Zacatecas the day following Urbina's departure. When all of Villa's forces had gathered, the Division of the North would field 22,000 troops, with fifty cannon, a formidable force.

Villa arrived at Zacatecas on June 22. He approved the plans his subordinates had drawn up and announced that the offensive would be launched the next day. Urbina's infantry had already driven in some of the Federal outposts on the north, and Natera's troops were ready on the south. Despite sporadic Federal fire and a driving rain, Angeles conducted Villa on reconnaissance around the position. Angeles planned to support the main attack on the north with thirty-eight guns and allocate another ten to support troops attacking from the south. Villa was confident that the enemy would be annihilated:

"I expect your cannon to win the battle." As a tactical general, Villa had come a long way.

Zacatecas, at an altitude of seventy-five hundred feet, was a natural mountain fortress. The streets were steeply inclined; in some places the slanting roads stopped, forcing the traveler to continue on his way by steps. The city was dominated by a range of hills that rose over a thousand feet above its streets. The northern approach, which Villa used, was dominated by two mountains, La Bufa on the northeast and El Grillo on the northwest. Other hills, leading up to those two, were secondary. Thus, from the outset, Urbina and Angeles focused their attention on La Bufa and El Grillo.

In order to achieve surprise, Angeles proposed to withdraw his artillery to new positions during the night. He would still be able to hit Federal batteries from the new firing sites, but his pieces would be temporarily invisible. By that ruse, he hoped to deceive the Federals into thinking Villa had left. Then, without warning, Urbina would take 5,000 men against La Bufa, and Villa would personally command another 5,000 against El Grillo. Natera would command the third force of 5,000 on the south. Two other forces, of 2,000 and 3,000 men, would complete the ring—20,000 men in the assault.

General Luis Medina Barrón, commanding the Federals at Zacatecas, had about 12,000 men but only ten guns. His overall strength was half that of Villa, but the advantages accruing to the tactical defense of a prepared position would normally have evened the odds. However, Villa held the initiative, and Barrón's men were all tied down in positions too far apart to permit mutual support, vulnerable to destruction one at a time. And the morale of Villa's men was high whereas many of Barrón's men were unwilling and frightened conscripts.

The assault jumped off, as planned, at 10:00 A.M., Tuesday, June 23. At that moment, all the infantry of the Division of the North advanced to seize the footholds leading up to the final objectives. Villa, in personal command of the wing attacking El Grillo, took the intermediate objective of Loreto Hill within twenty-five minutes. In like manner, Urbina, on his left, took Tierra Negra, in front of La Bufa. By 11:00 A.M., Villa had reorganized and was ready to move on. He instructed Angeles to move his artillery forward.

At that point, Villa was rocked by a loud explosion nearby. At first, he later wrote, he thought that some expert Federal gunner had pinpointed his position. But when the smoke and dust cleared away, he realized that the destruction had occurred because of an accident.

A shell had exploded in the hands of an ill-fated Villista gunner. The rest of the gunners in the battery were unharmed but immobilized by terror.

Villa rallied them quickly. "This is only an accident," he shouted. "It won't happen again. I am here with you. I will protect you!" As the men were weighing Villa's somewhat questionable reassurances, Angeles chimed in with a more logical argument. "Nothing has happened," Angeles shouted, "but something worse will happen if we slacken fire and the enemy defeat us. Then we will have died in vain!" The gunners went back to their pieces.

At 1:30 P.M., Villa believed that the enemy must be despairing, though Barrón's Federals on El Grillo continued to fight stubbornly and skillfully. Urbina had taken La Bufa, and Natera was making progress on the south. At 5:30 P.M., Villa had El Grillo in his possession, and from that point on Barrón had no defensive positions to fall back on. Eight thousand Federals broke into a retreat, taking refuge in houses within the city. Villa's men captured many of them. He executed all the Federal officers but spared whatever soldiers would join his army. Villa estimated that of all the Federals who had originally opposed him, only two hundred escaped. Other estimates claimed that between five thousand and eight thousand Federals were killed on the battlefield and another twenty-five hundred wounded.

Villa entered Zacatecas in person the next morning. As he surveyed the battlefield and the streets, he saw how devastating the battle had been. "Those who came to meet me," he exulted, "had to leap over corpses. Besides the enemy dead, many of my soldiers lay resting, sleeping in pools of blood." He immediately gave orders forbidding his men to loot the property of the inhabitants. He wanted to retain the good will of the shell-shocked people of Zacatecas.

The capture of Zacatecas left Huerta helpless, able only to buy time. His last natural terrain barrier was gone, and the defeat finished the process of demoralizing his army. To the world, it seemed that the Division of the North was invincible. So it was—to any armed enemy. In Mexico, at least, only the political power of Venustiano Carranza could stop it.

Pancho Villa and Felipe Angeles were in no mood to rest on their laurels after their victory at Zacatecas. Their fighting blood was up. In a flush of enthusiasm, Angeles asked Villa to give him four infantry brigades; with them, he would push on to Aguascalientes, the next important town on the rail line. Villa was not to be outdone: "Not four brigades, Señor General! Seven brigades! And before four days have passed, our cause will triumph at Aguascalientes!" Angeles set about making preparations.

But their zeal was quickly forgotten. Even during the battle, word had come in that Carranza, livid over his recent humiliation, had relieved Angeles of his position as deputy secretary of war, calling him an "unworthy revolutionary." And Carranza had an insult for Villa also. He quickly promoted both Pablo González and Alvaro Obregón to the rank of major general while pointedly ignoring Villa, who remained a brigadier. Carranza always referred to Villa's force, the most powerful army fighting Huerta, as only one division, subordinate to Obregón's Corps of the Northwest.

Normally, Villa and Angeles would shrug at these slights, but Carranza had a far more potent weapon in his arsenal: he cut off Villa's supply of coal and arms. Villa might have pushed ahead to Aguascalientes without the arms, but he was now so dependent on his rail transportation that he dared not push on without it.

For a while, Villa was tempted to march back to Monclova (Coahuila) and simply help himself to the coal in Carranza's stores. But such an action would cause more of a rupture in the Constitutionalist ranks than Villa was willing to bring about at that time. So Villa brought Angeles and his seven brigades back to Chihuahua. Villa had broken the back of Huerta's army at Zacatecas, but to others would go the glory of taking Mexico City.

While the generals in northern Mexico hobbled their military effort by feuding among themselves, the most immediate threat to Mexico City was that of Emiliano Zapata, in the adjacent state of Morelos. Tepic, Guadalajara, Zacatecas, and San Luis Potosí were all several days' marches away, but Cuernavaca, capital of Morelos, was only about sixty miles to the south. Thus, whenever the Huerta regime began to totter, the people of Mexico City looked anxiously toward the fierce, unrelenting Zapata.

At the age of thirty-five, Emilio Zapata was the revolutionary least encumbered by side issues. He was motivated solely by his concern for the small farmers of Morelos, who, like his own father, had lost their communal lands during the tyranny of Porfirio Díaz. Zapata's only criterion in deciding whether to support a national regime was the zeal that regime showed in pursuing his objective. Thus

Zapata had not shared Villa's worship of Francisco Madero; Madero, in Zapata's eyes, had failed on the only issue that interested Zapata. But Zapata always hoped; maybe the next president would be dedicated to land reform.

In other respects, however, Zapata had much in common with Villa. Like Villa, he had come from the people and was essentially illiterate. Both were bold and daring commanders, adored by their followers. And both held Carranza in contempt. Zapata was even more contemptuous of Carranza than was Villa, and he recognized Carranza only as the governor of Coahuila. Zapata had, in fact, once urged that Carranza be tried by court-martial for his effrontery in declaring himself First Chief.

Zapata and Villa recognized their common bonds from the outset. Although separated geographically by the territories held by Huerta, they did manage to exchange messages from time to time. After Villa's second capture of Torreón, Zapata invited him to send a representative to a convention he was planning to hold. Villa was busy preparing to attack Zacatecas when he received the invitation, and he could not accept. But he appreciated Zapata's gesture and came to look on him as a friend. In this, Villa was encouraged by his young adviser Martín Luis Guzmán, who warned him, "If you and Obregón do not unite against Carranza . . . [there will be] war with Obregón and González. You must be prepared. . . . *Get the revolutionary men of the South on your side.*" That was good advice. But Villa and Zapata were in no position to act in concert at this time.

With Villa immobilized in Torreón, the way was now clear for General Obregón, on the west coast, to take Mexico City in the name of Carranza. And that Obregón was about to do.

Alvaro Obregón was living up to his reputation as the stereotypical practical "self-made man" from Sonora. In working his way down the west coast in early 1914, Obregón was careful to avoid clashes with Carranza. He was not really Carranza's apostle; he probably would never have obeyed any of the First Chief's orders that he deemed detrimental to his own interests. But good relations with Carranza worked to Obregón's advantage for the moment, and he cultivated them.

Obregón understood how to deal with Carranza and was not too proud to handle him diplomatically. When the First Chief made unreasonable demands, Obregón always responded politely, and if his own interests dictated that he disobey Carranza, he took pains to appear to be merely interpreting Carranza's orders. His policy of accommodating Carranza forced him to keep Villa at arm's length. Thus, when Villa courted him as an ally, Obregón always answered courteously and correctly, advising Villa to remain loyal to Carranza and to work out his differences with their mutual political chief.

Obregón's first great victory over the Federals took place on July 8, 1914. At the Battle of Orendáin, he slaughtered the demoralized Federals and then moved on to occupy nearby Guadalajara. In the process, he seized eighteen military trains and thirty locomotives. Those actions cost Huerta's disheartened Federals two thousand dead. Obregón followed up this victory by pushing on toward the major rail junction of Irapuato. He was now within striking distance of Mexico City.

Victoriano Huerta knew that he was finished as provisional president of Mexico. On July 10, 1914, he called his cabinet together and swore in a new foreign minister, Francisco Carvajal. Carvajal now stood in the line of presidential succession right after Huerta and Blanquet. The world could sense that the time was near.

Early in the evening of July 14, a long procession of automobiles spirited Huerta's family through a dismal rain to the town of Guadalupe, three miles north of Mexico City. There Señora Huerta and her children boarded a train, along with a son-in-law and the members of General Blanquet's family. Huerta and Blanquet were not there. At 10:00 P.M., the train pulled out of the station in an easterly direction, led by a train carrying eight hundred Federal soldiers. The party's destination was presumed to be either Veracruz (still in American hands) or Puerto México (still in Federal hands). Anxiety for the safety of the families ran high, because the territory the trains would traverse was overrun by Constitutionalist rebels.

Throughout that day, Huerta had maintained a business-as-usual front. He attended the Bastille Day ceremony at the French ministry, and General Blanquet issued optimistic statements minimizing the significance of Obregón's seizure of Guadalajara. But their departure was only a matter of time. Everyone could see that trains were being held in readiness at the railway station, guarded by the Twenty-ninth Battalion. This combination of circumstances left no room for doubt.

At 4:45 P.M. on July 15, Huerta assembled a session of the deputies and senators to tender his resignation as provisional president. By 7:20 P.M., the resignation had been accepted by a vote of 121 to 17, and Francisco Carvajal took his place.

Huerta's short letter blamed all his troubles on President Woodrow Wilson: "You all know the immense difficulties which my Government has encountered owing to the scarcity of funds as well as to the manifest and decided protection which a great power of this continent has afforded to the rebels. . . ." But Huerta claimed that he had made progress in Mexico's struggle against the United States. Citing his record of good faith in dealing with adversity, he concluded with the claim that during his administration Mexico had "dealt death blows to an unjust power."

Reactions to Huerta's resignation were mixed. In Washington, the news was greeted with immense relief. The front pages of the papers carried favorable articles on Francisco Carvajal, who was known to be friendly to the Constitutionalist rebels, and they also praised Woodrow Wilson's policies. In Juárez, Pancho Villa told the press that Huerta would surely now take the field as a soldier and fight. Villa hoped to inflict on Huerta his last defeat. Even though he hated Huerta, he did concede that Huerta was "no coward."

Provisional President Francisco Carvajal lost no time in sending a message to Carranza, back at his favorite hideaway in Arteaga, near Saltillo. Carvajal offered to surrender Mexico City to the Constitutionalists, but he asked that Carranza consider granting generous terms to those governmental officials who had served in the Huerta administration. Woodrow Wilson joined in the chorus calling on Carranza to end the bloodshed. Carranza, however, was not to be placated. He would accept no compromise, he announced. The Revolution would demand unconditional surrender.

It is not surprising that Carranza took that position. His entire campaign was dedicated solely to placing himself in the seat of power in Mexico. Villa and Obregón had made Carranza's campaign a success, and he did not need to compromise.

After leaving the Chamber of Deputies on the evening of July 15, Huerta and Blanquet boarded a waiting train at Guadalupe and pulled out of Mexico City. They and selected members of their staffs were headed for Puerto México.

The trip was unhurried. It took two nights and nearly two days to cover a little over two hundred miles. With the territory overrun with rebels, Huerta deemed it advisable for the train to proceed cautiously and for the troops of the Twenty-ninth Battalion to dismount wherever an ambush might be lying in wait. Even though the train had left the capital in secret, Huerta had no assurance that the rebels were unaware of its departure.

Huerta's train pulled into Puerto México at 9:00 P.M. on Friday, July 17. In the fading light of a summer evening, spectators could see the former president sitting in the smoking room in shirtsleeves and with his collar off, trying to cope with the heat. Outside, troops mingled with a friendly crowd of curious people, including some dignitaries.

As soon as the train pulled to a stop, a visitor appeared. He was Captain Kohler, the skipper of the German cruiser *Dresden*. Huerta had not expected Kohler, and through the windows of the train amused onlookers could watch as Huerta and Blanquet scurried to don proper attire. Blanquet succeeded, receiving the captain in full uniform. Huerta was not so swift, however; he greeted his guest in shirtsleeves. After Kohler left, Huerta received the British vice consul, who offered him the services of the British cruiser HMS *Bristol* to take him to safety.

Even Huerta was unaware of the fate of Señora Huerta and the families that had left Mexico City with her. They were finally located, after a complicated journey. Their train had gone first to Veracruz, where they boarded the British cruiser HMS *Bristol*, which brought them to Puerto México. Like everyone else, Señora Huerta had been kept in the dark about the details of Huerta's plans. The old Indian trusted nobody.

That evening, Huerta spoke to a solemn and attentive crowd. There were no cheers. "When I assumed the Presidency," Huerta declaimed, "I said publicly that I would restore peace, cost what it might. I have paid—it has cost me the Presidency."

The next day, Huerta, his family, and his close associates boarded the German ship *Dresden*, bound for Spain.

13

****

The Convention at Aguascalientes

T he ouster of Victoriano Huerta as provisional president marked a critical moment for the Mexican Revolution. The various factions that had fought to oust the dictator now had a golden opportunity to bring peace to their war-weary countrymen. But the middle of July 1914 saw those factions, especially Carranza and Villa, at the point of fighting among themselves rather than trying to reach some sort of workable accommodation.

Many observers of the Mexican scene, Alvaro Obregón among them, foresaw the coming rupture between these headstrong personalities, but the man who actually took action to head off the crisis was not Obregón. He was Pablo González, a military commander more skilled at military politics than at fighting on the battlefield.

To break the impasse that had developed between Villa and Carranza over command arrangements and supply, González took it upon himself to invite a group of generals representing both leaders to meet at Torreón in mid-July. On their own recognizance, without the authority of either Carranza or Villa, the generals came up with a compromise. Villa, they recommended, should continue to command the Division of the North. If Villa recognized Carranza as First Chief, Carranza would supply Villa with coal and ammunition and allow him freedom of action "when circumstances demand." The Torreón conference failed to settle the sticky question of Mexico's overall leadership, because its influence was limited by Obregón's refusal to attend and by Carranza's refusal to discuss his own future. But it provided a way for both Carranza and Villa to save face, and as July drew to a close, the Constitutionalist structure was still intact—at least on paper.

On August 5, 1914, the *New York Times* carried fateful headlines:

ENGLAND DECLARES WAR ON GERMANY; BRITISH SHIP SUNK;
FRENCH SHIPS DEFEAT GERMAN, BELGIUM ATTACKED;
17,000,000 MEN ENGAGED IN GREAT WAR OF EIGHT NATIONS

In a sobering summary below, the *Times* gave the "Dual Alliance"— Germany and Austria-Hungary—a total of over seven million regulars and reservists. It gave the "Triple Entente"—headed by Britain, France, and Russia—nearly ten million men, regulars and reservists. The grand total of the men soon to be on the battlefield came to a startling 17,133,000 men. The First World War had broken out in Europe.

The whole world changed overnight. Old friends now became enemies. British and German officers who only three weeks earlier had been cooperating to rescue Huerta and his family in their flight from Mexico now stalked each other. The world's eyes would never again focus primarily on Mexico.

Two days before the outbreak of war in Europe, Alvaro Obregón and Pablo González rode out ahead of their respective armies to confer at Querétaro, a railroad junction a little over a hundred miles northwest of Mexico City, where their respective forces would soon converge. Later that day, Obregón sent a message to Provisional President Francisco Carvajal. He announced that he would soon be closing in on Mexico City and asked whether Carvajal intended to defend it. If Carvajal planned to resist, Obregón advised, foreign residents should be removed from danger.

Now thoroughly alarmed, Carvajal turned for advice to his minister of defense, General José Refugio Velasco. Velasco, as a soldier, insisted that the "honor of the Mexican Army" required at least a token defense of the city, but Carvajal had learned on what he considered good authority that the United States was preparing to march on the capital to protect American citizens in case of any danger. That word was questionable, but Carvajal knew that General Funston, in Veracruz, was agitating to do so. Carvajal therefore decided to surrender to Obregón.

Carvajal had no intention of playing the hero. On August 12, he resigned as provisional president and followed Huerta into exile. He left Mexico City in the hands of Velasco and ordered him to meet Obregón at Teoloyucan to arrange a surrender.

General Velasco enjoyed a good reputation in the Mexican army, so Obregón greeted him cordially when he arrived at Obregón's camp on August 13. Then the two generals, using the fender of a Packard touring car as a desk, signed the Treaty of Teoloyucan, which opened Mexico City to the Constitutionalists and declared martial law.

Two days later, Obregón entered Mexico City at the head of his troops. From a balcony of the National Palace over the Zócalo, he claimed the city in Carranza's name.

The people of Mexico City, elated at their liberation from the Huerta regime, spent the next week celebrating. They eulogized the late President Madero with a passion they had never shown during his lifetime. Obregón, the new military governor, visited Madero's grave as his first official act. During the following days, the bodies of Huerta's victims, including those of Senator Belisario Domínguez and Admiral Adolfo Bassó, were exhumed from their temporary graves and reinterred with great ceremony. When Carranza arrived in Mexico City five days later, he too participated in services eulogizing Madero.

Not everyone was overjoyed, however. In Morelos, just south of Mexico City, Emiliano Zapata was fuming at Obregón. One of Obregón's concessions to General Velasco, a very practical one, was to leave Federal troops at their posts guarding Mexico City. Obregón was willing to spare their lives and even their careers so long as they switched their allegiance to Carranza. Zapata could not stomach that concession; he was fighting a class war against the landowners, the "haves"; in his mind, anyone who had served under Huerta, including the Federal troops, fell into the category of the "privileged." Zapata would cheerfully have shot them all, at least the Federal officers. And he held Carranza and Obregón responsible.

Carranza wanted very much to placate Zapata. As a first step, he proposed that the two of them meet at some neutral point between Mexico City and Cuernavaca. Zapata, however, refused to meet in neutral territory. He insisted that if Carranza wished to confer, he must come all the way to Zapata's headquarters in the Morelos mountains.

Carranza persisted. Two weeks after entering the capital, he sent a trusted officer, General Antonio I. Villarreal, to meet with Zapata. Zapata received Villarreal at Cuernavaca but remained adamant in his terms. He insisted that Carranza (1) submit to Zapata's own "Plan of Ayala," (2) permit Zapata's troops to occupy his favorite town of Xochimilco, just south of Mexico City, and (3) resign his office or share power equally with one of Zapata's own representatives. Zapata reiterated his distaste for conferring with Carranza personally. He would talk only at his own headquarters—and the agenda for any such talks would be limited to exploring ways to implement the Plan of Ayala.

These conditions were obviously unacceptable to Carranza, as they would have been to anyone else.

At this point, Alvaro Obregón entered the Mexican political scene for the first time, emerging from his subordinate role as Carranza's loyal military chief. Even though Carranza held Obregón in mild contempt as a mere military man, it was the First Chief himself who created Obregón's new role.

Carranza needed Villa's help in dealing with the troubles that had broken out in the state of Sonora. He therefore called upon Obregón to act as his intermediary with Villa, since Carranza would never lower himself to ask a favor of Villa in person. Villa was delighted when, during the second week of August, he received Obregón's request for permission to visit him in Chihuahua. Villa had long been trying to develop a personal relationship with the Sonoran.

Obregón arrived by train at the Chihuahua station on August 24. Villa met him with a flurry of military fanfare. The atmosphere was friendly from the start. The tactful Obregón made no protest when Villa addressed him as *compañerito* (little companion), a term of instant familiarity. They talked frankly and at length, establishing a mutual rapport.

Once Villa was in a mellow mood, Obregón broached the situation in Sonora. He explained that Governor José María Maytorena and

Colonel Plutarco Elías Calles were political rivals, since Calles, as the strongman of the important border town of Agua Prieta, was challenging Maytorena's political primacy as governor. Maytorena and Calles had decided to settle their differences in the time-honored Mexican way, with bullets.

Villa and Obregón were on opposite sides of this issue. Maytorena was Villa's friend; Calles, as a Carrancista, was at least theoretically Obregón's military subordinate. But the differences between Obregón and Villa caused no hard feelings, and after two days of getting acquainted the two left Chihuahua together, determined to resolve the Sonora situation.

Though their ultimate destination was Nogales, it was easier and safer for the Mexican generals to travel by rail, first to Juárez and then across New Mexico and Arizona. Journeying to a Mexican town by way of Tucson may have appeared strange, but it was advisable. Not only was rail travel much easier than crossing the mountains by car or on horseback, but it was also safer for Obregón. Maytorena's followers had been so prejudiced against their fellow Sonoran that he would be at risk crossing through Maytorena's territory.

The stop that Villa and Obregón made at Juárez and El Paso was memorable for their meeting with Brigadier General John J. Pershing, who was commanding the U.S. Eighth Cavalry Brigade at nearby Fort Bliss. Pershing met the Mexicans at the midpoint of the International Bridge over the Rio Grande and escorted them through El Paso to Fort Bliss. There he rendered full military honors and entertained them at a banquet.

A famous photograph, taken at the time, reveals much about the attitude of each man. Obregón, in full uniform, seems reserved and uncomfortable, his military cap slightly askew on his head. Villa, the star of the show, looks relaxed in his loose civilian jacket and bow tie, his large Texas hat tilted carelessly on the back of his head. Pershing, still relatively unknown at the time, is noticeably stiff and awkward, effusive in his smile.

Obregón and Villa left El Paso by train on Thursday, August 27, traveling first to Tucson and then south to Nogales. They spent the night in the U.S. part of the divided town.

The Nogales conference turned out to be futile. Maytorena had no interest in meeting with Obregón, and their apparent agreements soon proved meaningless. But the fact that a conference was even being held impressed Washington. When Obregón and Villa reappeared at El Paso on September 1, General Pershing had in his hand a message to Villa from Secretary of State William J. Bryan. Bryan gave Villa credit for "valuable services" in "restoring order in Sonora." He added, "Your patient labors in this matter are greatly appreciated by the State Department and the President."

After they arrived back in Chihuahua, Villa and Obregón continued to visit amicably. This time, they focused on the future of the Mexican presidency. Obregón seemed to agree with Villa that Carranza, in accordance with the Plan of Guadalupe, should call a general presidential election, in which neither Carranza nor any general should be permitted to run. Obregón agreed to carry a formal proposal to that effect back to Mexico City. Villa's staff drafted the document, and the two men approved it.

Obregón returned to Mexico City in early September. On presentation of the Obregón-Villa agreement, the First Chief claimed that he approved of most of it—except for the provision excluding himself from the presidency. Carranza did agree, however, to call a council of generals and civilian officials, to meet in Mexico City on October 1. Its members would be appointed by Carranza himself.

During the period of the Villa-Obregón talks, Venustiano Carranza had been conducting Mexican affairs of state strangely. Some of his actions seemed designed to prove that he was not occupying the office of president: he snubbed the diplomatic corps, refused to reconvene the Congress, closed the doors of the courts of justice, and appointed only subministers of government. Other actions, however, lacked that kind of explanation: he declared the Huertista currency to be worthless and began a runaway inflation by printing 130 million pesos of Constitutionalist currency.

Carranza made one popular move. He pressured the United States to end its occupation of Veracruz. But his nationalistic zeal, though usually his political strong point, served in this instance only to delay the American departure. He refused to ensure the safety of those Mexicans who had accepted administrative positions with Funston's men. The United States therefore temporarily set aside plans to withdraw from the port.

Pancho Villa, in Chihuahua, soon recovered from the euphoria that had marked his visit with Obregón. He became increasingly angry at Carranza's snubs, and Obregón, in the Ministry of War, grew alarmed by the tone of Villa's messages. Obregón believed that he could solve whatever problems had arisen by building on the rapport he had established with Villa. He therefore decided to return to Chihuahua for further talks. It was a brave decision—and nearly his last.

Obregón arrived in Chihuahua on September 16, to find Villa a different man from the one he thought he knew. As usual, Villa put on a welcoming ceremony, but he now seemed intent only on impressing Obregón with the military might of the Division of the North. Obregón quickly concluded that Villa had given up trying to work with Carranza and that he, as Carranza's representative, was in dire physical danger. So concerned was he that Villa might force him to sign orders against his will that he sent a surreptitious warning message to his subordinates. Any instructions sent by him were to be ignored so long as he remained in Villa's hands.

Obregón was painfully right. Villa, at war with himself, ranged wide in his emotions. Several times, Villa threatened to shoot Obregón as a traitor, and after each such episode, Villa would abjectly apologize. During a whole week, Villa and Obregón never communicated in a lucid manner. Obregón lived in fear that Villa might make good on one of his periodic threats to execute him.

On September 22, Villa informed Carranza that he no longer recognized Don Venustiano as First Chief, after which Villa seemed to relax. While in one of his mellow moods, he put Obregón on a special train, accompanied by two of his most trusted generals.* After only a few hours, however, the train was pulled into a small railroad siding halfway to Torreón. A message had arrived ordering Obregón and his staff to return to Chihuahua.

Obregón underwent another harrowing day of threats. The reason for Villa's new fury, Obregón learned, was that Carranza, reacting to Villa's message, had directed all railroad traffic going to and from Chihuahua to be cut. Eventually, after another day of captivity and an uncertain train ride that night, Obregón made it through to Mexico City.

When Obregón stepped down from the train, his friends were astonished to see him. The press had reported his execution as a traitor by Pancho Villa.

Obregón had borne up admirably under his ordeal in Chihuahua. Even under the threat of a Villa firing squad, he had maintained his aplomb and his wry sense of humor. But the experience left a deep imprint on

*Eugenio Aguirre Benavides and José Isabel Robles.

him. Obregón was now convinced that Villa was a madman. In the future, circumstances might at times force Obregón to feign comradeship with Villa, but he had now become Villa's bitter and implacable enemy.

However, the might of Villa's Division of the North had greatly impressed Obregón. His facile mind could visualize the terrible consequences of a conflict between Villa's army and his own, under Carranza. Already on the train ride back to Mexico City, still shaken by Villa's choler, Obregón was considering ways to avert such a calamity, even at the price of unloading Carranza as First Chief.

Obregón acted immediately. On September 23, the day he got off the train, he called together a group of Constitutionalist generals to discuss some way to bring peace between the Villa and Carranza factions. At the informal conference, the generals decided to meet again as the "Revolutionary Convention" at Aguascalientes on October 10. Generals from all factions—Villistas, Carrancistas, and Zapatistas— were to be invited to attend.

Venustiano Carranza recognized instantly that his tenure of office was threatened. To counter the threat of a convention at Aguascalientes, he emphasized the importance of his own meeting, which he had previously scheduled for October 1. His ploy was to no avail, however. The Mexico City gathering took place as planned, but it was meaningless. All the participants were preoccupied by the prospects of the convention ten days later. The question of Carranza's political future, they had already concluded, would be decided at Aguascalientes.

The invitation list for the Convention of Aguascalientes reflected the political realities of Mexico at that time. No civilians were included unless "representing" someone recognized as having attained the rank of "general." Nevertheless, the membership constituted a remarkably democratic cross section of the Revolution. The "generals" tended to be young, idealistic, eager for peace—and recruited from the masses. And the provision for "representation" ensured that a good many of the intelligentsia were also present. Predictably, that group did much of the talking.

Would the lopsided breakdown of invitees—eighty-seven Carrancistas to thirty-seven Villistas—discourage the Villistas from attending the Convention? No, for the numerical quota was meaningless. Even the Carrancista generals were known to be fed up with Carranza, and the delegates were not voting in a democratic fashion. Most of the so-called generals, representing only small forces, wielded correspondingly small power. The purpose of the gathering, therefore, was to formulate a set of conclusions that all three of the main commanders—Obregón, Villa, and Zapata—could support. The achievement of that goal required Zapatista participation.

The town of Aguascalientes was a good choice for a meeting, located as it was about halfway between Mexico City and Chihuahua. It afforded peaceful surroundings, because the fighting of the Revolution had passed it by, and the buildings were relatively intact. Its major shortcoming lay in its small size. The delegates had to be housed somewhere, so the 45,000 townspeople were forced to accommodate many as houseguests. In view of the large number of ruffians attending, the prospective hosts understandably sought out such mannerly men as Angeles, Villarreal, and Obregón. To maintain order in the crowded streets, the authorities closed all cantinas. Yet plenty of tequila was somehow available, and the nighttime peace was continually broken by the noise of firearms as celebrants gaily emptied their pistols into the air.

The Aguascalientes Convention opened in the Teatro Moreles on October 10, 1914. By previous agreement, it was presided over by General Antonio I. Villarreal, a "radical" Carrancista who enjoyed the respect of the Villistas. The convention's first action was to declare its "sovereignty," in open defiance of First Chief Venustiano Carranza.

As the acknowledged sponsor of the Convention, Alvaro Obregón was called on to perform the first ceremonial acts. He presented a special flag, a Mexican standard with the words "Military Convention of Aguascalientes" printed across its face. Each delegate then climbed the steps to the platform of the theater and solemnly placed his signature on its white portion. The proper patriotic atmosphere had been established and the Convention's sovereignty emphasized.

Progress was slow. The delegates spent the first six days haggling over their credentials, despite the crippling absence of the Zapatistas. But the atmosphere remained cordial—an important thing in itself. On October 17, a week into the proceedings, Pancho Villa came for a visit from his encampment at nearby Guadalupe.

Villa, an imposing figure, was in his glory at the Convention. Invited to sit at the executive table, he accepted happily, though outwardly deferring to "men of greater intelligence and knowledge." Soon the cheering audience called on him to speak. He did so modestly, describing himself as a man "with a total lack of culture," who wanted nothing for himself, who had joined the Revolution only to do his duty. If Villa stretched the truth, he at least ended on a tactful and hopeful note: "In your hands you hold the future of the country, the destiny of all Mexicans, and if that is lost, the entire responsibility will lie upon you people of law and knowledge."

Before Villa left the meeting, he embraced Obregón, the man he had kept under constant threat of death three weeks earlier. The delegates cheered. Villa's performance was a personal triumph.

Once Villa had given the Convention his stamp of approval by appearing before it, the delegates settled down to serious business. The top order of the day was to induce Emiliano Zapata to send representatives. To that end, the membership designated Felipe Angeles to go by trian to Cuernavaca and see Zapata in person. Angeles arrived at Zapata's headquarters on October 22.

Zapata was a hard man to convince. Suspicious of all outsiders, he feared that the Convention would subordinate his goal of land reform to other considerations. Angeles, however, proved to be an effective emissary, not only because of his disarming personality but also because he represented Pancho Villa, the only man Zapata trusted.

But even Angeles could not completely convince Zapata. One of the obstacles was Zapata's concern that his young generals, though fearless fighters, were nearly all illiterate, unable to cope with the rhetoric of any large forum. However, Zapata had recently begun to gather around him a group of young men who have been described as possessing "great culture and knowledge." So Angeles finally prevailed on Zapata to confer instant military rank on twenty-six of these young intellectuals and send them to Aguascalientes as his delegation. Zapata insisted that they were to go only as "witnesses," not as delegates. At the same time, he illogically demanded that these witnesses be granted "voice and vote."

The train carrying Zapata's delegation passed through Mexico City unmolested and arrived at Aguascalientes on October 24. But it did not stop there. Members of the Convention who had gone down to the depot to greet the new arrivals were astonished to see the train continue right on through Aguascalientes, destined for Guadalupe.

The Zapatistas desired to obtain Villa's assessment of the Aguascalientes proceedings before joining. They returned to join the Convention two days later.

Zapata's "witnesses" were aloof and suspicious when they first entered the Teatro Morelos. After a day or so, however, they began to participate wholeheartedly. Shown much deference, they monopolized center stage and for a while made the most of it. Yet they fit in; the head of their delegation, Paulino Martínez, was described as "forthright and rousing."

A crisis occurred during the presentation by Antonio Díaz Soto y Gama, a young Zapatista lawyer. Díaz Soto may never have heard a shot fired, but he was strong on parliamentary oratory. His philosophy has been described as evolving from "liberalism" to "ill-defined anarchy." He was considered one of the " 'citified radicals' who brought to Zapatismo a new, articulate militancy," not exactly what the Convention had expected from Zapata.

Martín Luis Guzmán witnessed Díaz Soto's great moment. He saw Díaz Soto stride up on the stage wearing the tight trousers of the Mexican *charro*, a cotton jacket, and a broad-brimmed hat, the garb that symbolized Zapatismo at that time. For a while, Díaz Soto remained relatively conventional; he stressed the "excellence of Zapata's ideals" and the need to bring them down from the mountains of the south to the Plain of Mexico. His speech—"pyrotechnical, repetitive eloquence," Guzmán called it—quoted Buddha, Jesus Christ, Saint Francis, Karl Marx, and Zapata. His abstract radicalism in denouncing the great division of humanity into nation-states was quite acceptable to the amiable Mexican audience.

Once warmed up, however, Díaz Soto grew more and more defiant of his audience. He grasped the symbolic Mexican flag, which all the delegates had so proudly signed, and shouted, "What is the good of this dyed rag, bedaubed with the image of a bird and its prey?" Shaking the banner once more, he went on, "How is it possible, gentlemen of the Revolution, that for a hundred years we have been venerating this silly mummery, this lie?" The audience was becoming restive.

But Díaz Soto continued: "This rag and all it represents is but a mockery, an empty show, against which we must all . . ." He was now looking down the muzzles of four hundred guns, all pointed directly at his breast.

Villarreal, presiding, shouted, "More respect for the flag!"

But Díaz Soto stood firm. He faced the revolvers and insults, his arms folded. "When you have finished," he said, "I'll go on."

Díaz Soto's remaining remarks were far more moderate. He calmed down and explained that the flag was only a symbol; the important matter was the substance of the Plan of Ayala.

The Zapatista had accomplished more than he had probably expected. Colonel Roque González Garza, Villa's chief representative, sprang to his feet. "The Division of the North accepts as its own the Plan of Ayala!" he shouted. All in the Villa delegation agreed. Amid shouts of "Viva Villa!" and "Viva Zapata!" the alliance between those two factions was formalized at that moment.

The Convention proceedings continued beyond this climactic moment. Carranza himself did not appear, but his image, in the form of movie clips, was very much in evidence.

One of Carranza's many idiosyncrasies was his insatiable thirst to have his photograph taken. Public events were all too often dominated by his overweening desire to portray himself for history. That compulsion did not endear him to the conventioneers, who made their resentment clear one evening when they were entertained by patriotic moving pictures.

Martín Luis Guzmán, in *The Eagle and the Serpent*, describes the event in an amusing manner, even though what happened could have been fatal to him. Since the film promised excellent shots of the heroes of the Revolution, Guzmán and General Lucio Blanco decided to attend together. When they arrived at this gala event, they found the theater already packed. Squeezing into their reserved seats would have been close to impossible. Unwilling to miss the show, Blanco suggested that they go backstage, where they might find an armchair. They could watch the movies on the backside of the translucent movie screen. That they did, to the astonishment of the stage hands, and settled back to enjoy the evening.

The audience, Blanco observed, seemed to be getting bored with the Convention. The atmosphere in the theater was becoming raucous, and when the lights went out, the hubbub grew—"half humorous, half insulting guffaws." Then a loud voice shouted out.

"Long live the Revolution!"

"Long may it live!"

Then, as the projector vibrated along, the men began to calm down. Up came a picture of Obregón's Yaqui Indian soldiers—grim, sinuous, bronzed, feline in their rhythms.

"Long live the victors of the West!"

"Long may they live!" An ovation followed.

Then a picture of Obregón himself. "Long live the Army of the Northwest!"

"Long may it live!"

Then a picture of Carranza. "Long live the First Chief!"

Then a mixture of "Long lives" 's and "Down with" 's, of applause and stomping, protests, and hisses.

Then a picture of Pancho Villa, legendary and all-conquering. "Long live the Division of the North!"

"Long may it live!" More applause.

Throughout all this, however, the film sequence had sandwiched in one picture of Carranza after another, and the audience was beginning to lose patience. Hisses, hooting, and booing grew louder, culminating in an uproar.

Suddenly, shots rang out, aimed at an image of the First Chief's chest on the screen. Bullets whizzed past the heads of Guzmán and Blanco and struck the back wall of the theater behind them. One bullet passed eighteen inches above Blanco's head; another went right between his head and Guzmán's.

Guzmán later reflected that if the First Chief had entered Mexico City on foot rather than on horseback, the shots at his movie image would have been lower; he and Blanco would have been dead. But then, Guzmán mused, if the First Chief had entered on foot, he would not have been Carranza. In fact, there would have been no shots, not even the Convention itself.

The ebullient behavior of the rank and file did not distract the leaders of the Aguascalientes Convention from the tasks before them. Once the Villa delegation gave its wholehearted support to Zapata's Plan of Ayala, the Convention readily accepted it. The members then turned their attention to the mechanics of removing Carranza as provisional president and replacing him with someone else.

In Mexico City, Carranza was aware that he had no influence over the actions of his former generals at Aguascalientes and that the group favored his replacement. But Carranza was a fighter, and he knew how to use his political weapons. He did the only thing he could: he stalled. He sent a message to Aguascalientes announcing that he would be "disposed" to step down as First Chief under certain "conditions": (1) that the presidency not go to an "ambitious military man" and (2) that Villa and Zapata both step down from their military commands. He sneeringly added that only their military commands were at issue; neither was suitable even to entertain any thought of the presidency.

The Convention did not attempt to meet all of Carranza's conditions, especially not the demand that Zapata relinquish his military command. Villa, however, agreed to resign as commander of the Division of the North—provided that Carranza actually left his office as First Chief. The Convention therefore deemed that Carranza's "conditions" had been adequately met, and it accepted his "resignation" by a vote of 112 to 21.

The Convention then turned to selecting Carranza's successor. Since even such respected figures as Antonio Villarreal were deemed too close to Carranza, the delegates settled on a compromise candidate, General Eulalio Gutiérrez, a man who was not closely affiliated with anybody and who therefore had offended no one. Gutiérrez was elected by a margin of better than two to one.

A delegation headed by Obregón then left for Mexico City to notify Carranza of the Convention's action. On arrival at the capital, however, Obregón found the First Chief gone from Mexico City, supposedly on vacation. This action angered the Convention members even further, and on November 5 they voted to declare Carranza a rebel if he did not surrender his authority by the evening of November 10, 1914.

Carranza had never intended to return to Mexico City when he left it, and he continued his flight east to Puebla and from there to Córdoba, in Veracruz province. When Obregón finally reached him, Carranza was still determined to hold on to power in Mexico. Vainly, he sent orders directing his supporters to withdraw from the Convention. But his supporters had left him; even Obregón, the former Carranza loyalist, declared that he would support Gutiérrez.

The Aguascalientes Convention appeared to be a success. It had surmounted many obstacles. It had not, up to this time, been unduly influenced by the lurking power of Pancho Villa at nearby Guadalupe.

But Villa was not a patient man.

14

****

Villa's and Zapata's
Reign of Terror

Pancho Villa and Emiliano Zapata
had long admired each other—from a distance. Though the two had
exchanged emissaries and supported each other fully at the Aguascalientes Convention, they had never met in person. On Friday morning, December 4, 1914, Pancho Villa prepared to rectify that deficiency. Donning plain civilian clothes, the Centaur of the North left
his division at Tacuba, just north of Mexico City, and headed for
Zapata's headquarters in Xochimilco.

Much had happened during the month of November to bring this
opportunity about. Venustiano Carranza had refused to submit his
resignation as First Chief to the delegates in Aguascalientes, and he
was therefore declared a "rebel." General Eulalio Gutiérrez had been
inaugurated as president of Mexico, by the authority of the Convention.

At that time, prospects for peace seemed bright in Mexico. Carranza was officially in rebellion against the government, but his forces
had been denuded, very largely by simple demobilization. He was not,
for the moment, considered a threat. The one ominous cloud on the

horizon was Alvaro Obregón, who soon dissociated himself from the Convention, even though he was the man who had organized it.

The reason for Obregón's disaffection was the prominence that President Gutiérrez accorded to Pancho Villa. Because the Division of the North was the only organized force north of Mexico City serving under the Convention, Gutiérrez appointed Villa military chief of Mexico. That preferment of the man he hated the most was more than Obregón could stand. He withdrew his support for President Gutiérrez and left for Córdoba to join Carranza. Obregón's forces were weak, but he was capable of raising new ones. And Villa committed the gravest error of his career. He spurned the advice of Angeles and, out of deference to Zapata, whose forces were assigned to occupy Puebla, allowed Obregón to get away with his remaining troops.

Other significant things had happened in November. Carranza, who dearly wanted to use Veracruz as the base for his now minority government, swallowed his pride and declared amnesty for the Mexicans who had served General Funston's occupation force at Veracruz. The Americans happily disembarked from Veracruz, bands playing, on November 23. Carranza moved in on their heels and set up his administration in that major port.

Mexico City also changed hands. General Lucio Blanco, an ambivalent former subordinate of Carranza's, removed his ten thousand cavalrymen and headed for San Luis Potosí, his future allegiance unknown. Zapata's men occupied the city quietly, to the relief of the frightened inhabitants, and Villa moved the Division of the North (which he had never left) to Tacuba, on the outskirts of the city.

All this had happened in the course of a single month.

As Villa approached Zapata's headquarters, he had no idea what to expect. He came informally, accompanied by only a small escort, but when he met Zapata, he was surprised to find him wearing a short black jacket, lavender shirt, tight-fitting trousers lined with silver buttons, and sharp-toed, high-heeled Spanish boots. Zapata's wide-brimmed sombrero shaded his face, emphasizing his large black eyes and huge black mustache, the only features visible underneath. Zapata cut a dashing figure, though one somewhat inconsistent with his chosen role as the "peasant general."

The meeting between the two leaders was devoid of fanfare. After the customary *abrazo*, the two parties entered the village school, where they assembled their parties around a large oval table, joined by Leon Canova, a special agent from the United States. The group included Paulino Martínez, a prominent Mexican journalist, and Zapata's brother Eufemio, recently curator of the National Palace before being removed by the newly arrived President Gutiérrez.

Neither Villa nor Zapata was good at small talk, and the meeting started out slowly. Zapata offered Villa a glassful of cognac. Villa, a nondrinker, tried to drink it, but his coughs and teary eyes made it clear that he was doing so only to demonstrate his friendship for Zapata. Then the two revolutionaries admired each other's head-gear—Villa was wearing a British sun helmet. It was difficult for them to hear each other, because the village band never stopped blaring out the national anthem and other popular songs of the Revolution. To escape the noise, Villa and Zapata left the main room for a smaller one where they could talk in peace.

In this more intimate atmosphere, Villa and Zapata began to talk serious business. After each had vented his fury against Carranza, they addressed the problem of statesmanlike murder—they sought to agree on the names of the people they wished to execute. Zapata asked Villa to approve the execution of Guillermo García Aragón, the man Gutiérrez had appointed to take the place of Eufemio Zapata at the National Palace. That was fine with Villa; he had never liked Aragón in the first place. In turn, Villa asked that three generals currently with Zapata be turned over to him. Zapata demurred, since they were his personal guests. But Zapata was happy to surrender the journalist Paulino Martínez, who had once written a scathing article against Francisco Madero.

After the two finished drawing up their proscription lists, they joined the rest of their parties for a simple Mexican dinner. The most lavish toast that evening was proposed by the doomed Paulino Martínez.

Two days later, on December 6, Zapata and Villa held a joint parade through the streets of Mexico City. Fifty thousand men, from both armies, participated. After assembling in their respective villages—Xochimilco, San Angel, Mixcoac, and Tacuba—they marched into Mexico City by way of the Calzada de la Verónica. They then proceeded down the Paseo de la Reforma toward the Zócalo, ending up at the National Palace.

Villa and Zapata led the parade, sitting side by side in an open car. Villa was resplendent in a dark blue dress uniform, while Zapata wore the garb of a well-to-do hacendado, with a deerskin jacket embroidered with silk and gold. At the Zócalo, the two military chiefs met with President Gutiérrez and then assumed their places on the palace balcony. The ceremony over, Villa, Zapata, and General Tomás Urbina rambunctiously took over the President's Office and happily posed for photographs, with Villa taking the place of honor in the president's chair. Throughout this sequence of events, the man whom both Villa and Zapata acknowledged as the provisional president, Eulalio Gutiérrez, was given little notice.

Gutiérrez was keenly mindful of those snubs. The two caudillos had demonstrated their lack of respect for the civil government of Mexico. Gutiérrez could see that neither Villa nor Zapata, each a legend, could take him seriously as president. Both remembered him only as a mediocre general, elected president by the Aguascalientes Convention as a compromise candidate. But Gutiérrez himself took his new role seriously and became increasingly frustrated by the weakness of his position.

Gutiérrez's frustration grew when Zapata and Villa instituted their agreed-on reign of terror—in which he was allowed to play no part. It was serious enough when Zapata turned the journalist Paulino Martínez over to Villa for execution; even worse was the execution of Guillermo Aragón, an undersecretary in Gutiérrez's own cabinet. But the execution of Lieutenant Colonel David Berlanga was the most jarring of all. Martín Luis Guzmán, now in the entourage of Villa, learned about the outrage at first hand.

One evening, Rudolfo Fierro came to Guzmán's door in the hotel and asked to speak with him privately. Though somewhat taken aback to be sought out by this butcher, Guzmán hastily consented. Fierro checked the room—the furnishings, the carpet, the hangings, and the drawers. Then the man whom Guzmán had always considered "sinister" poured out his personal anguish at what he had just done.

Fierro had received orders from Villa to execute the young Colonel Berlanga as punishment for his role in a minor incident in a restaurant. Some drunken Villista *dorados* had refused to pay a proprietor's bill. Berlanga thereupon castigated them for their conduct and paid the bill himself. For this act, Berlanga was decreed to be a chronic troublemaker and was sentenced to die. To Fierro fell the task as a normal part of his job.

Fierro found Berlanga at about midnight, sitting in the Sylvain, a popular restaurant known to be his favorite. As Fierro approached, he could see that Berlanga had finished dinner some time earlier, for his cigar was half smoked, the ash still intact.

Fierro walked up to Berlanga. "I have orders from General Villa to ask you to come with me," he said. "Resistance would be useless, for I have enough men with me to make myself obeyed."

Berlanga scoffed. "Resistance?" he asked. "What good is resistance in such cases?" So he called over the waiter, paid his check, picked up his hat, and put it on calmly—all the while making sure that the cigar ash did not fall off.

Not another word was said until Fierro and Berlanga drove through the gate of the San Cosme barracks. Then Berlanga spoke: "Is it here that they're going to lock me up?"

"No. It is here we're going to shoot you."

Berlanga seemed surprised for the first time. "Shoot me? When?"

"Right away."

Berlanga asked for no further explanation. The two men got out of the cars and went to the guardroom. There Berlanga unbuttoned his coat, reached in his pocket, and pulled out a notebook and pencil. Then, by the faint light of a lamp, he wrote a long note, without even pausing. Not even the color in Berlanga's face changed.

Finally, Berlanga was finished. "If it is possible," he said, "I would appreciate it if you would give these things to my mother. I have put her name and address on this paper. . . . And I am at your orders."

As their steps crossed the courtyard of the barracks, the sounds seemed hollow to Fierro, strange, unreal. But he was spared the sight of Berlanga's face. The light was too dim. Then, after going through several doors, they stopped. Fierro ordered the squad of *dorados* to take up their positions in front of a wall and then turned and told Berlanga that everything was ready.

Berlanga fixed his eyes on Fierro for a few moments; then he bent his head toward the hand that held the cigar. "Yes, right away. I won't keep you waiting. . . ."

As Fierro finished telling this story to Guzmán, his hand was shaking.

"It was a horrible crime," Guzmán said at last.

"Horrible," Fierro answered. "The truth is, I am not as bad as they make me out. I have a heart too."

When President Gutiérrez received news of Berlanga's execution, he was both infuriated and frightened. He now realized what a terrible mistake he had made in appointing Pancho Villa the military chief of the Convention forces. Obregón, learning from his informers in Mexico City that a rift was growing between Gutiérrez and Villa, began subtly to court Gutiérrez. The Convention president, in turn, began to regard Obregón as his own best prospect for future support and started surreptitiously to reciprocate. As time went on, Gutiérrez became more vocal in his denunciations of Villa's actions, and he took advantage of Villa's absence in Jalisco to send a circular to all the generals, decrying the recent assassinations. When Villa returned to Mexico City, he heard that Gutiérrez was preparing to flee.

In the early morning of December 27, Villa sealed off all the exits from Mexico City. He lined the Paseo de la Reforma with his cavalry and proceeded to the Chamber of Deputies, where the Permanent Convention had been meeting ever since its move to Mexico City. The members prudently sympathized with Villa's protests about Gutiérrez's plans, but they refused to take action to prevent his leaving. So Villa, after consulting Urbina and Fierro, placed an armed guard around Gutiérrez's residence on the Paseo de la Reforma. He entered the front door and confronted the president and his minister of defense, José Isabel Robles.

The presence of Robles as minister of war in Gutiérrez's cabinet upset Villa. Robles had previously been one of Villa's most trusted subordinates, one on whom he had lavished unusual affection. So, throwing tact aside, Villa demanded bluntly to know what Gutiérrez was up to. Gutiérrez admitted that he was planning to leave the city for San Luis Potosí, and Villa for some reason calmed down. Once more assuming the role of the loyal subordinate, Villa asked, "Don't you know, Señor, that you are the President of our Republic, and my troops are charged with protecting you? Where would you be without me if you run the risk that nobody will protect you?"

"I want to be a long way from you and Emiliano Zapata, Señor General," answered Gutiérrez; "I want to free my conscience of the crimes the Villistas and Zapatistas are committing under my government."

"Very well, Señor, but I will not let you go. I have already stopped the departure of all trains."

"If I have no trains at my disposal, I will even ride a burro to get away from you."

Villa suppressed an urge to shoot Gutiérrez on the spot and said,

"Tell me, Señor, what complaints you have, and I promise to correct them."

"Your men executed Berlanga, who was a good Revolutionary."

"I have told you, Señor, that his death was in our best interests."

Communication was impossible. Villa could not understand how Gutiérrez could misinterpret his own good deeds in order to incriminate him. So Villa replaced the usual security forces around the house with his own men in the interest of the president's "safety." Eulalio Gutiérrez was now Pancho Villa's prisoner.

At this point, Robles stepped in, promising Villa that he himself would see to it that Gutiérrez did not leave. Villa removed his guard from the house and left.

Villa took some time out to enjoy the comforts of Mexico City. While doing so, he continued to act in a manner that was for him not unusual. Taking a fancy to a comely receptionist in a French hotel, Villa ordered that the young lady be delivered to his hotel room that afternoon. The hotel's proprietor came to her rescue, but word of the incident spread. Unaccustomed to Villa's ways, the people of Mexico City were shocked.

Villa's sojourn in Mexico City was interrupted in early January 1915 by a message from his old friend Major General Hugh L. Scott. Scott asked Villa to meet him in Juárez. Villa left jubilantly by the first train.

This conference was not going to be pleasant, because Scott, now U.S. Army chief of staff, had been sent from Washington to induce Villa to intercede with his close ally José María Maytorena, governor of Sonora. Maytorena had driven his Carrancista opponents into the town of Naco, on the U.S. border, and stray bullets from the fighting had killed one American civilian and wounded twenty-six others on the U.S. side. The U.S. Tenth Cavalry had in fact been forced to move back to a site four miles north, a great humiliation.

Villa became aware of the issue while on the trip from Mexico City to Juárez, so when he met Scott at the International Bridge, the atmosphere was unusually hostile. Villa hated being forced to pressure Maytorena to suspend his attack on Naco, since cornering the Carrancistas had cost Maytorena eight hundred casualties.

Nevertheless, as Scott continued to press, Villa knew that he would eventually concede. Carrancista agents in Washington were already driving a wedge between Villa and the Wilson administration—even between Villa and Scott. Villa thus signed the agreement Scott had brought, muttering, "Carranza will be grateful to you, Señor."

When Maytorena received Villa's order to withdraw from Naco, he signed it, dropped the pen on the floor, and wept.

When Villa reached Chihuahua on his return from Juárez, a message from Felipe Angeles in Saltillo was waiting for him. Having taken the city, Angeles had seized the belongings of General Antonio Villarreal, and among them he had found a letter from President Gutiérrez proposing that the Conventionalists join the Carrancistas to fight Villa "like a bandit." The letter also proposed that Carranza be removed, but the references to Carranza were less contemptuous.

Villa felt hurt and betrayed. Even his onetime protégé José Isabel Robles had joined in the Gutiérrez plot. If Robles went, who would remain loyal?

One who did remain loyal was General Roque González Garza, the young man who had served as Villa's delegate to the Aguascalientes Convention. González Garza was now back in Mexico City reporting events to Villa by way of telegraphic conferences. In mid-January, González Garza informed Villa that Gutiérrez had left Mexico City for San Luis Potosí. (Gutiérrez had taken with him more than half the money in the treasury.) Then, on January 20, González Garza informed Villa that the Convention had appointed him, González Garza, Convention president in place of Gutiérrez. In his new capacity as Villa's political chief, González Garza urged Villa to return to Mexico City. Obregón, he advised, had taken Puebla from Zapata and was now ready to march on the capital.

Villa was reluctant to return to Mexico City. His armies were fighting hard against the Carrancistas, but with mixed successes, having taken Saltillo but lost Puebla. His troops in the field required his personal attention, Villa reasoned; cities were secondary. So Villa decided not to return to the capital. The impropriety of disobeying orders from his new president never occurred to him.

Without Villa's protection against the advancing Obregón, the members of the Permanent Convention then abandoned Mexico City and sought Zapata's protection in Cuernavaca, Morelos. Villa had no incentive for returning to Mexico City. On January 31, he therefore decided to appoint himself governor of the territories he occupied. He called in his legal advisers and drew up a manifesto.

Villa's manifesto denounced both Carranza and Gutiérrez, and it proclaimed that the armies of Villa and Zapata, now separated, would once more operate independently. Villa would govern in the north and Zapata in the south.

Alvaro Obregón's troops entered Mexico City in late January, and for a second time Obregón claimed the capital in the name of Carranza. He then moved into the most controversial and tragic period of his otherwise admirable career.

When Obregón took control, the infrastructure of Mexico City was crumbling. Yet he did nothing to restore mail service or repair the damaged pumping station at Xochimilco, upon which sanitation in the city depended. He did nothing to restore the supply of food, which was cut off by the Zapatista blockade. Starvation became so serious that even Secretary Bryan and President Wilson sent protests from Washington regarding the prevailing conditions. Because Carranza showed no sign of moving from Veracruz, Obregón went about methodically stripping Mexico City of factory equipment, hospital beds, cars, and horses—all to be shipped to Veracruz.

Obregón's callous administration of the city reflected vindictiveness. He was angry at the people of Mexico City for the joy they had shown when he had been forced to evacuate during the previous November. He regarded the city as a hotbed of Villa supporters—the clergy, the houses of commerce, the bankers, the industrialists, and the foreigners. "I had to choose between two alternatives," he later wrote, "to withstand all the enemies of the Revolution or, yielding to the pressure of those perverse influences, to confess myself beaten. The former a thousand times sooner than the latter. . . ."

In mid-March 1915, Obregón and his growing army left Mexico City to seek out Villa's army. The people of Mexico City heaved a sigh of relief.

Pancho Villa, in the meantime, was absorbed in consolidating his vast territories, which spread all the way from Guadalajara to Matamoros. His main supply route was still the railroad line between Juárez and Mexico City, which he controlled all the way to Querétaro. To facilitate central control, he set up his command post at Irapuato, a town about halfway between Querétaro and Aguascalientes—and the place where the railroad line ran closest to Guadalajara.

Villa's most immediate trouble spot was Guadalajara, where Rodolfo Fierro had recently been defeated by the Carrancistas. Therefore, Villa determined to go to Fierro's aid. He turned due west from his base at Irapuato and he retook Guadalajara on February 12.

At about this time, however, Villa received word that Angeles was beset at Monterrey by three forces coming from north, east, and south. Although Angeles was in no panic, Villa left Guadalajara for Monterrey, placing Fierro in charge once again.

At Monterrey, Villa found Angeles well in control, only awaiting his own arrival. The reunited armies of Angeles and Villa quickly crushed the three Carrancista armies closing in on Monterrey. Villa was jubilant: "You see, Señor General. These Carrancistas flee at the jingle of my spurs."

Villa's triumph was short-lived. Fierro had been trounced again at Guadalajara, and Obregón had left Mexico City, reported to be preparing a position at Celaya, near Querétaro, between Villa's army and what was left of Fierro's. Angeles recommended that Villa finish off the campaign in the northeast before heading south. But Villa's mind was made up. He would make an all-out assault on Obregón at Celaya.

15

****

Carranza
by Default

As the armies of Villa and Obregón converged on Celaya in April 1915, the stage was set for a showdown of the two great commanders of the Mexican Revolution. On paper, Villa seemed to be the odds-on favorite. His Division of the North was larger than Obregón's newly recruited army, and Villa's commanders were accustomed to working together as a team. The Division of the North had never suffered defeat in any battle when Villa himself was in command. To Mexican eyes—and to the eyes of the world—Villa seemed invincible.

Other factors, however, were working against Villa. One was the way his army was spread out over northern Mexico. By dispatching Fierro to Jalisco and sending Angeles to Tamaulipas, Villa had reduced the number of troops in his main body to only eight thousand men. He estimated that Obregón's army boasted as many as twelve thousand.

Another intangible was even more important than numbers. Obregón had developed a critical advantage in the use of modern techniques of warfare, thanks to his study of the experiences of the Europeans, who had been at war since early August 1914. Fighting on the Western Front, between the British and French on one side and the Germans and the Austrians on the other, had developed deadly new defensive tactics. The introduction of barbed wire and machine guns on a large scale made frontal attacks on entrenched positions suicidal. Obregón had learned about these techniques from a German adviser, Colonel Maximilian Kloss, and he was shrewd enough to realize that with these methods he could easily repel Villa's headlong charges, no matter how aggressively Villa might execute them.

Accordingly, Obregón decided to fight Villa by assuming the tactical defensive and luring Villa into attacking nearly impregnable positions. He selected a critical position at Celaya, one that he believed Villa would have to take in clearing the path to combine forces with Fierro. Obregón prepared European-style defenses at that position, taking full advantage of the numerous canals and ditches in the region and tied into a coordinated defense. Obviously, he made ample use of barbed wire and machine guns. There Obregón waited.

Obregón's trap did not snare Villa at first. Knowing the territory far better than did Obregón, Villa followed back roads that allowed him to bypass Obregón's position. So Villa returned to his base at Irapuato and then rejoined Fierro. Obregón was not dismayed; he could afford to wait; he was being resupplied amply from Mexico City and Veracruz, and he knew that Villa would have to attack his Celaya position soon, because Villa's supplies were running low. So, as Obregón had planned, Villa mounted his attack before he was completely ready, straight into Obregón's trap.

The First Battle of Celaya, April 6–7

On the night of April 5, Villa concentrated his reunited army near Salamanca, a suburb of Celaya. By late in the morning of April 6, he had joined battle, impatiently committing his forces as they arrived on the scene. His attack went well at first. By 10:00 A.M., Villa's advance guard had brushed Obregón's cavalry aside and then, flushed with success, pushed on to the outskirts of Celaya. There, however, he first met Obregón's main battle position, the dug-in infantry of General Benjamín Hill. Once Villa had hit that line, he went no farther; the initial day of the battle came to a close without a clear-cut advantage falling to either side.

The heavy fighting had caught Villa by surprise, and he carelessly wasted much of his high-quality artillery ammunition. But though he was now dependent on makeshift shells crafted by his own men, Villa was not overly concerned. Victory seemed to be in the air. He was surprised, in fact, that Obregón had dared to remain at Celaya.

Many of Obregón's officers agreed with Villa's assessment. That evening, a group of them urged Obregón to withdraw to Querétaro. Obregón, however, was determined. He saw no alternative to remaining in place.

Villa resumed the attack early on the morning of April 7, again attempting to penetrate Obregón's fortifications. Intensive Carrancista artillery and machine-gun fire took a fearful toll, however, and Villa's troops sustained heavy losses as they pushed forward. The attack penetrated to the center of the city, and in their brief moment of triumph Villa's men rang a church bell. But triumph was short-lived, and they were soon ejected. Villa's proud cavalry, the *dorados*, were virtually wiped out. Obregón launched a cavalry attack on Villa's flanks, and a puzzled Villa, out of ammunition, fell back to Irapuato at the end of the day, leaving two thousand of his best men dead on the field.

Villa did not learn from that defeat. Furious and frustrated, he vowed to return to Celaya for revenge. Since Obregón expected Villa to react in that manner, he remained at Celaya. He spent his time improving his position and amassing large quantities of ammunition—and waiting.

The Second Battle of Celaya—Villa's Waterloo

By April 12, Villa had refitted his army and was ready to fight again, determined to destroy Obregón. He now sensed that he was facing a momentous task in dislodging Obregón from his strong position, but he believed that victory had nearly been his in the first battle. Furthermore, his army had since been reinforced. And Villa was impatient. "Obregón would never fight," he wrote later, "unless he was fortified and entrenched. I would have to conquer him like that or let myself be conquered." He resumed the attack on the same position he had failed to take a week earlier.

Villa's 20,000 men began their attack on Obregón's 15,000 during the early hours of April 13. The battle raged for three days. Time and again, Villa's soldiers assaulted Obregón's defenses, only to be repulsed. But his attacks had their effects in Obregón's camp. Reeling under the virulence of Villa's onslaught, some of Obregón's pessimistic officers urged him to break off and retreat. But as before, Obregón

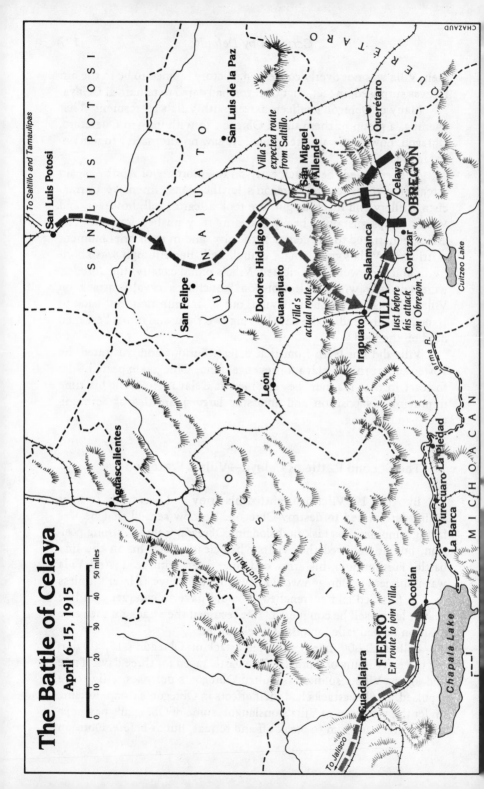

The Battle of Celaya
April 6–15, 1915

To Saltillo and Tamaulipas

San Luis Potosi

SAN LUIS POTOSI

San Luis de la Paz

San Felipe

GUANAJUATO

Villa's expected route from Saltillo.

San Miguel el Allende

Querétaro

QUERÉTARO

OBREGÓN

Celaya

Dolores Hidalgo

Guanajuato

Villa's actual route

Salamanca

Cortazar

VILLA
Just before his attack on Obregón.

Irapuato

León

Lerma R.

Cuitzeo Lake

AGUASCALIENTES

Aguascalientes

J A L I S C O

Lerma R.

Yurécharo La Piedad

MICHOACAN

La Barca

Ocotlán

FIERRO
En route to join Villa.

Guadalajara

To Jalisco

Chapala Lake

0 10 20 30 40 50 miles

CHAZAUD

stayed where he was; for three days, he held a strong force of 6,000 cavalry in reserve while the infantry of both armies slugged it out. Then, on April 15, Obregón committed his cavalry northward around Villa's left flank; when the blow struck Villa's rear, the Division of the North broke into flight.

The Battle of Celaya was the largest land battle fought on the North American continent since the American Civil War. Though Villa later claimed that he had sustained only 3,500 casualties, an American observer placed the number at 9,000, including 5,000 prisoners. A significant measure of Villa's defeat was his confirmed loss of twenty-eight of his thirty-four cannon. But if Villa refused to admit the extent of his losses, so did Obregón. The Carrancista general declared he had suffered only 200 casualties, including both dead and wounded.

Villa could conceal the severity of his defeat for a while. By virtue of his remote location in the interior of Mexico—and with the cooperation of his friend George Carothers—he was able to minimize his losses. As late as April 15, the final, crushing day of the Second Battle of Celaya, the *New York Times* reported that the Villistas had Obregón surrounded. Nevertheless, the truth gradually leaked out. Newspapers in the United States began speculating that perhaps Villa was finished. Although those pundits were writing Villa off prematurely, his path was downhill from this point on.

After the Second Battle of Celaya, Villa fell back to Aguascalientes. Obregón, whose forces had suffered more heavily than he admitted, followed in Villa's tracks slowly up the railroad line to the town of León, about halfway up from Celaya. Here Villa decided that he had retreated far enough, and he determined to attack Obregón once again. Felipe Angeles, who had just rejoined Villa, restrained him for a while. Angeles analyzed the two Celaya battles and concluded that Villa's frontal attacks could no longer succeed. Angeles urged Villa to employ the same tactics Obregón had used—dig in and force the enemy to attack. Villa disdained such conservative tactics. Furthermore, he was certain that Obregón would never risk an attack. Nevertheless, Villa heeded Angeles's advice for the moment and prepared entrenchments.

As Villa had predicted, Obregón refrained from attacking his entrenchments. He followed Villa cautiously as far as León and stopped there. Beginning in late May, the two armies faced each other on the defensive. There they remained for forty days, pounding each other with artillery, machine guns, and even hand grenades but never making any all-out assaults.

The Battle of León came close to being Obregón's last. One of Villa's shells burst near Obregón's headquarters and mangled his right arm. In his pain, Obregón reached for a gun to commit suicide; the weapon was unloaded. His aides rescued him, stopping the flow of blood and putting him in the hospital.

Villa finally lost the war of nerves; his patience ran out. In the attack that Obregón was waiting for, Villa led his cavalry out of camp and attempted to outflank Obregón's army to the east and cut his supply line back to Mexico City. Villa's attack was repulsed, however, and two days later General Benjamín Hill, who had replaced the wounded Obregón, broke through Villa's weakened lines. Again the Villistas headed north in a rout.

The defeat at León was not the last of Villa's setbacks. The Division of the North was soon driven out of Aguascalientes, then Zacatecas, and finally even Torreón. The outside world came to realize that Villa had lost all of northeast Mexico—Coahuila, Nueva León, and Tamaulipas. His domain was now reduced to the line of the railroad he had occupied in late 1913—from Juárez on the U.S. border to the southern border of Chihuahua.

During these months of his declining fortunes, Villa's followers began to desert him. Some, such as Luis Aguirre Benevides and Martín Luis Guzmán, found excuses to depart peaceably. Even Angeles left on a "temporary" mission to Washington to plead Villa's cause—with Villa's blessings, of course. But many of Villa's former friends rebelled against him. Among these was Villa's old compadre Thomás Urbina, one of the eight men who had crossed the Rio Grande with Villa in March of 1913.

Shortly after the Battle of León, Urbina absconded to Durango with gold worth thousands of pesos. When Villa heard of this desertion, he loaded two hundred men on a train and surprised Urbina at his hacienda in the middle of the night. Urbina was wounded and fell into Villa's hands. For a moment, Villa felt compassion for his old friend and even considered sending him back to Chihuahua for hospitalization. Villa's compassion disappeared, however, when Urbina refused to disclose where he had hidden the treasure. Villa thereupon turned Urbina over to Fierro for execution.

The American author Ambrose Bierce was also said to have met his end at about this time. How Bierce actually died will remain an unsolved mystery, but one of Villa's biographers, Elias L. Torres, has claimed to have been a witness to his death and has supplied a plausible account.

At dinner one evening, according to Torres, Villa and Bierce were eating together, with Fierro and two other men. Villa was in a good mood, expecting the usual jokes from the American to enliven the evening. But Bierce, who had been mysteriously absent from Villa's headquarters for three days, seemed unusually morose.

In the course of the meal, Bierce told some trivial, rather disappointing story to his attentive audience and then said brusquely that he was tired of accompanying Villa, that Villa's actions no longer seemed to adhere to reason or justice, and that Villa's purported "army" was really nothing but a band of thieves and assassins. When Villa realized that Bierce was not joking, he ceased smiling.

Bierce did not notice the terrible look on Villa's face. Nor did he see Villa signal one of his men to slip outside. With Villa's encouragement, Bierce continued. He was off to join Carranza, "the only man of worth in Mexico," he declared. He had his orderly and his horse waiting for him.

"That's very well thought out, Mr. Bierce," said Villa, smiling again. "I'm very sorry about your determination because I've grown used to your tales and stories. But I never hold anyone back by force. Give this bandit an abrazo and may it please God that Carranza receives you better than I."

The two men embraced and shook hands. Bierce left the room. Villa went on eating. Outside there were the sounds of voices, of horses' hooves, and shots. Villa turned to Fierro.

"Let's see if that damned gringo tells his last joke to the vulture of the sierra."

The vultures did their job; nobody dared remove the bodies of Bierce and his orderly.*

*Elias L. Torres, *Twenty Episodes in the Life of Pancho Villa* (Austin, 1973), pp. 36–37. C. Hartley Grattan, *Bitter Bierce* (Garden City, N.Y., 1929), p. 80, says, "If the number keeps on increasing as many Mexican towns will claim to have been the death place of Bierce as Grecian towns claimed to be the birthplace of Homer."

As Villa was reeling from a series of military defeats at the hands of Obregón, he also suffered diplomatic defeats at the hands of Carranza. The two spheres—military and political—were of course linked, for the military governed the political sphere in the Mexico of 1915. However, Villa's political defeats could not be hidden. Villa might cover up military disaster for a while by issuing false reports, but political setbacks were blazoned on the front pages of all the major newspapers in both Mexico and the United States.

When Carranza first established his provisional capital at Veracruz, in November of 1914, his stock with foreign powers, especially with the United States, was low. Not only did his political future seem dim, but he continued his abrasive attitude toward the United States. President Wilson and Secretary Bryan agreed that Carranza never passed up a chance to offend them. Wilson expressed his distaste succinctly when he wrote, "I think I have never known of a man more impossible to deal with on human principles than this man Carranza." Villa, on the other hand, always worked on convincing the Americans that he would establish a government they could control. (His friends George C. Carothers and Hugh Scott assisted him in this.)

But the First Chief, arrogant though he was, showed remarkable flexibility when his prospects looked most bleak. The winter of 1914–15 was one of those times. During the months at Veracruz, Carranza listened to the counsel of his advisers and finally decided to swallow his pride.

Shortly after arriving at Veracruz, therefore, Carranza issued a manifesto that revised his Plan of Guadalupe. He promised measures to meet the economic, political, and social needs of the country. Then, on January 6, 1915, he published his "Agrarian Decree," which in principle began the process of returning Indian communal lands to their rightful owners. Soon at least one governor under Carranza's control began to distribute land to peasants. It marked a major step in the rise of Carranza's fortunes.

For internal political reasons, Carranza continued to trumpet his anti-American rhetoric in public; but behind the scenes he began to make friendly overtures. In February, Carranza sent three agents to the United States for the sole purpose of developing support for the Carrancista cause among influential men. His representatives met with some success in California and later in Washington; the circle of Carranza supporters included John Lind.

Carranza's agents then drafted the "Manifesto to the Mexican

People." In April, at about the time of the battles of Celaya, they delivered their handiwork to Secretary of State Bryan. President Wilson studied it and made suggestions. The processed draft was then returned to Carranza's Washington agent, who passed it on to the First Chief in Veracruz.

As the great Battle of León was raging in May and June 1915, President Wilson seemed to be despairing over the continued bloodletting. He issued a statement that decried the tragic conditions then prevailing in Mexico and added a veiled threat of intervention. In these circumstances, he stated, "the people and government of the United States cannot stand by indifferently." Wilson denied any desire to interfere in Mexico's affairs, but he seemed to see no inconsistency when he added that the United States must "lend active moral support" to a man or group that could rally the people of Mexico, adding that if the Mexicans could not resolve their differences, the U.S. government would soon have to "decide what means should be employed by the United States in order to help Mexico save herself."

On June 9, Carranza issued the manifesto that Wilson had helped to shape. In an obvious reference to Wilson's search for a regime that could bring stability, Carranza made the claim that the Constitutionalists controlled seven-eighths of Mexico's territory and commanded the loyalty of twenty governors out of a total of twenty-seven—that is, he claimed that he now governed thirteen million of Mexico's fifteen million people. Carranza's claims were exaggerated, but his manifesto—and his ingratiating collaboration with Bryan and Wilson—did much to bolster his recognition by the United States.

At the end of June, William Jennings Bryan stepped down as secretary of state, and Robert Lansing replaced him. This change in the State Department profoundly affected Mexican-American relations. In contrast to the reticent Bryan, the self-assured Lansing held strong beliefs regarding Europe, and he was determined to put relations with Mexico out of the way. That objective meant, in his view, finding one government in Mexico that the United States could support—and then throwing the weight of the United States behind it. That policy accelerated the already rapid decline of Pancho Villa.

Lansing's determination to back one Mexican regime was reinforced by an unlikely figure, the former Mexican dictator Victoriano Huerta. Huerta's plotting, a real annoyance, further strengthened Secretary Lansing's resolve.

After Huerta sailed from Puerto México the previous July, he settled in Barcelona, Spain. In that haven for fugitive Latin American dictators, he found relative safety from everything except acute boredom. The ennui was so oppressive that Huerta was highly vulnerable to the blandishments of a German operative who approached him one day in February 1915 and offered to help him return to power in Mexico. The agent proposed to reestablish Huerta as president by organizing an invasion of Mexico from the United States.

The agent's name—or at least one of his names—was Captain Franz von Rintelen, Imperial German Navy. The aggressive and persuasive Rintelen explained that since relations between President Wilson and the kaiser's government were deteriorating so rapidly, it was in Germany's interest to divert the American public's attention from Germany. That could be accomplished by creating unrest in Mexico. A counterrevolution by Huerta in Mexico would therefore receive substantial support from the kaiser.

Rintelen had little difficulty in persuading Huerta, so in early April 1915 the two men traveled separately to New York. Rintelen, carrying a forged Swiss passport, arranged for the purchase of eleven million rounds of ammunition to sustain Huerta's force—whenever such a force should be assembled. At the same time, he deposited $800,000 in Huerta's name in the Deutsche Bank of Havana. He also persuaded a willing Félix Díaz to lead a simultaneous uprising in southern Mexico.

Huerta arrived in New York in mid-April, much noticed in the American press. He handled the situation well. The soul of tact in dealing with hordes of newspaper reporters, Huerta convincingly denied any complicity in President Francisco Madero's death. When the thirty members of Huerta's family arrived (with one hundred steamer trunks), he moved from his New York hotel to a pretentious home in Forest Hills, on Long Island. There he posed for photographers as a settled, domesticated family man. He even posed for the photographers while ostentatiously mowing the lawn.

On Thursday, June 24, however, Huerta slipped out of New York under the pretext of visiting the Panama-Pacific Exposition, in San Francisco. When his train reached Kansas City, he switched trains and headed south toward El Paso, Texas. Pascual Orozco, who had taken refuge in the United States after Villa had chased him across the border at Ojinaga, joined Huerta at Newman, a railroad stop twenty miles north of El Paso.

Unfortunately for Huerta and Orozco, the American collector of customs at El Paso, Zach Cobb, was a suspicious sort of man, and he sensed that a plot was afoot. Huerta and Orozco were arrested by Department of Justice agents and taken to an El Paso jail, charged with violation of neutrality laws.

Huerta, however, had many resources to draw on. He somehow managed to be represented in court by none less than Tom Lea, the mayor of El Paso. As a result, Huerta and Orozco were soon out of jail on bail. Orozco's stormy career soon came to an end when he jumped bail and died in a shoot-out following a robbery in western Texas. The U.S. authorities thereupon incarcerated Huerta at nearby Fort Bliss to prevent him from jumping bail also. But Huerta's health had taken a turn for the worse, and for the next few weeks the general spent part of his time in custody and the rest consigned to the care of his family in El Paso.

Huerta's scheming alerted the agents of the U.S. Justice Department to the activities of Captain Rintelen. It also brought President Wilson around to Lansing's view that the United States must back one regime in Mexico. So Lansing, on Wilson's behalf, called a meeting of Latin American diplomats to discuss the Mexican situation. They met in Washington on August 5.

From that meeting came a call for all Mexican revolutionary leaders to confer in neutral territory and take the "first steps necessary to the constitutional restructuring of the country—and to issue the first and most essential of them all, the immediate call to general elections."

Villa, Zapata, and the moribund Aguascalientes Convention government responded favorably to Lansing's summons—they had nothing to lose. But Carranza waited a full month before bothering to reject "any conference with the chiefs of the rebel party." Carranza's defiance was well calculated. Instead of offending the new secretary of state, it seemed to impress him.

Lansing had earlier written a note to himself that "we must recognize one faction as dominant in Mexico." He now put that principle into effect. On October 9, Lansing and the Latin American diplomats decided that a de facto government of Mexico must be recognized—and that it should be that of Carranza.

Ten days later, the decision became official. The United States recognized Carranza's regime as the de facto government of Mexico. At the same time, President Wilson issued a proclamation leveling an arms embargo on any faction in Mexico other than Carranza's. The governments of Britain, France, Italy, Russia, Japan, Germany, and Spain soon followed Wilson's lead.

U.S. Army Chief of Staff Hugh Scott, still Villa's friend, was indignant: "The recognition of Carranza had the effect of solidifying the power of a man who had rewarded us with kicks on every occasion, and of making an outlaw of the man [Villa] who had helped us." But Scott was a soldier, not a policymaker, and Villa had very few friends like Scott in the United States.

16

****

Blood on the Border

During the last half of 1915 and
early 1916, the pace of violence along the Mexican–U.S. border quick-
ened dramatically. Raids across the border increased, and more than
property was at stake. Blood flowed on both sides.

With more violence came heightened tensions and desperate demands from U.S. citizens in southern Texas and New Mexico for
their government to do something to end it. Those demands formed
the backdrop to President Wilson's action in sending the Punitive
Expedition into Mexico in March of 1916. Ordinarily, such a radical
step on the part of a nonviolent man would be considered a gross
overreaction, but the atmosphere that caused it is worth looking at.

Many factors contributed to this increased tension, but at least
three stand out: the U.S. assistance to Carranza forces at the Battle of
Agua Prieta, which embittered Pancho Villa against the gringos; the
planned rebellion of Mexican-Americans in the vicinity of Brownsville, Texas, and Matamoros, Tamaulipas; and the wanton murder of
seventeen American citizens at the Cusi mines, near the city of
Chihuahua.

The Battle of Agua Prieta

By late summer of 1915, Pancho Villa's Division of the North was critically wounded but not quite dead. Villa still had force enough for one last effort to recoup his fortunes. His defeats at the hands of the Carrancistas had cost him nearly all the vast territories he had once occupied; his domain now consisted only of the state of Chihuahua, with just one significant point of entry, Juárez, through which to import illegal arms from the United States. Villa's state of mind made his prospects even worse. Those close to him noticed that he had lost his usual energy and decisiveness. He failed to perceive that Obregón's troops, despite their victories, were tired and low on ammunition. Villa's force, concentrated once more, now numbered some fifteen thousand men. With that many on hand, he could have struck Obregón once again, perhaps successfully. But he did not. He missed this one, fleeting chance.

At that point, however, Villa's spirits received a temporary lift. Adolfo de la Huerta and José María Maytorena, in the adjacent state of Sonora, suggested that Villa cross the Sierra Madre, destroy the Carrancista garrison at the border town of Agua Prieta, and with undisputed possession of Sonora launch a brand-new revolution.

Villa leaped at that suggestion. With a surge of life, he concentrated his army at the road junction of Casas Grandes and on September 16 received word that his advance guard had succeeded in seizing the dangerous Púlpito Pass, where a small but determined force might hold up his whole division. With that obstacle surmounted, Villa and his army disappeared into the Sierra Madre. He did not yet know that President Wilson had given de facto recognition to Carranza.

The march across the Sierra Madre was arduous but uneventful—except for the loss of Rodolfo Fierro, who had stuck by Villa when fainter-hearted men had deserted him. Fierro was occupying Juárez when he received news of Villa's march, so he decided to take a direct route to join Villa in Sonora. At a point just south of Columbus, New Mexico, Fierro found his path blocked by Lake Guzmán, a wide flat full of dangerous quicksand. When his men hesitated, Fierro plunged impetuously forward, shouting words of contempt for their cowardice. His horse soon stumbled, throwing Fierro forward into the mire. He sank beneath the surface, dragged under by the weight of the gold he was carrying in his pockets. Villa was the only one who mourned Fierro; the rest of his entourage felt safer with him dead.

Villa's journey across the Sierra Madre was slow along the restricted road net. And even though they still had a faint hope of success, his officers and men had lost their old sense of urgency. Villa's army was now, as his biographer Haldeen Braddy describes it,

> a multitude of fifteen thousand souls, women and ripe girls and children, *peones* and Indians and *Dorados*. . . . The women nursed their crying babes and cooked *frijoles*; the moon-bosomed girls made promiscuous love; the *peones* swigged their *sotol* and waxed fat from inaction. Villa's rabble included long-haired Indians, some of whom smoked *marihuana* at night and threw fits or danced wildly about the campfires. Everywhere the "campers" reeked of filth and, worse still, of gluttony and sloth.

Even their songs reflected resignation:

> *I am a soldier of Pancho Villa.*
> *I am the most faithful of the "dorados."*
> *It matters not if I lose my life*
> *Or that I die for him against any man.*

Once Villa had crossed the Sierra Madre, he stopped to await Maytorena, who had promised to join him with several thousand troops. Villa felt no urge to move quickly, so he made camp east of Agua Prieta, obtaining beef at several ranches, one of which was that of "Texas John" Slaughter, a retired American lawman from nearby Tombstone, who was sympathetic to Villa's cause. Slaughter's Ranch, on the U.S.–Mexican border, also provided water from the artesian wells on the property. Though Villa was now encamped only eighteen miles from Agua Prieta, he hoped to remain out of sight for the time being.

Plutarco Elías Calles, commanding the Carrancista forces in Agua Prieta, had a strong position, virtually immune to a sneak attack. The city lay in a flat valley, and the lack of vegetation made it easy for Calles's scouts to detect Villa's advance. Moreover, Calles had heeded Obregón's advice, walling in the town and bolstering his defenses with strong barbed-wire entanglements and mines. Supply presented no problem for Calles; plenty of food and ammunition were available.

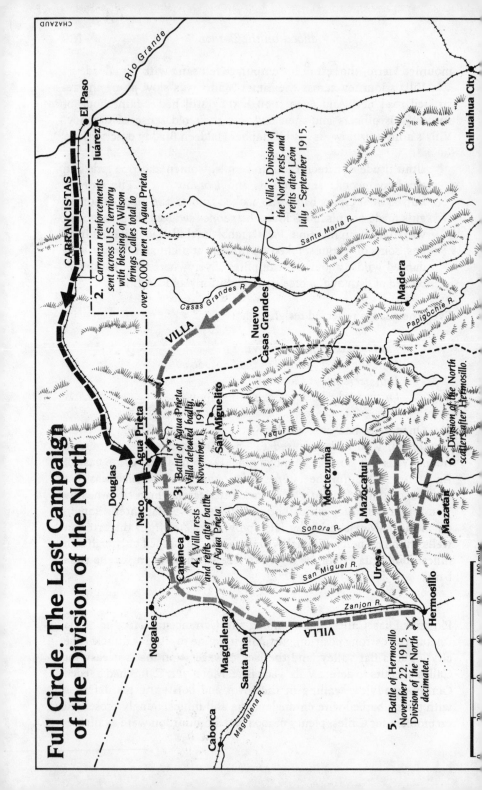

Full Circle. The Last Campaign of the Division of the North

CHAZAUD

CARRANCISTAS

VILLA

VILLA

1. Villa's Division of the North rests and refits after León July - September 1915.

2. Carranza reinforcements sent across U.S. territory with blessing of Wilson brings Calles total to over 6,000 men at Agua Prieta.

3. Battle of Agua Prieta. Villa defeated badly. November, 1915.

4. Villa rests and refits after battle of Agua Prieta.

5. Battle of Hermosillo November 22, 1915. Division of the North decimated.

6. Division of the North scatters after Hermosillo.

El Paso
Juárez
Rio Grande
Chihuahua City
Santa Maria R.
Madera
Casas Grandes R.
Nuevo Casas Grandes
Papigochic R.
Douglas
Agua Prieta
Naco
San Miguelito
Yaqui R.
Moctezuma
Mazocahui
Mazatán
Cananea
Sonora R.
Ures
Nogales
San Miguel R.
Magdalena
Santa Ana
Zanjon R.
Hermosillo
Caborca
Magdalena R.

100 miles

The most important asset that Calles enjoyed was the cooperation of the United States. The extent of that cooperation, in fact,
constitutes the major significance of the battle. President Wilson and
Secretary Lansing, once they had recognized Carranza, followed up on
Lansing's policy of giving support wholeheartedly to the dominant
faction. During October 1915, the U.S. government assisted Carranza
by allowing him to use the railroad across New Mexico and Arizona.
Carranza brought fresh troops across U.S. territory from as far away as
Laredo, Texas, thence through Lordsburg, New Mexico. These troops
arrived at the Fifteenth Street station in Douglas and crossed the border immediately into Agua Prieta. At a stroke, Calles's total force
jumped from only three thousand men to sixty-five hundred, a number more than adequate to sustain a defensive position behind well-
prepared field fortifications.

The Americans were well aware that a battle at Agua Prieta was
imminent. American soldiers and civilians would not, of course, be
immune from stray bullets coming from the battle, but Frederick Funston, now a major general commanding the army's Southern Department, was determined to prevent any incursions into U.S. territory.
Funston bolstered the garrison in Douglas to a force of three infantry
regiments, one regiment of field artillery, and several troops of cavalry. Never one to miss action, he assumed personal command of the
American garrison.

On October 30, a detachment of Calles's scouts discovered Pancho Villa's force at Slaughter's Ranch, and Calles immediately made
this news public. Word reached Douglas of the pitiable condition of
the women and children with Villa, and sympathetic women, both
Mexican and Anglo, carried food out to ease their hunger. An American newspaper reporter also received the news, and he headed straight
out to the ranch to interview Villa. At that meeting, Villa learned for
the first time that the United States had recognized Carranza as de
facto president. Villa swore revenge and declared he would attack
anyone, even Americans, in continuing his fight against Carranza.
But Villa apparently did not hear about U.S. help in bolstering Calles's
command. Had he known that, he might have retreated back into the
Sierra Madre.

The story of the fight at Agua Prieta reads like a grim repetition
of Villa's other recent defeats. Two days after spotting Villa at Slaughter's Ranch, Calles decided to bring the battle on, perhaps as an act of
sheer defiance. He sent a force of heavy artillery across the plain
between them, and from a position near Villa's camp his cannon

opened fire. Villa's cannoneers answered. Calles's guns fell back into their entrenchments, and Villa's *dorados* followed on their heels.

When Villa's *dorados* reached the edge of Agua Prieta, they encountered a strong wind that blew dust in their faces. In the confusion, some of them mistakenly fired into their fellows. Nevertheless, they charged into the main part of town, shouting, "Viva Villa! Viva Mexico!" But the noise of Carrancista artillery and machine guns deafened them. The well-entrenched Carrancistas poured volley after volley into their ranks. Soon Agua Prieta had become "a slaughterhouse of wind and smoke, of gray dust, and of short, stabbing flames of gunfire." Villa launched three such attacks. All failed.

Americans across the railroad in Douglas, Arizona, witnessed this battle. Despite General Funston's concern for their safety, the townspeople regarded the unfolding drama as a social outing and flocked to the railroad tracks to see what they could. Some stood on boxcars with binoculars; others climbed to the tops of buildings; some had to watch from the ground. They paid little heed to the possible danger of stray bullets.

One of the witnesses was a spunky twelve-year-old girl named Winifred Paul. Winifred's mother, Mabel Paul, had promised to take her along when the expected battle took place, but when Winifred arrived home from school at about four in the afternoon, she found her parents gone. The maid, however, told her that they wanted her to take a bath and do her homework.

Winifred was not willing to miss the excitement. She ran down to the railroad tracks, a mile away, as fast as her legs would carry her. When she arrived, she found that all the vantage points had been taken; she would have to watch from the ground. From there, she could see little in the clouds of dust to the south, and the noise was deafening. Still she stayed.

All of a sudden, a stray bullet from Agua Prieta hit a rock near Winifred and ricocheted around, nicking her in the left ankle. No bones were broken, but it hurt. Worse than that, it tore a hole in her long black stocking. Her distress was complete when she heard the voice of one of the neighbors calling her mother over the noise: "Mabel, Winifred has been shot!"

Her mother came. But instead of sympathy, Winifred received a mild thrashing and orders to go home.

A troop of Pascual Orozco's *colorados,* the men to whom Pancho Villa gave no quarter. (Aultman Collection, El Paso Public Library)

First Chief Venustiano Carranza visits his troops in Torreón, 1913. (Library of Congress)

The historic meeting of future enemies. Brigadier General John J. Pershing, commanding the Eighth Cavalry brigade at Fort Bliss, greets the Mexican generals Alvaro Obregón and Pancho Villa on the International Bridge between Juárez and El Paso, September 1914. (Aultman Collection, El Paso Public Library)

Famous photograph of Villa and Zapata occupying the President's Office of the National Palace, Mexico City, in December 1914. Villa sits in the president's chair with Zapata on his left. On Villa's right is his old comrade Tomás Urbina. Watchful as ever is Villa's bodyguard, Rodolfo Fierro (standing). Notably absent: President Eulalio Gutiérrez. (Aultman Collection, El Paso Public Library)

Villa confers with his old friend Major General Hugh Scott, chief of staff, U.S. Army, January 1915. Scott and Villa met several times at Juárez and El Paso. Scott always remained Villa's friend, even after Villa had lost the Division of the North. (Aultman Collection, El Paso Public Library)

General Alvaro Obregón.
(Library of Congress)

**Robert Lansing, who
succeeded William J.
Bryan as secretary of state
in June 1915. Lansing's
impatience to recognize a
single faction in Mexico
precipitated Villa's
downfall as caudillo of
Chihuahua.**
(Library of Congress)

Below: **The U.S.–Mexican border running along International Avenue in Nogales, Arizona. This photograph, while obviously doctored, brings out the easily forgotten fact that no river divides U.S. and Mexican territory west of El Paso. Both Naco and Nogales have Mexican and American sectors.** (Courtesy Fort Bliss Museum, Fort Bliss, Texas)

NOGALES, ARIZONA   NOGALES, SONORA, MEXICO

Columbus, New Mexico, after the Villista raid of March 9, 1916. (National Archives)

Opposite page (top): **Villa's men, captured and hanged by General Francisco Murguía at Chihuahua in 1915. The mass hangings occurred on an avenue always remembered thereafter as the Avenue of the Hanging Men.** (Aultman Collection, El Paso Public Library)

Troopers of the Thirteenth U.S. Cavalry burning the bodies of dead Villistas after the raid on Columbus on March 9, 1916. (National Archives)

Brigadier General (later general of the armies) John J. Pershing. (Courtesy Fort Bliss Museum, Fort Bliss, Texas)

General Pershing and the staff of the Punitive Expedition, 1916. *Left to right*: **unidentified, Lieutenant Colonel De Rosey C. Cabell, unidentified, Pershing, First Lieutenant George S. Patton, Jr., Major John L. Hines, unidentified.** (Courtesy Fort Bliss Museum, Fort Bliss, Texas)

U.S. cavalry in pursuit of Pancho Villa, Chihuahua, 1916.
(Aultman Collection, El Paso Public Library)

**Apache scout,
Punitive Expedition,
1916.**
(National Archives)

Wagon supply train, Punitive Expedition, Chihuahua, 1916.
(National Archives)

Opposite page (bottom): **U.S. Army JN-3 observation plane, Pershing's abortive "eyes" for the Punitive Expedition.** (National Archives)

Pershing in his touring car, with De Rosey C. Cabell and Lieutenant James L. Collins (aide). (National Archives)

Colonel (later Brigadier General) George A. Dodd. (Special Collections, United States Military Academy Library)

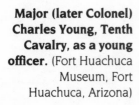

Major (later Colonel) Charles Young, Tenth Cavalry, as a young officer. (Fort Huachuca Museum, Fort Huachuca, Arizona)

Meeting between General Alvaro Obregón and General Frederick Funston, Juárez, Mexico, April 1916. (Courtesy Fort Bliss Museum, Fort Bliss, Texas)

**Captain
Charles T. Boyd,
Tenth Cavalry.**
(Special Collections,
United States Military
Academy Library)

**American soldiers of the Tenth Cavalry held by the Mexicans, June
1916.** (Courtesy Fort Bliss Museum, Fort Bliss, Texas)

American camp at Colonia Dublán, 1916.
(National Archives)

Withdrawal of the Punitive Expedition, February 5, 1917.
(National Archives)

That evening, Pancho Villa decided to attack again. This time his Yaqui Indians led, employing their usual tactics for night assaults. Crawling on their bellies into the barbed wire, they counted on achieving surprise. Suddenly, they were discovered—and blinded—by overpowering light beams cast by three giant spotlights. The Yaquis, hopped up on marijuana, then stood up and charged forward into the barbed wire. They never had a chance; they were slaughtered, while Calles's men were nearly untouched.

The next day, nothing was heard from the Villista army. By November 3, the Division of the North had slipped away from Agua Prieta and headed toward Naco, thirty miles to the west.

When the survivors of Villa's force reached Naco, they camped for several days and attempted to recover from the disaster at Agua Prieta. The wounded were in pitiful condition, lacking medical supplies, such as morphine.

Word of the suffering of Villa's men reached George Kingdon, the manager of the Consolidated Copper Mine, at Cananea. Distressed at what he heard of the tragedy, Kingdon sent two American physicians, Drs. Thigpen and Miller, to tend the wounded Villistas. Villa gratefully acknowledged Kingdon's aid and received the American doctors warmly. Soon, however, word came to Villa—surprisingly, the first word—that the United States, by rendering critical aid to Calles at Agua Prieta, had virtually brought on his crushing defeat.* Villa became blinded with rage against all Americans, and he took leave of all reason. He summoned the two doctors and demanded to know whether they masqueraded as spies. Both, of course, denied any such allegations, but Villa threw them into jail anyway and condemned them to be shot.

For several days, the fate of the two doctors hung in the balance. Kingdon, justifiably alarmed, sent representatives from Cananea to entreat Villa to spare their lives. The Cananea mine finally wound up paying Villa $25,000 in "taxes," in exchange for the release of the doctors. But Villa did not return Thigpen and Miller to Cananea;

*Besides allowing the Carrancistas to use the railroad from Laredo to Douglas for reinforcements, the Americans also undoubtedly supplied the power for the searchlights that blinded Villa's Yaquis the night of November 1, at Agua Prieta. Douglas was a modern town, the site of a smelting plant. Agua Prieta was at that time a primitive barrio, without electricity.

instead, he dropped them off in a small town several miles from Naco. The two almost died on the way back to Arizona, and the overweight Dr. Miller later succumbed from the effects of the ordeal.

Finally, Villa and his men left Naco, heading south toward Hermosillo, the capital of Sonora, two hundred miles away, hoping once more to join Governor Maytorena's army. On arrival at Hermosillo, however, Villa found no trace of Maytorena.* So he decided to attack Hermosillo alone.

On November 22, Pancho Villa launched his last attack as the commander of a major unit, this time against Hermosillo. He sent his troops in broad daylight against strong Carrancista defenses in his old, slashing style. Again Villa's men were cut down in swaths by machine-gun and rifle fire. This time, the surviving Villistas broke and fled. Most of them headed in the direction of Nogales, spreading death and destruction in their path. After thirty hours of fighting at Hermosillo, Villa's once proud Division of the North no longer existed.

That was the end, and Villa knew it. He retreated to Chihuahua and there made a final speech to his remaining followers. He admitted that the people of Mexico had "erroneously" turned to Carranza rather than to himself. For his part, he would return to the Sierra. But he would rise again if Carranza had not pacified the country within six months.

On the day before Christmas 1915, Pancho Villa and his small band left Chihuahua and disappeared into the hills. A week later, a Carrancista force occupied Chihuahua and accepted the surrender of about four thousand Villista officers (including forty-four generals) and eleven thousand men.

Violence at Brownsville and Matamoros: The Plan of San Diego

While Venustiano Carranza was gaining ascendancy over Pancho Villa during 1915, tensions between Mexicans and Americans were growing all along their common border because of a marked increase in bandit raids on both sides. The growing number of raids boded ill for the future of Mexican-American relations.

The most serious situation developed in the lower Rio Grande valley, the area around the Texas town of Brownsville and the Mexi-

---

*Villa later learned that Maytorena had been "defeated" by a Carrancista force at Nogales and had found it prudent to flee to the United States.

can town of Matamoros. It was set off by disorder on the Mexican side growing out of a citizens' uprising against Carranza's troops, who had held Matamoros since early June 1913. The rebellion was quashed, but in the ensuing confusion shots fell in Brownsville, across the river, and endangered the lives of American citizens.

The situation alarmed the governor of Texas, Oscar B. Colquitt, who sent reinforcements of state guardsmen to Brownsville, meanwhile pressuring Washington to dispatch more federal troops to the Rio Grande. Colquitt's rhetoric even surpassed his actions. He ordered his guard commander to warn his Mexican counterpart that "if he harms a single Texan, his life will be demanded as a forfeit."

President Wilson, Secretary Bryan, and Secretary of War Garrison all feared that Governor Colquitt's dramatics might bring about a war if he followed through on his threat. To keep the governor in some sort of harness, therefore, the War Department ordered General Funston, commanding at San Antonio, to "cooperate" with the Texas state authorities. Once the federal government accepted the primary responsibility for security on the border, Colquitt calmed down.

Funston's Southern Department, U.S. Army, was faced with a difficult job to perform. Only twenty thousand men were assigned to guard the 2,000-mile frontier against Mexican encroachment—ten men to the mile. But Funston was not unduly alarmed. He noted officially that cattle rustling had been going on for years and that it was not surprising for robberies to occur "when on one side of an easily passable boundary there is the direst poverty among the people, some of whom are of low intelligence and desperate character, while on the other side there is wealth and plenty." Besides, in the twenty-five incidents reported within U.S. territory during the latter half of 1915, only eleven Americans had been killed, in contrast to a far larger number of Mexicans.

Funston was certain that First Chief Venustiano Carranza was at least indirectly responsible for the current rash of violence; he saw behind the Mexican raids a "fixed purpose and design to invade our territory, promote strife, and make war upon our people." Specifically, Funston pointed to a Carrancista faction named the de la Rosa group, after their leader, Luis de la Rosa. These men, he believed, were "tolerated and even encouraged in their plans and acts" by the Carranza government in Mexico.*

The de la Rosa group took as its credo a manifesto commonly

*Funston's report was written in July 1916. Subsequent events involving Carranza might well have influenced his views at the time of writing.

known as the Plan of San Diego, named for a Texas town located between Corpus Christi and Laredo. The document called for Mexicans and Mexican-Americans to rise up against American authorities on the Texas side of the border, to declare their independence from the United States, and then to invade the rest of Texas, New Mexico, Arizona, California, and Wyoming. The states mentioned covered about the same territory that the United States had wrested from Mexico as the result of the war of 1846–48. The date for the uprising was set as February 20, 1915.

The Plan of San Diego was an elaborate scheme. Its other features included a subsequent annexation of six additional states of the Union, these to be turned over to the "Negroes," who were expected to form their own independent republic. The Apaches were to be given back their lost lands, and all white American males over the age of sixteen were to be killed.

General Funston attached enough importance to the Plan of San Diego to include its entire text in his 1916 annual report, but the plan was not at first taken seriously by other U.S. authorities. When one of the de la Rosa conspirators was captured and brought before a court in Brownsville, the judge told the defendant, "You ought to be tried for lunacy." The threat inherent in the plan lost urgency when the target date of February 20 came and went without incident.

However, many Mexicans along the lower Rio Grande took the Plan of San Diego seriously. It reappeared in a somewhat modified and expanded form in March 1915, after which Mexican raids into Texas increased.

Toward the end of July 1915, the Texans of the lower Rio Grande responded with actions on their own. They formed a vigilante group called the Law and Order League, and under that guise began to summarily execute Mexican-American suspects without trial. The mayor of one small town appointed every man in town between the ages of twenty-one and sixty as "special policemen," who at one time shot fourteen Mexican-Americans and stretched their bodies along a roadway as a warning to others.

Shortly thereafter, a Texas Ranger detachment arrived in the area, but the situation for Mexican-Americans grew worse, not better. Known as *rinches* to the Mexicans, these men often behaved more like bandits than the bandits themselves did. A young Mexican-American girl named Cecilia Almaguer Rendón described a nightmarish experience when the *rinches* paid her family a visit in Brownsville. Her cousin Encarnación Garza had come to her farm to see her mother. He slept outside to avoid crowding the hot house, even though the family warned him against it. In the early morning hours, the *rinches* came and seized Garza. They handcuffed him and stood him in the headlights of their car while they entered the house and searched it. They then took Garza to a nearby cemetery and shot him. They left his body where it lay; the family buried it the next morning.

Cecilia Rendón told only one side of the story—Garza may have been a murderer—but the arbitrary way in which the Texas Rangers ignored the basic civil rights of Mexican-Americans did much to heighten tension.

Antagonism between Anglos and Mexicans grew, and the U.S. authorities came to believe that the Carrancistas were openly supporting the de la Rosa faction in Texas. That belief was bolstered by the appearance in the Mexican press of articles such as that of August 26, 1915, in the Monterrey newspaper *El Democratica*. Funston considered *El Democratica* "the official organ of the Constitutionalist Government":

TO OUR COMPATRIOTS, THE MEXICANS IN TEXAS

A cry of indignation and ire has been brought forth from the depths of our souls upon seeing the crimes and abuses which are daily being committed on defenseless women, old people, and children of our race by the BANDITS AND MISERABLE RANGERS WHO CARRY ON vigilance along the Rio Grande . . . savages who would put to shame the hungry tiger and nauseate the hyena. . . .
Enough of tolerance, enough of suffering insults and scorn. . . . The moment has arrived! Long live the INDEPENDENCE of the states of Texas, New Mexico, California, Arizona, part of Mississippi, and Oklahoma, which shall be known from this day henceforth as THE REPUBLIC OF TEXAS. . . .

The augmentation of the American military at the Rio Grande did not stop the violence. On August 8, Mexican raiders attacked the Las Norias flag station on the Kingsville–Brownsville rail line, seventy miles north of Brownsville. Unexpectedly encountering a force from the Eighth U.S. Cavalry, they lost four men killed. The remarkable thing about this raid was not its size but its daring. The maraud-

ers penetrated far into Texas territory and threatened the touted
Kennedy-King Ranch, a "symbol of Anglo domination" in that part of
Texas. Another raid took place on October 18, when Mexicans de-
railed a St. Louis–Brownsville–Mexico Railway train just north of
Brownsville. Funston later claimed that the mayor of Matamoros,
Emiliano P. Nafarrete, was behind the October 18 raid and that the
killers were crying "Viva Carranza!"

The people of Brownsville were now up in arms. American artillery pieces were trained on the bridge leading into Matamoros, and
army reserves came pouring into the area. The feeling was likewise
strong on the Mexican side. Fortunately, war was averted through
diplomatic channels. Venustiano Carranza agreed to remove the sus-
pect Mayor Nafarrete, and the raids ceased almost immediately.

Though the extent of Carranza's involvement in the violence
along the lower Rio Grande is uncertain, the First Chief certainly used
the tragic situation skillfully to further his own ends. While negotiating with Washington on the subject, Carranza indirectly, but definitely, linked that question to his desire for recognition as the legiti-
mate executive of Mexico. By some curious coincidence, the raids
tapered off when the United States granted Carranza de facto recognition, on October 19, 1915.

But the damage had been done. By the end of 1915, Americans
all along the Rio Grande border were fed up with the Mexican incursions. They expected the U.S. government to do something about
them.

The Massacre at Santa Isabel

The sporadic raids that discontented Mexicans made on the Anglos in the lower Rio Grande valley may well have been abetted by
radical Carrancistas. But no question was ever raised regarding the
responsibility for the notorious Santa Isabel massacre, which dwarfed
any atrocities committed near Matamoros. That outrage was definitely the work of Villa—or at least of Villistas.

During the period of Villa's decline in late 1915, most of the
American mines in Sonora and Chihuahua had prudently closed
down. After Villa's defeat at Hermosillo, however, a prematurely confident Alvaro Obregón declared that Sonora and Chihuahua had been
"pacified." To spur the locals into action, Obregón urged that those
American mines be reopened. Since many Americans had faith in

Obregón, a number of American miners, despite warnings from the State Department, began to cross the border to resume operations.

One of the companies whose management believed Obregón's rosy promises was the Cusi Mining Company, located at Cusihuiriáchic, in the Western Sierra Madre of Chihuahua. On January 9, 1916, seventeen American Cusi Mining officials and engineers boarded a train in Chihuahua City. Along with twenty Mexican employees, they intended to resume mining operations when they arrived. As was customary at the time, the Americans rode in one car and the Mexicans in another.

The train left Chihuahua in a southwesterly direction at first. Then, as the tracks bent northward near the ranch of Santa Isabel, the train suddenly ground to a halt. A barrier had been thrown across the tracks, and the train was obviously going to be held up.

One of the Mexicans, José María Sánchez, retained vivid impressions of the atrocity, and he freely gave them in subsequent interviews. Sánchez described the group of bandits who swaggered into the stalled Mexican railroad car, the leader of whom he claimed to recognize as a Villista colonel, Pablo López. Sánchez watched López carefully.

The bandits showed little interest in the Mexicans in the second car. They contented themselves with robbing the terrified workers of all their possessions and did them no further harm. Their targets were the Americans. Sánchez later reported that López was enjoying himself. He turned to the cowering Mexican laborers and shouted, "If you want to see some fun, come watch us kill these *gringos*. Come on, boys!"

The bandits then ran from the coach, shouting "Viva Villa!" and "Death to the *gringos!*" Sánchez heard a volley of rifle shots and peered cautiously out the window. As he watched in horror, he saw the Cusi general manager, Charles Watson, running toward the Santa Isabel River. Four other Americans were running in another direction. All were hotly pursued. The bandits were shooting, some of them dropping to their knees to take better aim. Watson was hit. He stumbled, continued a short distance, and finally threw up his hands and fell forward.

Panic then broke out among the Mexicans in the second car, but Sánchez could not resist peeking out the window again. By then, Americans were lying on the ground, and a few, as yet unharmed, were being lined up. Colonel López selected two men as executioners, much to the disappointment of those other bandits who were denied the honor. The two executioners then went down the line taking turns shooting the Americans in the head with Mauser rifles.

Soon all the victims were lying on the ground, "some gasping and writhing in the cinders." López ordered his men to put those still alive out of their misery. Then the men stripped the bodies of all clothing and shoes. Finally, they mutilated the bodies.

One of the seventeen Americans survived. Thomas B. Holmes, who made a break at the same time as Watson, was left for dead when he fell in the bushes. Holmes later crept into some thicker undergrowth and waited until he could get away safely.

When word of the Santa Isabel massacre reached El Paso on January 14, 1916, the townspeople were enraged. Certain hotheads urged revenge on whatever Mexicans the citizens could get their hands on. That rage subsided, only to be revived when the mutilated corpses of the victims were delivered to El Paso. At that point, the desperate U.S. authorities resorted to declaring martial law. Only under that stringent authority could the law enforcement officials prevent maddened Americans from crossing the Rio Grande to wreak vengeance on innocent people in Juárez.

Villa quickly denied any involvement with the Santa Isabel massacre, blaming it solely on Colonel Pablo López. First Chief Carranza went even further. Shortly after the incident, Obregón's men seized one of the alleged murderers, General José Rodríguez, and executed him. The Mexicans displayed the corpse conspicuously in Juárez, where it could be viewed by the Americans. Six months later, Pablo López was also apprehended by the Carrancistas and executed.

Carranza's elaborate show of remorse for the Santa Isabel massacre quickly mollified Woodrow Wilson, but not the frightened Americans along the border. The aroused citizenry again demanded that the United States *do something.*

17

****

Villa Raids Columbus

In the dark morning hours of March 9, 1916, a band of nearly five hundred Villistas crossed the border between Mexico and the United States. Three miles north of the border, they raided the small town of Columbus, New Mexico, robbing, burning, and killing. In numbers, Villa's Columbus raid was a relatively small affair—seventeen Americans and probably over a hundred Villistas killed. But such an outright violation of U.S. territory was infuriating to the American public, and many people, especially those living in fear near the Mexican border, demanded retribution.

Columbus itself seemed to offer very little to tempt even a reckless bandit to raid it. Troops of the U.S. Thirteenth Cavalry Regiment were stationed at Columbus only as part of an overall scheme to protect the American side of the Mexican-American border. The cavalry regiments assigned to that mission provided a degree of security for the Americans of the region by holding only the principal towns; they relied on patrols between the towns to deal with any incursions in the areas between them. The sector assigned to the Thirteenth Cavalry, like those assigned to other regiments, was long; it extended across sixty-five miles, from Noria in the east to Hernanas in the west.

Colonel Herbert J. Slocum, commanding the Thirteenth Cavalry, was a crusty, hard-drinking veteran of forty years of Indian campaigns, and he deployed his troops in a standard manner. He posted two of his seven rifle troops at Gibson's Line Ranch, fourteen miles west of Columbus; another he placed at the Border Gate, where the Guzmán (Mexico)–Deming (New Mexico) wagon road crossed the border south of Columbus. He kept his headquarters, his machine-gun troop, and four rifle troops at Columbus. Of Slocum's total force of 550 officers and men, about 350 were at Columbus.

The town of Columbus, "a cluster of adobe houses, a hotel, a few stores and streets knee deep in sand, combined with the cactus, mesquite, and rattlesnakes," boasted about 350 souls, a number about equal to that of Colonel Slocum's men. Geographically, the civilian-military community was neatly divided into four quadrants by a railroad (the El Paso & Southwestern) that ran roughly east–west, and the wagon road (Guzmán–Deming) that ran roughly north–south. The northeast quadrant contained the business district and most of the private residences. The southeast quadrant consisted of the temporary structures of Camp Furlong, the army post that housed the cavalrymen. Only scattered adobe houses were located in the northwest quadrant. The southwest quadrant had very little habitation at all, being filled almost entirely by a rocky, cactus-ridden knoll known as Cootes Hill.

Camp Furlong itself provided no space in which to house the families of the married officers. Though the enlisted men lived in the camp barracks, nearly all the officers lived in town. There was nothing unusual about this separate living arrangement. This was garrison, not field, duty. The United States and Mexico were at peace.

Like everyone else on the border, Colonel Slocum had been concerned about Pancho Villa's whereabouts ever since the murder of the sixteen Americans at Santa Isabel on January 9. However, Slocum's hands were tied. He was prohibited from sending scouting patrols across the Mexican border, but since Columbus was only three miles from the Border Gate, Villa could conceivably approach very close while still in Mexican territory.

Villa had truly disappeared. He was last seen at the time he left Chihuahua for the Sierra Madre in early December 1915. He had good reason for staying out of sight. The Carranza government had officially declared him a "bandit," so he was wanted by the Mexican law enforcement authorities. As a result, he adopted a totally new way of operating. One authority, Haldeen Braddy, has said,

In the Revolution [Villa's] presence at the head of his charging cavalry had created an idealized image of a fearless and intrepid officer. In those days wherever there was fighting, there was sure to be Villa. As a harried irregular, however, [Villa] had to follow the pack and direct it from out of sight. Perhaps this explains why he did not appear in person at Santa Ysabel. His accomplices Rodríguez and López had paid for Santa Ysabel with their lives— Villa himself had come off unscathed.

As concern increased among the Americans, rumors proliferated. According to some, Villa was still in a rage against the Americans; according to others, he was seeking a reconciliation. An Associated Press correspondent named George L. Seese actually sent Villa a letter inviting him to visit the United States under Associated Press auspices; Seese was later told to drop the scheme.

On March 3, 1916, the U.S. government warned that Villa was moving toward Columbus, and on March 6 the Mexican general Gabriel Gavira, commanding at Juárez, warned of Villa's presence in that area. But most believed an article in the *El Paso Times* on March 7 indicating that Villa intended to attack Palomas, the Mexican town six miles south of the border.

Colonel Slocum was not overly worried. Rumors of imminent Mexican or Indian attack were common. Slocum had noticed a great many Mexicans walking the streets in Columbus, but strangers from Palomas and the Mexican detachment at the Border Gate regularly came to Columbus to buy supplies. So Slocum could only shrug.

In the late afternoon of March 7, two Mexicans rode into Columbus from the south and claimed that they had just escaped with their lives from a band of Villistas near Palomas. One was a middle-aged man named Juan Favela and the other an elderly man named Antonio Muñoz. At 8:00 A.M. that day, the Mexicans said, they had been riding with an American cowboy toward Columbus when they encountered a party of five hundred Villistas along the Boca Grande River. The cowboy, for his own reasons, had left them to join the Villistas,* but Muñoz and Favela had spurred their horses and made their escape. They sought Slocum in order to warn him of what they had seen.

Slocum knew both men slightly; Favela, in fact, was a resident of

*The cowboy's name was William Corbett, and his reason for joining the Villistas was to try to persuade them to release Arthur McKinney, a friend of Corbett's in their custody. Instead, both were hanged that day. The grisly story of their deaths is told in Frank Tompkins, *Chasing Villa* (Harrisburg, 1934), pp. 61–62.

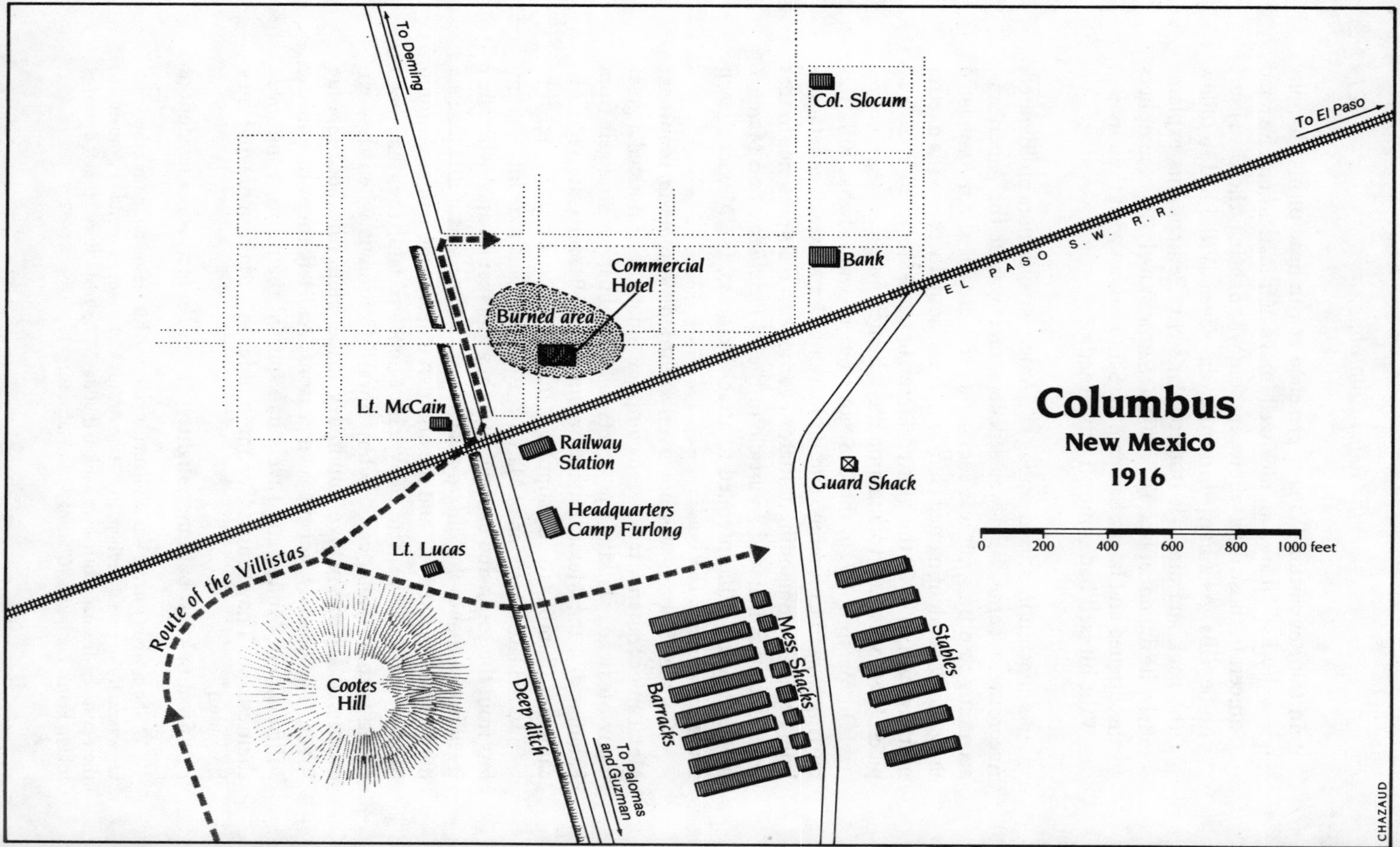

Columbus
New Mexico
1916

CHAZAUD

To El Paso

E L P A S O S. W. R. R.

1000 feet
800
600
400
200
0

Col. Slocum

Bank

Commercial Hotel

Burned area

Railway Station

Headquarters
Camp Furlong

Stables

Guard Shack

Mess Shacks

Barracks

To Palomas
and Guzman

Deep ditch

To Deming

Lt. McCain

Lt. Lucas

Cootes Hill

Route of the Villistas

Columbus. So Slocum finally decided to follow up the report, offering Muñoz twenty dollars to go back to Palomas and take another look. Muñoz was terrified, but twenty dollars was a fortune, and he went.

The next evening, March 8, Muñoz returned. He had revisited Villa's camp, he claimed, but had found it deserted. The ashes of the campfires suggested that Villa had broken camp early that morning, and the tracks indicated that Villa was heading away from, not toward, Columbus. Slocum gave Muñoz his twenty dollars.

Slocum stepped up his readiness. He ordered additional patrolling and ensured that his interior guard in Columbus was functioning: three regular posts; a watchman; and a roving patrol of four men, sometimes mounted. Unfortunately for them, the streets and most of the houses in Columbus were dark; Slocum's requisitions for oil and street lamps had been disapproved. There was no moon. Nevertheless, Slocum had done what he could. He left Columbus for a visit to Deming during the evening of March 8.

It is little wonder that no American could guess what Villa was up to, because Villa himself had not decided. To help him decide, he sent a scout from his base camp at Boca Grande to reconnoiter Columbus. He wanted particularly to know the state of readiness of the troopers at Columbus.

The scout may never have reached Columbus; at least, the word he brought back was worse than no word at all. He estimated the strength of the American garrison at Columbus to be only some thirty men. On the basis of that misinformation, Villa decided to make an assault. At 4:00 P.M. on March 8, Villa's 485 men were on the road northeast toward Columbus. The next day, at 2:30 A.M., his party crossed the border at a point west of the Border Gate. They stopped for final orders at a point just west-southwest of Cootes Hill.

In the pitch dark, Villa gave his last instructions. The advance guard would consist of eighty men. The rest of his force would be divided into five main groups of about eighty men each. He sent three groups eastward along the railroad to seize Cootes Hill. Once those three groups had reached the Deming–Guzmán road, two were to swing to the left and encircle the town from the north. The third was to enter Camp Furlong from the south and west. The two remaining groups were to stay with Villa in reserve behind Cootes Hill. Villa was sticking to his new way of operating, commanding from the rear.

At midnight of March 8, the "Drunkards' Special" from El Paso creaked into the Columbus railway station. Aboard the train was First

Lieutenant John P. Lucas, age twenty-six, commander of the machine-gun troop, Thirteenth Cavalry. Lucas was returning to Columbus from a week's leave in El Paso, where he had occupied himself playing polo with the army polo team. He could have stayed over in the city one more night and returned the next morning, but a "hunch" had caused him to return this evening.

As Lucas jumped off the train in the dark, he greeted the officer of the day, Lieutenant James C. Castleman, who was on hand to see that everything was in order. Lucas did not delay to make idle conversation; the hour was late. Instead, he stumbled through the dark to his quarters, a small adobe hut located only fifty yards west of Camp Furlong, across the Deming–Guzmán road.

Once in the hut, Lucas checked his revolver and found its chambers empty. His roommate, Lucas thought casually, had probably taken the ammunition with him when leaving for detached duty at the border the evening before. Lucas would ordinarily have waited until morning to reload his weapon, but another hunch made him search through the boxes in the corner of his room. After much difficulty, he found a box of shells and loaded his firearm before going to sleep.

Lucas did not sleep long. At about 4:30 A.M., he awoke to the sound of horsemen thundering past his hut. He peered through the window, and despite the general darkness thought he could make out the intruders. The horsemen pounding the streets, he was sure, were Mexicans, probably Villa's men. Whoever they were, Lucas had no doubt that they were attacking Columbus!

Lucas, as he later reported, was convinced that his time had come. But if he was going to be killed, he would take some of the enemy with him. So he drew his revolver, assumed a position in the middle of the room, and faced the door. He would at least get in the first shot if somebody were to break in.

Nobody came to the door, however, and Lucas stumbled back to the window. Across the road, he saw the flashes from an exchange of small-arms fire. Mexicans who had swept by his hut had encountered a sentry, Private Fred Griffin, Troop K, Thirteenth Cavalry, who barked out a challenge and was answered by a shot. Griffin, Lucas later learned, was hit in the belly, but as he reeled back he returned fire, miraculously cutting down his assailant. In quick succession, Griffin hit two others before he died. The Villistas, apparently surprised, spurred their mounts and could be heard charging down the streets of the camp, headed toward the stables. All this happened in a matter of seconds, as Lucas watched spellbound.

Lucas quickly recovered from his surprise and headed out the door, not bothering to find his boots in the dark. He jumped the ditch and dashed across the road, headed for the Camp Furlong barracks. No other officer was in sight, so he determined to assemble his machine-gun platoons and put them into action. He ran into the guard tent and obtained keys from the acting first sergeant and then, with two men, rushed out into the street and headed for the arms room in order to unlock his weapons. On the way, he was confronted by a Mexican, who fired at him with a rifle and missed. Lucas fired back. The range was so close that Lucas, no expert with a revolver, killed the man instantly.

At this point, Lucas confirmed what he had already suspected: he was the only officer in camp. His roommate was at the border, and the other regimental officers were at home in the town, cut off from the camp by the rampaging Mexicans. Lucas also learned that Lieutenant Castleman, the officer of the day, had taken a troop of soldiers into town. Lucas decided that his first priority should be the defense of the camp, so he set up his machine gun at a point where he could cover the crossings over the railroad. But lacking targets in the dark, Lucas and his crew merely fired their weapons in the direction of the flashes from the Mexican firearms.

In a short time, Lucas had assembled most of his machine-gun troop. When Captain Hamilton Bowie arrived at Camp Furlong and assumed command, Lucas moved one machine-gun detachment into town. There he found Castleman, set up in a position protecting the National Bank. Lucas tied his line in with that of Castleman.

Lucas then realized that throughout the action he had remained barefoot. It took him six months, he later wrote, to pull all the burrs and thistles from the soles of his feet.

From Cootes Hill, it will be recalled, Pancho Villa had sent some of his raiders northward, to circle around Columbus, and the rest into Camp Furlong. Of those entering the camp, some went past Lucas and others looped around to the south, trying to reach the stables from that direction. But since Villa had been counting on meeting only a tiny garrison, his raiders were surprised when they encountered a large number of Americans. Heavy fire, therefore, forced them to seek cover in small groups.

Some of the bewildered Villistas encountered serious trouble. A group that tried to take refuge in one of the bulletproof adobe kitchens ran afoul of some desperate American cooks. As the Mexicans burst through the door, they were doused with large potfuls of boiling water. Other cooks attacked them with axes and even baseball bats. None of the fugitives who entered the kitchens survived. A witness later went through the company streets outside and found "pieces of human skull as large as [his] hand, with the long hair of the Yaqui Indian attached."

In the center of Columbus, however, the Villistas met little resistance. One band swept down the railroad tracks to the nearby Commercial Hotel, a flimsy, two-story building located a long stone's throw from the railway station. Nine guests were registered there. Four of the nine were murdered, all of them men. One was the young Walton R. Walker, who was dragged away from his bride of less than a month and shot on the stairway. Two others, H. M. Hart and Charles D. Miller, were shoved out into the street before being gunned down.

The proprietor of the Commercial Hotel, William T. Ritchie, had hidden his wife and three daughters on the top floor of the hotel when the raiders arrived. When his family was taken prisoner, Ritchie readily obeyed his captors, following them down the stairs—to be shot on the ground floor. The four Ritchie women cowered upstairs, terrified but alive.

One guest escaped harm by a ruse. Fluent in the Spanish language, he told his captors that he would give them all his money. While they were scrambling for the coins that he had dropped on the floor, he crawled out the back window of the room.

At about that time, some Villistas set fire to the grocery store across the street from the Commercial Hotel, and the flames spread to the hotel. The four Ritchie women were rescued by Juan Favela, Slocum's Mexican informant, and by a young customs official named Jolly Garner. Garner later married one of the Ritchie daughters.

Several other American civilians were also killed, at various places. Most of the deaths seemed to stem from random shooting at lighted houses. Three men and one woman were killed in the town, probably by chance. But in their home a mile south of town, Mrs. J. J. Moore saw her husband and child killed, while she was painfully wounded in the leg. A total of nine American civilians and eight American soldiers eventually died in the Columbus raid.

Plunder, not murder, seemed to be Villa's main objective, however. His men looted stores and stole horses. The main Villista target was the store of Sam Ravel, the man who had done a lucrative under-cover business with Villa in happier days. Ravel's zest for such busi-ness had ebbed along with Villa's fortunes, and Ravel still owed him money. Happily for Ravel, he was away in El Paso undergoing minor surgery at the time of the raid. His sons Arthur and Louis, however, were taken prisoner while asleep in the store. The Villistas marched the boys down the street to the Commercial Hotel, but the boys were freed when some American sniper picked off both of their captors. The bandits had been silhouetted by the fires their fellow raiders had lit.

Amid all this wanton murder, women were generally treated with something resembling consideration. Mrs. Thomas Ryan, wife of a captain absent on patrol duty, was accosted by a Mexican as she tried to flee her home to take refuge in her bulletproof garage. The Mexican grabbed her by the arm and demanded where she was going. "Nowhere," she answered in her best Spanish. The man released her.

Another woman, Mrs. Maud Wright, was released by Villa after having been his captive for over a week. Picked up by Villa at her ranch near Chihuahua, Mrs. Wright had been forced to leave her hus-band and baby, and during her time as a prisoner she underwent much hardship. She rode a mule, slept on the ground, and survived by pick-ing over the leavings of the food eaten by Villa's horsemen. Mrs. Wright was released that morning in Columbus because she had earned Villa's admiration. Her testimony gives convincing evidence that Villa himself was *near*, but not *in*, Columbus during the raid.

Mrs. Wright did not collapse when she was released south of town. By chance, she came across the wounded Mrs. Moore and stopped off in Mrs. Moore's home to take care of her.

Other harrowing stories came out of the Villista raid on Colum-bus, several of them occasioned by the isolation of officers' families. Mrs. William A. McCain, mother of a little girl, had one of the grim-mest experiences. When the first swarm of horsemen engulfed the McCain house, her husband was able to hide his family and his or-derly in a dark spot in the mesquite outside. Soon a figure crept up in the dark; it turned out to be Captain George Williams, the regimental adjutant. Between them, the three men had only one pistol and one shotgun.

As the Mexicans began to retreat in the dark, one of them discov-ered the McCain family group and opened his mouth to shout. The Americans acted quickly, however. Before the man's warnings were understood by his fellows, McCain's orderly blasted him point-blank with the shotgun. The noise did not immediately reveal their position because of the confusion, but the fine shotgun pellets failed to kill their victim. McCain and Williams pulled the man into the bush, not daring to shoot him for fear of giving away their location.

But the man had to be killed, so McCain and the orderly tried to cut his throat with McCain's pocket knife. When the knife blade proved to be too dull, the Americans frantically hammered the man's head with the butt of a pistol. Finally, the Mexican was dead. Mrs. McCain and her young daughter huddled together in terror throughout the gruesome business, close enough to touch the victim while the struggle was going on.

Villa's men remained in Columbus only two hours. Once the raiders discovered that they had attacked a much larger garrison than expected, they gradually made their way out. American officers managed to reach camp, and by dawn, shortly after 6:00 A.M., Colonel Slocum resumed personal command of the regiment. By then, the Villistas were almost all gone.

As soon as Columbus was clear of invaders, Major Frank Tompkins reported to Colonel Slocum on Cootes Hill, requesting permission to follow the fleeing Villistas. Permission readily granted, Tompkins left with about thirty-two men, mostly from Troop H. They pursued the Mexicans until the Villistas took up a position on a ridge across the border. At that point, Tompkins realized that he had violated the War Department restriction against border crossings, so he sent a note back to Slocum requesting permission to stay in "hot pursuit." Slocum agreed, and Tompkins attacked the ridge and continued to follow the retreating Mexicans.

Tompkins kept up his pursuit for several hours, he reported. Then the Mexicans turned around and faced him. Tompkins now realized that he was outnumbered by ten to one, his ammunition was low, and his men were at the limit of their endurance. He began the long trip back to Columbus, reporting to Slocum in the early afternoon. Tompkins later claimed that his men had killed between seventy-five and one hundred Villistas on that foray alone.

The troopers of the U.S. Thirteenth Cavalry did not take the raid on Columbus in a cool, professional manner. They were enraged by the deaths of their comrades and of the people of Columbus, and they treated Mexican prisoners with contempt. Several Mexican residents of Columbus were later tried and hanged as conspirators, though some were given lighter sentences and at least one was acquitted.

When it came to cleaning up the streets after the raid, Colonel Slocum was personally accused of brutality. Slocum did nothing, the accusation said, to help Mexican wounded. As one man lay dying in the streets, Slocum snorted, "Let him bake in the sun." One account further insists that the same Villista was still alive when the burial party found him. The troopers merely hit him on the head and threw him into a wagon hauling bodies off to be cremated.

Tactically, Villa's raid on Columbus was a failure. If his objective was to attain booty, the cost to him was hardly worth it, as the Villistas lost most of the money and valuables while escaping. If Villa came only to kill gringos, he paid a high price, for he probably left well over a hundred Villistas dead behind him.

But despite his tactical rebuff, Villa scored a great psychological success at Columbus. His raid heightened panic among the Americans on the frontier, and it proved conclusively that the Carrancista government could do nothing to control him, at least in northwestern Mexico.

If Villa hoped to cause a war between the United States and Mexico, he nearly succeeded. But even though that ambitious scheme failed, his raid triggered one of the most remarkable episodes in the stormy history of Mexican-American relations—the Punitive Expedition.

18

****

"You Will Promptly Organize . . ."

As the raiders galloped south from Columbus during the morning hours of March 9, 1916, the terrified citizens of Columbus were half expecting Villa to return, and rumors grew during the day that he would be back that night. Word of the raid reached the outside world through the efforts of the Associated Press correspondent George Seese, who had spent the night in the Columbus Hotel. As the result of Seese's telegraphed messages, President Wilson learned of the raid only three hours after Villa had recrossed the border into Mexico.

Wilson took no immediate action, but Generals Funston and Pershing reacted rapidly, sending troops to reinforce border security and to control civilian panic. Sympathizing with the feelings of the townspeople of Columbus, Colonel Slocum and his troops allowed many of them, principally women and children, to take refuge in Camp Furlong that evening. Some slept on the floor of the camp hospital; others in the bulletproof adobe mess shacks. The camp quartermaster issued blankets and pillows, and the refugees felt relatively safe. Other civilians stayed in the schoolhouse in town. Next morning, the frightened people were happy to see hundreds of American soldiers coming in by train to bolster the Camp Furlong garrison. Some of the troops were New Mexico state guardsmen from nearby Deming; others were regulars from El Paso.

Columbus was not the only border town receiving additional protection. Other units went to such places as Nogales. These units included the Tenth Cavalry, stationed at Fort Huachuca, Arizona. One officer who found the sudden movement a bit inconvenient was Captain George B. Rodney, newly assigned commanding officer of its G Company.

Rodney was an old hand on the frontier, having served at Fort Huachuca for some years before his reassignment to Fort Leavenworth, Kansas. Leavenworth was pleasant enough, but Rodney itched to return to Arizona, so he sought out a vacancy as a troop commander in the Tenth Cavalry. The headquarters of the regiment was located at Fort Huachuca, but Rodney's G Troop was posted at Naco, a town on the U.S.–Mexican border. Because Naco was such a small town, the army provided only limited family housing there. Rodney, like the other officers stationed in Naco, therefore set his wife up at Fort Huachuca and reported at Naco to the squadron commander, Major Ellwood W. Evans.

The Tenth Cavalry was a regiment of African-Americans officially designated a "Negro" regiment in the segregated army of the time. Its members were commonly referred to as Buffalo Soldiers. The term "Buffalo Soldiers" is of uncertain origin, but it carried an agreeable rough-and-ready aura, and the designation made the members of the Tenth Cavalry proud. Rodney had never served with the Buffalo Soldiers before, and he was ill prepared for its traditional way of functioning—specifically the degree to which the first sergeant literally ran the outfit. So he was startled when he reported to Major Evans, an old friend, who suggested that he wire his wife and ask her to take the train down from Fort Huachuca that afternoon. The Rodneys were invited for dinner at Evans's quarters, and to a dance at the Warren Country Club afterward.

Rodney protested; he had just been assigned the command of a troop, he told Evans, and he was anxious to join it. But Evans was unmoved. "You can attend to that later. The troop runs itself. Rather the first sergeant runs it like a clock. He's been more than thirty years in the regiment." So Rodney wired his wife at Fort Huachuca, twenty-five miles away, and that evening they joined the Evanses as planned. The evening provided a pleasant reunion with many old friends.

At about midnight, Major Evans was called from the table. When he returned, his face bore a serious expression. He nodded to Rodney and to four other officers. In a moment the six men met on the porch.

"Get your wives out quietly and arrange to leave for camp at once," Evans said. "Long distance called me up a minute ago. Villa jumped Columbus early this morning and raided and burned the town. He killed a lot of civilians and the 13th had a hard fight. The Regimental Adjutant wired me to stand by for orders. The regiment has got orders and leaves at daylight."

Rodney's wife returned to Fort Huachuca by the morning train. Rodney did not see her again for months.

March 10, 1916, was the first day in office for Woodrow Wilson's new secretary of war, Newton D. Baker. Baker was at first out of his element in his new position. Besides being unfamiliar with the workings of the War Department, this avowed pacifist was serving for the first time anywhere in the federal government. He was glad, therefore, to find the army chief of staff, Major General Hugh L. Scott, to be so affable. Scott was proud of his reputation for tact in dealing with those less tutored than himself, and he was grateful that Baker had retained him as chief of staff. Baker could have selected any one of a number of officers to serve in Scott's stead. The two men instantly found themselves compatible, and Baker was willing—perhaps too willing—to accept Scott's advice.

Baker needed Scott's help on his first morning in office. In a cabinet meeting that day, the president and his department heads were discussing how to react to Villa's raid on Columbus. Wilson had earlier decided that he would probably have to send an expedition into Mexico, but for the moment he directed Baker to send only a warning order to the units in the field. Orders to execute that warning order would be issued later.

Baker went straight from the cabinet meeting to Scott's office. "I want you to start an expedition into Mexico to catch Villa," he said.

Scott respectfully demurred. "Mr. Secretary," he asked, "do you want to make war on one man? Suppose Villa should get on the train and go to Guatemala, Yucutan, or South America: are you going after him?" Baker saw Scott's point and agreed. Later that day, the War Department sent orders to General Funston that did not mention Villa by name: "You will promptly organize an adequate military force of troops from your department under the command of Brigadier-General John J. Pershing and will direct him to proceed promptly across the border in *pursuit of the Mexican band which attacked the town of Columbus,* New Mexico, and the troops there on the morning of the ninth instant."

The wording of this directive was unusual in that it designated the officer who was to command the expedition. Normally, that choice would have been left to the department commander—in this case, Funston. The departure from the norm was no mere oversight. Funston, Scott knew, was thirsting to command the expedition and would, if the decision were left to him, assume it himself. But Scott preferred Pershing for this task, and Baker had no basis on which to override him.

Scott's and Baker's care to avoid specifying Villa as the target of the projected expedition had been well taken. Nevertheless, their position was soon reversed by political considerations. Relations between the United States and Mexico were extremely delicate, and in hopes of making the expedition as palatable as possible to Carranza, Wilson and Lansing focused the objective on the capture of the "bandit" Villa. That device, Wilson hoped, might smooth over the bald fact that U.S. troops were about to invade Mexican territory. Thus the order that went out that same afternoon mentioned Villa by name: "President has directed that an armed force be sent into Mexico *with the sole object of capturing Villa and preventing any further raids by his band,* and with scrupulous regard for sovereignty of Mexico."

Once that presidential order was issued, the State and War departments went to work in their separate spheres. The War Department's task was to find troops and supplies for Pershing's force; the State Department's was to secure the blessing of the Carranza government. As the United States drifted ever closer to involvement in the European war, President Wilson was exceedingly anxious to avoid provoking any kind of war with Mexico.

Unfortunately, communications between Wilson and Carranza were conversations between the deaf and the dumb. Both men were on the spot politically at home, and both were therefore forced to assume a more bellicose position in public than they desired in private. Wilson, though concerned about Mexico's reaction to any Yankee incursion, felt an even stronger pressure from public opinion in the United States, which called for action. Carranza was in a similar dilemma. Since his own political position was precarious in Mexico, he personally needed the continued support of the United States. But Carranza could not allow the Mexican population to see him as knuckling under to the gringo, so in public he had to stand firm.

Carranza was not, however, hypocritical in maintaining a defiant stance toward the Yankees. He always remained sensitive to anything that appeared to violate Mexican sovereignty. His truculence in defending that sovereignty represented Carranza's strongest asset as a leader of the Mexican people.

Carranza therefore tried earnestly to convince the Wilson administration that pursuit of Villa was totally unnecessary. As early as 3:00 P.M. on March 9, General Luis Gutiérrez, in Chihuahua, hastened to assure the American consul that "orders [had] been given for the capture of the banditti from the Mexican side." Three hours later, he reported that 250 Carrancista cavalry were on the way to intercept Villa and that 350 others were being sent to protect Ojinaga, the town on the border between Texas and Chihuahua. Gutiérrez expressed "willingness to cooperate with the Government of the United States to capture Villa."

But the outraged American public, especially the citizens along the Mexican border, would never settle for mere assurances of "cooperation." They demanded both apologies from Mexico and revenge on Villa. Responding to that strong demand, Secretary Lansing sent a harsh message to Carranza that described the current situation as "the most serious which has confronted this Government during the entire period of Mexican unrest." Carranza was expected to "do everything in his power to pursue, capture, and exterminate this lawless element which is now proceeding westward from Columbus."

Lansing's "expectations" presented a tall order, considering that Carranza had been trying to capture Villa for about a year, so the First Chief played for time. First he tried to avoid meeting with the U.S. special agent, John Belt, who was charged with delivering the message. But Belt refused to be shunted off to Minister of Foreign Affairs Jesús Acuña. He insisted that Carranza receive the message personally. Finally, the three men met together. Acuña presented a creative version of the Mexican situation as it pertained to Villa: "The fact that Villa and his forces have entered the United States territory is evidence of the strength of the de facto Government's forces."

After Carranza left the meeting, Belt gave Acuña a set of written questions so blunt that he had been reluctant to give them to the First Chief in person:

   a. Was Carranza aware that Villa was in the Casas Grandes area?
   b. Was Carranza asked for reinforcements by his consul at El Paso?

    c. What action had Carranza taken?

    d. What action did Carranza plan to take to pursue, capture, and punish Villa?

    e. Would Carranza return to Mexico City from Querétaro in light of this serious matter?

    f. What else would Carranza like to say to the U.S. government?

Acuña, still feeling defensive about the Villa raid, promised to take the questions up with Carranza.

Acuña sent a reply that same evening. Still feeling at a disadvantage, he referred to the "courteous note" Belt had given him and asked Belt to assure President Wilson that the First Chief was "pained to hear of the lamentable occurrence at Columbus, New Mexico." He added that Carranza, at the request of the governor of Chihuahua and the Mexican consul at El Paso, had recently ordered an additional twenty-five hundred men, under command of General Luis Gutiérrez, to pursue the bandits. But he reiterated that these bandits had "made this move doubtless because they were driven to it by the persistent pursuit" of the men under Gutiérrez.

Carranza's message offered not only assurances but also an important proposal, designed to promote a new understanding along the border. It harked back to a similar problem that had faced the two countries during the 1880s. At that time, Apache Indians from government reservations in the United States had conducted raids into Chihuahua and Sonora. The United States and Mexico had thereupon agreed that "armed forces of either country might freely cross into territory of the other to pursue and chastise those bandits." Carranza's message specifically proposed "that Mexican forces be permitted to cross into American territory in pursuit of the aforesaid bandits . . . upon the understanding that, reciprocally, the forces of the United States may cross into Mexican territory, if the raid effected at Columbus should unfortunately be repeated at any other point on the border."

That communication led Wilson and Lansing to hope that Carranza would cooperate. The next day, however, the First Chief seemed to reverse himself, or at least to interpose prohibitive conditions: "If the Government of the United States . . . insists in sending an operating army into Mexican soil, my Government shall consider this act as an invasion of national territory."

That message seemed clearly to withhold permission to send troops into Mexico—provided that the reader was willing to take Carranza seriously. But Wilson quibbled by differentiating between "mutual permission to cross over" into each other's territory and "sending an operating army." Wilson therefore chose to ignore Carranza's threat. As he summed it up, *(a)* Carranza was incapable of policing Chihuahua and tracking Villa down, and *(b)* the United States, in the light of the public uproar, simply had to "do something." Wilson was conscious that, in the upcoming 1916 presidential election, he must not look "weak" to the electorate. One cabinet officer, in fact, declared that if the president failed to take action in Chihuahua, "he might just as well not contemplate running [for the presidency], in 1916, since he would not get a single electoral vote."

Still Wilson paused. Carranza had just issued an "appeal" in which he exhorted the Mexican people to "exercise the utmost prudence and maintain order while extending every guaranty to the American citizens residing in your state" but at the same time had asserted that the Constitutionalist government "will not admit, under any circumstances . . . that the territory of Mexico be invaded for an instant and the dignity of the Republic outraged."

That public appeal would ordinarily have stopped President Wilson, but he had already gone too far. So preparations for the expedition continued. On the evening of March 14, the State Department informed all U.S. consular officers that Carranza had "proposed that reciprocal privileges be granted should armed bands from the American side raid Mexican territory."

Wilson's message ended by announcing, "This Government's expedition will shortly enter Mexico with sole object of pursuing and capturing Villa and his band. . . ."

John J. Pershing, at Columbus, could sense that his superior, Frederick Funston, was unhappy with Pershing's designation as commander of the Punitive Expedition. Funston's first orders to Pershing had gratuitously emphasized the reason for that designation: he had been so named by the secretary of war. More serious to Pershing, however, was the tone of Funston's order, for it hinted that Funston, though not in direct command, intended to manage every detail of the expedition. His order specified that the expedition would be sent in "two columns, one to enter from Columbus and the other from Hachita, via Culberson's Ranch." It went on to prescribe the composition of each column down to the last cavalry troop, even the individual airplanes.

Then it asked whether Pershing had "any recommendations to make."

Pershing did not answer in writing, but he probably complained informally, for Funston's next order was reassuring: "As commander of the expeditionary force, the Department Commander leaves you free to make such assignments of the troops under your command as you think best. . . . From the time the troops report to you they will be subject to your orders."

General Hugh Scott had his own, definite reasons for preferring Pershing over Funston as the man to command the Punitive Expedition. Funston held a higher rank and enjoyed an unparalleled reputation as a fighter, but Pershing's combat record was also creditable. Pershing had fought against Indians, Philippine insurrectos, and even Chinese in the Boxer Rebellion. But, as Scott was aware, command of the Punitive Expedition would call for restraint and tact at times, and Pershing's experience in the settlement of international disputes would make him the ideal agent to cooperate with the Carrancista forces. In diplomacy—and even in common tact—Funston was seriously lacking.

At the age of fifty-five, Pershing was a favorite in the army. Commissioned in the West Point Class of 1886, he quickly gained experience in the West, where he helped reestablish peace after the Battle of Wounded Knee, in 1890. He performed exemplary service in the Spanish American War (1898) and later in the Philippines, among the Moros of Zamboanga and Sulu. A bachelor for forty-five years, he was advantageously and happily married in 1905 to Frances Warren, daughter of Senator Francis E. Warren of Wyoming. President Theodore Roosevelt attended the ceremony in the Washington Cathedral. During the next year, 1906, Pershing was promoted from the rank of captain directly to that of brigadier general. President Theodore Roosevelt bypassed eight hundred higher-ranking regular officers to make that appointment.

In 1914, Pershing left his wife and four children at the Presidio, a headquarters post on San Francisco Bay, so that they could be comfortable and safe while he went to take command of the Eighth Cavalry Brigade at Fort Bliss, Texas. Then tragedy struck: on August 27, 1915, Pershing's wife and three daughters were burned to death in a raging fire. Of his children, only Warren, age six, survived.

Pershing was devastated. Returning to Fort Bliss after burying nearly his whole family, he smothered his grief by throwing himself wholly into his duties. Whether or not this tragedy influenced his selection to command the Punitive Expedition, the challenge turned out to be a tonic for the shattered Pershing.

Pershing's mission, to capture Villa, was almost chimerical but not quite. If certain assumptions held, it just might be accomplished. The president assumed, first of all, that Carranza wanted to capture Villa and would therefore render the Americans his full and unstinting cooperation. That in turn presupposed that Carranza would allow Pershing to ship men and supplies over the Mexican Northwestern Railway. Wilson's third assumption, the most unrealistic of all, was that the Mexican people in the region would be eager to help capture Villa.

None of these assumptions even approached the true state of affairs, but it would take considerable time and diplomatic bickering before the Americans would realize their fallacy. Carranza had no intention of cooperating with the Americans, especially of granting the use of the Northwestern Railway, though at first he hesitated to say so directly. And any prospect of help from the people of Chihuahua was nil. The Mexicans, it is said, were about as eager to help the Americans in capturing their hero as were the people of Sherwood Forest to help the Sheriff of Nottingham capture Robin Hood. So Pershing would have no help from anyone outside the U.S. government. But it was not for him to argue on the feasibility of his mission but to execute it.

Pershing's organization for the expedition, governed largely by the locations of the various component troop units, followed closely the general outline of Funston's first order. The expedition would consist of three brigades, two of cavalry and one of infantry. The main body, comprising one cavalry and one infantry brigade, would cross the border at Columbus, and the other brigade, all cavalry, would leave from Culberson's Ranch, about 80 miles to the west. The two brigades would converge on Casas Grandes, 120 miles into Mexico from Columbus.

If luck smiled on the undertaking, these columns might surprise and capture Villa even before they reached Casas Grandes. The Second Cavalry Brigade, which left from Culberson's Ranch, held the best promise of trapping Villa, so Pershing decided to accompany that force in person.*

The commanding officer of the Second Cavalry Brigade was an ideal man to lead a swift cavalry strike. Colonel George A. Dodd was a hard-bitten, sixty-three-year-old trooper, due to retire in a couple of months. Because of Dodd's advanced age, Pershing had harbored some doubts at first about retaining him in command. Dodd, however, insisted that he could "outride any man in his command," and his unexcelled reputation as a professional cavalryman led Pershing to take a chance on him. Dodd's brigade consisted of George A. Custer's old Seventh Cavalry Regiment, the "Garryowens," and Pershing's Tenth Cavalry, the Buffalo Soldiers.

Pershing selected Lieutenant Colonel De Rosey C. Cabell, Tenth Cavalry, to be his chief of staff. Cabell was a fortunate choice. Like any good chief of staff, the fifty-four-year-old trooper was well equipped to anticipate Pershing's desires without asking him and, therefore, able to represent his chief when necessary—a privilege he never abused. Unfortunately for the record, Cabell's version of the Punitive Expedition has been lost to history. In the National Archives in Washington, one finds the following note:

> In reply to your letter of Aug. 25th . . . I wish to say that two months ago I burned all my husband's official papers. Had I known that the War Department wanted them I would have been glad to have sent them. Sincerely, /s/Martha Otis Cabell, Aug 31—1927.

As preparations for the Punitive Expedition began, the atmosphere among American troops along the Mexican border became electric. This promised to be the first action the army had seen since the Philippine Insurrection, some fifteen years earlier. Everyone wanted to go along. But not every regiment in the Southwest was

---

*The First Cavalry Brigade (Colonel James Lockett) consisted of the Eleventh Cavalry, the Thirteenth Cavalry, and Battery C, Sixth Field Artillery. The Second Cavalry Brigade (Colonel George A. Dodd) consisted of the Seventh Cavalry, Tenth Cavalry, and Battery B, Sixth Field Artillery. The First Infantry Brigade (Colonel John H. Beacon) consisted of the Sixth Infantry, the Sixteenth Infantry, two companies of the Second Engineer Battalion, and signal, ambulance, medical, and aviation units.

Frank Tompkins, *Chasing Villa* (Harrisburg, 1934), pp. 72–73.

scheduled to participate, and one of those left out was the Eighth Cavalry, at El Paso.

One of the lieutenants in the Eighth Cavalry resolved that he, for one, was not going to be left behind. George S. Patton, Jr., was willing to pull every string necessary in order to get his way. It so happened that Patton had a personal tie to General Pershing; his sister Nita, though twenty-five years younger than Pershing, had been keeping proper company with the general in El Paso, helping him sustain the grief of the loss of his family. Lieutenant Patton could not draw too heavily on that relationship to justify favoritism, but he could be a little bold.

Patton was lucky. One of Pershing's regular aides, Lieutenant James L. Collins, was away on temporary duty, and Patton decided to try to go in Collins's stead. Patton was careful to observe propriety, however, and he submitted a proper application through channels, to the adjutant of the Eighth Cavalry. At the same time, Patton went to the adjutant general of the forthcoming expedition and to Pershing's other aide, Lieutenant Martin C. Shallenberger, asking each officer to recommend him. Pershing finally received the word and sent for him.

Patton reported on the evening of March 13, at Columbus. Pershing presented his usual gruff appearance. "Everyone wants to go," he demanded. "Why should I favor you?"

"Because I want to go more than anyone else, sir."

For the moment the general brushed Patton off with a terse "That will do." Patton returned to his quarters and packed his bed roll, ready to report for duty in a moment.

The next morning the telephone rang at 5:00. "Lieutenant Patton, how long will it take you to get ready?" Pershing's voice asked. "Right now," Patton answered.

"Well I'll be goddamned!" Pershing exclaimed. "You are appointed aide."

Not everything else was so easy. When General Pershing arrived at Columbus on March 13, the camp presented a picture of confusion. As the infantry and cavalry troops arrived from various directions, they found nobody to guide them to their campsites. Nobody advised them where to draw supplies; they even lacked official orders.

The supply situation was even worse. Railroad boxcars sat untouched on the railway sidings, because no chief quartermaster was available to designate depots, classify shipments, and sort the freight from unmarked cars. Escort wagon bodies arrived at Columbus without wheels, axles, or whiffle trees. Parts of trucks arrived disassembled without directions, tools, or anyone who knew how to fit them together.

Ordnance and medical supplies were in no better shape, as neither depots nor hospitals were available. Since hospitals were of top priority, desperate medical officers quickly began to assemble the elements of an evacuation field hospital and an ambulance company, but progress was slow.

Communications equipment was also lacking, a situation that would grow serious when units became separated by long distances. No field telegraph wire was on hand, but someone tried, with limited success, to substitute galvanized-iron wire. The pack radio sets for the cavalry units did not inspire confidence. There was some hope for the large wagon sets and tractor transmitters, but such heavy equipment could not accompany the lead cavalry troops.

One unit that gave great promise was the First Aero Squadron, commanded by Captain Benjamin D. Foulois, of the Army Signal Corps. The squadron of eight primitive JN-3 biplanes reached Columbus in midmorning of March 15. Since Columbus was far away from the squadron's home base at San Antonio, Foulois and his men had prudently disassembled its planes and carted them like Tinkertoys on the squadron's open trucks. The aviators began to unload and assemble the planes as soon as they arrived. It was a source of great pride to Foulois that they managed to put together one plane and make a twelve-minute test flight that very day.

That first test flight would be remembered as a landmark in the history of American air power, but the First Aero Squadron's most significant contribution to solving Pershing's problems involved its organic trucking equipment, not its flimsy airplanes. As commander of the only completely motorized unit in Pershing's force, Foulois was soon able to free seven trucks to carry supplies around the camp. He was rewarded by being placed temporarily in charge of all transportation for the expedition.

It added to Pershing's difficulties in organizing the expedition that he was pushed for time. By March 13, the exchange of notes between the United States and Mexico seemed favorable—or at least fuzzy—enough to allow President Wilson to presume Carranza's acquiescence to the entrance of U.S. forces. Frederick Funston, not always the most subordinate of officers, became worried lest some unwelcome new twist in the diplomatic exchange might dim

any chances of a pursuit into Mexico. On the evening of the thirteenth, therefore, Funston sent Pershing orders to cross the border at
6:00 A.M. on the fifteenth.

The same evening, however, a snag appeared. The Mexican officer in charge of the Border Gate, three miles south of Columbus,
declared that he would oppose any American entry into Mexico. He
had orders to do so, the officer insisted, and his personal honor also
dictated such opposition. Since Pershing had been warned to avoid
clashes with Carrancista troops, this Mexican's attitude was a serious
matter. Pershing duly reported the circumstances to Funston.

Funston seemed unimpressed by the prospects of a small fight.
He allowed Pershing to delay his departure only until noon of the
fifteenth. When the Columbus column set out shortly after noon, it
found that the Mexican force at the Border Gate had disappeared. At
least that problem had been averted!

Once Colonel Lockett's First Brigade had crossed the border from Columbus, General Pershing departed by automobile to join the Second
Cavalry Brigade at Culberson's Ranch. It was a long trip, and the dirt
road was narrow and rutted. Along the way, his automobile had an
accident that injured nobody but caused considerable delay. At Culberson's Ranch, Dodd waited dutifully. When Pershing finally arrived, six hours late, the two cavalrymen led the brigade into Mexico,
crossing the border at about 1:00 A.M. on March 16.

The following day, the U.S. Congress passed a resolution. Assuming
the consent of the de facto government of Mexico, it declared that
"the use of the armed forces of the United States is hereby approved."

19

****

Pancho Villa's
Narrow Escape

As Brigadier General John J. Pershing crossed the Mexican border during the early hours of March 16, 1916, he had no idea where Pancho Villa was. He was not even sure that Villa was in northern Chihuahua. After all, even the sketchy reports of the bandit's presence at Columbus were unsubstantiated.

Nevertheless, enough reports placed Villa in the general area that Pershing hoped to trap him quickly. Surprise gave Pershing his best prospect for success. If Villa could not be caught immediately, operations to find him would be drawn out. Pershing would then have to count on Mexican cooperation. A force under General Jacinto Treviño, commanding in Chihuahua, just might seal off the southern border of the state, helping Pershing's cavalry snare him by beating every bush between Treviño in the south and the United States border in the north. But a quick capture, based on surprise, was far preferable.

In any event, Pershing thought it necessary to make plans for an organized search; he would establish a secure camp at Casas Grandes and send out small, fast-flying columns. He selected Casas Grandes because it was the last town considered to be in territory "known" to the Americans. Beyond Casas Grandes, the relatively broad northern plain of Chihuahua breaks up in the Sierra Madre Occidental.

The Casas Grandes area offered another inducement for Pershing. Only two miles to the northeast stood Colonia Dublán, a small Mormon settlement on the railroad from Juárez. The population of Colonia Dublán had diminished in recent months, but it was still a hospitable haven to serve as headquarters for Pershing and some of his troops.

Taken together, Casas Grandes and Colonia Dublán also provided a good location for Pershing's supply depots. The land surrounding them was flat enough to allow Pershing's engineers to construct an airstrip to accommodate his fledgling air force. Pershing had brought along plenty of infantry troops to secure the bases and the airstrip.

But Casas Grandes, Dublán, and the airstrip were part of the long-range plan. The striking arm of Pershing's expedition, on which he pinned his hopes of a quick success, was his cavalry. And to move his cavalry southward in a hurry, Pershing drove Dodd's troopers relentlessly. The Second Brigade marched twenty-five miles in the dark the first night, arriving at Geronimo's Rock at 6:00 A.M. Pershing allowed the men and horses to rest until noon and then had them back on the road for another thirty miles, making a total of fifty-five miles in less than twenty-four hours. On March 17, Pershing's column marched a whopping sixty-eight miles, arriving at the Casas Grandes–Colonia Dublán complex at 8:00 P.M.

This march broke all previous records for endurance. The Second Cavalry Brigade covered the longest distance ever recorded in the annals of the U.S. Cavalry. Moreover, the troops accomplished this under grueling conditions. The terrain was rough and parched, no rain having fallen since July of the previous year. White alkaline dust forced the men to cover their noses and mouths with bandanas. They even found it necessary to spread cloth over the noses of their mounts to preserve some moisture in their nostrils. The air was frigid, for it was only mid-March, and they were at an altitude of five thousand feet. Fortunately, Pershing's men were all seasoned regulars, most of them hardened by years of experience fighting the elements in the West. Less hardy troops could never have held up.

Pershing did not take time to relax upon arrival at Colonia Dublán. The same evening, he accepted an invitation to dinner with the local Mormon bishop, but he then excused himself early. He assembled his staff and stood under a tree, his map illuminated only by a flashlight, to outline his plans to his staff. Those plans did not call for rest and recuperation.

Pershing presumed that Villa had taken refuge in the Mexican state of Chihuahua, somewhere west of Chihuahua City. It is forbidding country, once dramatically described as "a stage five hundred miles long and a hundred miles across which snow, sandstorms, tropical heat and sharp cold." This territory is roughly the size of the states of Virginia, North Carolina, and South Carolina, with roads so winding that a north–south air distance of about 350 miles translates into 550 miles on the ground, or about the distance between Washington and Atlanta.

The land was primitive. Even today, over seventy-five years later, the small towns of the region remain connected to each other only by narrow, dusty roads. And it is rugged. In the western part of Chihuahua the Continental Divide runs along the crest of the Sierra Madre Occidental, many of which, over 10,000 feet, rise abruptly from the 5,000-foot plain below.

A rather poetic description ends with the solemn observation "It is a country without grace. A man wishes for a sound. It is a country of no answers." And somewhere in that desolate wasteland John J. Pershing's meager force of ten thousand Americans was ordered to find an individual named Pancho Villa.

As Pershing stood under the tree at Colonia Dublán, he told his staff of some new information that might lead to his quarry. Villa was reported to be resting at a place called San Miguel Babícora, about sixty miles south of their current location. The report was admittedly questionable, but the prospect of nabbing Villa quickly was enticing. Pershing decided to follow up the lead even though his men and horses were exhausted.

One fact about Babícora made that report of Villa's presence seem plausible: Babícora was the site of a vast ranch belonging to the American newspaper magnate William Randolph Hearst. Since the ranch served as a trading post, it seemed logical that Villa could be there for resupply. Furthermore, Babícora was located in Villa territory on a plateau above the Santa María River, the source of Villa's current strength. This river ran northward on the eastern edge of the plateau. On the western side of the Babícora plateau was another valley, less

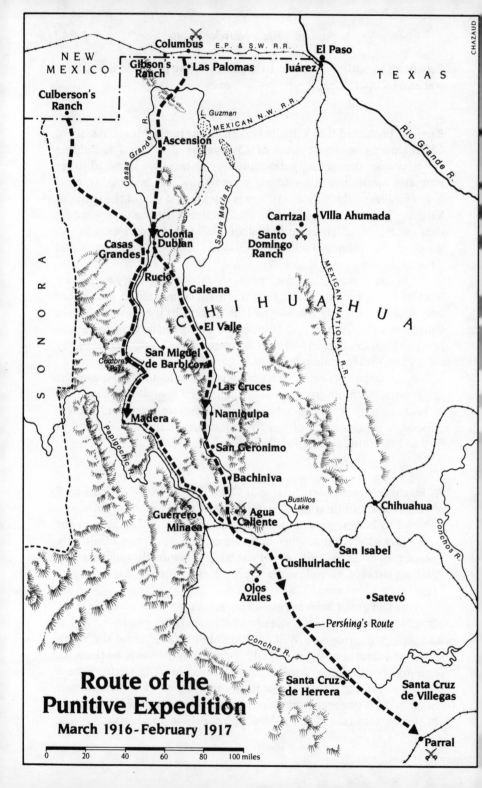

Route of the
Punitive Expedition

March 1916 - February 1917

pronounced but served by a railroad capable of carrying troops. The two valleys converged near Casas Grandes. So Pershing determined to send two forces southward, one up each valley, hoping that they could approach Babícora simultaneously, one from the east and the other from the west.

In the absence of fresh troops to perform this mission, Pershing had no choice but to use Dodd's weary Second Brigade. The infantry-cavalry column from Columbus would not arrive at Casas Grandes until noon on March 20, and Pershing had no intention of waiting that long. But of Dodd's two regiments, only the Seventh Cavalry could be sent right away. The Tenth had traveled 250 miles from Fort Huachuca just to reach Culberson's Ranch; so exhausted were they that not even a hard-driving man like Pershing could order them back into the saddle without some respite.

The Seventh Cavalry would therefore leave for Babícora by way of the Santa María valley right away. The Tenth Cavalry would follow through the western valley by train after a day of rest. Since First Chief Carranza was still vaguely promising cooperation, Pershing ordered an American train from the El Paso & Southwestern Railroad to run on the Mexican Northwestern Railroad track to carry the Tenth Cavalry. With this help, Pershing hoped, the Buffalo Soldiers would catch up with the Seventh in a couple of days.

At 3:00 A.M. on March 18, Colonel James B. Erwin's Seventh Cavalry "Garryowens" trotted out of Casas Grandes with about seven hundred officers and troopers. After a few miles on the trail, the regiment picked up the Santa María River and headed south. It would be out of touch with Pershing for several days.

The train that Pershing had ordered to carry the Tenth Cavalry rumbled into Casas Grandes the next day, March 19. When the quartermaster inspected it, however, the old wood burner turned out to be a wreck. Before it could carry troops and horses, the railroad men would have to hack holes in the sides of the boxcars for ventilation and repair the flooring where hobos had built fires to keep warm. Several hours later, when the train was ready, the Tenth Cavalry loaded up. The men placed their mounts inside the boxcars and lined the tops of the cars with bales of hay to prevent their falling off when asleep. They also demolished a set of loading pens to provide wood to fuel the locomotive. The U.S. government later had to pay the Mexican owner $1,900 for that line of fencing.

Babícora could be approached from three directions. Pershing therefore decided that he needed three rather than only two columns to seal them all off. He divided the Tenth Cavalry into two task forces, each a squadron. One of those squadrons was to dismount from the train at Rucio, only about forty miles from Casas Grandes, and from there to move on Babícora from the north. The other was to ride the train all the way to Madera and approach Babícora from the south. One squadron was to be commanded by Colonel W. C. Brown, the regimental commander; the other, by Major Ellwood Evans.

The railroad scheme was a fiasco from the beginning. The Buffalo Soldiers left Colonia Dublán at 5:30 P.M., March 19, expecting to arrive near Babícora at about daybreak. The conductor, however, refused to stop for fuel at Casas Grandes, fearing raids by Carrancista troops. As a result, the train ran out of firewood at a desolate spot somewhere down the line. Reloaded with wood, it soon ran out of water. Early the next morning, Colonel Brown found it necessary to bribe the exhausted engineer to continue, only to discover that the engine could not pull the twenty-five boxcars up the grade to Rucio. So Brown detrained his squadron at the foot of the hill and left on horseback for Babícora, some seven hours behind his projected schedule.

When Brown's Buffalo Soldiers finally reached Babícora, they found no Villistas. Nor had any Villistas been there at all.

The fate of Major Evans's squadron was even worse. The shortened train was able to reach Rucio, but soon thereafter several of its boxcars overturned at a switchback near the Cumbre Pass. One car rolled down a steep embankment, injuring eleven men, a couple of them badly. Evans cared for the injured men as best he could and ordered the injured horses desaddled and shot. He sent the casualties ahead to Madera on the train but took the rest of his squadron across country directly to Babícora.

The next few days offered plenty of frustration for the Buffalo Soldiers. Every place they stopped they heard rumors regarding the whereabouts of Villa—always false. The Tenth Cavalry would ride for thirty-two days, until April 20, without government supplies, living off the land.

After his first effort to capture Pancho Villa failed, Pershing put his longer-term plan into action. He ordered the Seventh Cavalry to continue its march south up the Santa María River valley and the Tenth Cavalry Buffalo Soldiers to continue down the railway line—but not on the train, of course. Both units were to send detachments to search out the plateau between those two lines. By so doing, Pershing screened a large portion of the Chihuahua plain.

Pershing realized, however, that he could not keep in personal touch with his columns from his headquarters at Colonia Dublán. To coordinate their efforts, he sent Colonel George Dodd, their brigade commander, to accompany them in the field. Dodd left to join the Seventh Cavalry at Galeana on March 21, two days after the Tenth Cavalry had begun its disastrous railroad trip. The Tenth Cavalry would also come under his authority, though he would personally accompany the Seventh.

Pershing had found the right man in Dodd. This veteran officer soon proved that he could indeed, as he had boasted, "outride any of them." And that he did, driving even the hardy Seventh Cavalry to exhaustion.

As Dodd led the Seventh Cavalry up the Santa María valley, he did not know where to search first. At El Valle, the first town he reached after leaving Galeana, he met a Carrancista unit commanded by a Mexican colonel named Salas. Once Salas was convinced that Dodd possessed proper authority to be in Mexico, he seemed willing to help in the effort to trap Villa. Villa, he advised, was probably at Namiquipa, one of the larger towns in the area, located about fifty miles due south. Since Salas seemed to be open in his demeanor, Dodd gambled that the Mexican was telling the truth. After camping at El Valle that night, he broke camp early on March 23 and headed his command toward Namiquipa.

Dodd covered the fifty miles to Namiquipa in one day. That evening, he pitched camp in the nearby hills, intending to attack the town the next day. That night, however, he learned that Villa had left. Dodd checked Namiquipa to confirm that the town was clear of Villistas, but he could not induce the local Carrancista commander to disclose where Villa had gone. Dodd concluded then and there that he was going to receive no real help from the Carrancistas.

As Dodd was pondering his next move, he received a report from Colonel Brown, whose Tenth Cavalry was resupplying and resting back at the Hearst ranch at Babícora. Brown believed that Villa had gone south. Dodd therefore considered it useless to search further in the area where he was. Villa had undoubtedly escaped to the south, so Dodd resolved to pursue him in the Bachíniva–Guerrero area. But first he turned the Seventh Cavalry back toward Babícora for needed refitting.

For two days, March 24–25, the Seventh Cavalry fought its way through a freezing gale to Babícora. The troopers then enjoyed a short rest and resupplied themselves at the Hearst ranch. Their enjoyment was marred, however, by the cold weather in that 7,000-foot altitude; they were only too happy to remount and head for Bachíniva, at the end of the Santa María valley.

On reaching Bachíniva, Dodd received his first credible information: Villa had been involved in a battle at the important military center of Guerrero, about forty miles away.

On March 28, a U.S. Army biplane bumped and skidded to a halt on the rough ground near Bachíniva. Lieutenant Herbert A. Dargue climbed out of the cockpit and delivered a message to Dodd from Pershing. Well aware that Dodd's men and horses had marched fourteen out of the past fifteen days, covering an amazing four hundred miles, Pershing had concluded that they should take a rest. A provisional squadron of the Eleventh Cavalry, under Major Robert L. Howze, would soon arrive in the area to take over Dodd's mission.

Dodd mulled over Pershing's message and decided to pass up the chance for a rest, at least for the moment. He had learned that Villa was not far distant. So he gave Dargue a message to take back to headquarters. He would "proceed farther south and continue in such touch as is possible to attain with Villa. At any rate, until fresh troops arrive."

Where had Villa been all this time? Accounts vary, but most evidence indicates that he had returned to the Santa María valley right after his raid on Columbus two weeks earlier. According to one witness, Villa stopped to rest at El Valle and there called for volunteers to join him. Forty men stepped forward, and those who refused were immediately placed under guard. Villa did not release his prisoners; he marched them up the Santa María valley to Namiquipa along with his band. Villa arrived there the night of the eighteenth, just as Pershing was entering Colonia Dublán.

By March 20, Villa had led his men thirty-five miles to the vicinity of Guerrero, on the Mexican Northwestern Railroad line, there to rest. His force had now been reduced to four hundred men, many of them very recent "volunteers." Villa's *dorados* were nearly gone; only sixty of them had survived the killing grounds of Celaya, Agua Prieta, and Hermosillo.

At 4:00 A.M. on March 28, Villa's band surprised the sleeping Carrancistas at Guerrero and chased the frightened soldiers out of town without firing a shot. He was not so successful, however, at the little village of San Isidro, across the valley. There the alert garrison, reinforced by many of the Carrancistas who had fled Guerrero, repulsed the Villistas. Soon a fight was under way between the Villistas and the remnants of the two Carrancista garrisons.

At this point, a twist of fate saved Villa from imminent capture by the Yankees: he was wounded by his own men. Because of the difficulty of the fight at Guerrero, Villa had issued rifles and ammunition to the unwilling "volunteers" he had taken at El Valle, expecting them to join the battle on his side. That they did—ostensibly. But in the firefight one enterprising prisoner spied Villa's huge bulk bounding forward, and he shot not at the Carrancistas but at Villa. Down went the Centaur of the North, his right shin shattered just below the knee.*

Villa was out of action, in severe pain; doctors removed splinters of bone from his wound and bound his leg in a splint. Shortly after midnight, he was carried out of Guerrero by wagon, headed toward Parral, with an escort of only 150 men.

Thus Villa had left Guerrero to the north by the morning of March 29, as Dodd approached from the south.

Colonel George Dodd had allowed the men of the Seventh Cavalry to rest and refit for a few hours at Bachíniva on March 28. At 11:00 P.M., they swung into their saddles for the night march to Guerrero, with high hopes of catching Villa. Unfortunately for the Americans, Dodd's previously reliable guides now found themselves in unfamiliar country. Only his chief guide, J. B. Barker, had been to Guerrero before, and that had been some time earlier. Dodd attempted to press local men into service, but even bribery could not make them cooperative, so Dodd decided to follow Barker's circuitous route. His command therefore did not reach Guerrero until 6:00 A.M. on March 29, much later than he had hoped.

The town of Guerrero lay west of the railroad, in a horseshoe-shaped canyon, with the open end to the north, hidden from the view of Dodd's column as it moved from the east around to attack the

---

*The prisoners later claimed that they had intended to kill Villa and then join the enemy, but at just that moment the Carrancistas gave way and ran. All the prisoners could do was to pretend that the shot had been a mistake and declare their loyalty to Villa.

southern end. The Villistas, however, had detected Dodd's horses as they struggled over the rough ground. They had predicted Dodd's intentions long before he arrived. Most of them therefore slipped out of town to the north.

The "battle" of Guerrero amounted to little. Dodd attempted to approach the town by first occupying the three sides of the horseshoe and later closing the open end. He sent one squadron to the left in order to sever Villa's line of retreat westward, while the rest of the regiment proceeded northward along the eastern edge. The two columns might have closed the northern gap had they taken their prey by surprise. As it was, Dodd's men saw Villistas escaping into the northeast before his men could shut the trap. Dodd sent a force in pursuit, but the gesture was futile. The Seventh Cavalry troopers were forced to break off the chase; their mounts were too worn out to go farther.

Pancho Villa had escaped a "near-run thing," as Wellington described Waterloo. His draftees had unwittingly saved him from capture by wounding him. But the loyalty of other people helped him, by keeping Dodd in the dark and heading him in wrong directions. Had Dodd known how to go directly from Namiquipa to Guerrero, he would have encountered Villa's wagon along the way.

The Americans would never again come so close.

Despite the disappointment, Colonel George A. Dodd's men had performed a remarkable feat. And Dodd received the recognition that was his due. Just before his retirement from the army three months later, he was promoted to the grade of brigadier general, and his deeds were highly praised in the halls of Congress.

But Pancho Villa was still at large.

20

****

Colonia Dublán

While George A. Dodd was driving his troopers through the mountains of Chihuahua in search of Pancho Villa, Black Jack Pershing* was organizing his base of operations at Colonia Dublán for the long haul. In order to conduct a methodical search, he needed a full staff to gather intelligence regarding Villa's whereabouts, to draw up plans, to arrange for supply, and to deal with the demands of Washington. This big task did not daunt Pershing. He was a veteran of numerous similar campaigns in the Philippines.

Besides his reliable chief of staff, the "shrewd and tough horse-soldier" De Rosey C. Cabell, Pershing was also fortunate in his selection of an adjutant, Major John L. Hines, forty-seven years of age and destined to succeed Pershing as army chief of staff nearly a decade later. Intelligence functions were performed by Major James A. Ryan, detached from the Thirteenth Cavalry. But Pershing's staff lacked an operations and training officer. Pershing and Cabell intended to do their own operational planning.†

---

*Pershing's nickname, intended to be unflattering by the West Point cadets who gave it to him, turned out to be the affectionate name by which he is best known.

†Since the reorganization of the army staff in 1903, the standard staff had been

Pershing had no way of knowing how long the Punitive Expedition would be in Mexico, nor could he predict how far he would have to penetrate into Chihuahua. So for a while, at least, he determined to keep his headquarters at Colonia Dublán, where the members of the Mormon colony welcomed the protection of his force. Pershing's supply base would be situated at nearby Casas Grandes, a couple of miles down the railroad. There he would store supplies, including food, ammunition, guns, and organizational equipment. The names Casas Grandes and Dublán were used interchangeably in referring to Pershing's base.

The most vital problem facing Pershing was that of supply. The capture of Villa was, in the final analysis, secondary to the survival of his men. Providing food, water, forage, and ammunition for a force of ten thousand men would be difficult. Sufficient supplies were on hand in the United States, and they could readily be delivered to Columbus and El Paso; but getting them to Casas Grandes and beyond was another matter. To do so, Pershing would have to resort to all means available—rail, truck, wagons, and muleback.

It would have been ideal, of course, to deliver supplies via the Mexican National Railroad from El Paso through Juárez and the city of Chihuahua to some forward supply depot farther south. Carranza, however, continued to withhold permission for the use of the National Railroad, without prohibiting it outright. Even though army agents were able to arrange some delivery of supplies by railroad as far as Casas Grandes, Pershing could never establish a railroad capacity that even came near to meeting his tonnage requirements.

Nevertheless, Pershing's quartermaster reported that the supply needs at Casas Grandes were met "to a considerable extent" by rail shipments from El Paso. Hay, oats, flour, salt, building materials, wood, sugar, potatoes, and onions—an odd mixture—were sent by this means.

Truck transportation of army supplies came into its own with the Punitive Expedition. Pershing established a quartermaster base at Columbus, on the site of the old Camp Furlong, but since motor transport was new at the time, the army was deplorably short of trucks. Bold action on the part of General Hugh Scott, army chief of staff in Washington, made up a portion of the deficiency.

---

organized along the following lines: G1 (personnel, including staff organization and command posts); G2 (intelligence, including air reconnaissance); G3 (operations and training); and G4 (supply and logistics).

Concerned about the problem, Scott called in the quartermaster general. "Have you enough trucks to supply Pershing from Columbus with food, clothing, and ammunition?" he asked.

"No," answered the quartermaster general. It would take $450,000 of as yet unappropriated funds to buy them.

According to Scott, he then took matters into his own hands. "Send right out and buy those trucks, with the necessary garages and mechanics," he ordered. "Send them by express to Columbus. . . ."

Scott informed Secretary of War Newton D. Baker about what he had done. "You will have to use your good offices with the President, Mr. Secretary," he said, "to keep me out of jail. I have just expended $450,000 of public money that had not been appropriated by Congress—a penitentiary offense."

"Ho," answered Baker. "That's nothing. If anybody goes to jail I'll be the man." The trucks were sent.

Army motor transportation was not formalized before the quartermaster at Columbus put his hand to doing so. Because motor transportation units did not exist in early 1916, the quartermaster at first resorted to organizing each convoy individually, generally assigning about thirty trucks per train. Each train included security troops and cooks as well as drivers and mechanics. Shortly thereafter, the quartermaster organized trucks and drivers into standard truck companies. The Columbus base soon included maintenance shops. The drivers were required to be soldiers, since they were operating under combat conditions, but the quartermaster staffed the machine shops with civilian mechanics, because mechanical skills were in short supply among regular soldiers.

The efforts paid off. Ten thousand tons of supplies eventually made their way by truck into Mexico during 1916, much of the cargo consisting of forage to feed the animals that would carry supplies southward from Casas Grandes.

Organizing motor transport was no mean feat, and General Pershing, in his report, saw fit to laud the quartermaster handsomely. Noting that some of the trucks operated at a distance of four hundred miles from Columbus over "deplorable" Mexican roads that ran "at random over the dry alkaline flats and sandy plains of the desert," he wrote, "Contemplation of the supply of an army under such adverse conditions might dishearten the most courageous, hence actual accomplishment under the circumstances is all the more creditable to the officers concerned. . . . The successful handling of supplies by truck trains . . . has been steadily developed to a degree never before attained in our service." Even allowing for the military's penchant for hyperbole in giving praise, the delivery of supplies by truck transport was a remarkable achievement.

Nevertheless, Pershing still had to rely to a large extent on the heretofore time-honored army means of supply—wagons and mules.* But not even animal transport was easy. Roads depicted as adequate on the available maps turned out on inspection to be nothing but trails; during wet weather, they became mires that hardened into ruts when they dried out. Forage was scant in that high country, and a good portion of the animals' carrying capacity had to be devoted to their own food. When the far-ranging cavalry squadrons set out in pursuit of Pancho Villa, they were forced to live off the land.

The fledgling air service, for which Pershing held high hopes, turned out to be a severe disappointment. The small air section that Captain Benjamin Foulois had brought to Columbus from San Antonio consisted of only eight tired aircraft, totally inadequate for the missions they were intended to perform.

This development reflected incredible shortsightedness on the part of the U.S. government. Although invented in the United States, the airplane was neglected in this country while it was being developed as a potent weapon of war in Europe. In contrast to the dangerous aircraft the Americans were flying, European commanders on the Western Front in 1916 had planes available that could reconnoiter, photograph, and use radio to adjust artillery. Their machine guns fired through their propellers, and the European aircraft could engage in dogfights with each other and even perform bombardment missions. These aircraft could reach speeds exceeding 110 miles per hour and climb to altitudes of 15,000 feet. Nevertheless, the United States seemed so oblivious to these military applications that Pershing was denied the asset of an air arm throughout his campaign in Mexico.

The deficiencies of the First Aero Squadron were not the fault of Benjamin Foulois, who had campaigned for improved equipment ever since his days as a flying student under Orville Wright. By the age of thirty-four, Foulois had risen through the ranks of the army to become

---

*A wagon company in 1916 consisted of one wagon boss and three assistants (all sergeants). It also included one cook, one saddler, two blacksmiths, and twenty-eight soldiers. It was equipped with twenty-seven wagons, 112 mules, and six horses. See Frank Tompkins, *Chasing Villa* (Harrisburg, 1934), p. 75.

the first American dirigible pilot. From November 1909 to spring 1911, Foulois was the only pilot and navigator in the army's heavier-than-air division. At that time, students in training suffered one fatality for every hundred hours of flight, and though the United States had produced good aeronautical engineers—Glenn Martin, Thomas Morse, Glenn Curtiss, and others—the U.S. government had spent less than half a million dollars for aeronautics between 1908 and 1913, a period during which Germany spent $28 million.

Foulois's awareness of his equipment's inadequacies was heightened by a bad experience in late November 1915. As he led the six airplanes of the First Aero Squadron from Fort Sill, Oklahoma, to Fort Sam Houston, Texas, the formation was scattered. His six planes managed to reach their destination, but only after seven days of flying and numerous forced landings.

That sobering trip came barely four months before Foulois was ordered to take his squadron from San Antonio to Columbus. He and General Funston were wise when they decided to disassemble the planes and send them by truck. The 520 miles would have been too far for them to fly.

On March 19, four days after their arrival at Columbus, Foulois and his squadron completed assembling all eight of the First Aero Squadron's planes. They tested the performance of their aircraft at the 4,000-foot altitude of Columbus and found no adverse effects. Therefore, when Pershing ordered the squadron to join him at Casas Grandes, Foulois did not delay. His squadron took off at 5:10 P.M., March 19.

Foulois's departure at sundown may have been a tribute to his bravery and dedication, but the decision to go was imprudent, to say the least. The JN-3's ("Jennies") were unsuitable for flights longer than fifty miles, and the distance was well over a hundred miles. Furthermore, none of the pilots except T. F. Dodd had ever flown at night, and none had any idea where Casas Grandes was. Without maps, instruments, or landing lights, Foulois's pilots navigated by following the plane ahead; the field at Casas Grandes was to be identified by fires lit on the runways.

None of the Jennies made it to Casas Grandes that night. Of the eight planes that took off, one developed engine trouble right away; four made it to Ascensión (about halfway), one to Janos, a little farther, and one to Ojo Caliente. The eighth crashed at Pearson. Since the last plane was badly damaged, Foulois permanently lost two of his eight Jennies in a single night. Fortunately, all the pilots survived.

Despite Pershing's concern for the safety of his young airmen, he intended to use them. So on March 20, as the remnants of Foulois's squadron came one at a time into Casas Grandes, he sent Dodd and Foulois off again to locate the units of the Tenth Cavalry that had run into trouble aboard the train at Cumbre Pass.

For risky missions such as this, Foulois always flew with Dodd. Dodd would handle the controls, and Foulois would perform the more dangerous job of observer, sitting in front. On this mission, Foulois learned how inadequate the test flight four days earlier had been. Here the Sierra Madre rose to elevations of 10,000 feet—and to 12,000 feet an hour away from Casas Grandes. "Whirlwinds and terrific vertical currents of air" forced them to turn back to their base after traveling only twenty-five miles.

On the following day, the same two pilots had better luck: they landed at a spot near Colonel Erwin's Seventh Cavalry and transmitted his request for supplies back to Pershing. The next day, six supply-laden trucks lumbered out of Casas Grandes to find Erwin.

Despite this and other limited successes, Foulois pulled no punches in making his plight known:

> The aeroplanes are not capable of meeting the present military needs, incident to this expedition. Their low power motors and limited climbing ability with the necessary military load makes it impossible to safely operate any one of these machines in the vicinity of the mountains which cover the present theatre of operations. . . . Even the united efforts of the entire technical ability in this command cannot make these aeroplanes suitable to meet present military needs.

Foulois then pleaded for ten new airplanes—two each of five different makes. Pershing approved the request and sent it along to General Funston, who passed it on to Washington. There it was turned down by Secretary Newton D. Baker with the terse comment "All airplanes available for service are already with the Pershing Expedition."

Since the equipment assigned to the First Aero Squadron could never have negotiated the Sierra Madre range, Foulois recommended to Pershing that his planes be used to supplement the other means of communication—trucks, motorcycles, and radio telegraph—in keeping contact with the key points on Pershing's main supply route. Because that line stretched from Columbus all the way through Casas

Grandes to Namiquipa, the new method of employment called for concentrating the squadron at Namiquipa, the advanced base. The planes would then focus on communications between Namiquipa and the forward troops. A telegraph line would soon link Namiquipa with Dublán and Casas Grandes.

Pershing approved the plan, and it went into effect on April 1, 1916. Foulois retained his faith in his airplanes' ability to contribute, but for the moment their contribution would be limited.

On the afternoon of Thursday, March 23, a small contingent of newspaper reporters bounced into the headquarters area of Colonia Dublán. These journalists were not the most famous ones—at least not yet. The Battle of Verdun, raging in eastern France, relegated even the Punitive Expedition to secondary significance. Nevertheless, the public was beginning to show an interest in Pershing's challenge, so the stories filed in Mexico would at least appear in papers throughout the United States, even if they did not receive top billing. For young reporters on the way up, this offered a great opportunity.

Among the new arrivals was the twenty-nine-year-old Floyd Gibbons, a man later dubbed the "premier war correspondent of his generation." Gibbons was familiar with Mexican affairs and formerly on friendly terms with Pancho Villa, who had allegedly outfitted a railroad car for Gibbons's personal use. However, the greatest impression on the public would be made not by Gibbons, but by Frank B. Elser, correspondent for the *New York Times*. Not only did Elser provide occasional headlines for the nation's most prestigious newspaper; he also wrote, four years later, an article on the expedition that has become the most quoted account of that period.

Elser and his associates were greeted by a bleak scene. The countryside, except for the cottonwoods on the banks of the Rio Casas Grandes, was sheer desert, and a sandstorm raged among the tents and wagons. The tents, which Elser described as "innumerable triangular little piles of sand," were double-staked and stone-weighted to keep them from blowing away. Disgruntled men lay flat on their bellies inside the tents; most of them wore sand goggles and kerchiefs tied over their mouths. As the men leaned against the wind, they appeared to Elser to resemble things under water.

The correspondents arrived only one week after Pershing's troopers had departed from Columbus, and already the Seventh, Tenth, and Thirteenth cavalries were scouring the countryside in search of

Villa. Pershing's headquarters was out of touch with them most of the time. The field telegraph of insulated wire that snaked its way across the desert ran back to Columbus, not southward. As Elser described the communications line, "where the general was, it ended."

All the correspondents considered Pershing's censorship to be strict, but they saw the need to cooperate and put up with it in good humor. To Major Hines, as adjutant, fell the touchy assignment of censoring the dispatches. Pershing's instructions to Hines were simple: he wanted nothing "derogatory to the Expedition or anything informatory to Villa to be sent out by reporters." Hines did his job conscientiously and "wielded a very heavy blue pencil, even searching photographs for any items of intelligence value to Villa."

Nevertheless, the correspondents found the aloof and dignified Pershing to be a man they could sympathize with. To their astonishment, he even had a sense of humor. Elser described one incident with relish:

At dusk a few days after [we arrived], the general issued to correspondents the first communiqué of the campaign. Orderlies had erected a wind-break of cottonwood and willow-brush near his tent, and standing beside it, his campaign hat pulled well down on his head and a campfire at his back—it must be remembered that Chihuahua evenings have sting in March—he summarized the troop movements to date and traced Villa's line of retreat to and beyond the town of Namiquipa, where [Villa] had met and defeated the Carranza command.

"Our troops seem to be pressing him," said the general, "but I won't hazard any predictions. Villa is no fool. It may be that the campaign has just started."

A scout in a red shirt, a real border character, albeit he looked more like a movie one, glanced up from where he squatted on his haunches, chewing a straw.

"As I figure it, General," he said, "we've got Villa entirely surrounded—on one side."

He allowed in his drawl just the requisite pause. Will Rogers couldn't have done better.

Pershing laughed; everybody did. It brought the delivery of the communiqué to an end. . . .

By the evening of March 27, Pershing could tolerate his isolation from the lead cavalry units no longer. Here he was, marooned at Casas

Grandes, depending on air couriers to communicate with Dodd and others to the south—this at a time when Dodd seemed to be closing in on Villa. Pershing therefore decided to move on to San Geronimo Ranch, 110 miles south, where he could be in closer touch.

Pershing's move was not only bold; it bordered on the insubordinate. Since telegraph wire could never be laid through the mountains to San Geronimo, his displacement would cut him off from all communications with Washington. To keep Funston and Washington mollified, if not happy, Pershing left his chief of staff, De Rosey Cabell, in charge of his main headquarters at Dublán.

The command group that Pershing took with him when he left on March 28 was the smallest he considered necessary to conduct operations. It consisted of Major Ryan (intelligence); Lieutenant Patton (aide); a stenographer; Johnnie Booker (cook); three drivers; and four riflemen for security. Frank Elser, with two other correspondents, followed Pershing in a battered secondhand car.

As the small convoy set out and members of the party gazed back on the adobe shacks of Casas Grandes, someone spied another car, speeding as fast as it could go. In it were two correspondents, one of whom was Floyd Gibbons. They had bought an old vehicle from some "wandering spirit," paying for it with a check written on wrapping paper. The entourage that would accompany Pershing to the limits of Chihuahua was now complete.

To Pershing and the military members of his command group, this departure from base camp was no great novelty. But to the correspondents—"bandoliered, pistoled, draggled with paper, typewriters, cameras, canteens, tents, and an eye-catching assortment of Fords, Dodges, and Hudsons somehow purloined in El Paso"—it was something new.

Soldiers and reporters alike were leaving Dublán on a dangerous but heady adventure.

21

****

Gunfight at Parral

Young Modesto Nevares was feeling very lucky. As one of the unwilling conscripts Villa had taken at El Valle, he had faced a future that looked bleak, to say the least. But he had now been made a wagoneer. Driving a wagon was easier than walking; besides, this freer activity might afford him a chance to escape. But not for the moment; his wagon was selected to carry the wounded Pancho Villa to Parral, far away.

As the guerrilla leader was hoisted into his wagon, Nevares was unmoved by his pitiable condition. Villa's shattered leg, Nevares noticed, had been bathed in a strong disinfectant and wrapped in cotton, his trousers torn off to the hip, the limb wrapped in splints and bandages. From time to time as the wagon creaked along, Nevares glanced around. He observed that Villa's leg was beginning to turn black above and below his wound. Villa was lapsing into a coma, punctuated by moments of fear. Every time the wagon hit a rock, Villa would curse and cry like a child.

The man caring for Villa was his brother-in-law, Manuel Corral. After a time, Corral decided that his chief might ride more comfortably on a litter. So he called together a detail of men, fashioned a litter out of four poles, and lifted Villa onto it. Nevares was told to follow in the wagon. Villa was, in the young Mexican's words, "the most scared man I ever saw."

Corral did not allow his sense of family responsibility toward Villa to dampen his own lust and greed. One night, when the party reached the Rancho Cienégita, Corral made advances to the overseer's wife. When the frightened couple resisted, Corral ordered them locked in a house and riddled it with bullets. The overseer was killed and his wife wounded. Then Corral stole their savings. Nevares later heard that Corral had removed some 2,500 silver pesos.

Nevares's account of Villa's tribulations ends at the point where the party reached the Rancho Casa Colorado, about halfway to Parral. The opening he had hoped for suddenly appeared, so he and a friend ducked off and fled, eventually making it home to El Valle.

As Pershing bumped along in his rented touring car, he and his small staff found the trip fairly easy at first. There were no real roads to follow, but the trails were well identified; Dodd and others had passed through the territory only a couple of days earlier. Pershing's personal "headquarters" consisted of a box he occasionally plunked down in front of the car's headlights. Living was far from luxurious; everyone slept on the ground without a tent; Pershing had allowed himself only one blanket, so he doubled up with Lieutenant Patton to sleep, sharing an extra blanket and body warmth. But no adverse conditions could prevent the general from shaving every morning; Black Jack Pershing would never let his men see him with a stubble of beard.

Pershing entered the Santa María River valley at a point near Dublán. He then followed the valley south toward Namiquipa by way of El Valle. This was the road he intended to use as his main supply route, as he planned to establish his advance base at Namiquipa. For part of the way, Pershing could maintain radio contact with his main headquarters at Dublán, so at El Valle he greeted the newspaper correspondents at breakfast on the morning of March 29 with hopeful words: "I think we've got Villa." Almost as he was saying that, George Dodd was attacking the Villistas at Guerrero. Pershing did not wait for further news. He continued on to Namiquipa and then thirty miles farther to San Geronimo Ranch, near Bachíniva.

Pershing reached the ranch late on March 30. He and his party soon discovered that he had picked a poor location, at least from the viewpoint of physical comfort. San Geronimo sits at an altitude of 7,500 feet in the foothills of the Sierra Madre, and a sandstorm mixed with snow greeted the party. Eyes, hair, and clothing filled with sand, which cut through outer garments like a knife, filling boots and even underclothing. The horses, when able, turned their backs to the wind and stood with their heads down, like cattle before a blizzard.

That evening, Pershing learned the details of Dodd's fight at Guerrero, and the circumstances of Villa's departure from that town convinced him that Villa had fled to the north. Hoping that he had his quarry trapped, Pershing placed three of his units in positions astride the main north–south trails—Dodd and the Seventh Cavalry were to stay at Guerrero; Tompkins's squadron of the Thirteenth Cavalry was to take position at Providencia, near Guerrero; and Brown's Tenth Cavalry was to wait at Bachíniva, on the east. With those three escape routes blocked, Pershing expected Major Robert L. Howze's Eleventh Cavalry, coming down from the north, to trap Villa in a vise—provided that Villa was located somewhere north of Guerrero. Unfortunately for the success of Pershing's plan, Villa had already made his escape to the south.

The newspaper correspondents with Pershing were soon caught up in his optimism. Elser, carried away, prognosticated that Villa "may come this way, right up the valley, like a hare in a lane. . . . An airplane has just lighted, and *when he takes flight again, he will carry this dispatch, which may or may not reach New York before Villa is dead or a prisoner.*"

Pershing read Elser's dispatch in the back of his car. When he reached the last sentence, he shook his head and frowned. "You fellows mustn't be too sanguine," he said. "It may require weeks, perhaps months. It's like trying to catch a rat in a cornfield."

In the meantime, the Mexicans in Chihuahua, especially the Carrancistas, were becoming ever more resentful of Pershing's penetration so deep into their territory. The Americans had already suspected as much, but the first overt sign was the way the people of Chihuahua City treated Pershing's chief aviators, Benjamin Foulois and Herbert Dargue. Assigned to deliver dispatches by air to that city, Foulois had prudently written two copies of the message. He carried one copy in each of two airplanes, which were to land on opposite sides of the city.

The precaution was wise. One of Foulois's planes was actually fired upon as it landed. Foulois himself was arrested and marched into town, surrounded by large, angry mobs. But an American in the crowd reported his plight, so as Foulois was cooling his heels in the city jail, the American consul arrived and secured his release.

The American airmen were harassed again as they left the city, and at the airstrip they found that someone had damaged the planes with knife cuts and cigarette burns. The portent for future relations with the Mexicans was anything but promising.

Although concerned about the attitude of the people in Chihuahua, Pershing had a more pressing concern. A sizable Mexican force under a maverick Mexican general, Luis Herrera, was located somewhere in his vicinity, and Pershing did not know what he was up to. Herrera had just been deposed as governor of Chihuahua by First Chief Venustiano Carranza, and he had simply led his command out of Chihuahua City, disappearing somewhere in the countryside. Herrera had publicly denied any intention of joining the Villistas, but nobody knew whether he was telling the truth.

Pershing was well aware of Herrera's disappearance, and he kept his eyes open as he drove to San Geronimo, but Herrera had not been seen up to then. Now Herrera suddenly appeared at San Geronimo with an escort of about two hundred men. Pershing was uneasy. He had retained a security detachment of only about forty troopers when he sent the Tenth Cavalry from San Geronimo to entrap Villa at Bachíniva. As Pershing's party watched, Herrera and his men cautiously approached the American camp, apparently suspecting a trap.

Finally, Herrera led his group into Pershing's enclosure, and the general met them with elaborate ceremony. He sent orderlies to hold the Mexicans' horses as they dismounted, and Pershing himself strode out to grasp Herrera by the hand. Introductions were made all around, and Pershing's cook, Booker, swept the camp litter aside, creating a clear space. The conferees gathered in a semicircle and sat on boxes and gas cans.

The correspondent Frank Elser was present at this strange meeting, eagerly taking notes. The Mexicans, he observed, were all armed "with double rows of cartridges, spurred as only Mexicans can equip their heels, and riding pinto, roan, gray, sorrel, black, white, and bay mounts and weighted down with accoutrements."

Elser also noticed that Herrera's officers, nearly all of them in their thirties and forties, were alert, watchful, and curious. They laughed and smiled easily. Elser remarked on their white teeth. They spoke so softly that Elser could hardly hear them from only ten feet away.

Herrera's purpose in coming was obviously to elicit some commitment from Pershing as to his future intentions. What, Herrera asked, did Pershing know of Villa's whereabouts? Did Pershing believe that Villa had succumbed to his wound? How many men did Pershing have? *How much farther south were Pershing's men going?* That last question made Elser and others sit up and take notice.

Pershing gave no direct answers. He refused to disclose the details of his dispositions, and he countered questions with questions. When asked about his troops, he in turn asked about Herrera's.

Finally, Herrera tired of the exchange. He could see from the general's manner that "he was not a garrulous sort of person," so he suddenly ended the parley and rode away.

The meeting with Herrera prompted Pershing to reconsider his situation. The Mexican had avoided disclosing his own attitudes about Pershing's presence, but he obviously did not welcome it. Pershing, himself a man of honor, assumed that if Herrera were hostile, he would say so, but he now began to have serious doubts. He suspected that all the Carrancista officers—certainly the ones the Americans had encountered—had known of Villa's whereabouts but had made no effort to subdue him. The villages along the Santa María valley, Pershing acknowledged, were hotbeds of Villista sympathizers—the same towns that had furnished Villa with the men for the Columbus raid. Many of the people, "would consider it a national disgrace if the Americans should capture Villa." So Pershing now concluded that he would receive no Carrancista assistance. He would have to catch Villa on his own.

Major Frank Tompkins, Thirteenth Cavalry, lived and breathed the mounted arm of the service. An aggressive soldier, with the zest for fast movement that characterizes a good trooper, Tompkins seems to have savored every minute of the Mexican campaign. His later written account of the Punitive Expedition provides such encyclopedic detail that it has come to be recognized as the authority to whom all others defer.

According to Tompkins, Pershing sent for him on the evening of March 31, at San Geronimo. As the two of them sat by a fire, Pershing had one thing on his mind: "Tompkins, where is Villa?"

"General, I don't know, but I would like mighty well to go find out where he is."

"Where would you go?"

"I would head for Parral and would expect to cut his trail before reaching there."

"Why?"

"The history of Villa's bandit days shows that when hard pressed he invariably holes up in the mountains in the vicinity of Parral. He has friends in that region," said Tompkins, now feeling somewhat on the spot.

Before the talk ended, Tompkins had boasted that his small squadron of two troops, if provided with a dozen additional mules, could move faster than a larger command, could live off the land, and could conceal itself easily. A bonus: the squadron's small size would tempt Villa to attack it.

Tompkins was sure that Villa had gone south. The various Villista bands roaming around the San Geronimo area, he insisted, were there only to keep the Americans occupied while the wounded Villa was transported to Parral.

Typically, Pershing said little in response to this presentation, but Tompkins felt that he had made an impression.

The Battle of Agua Caliente

The night that Pershing sat conferring with Frank Tompkins was cruel for all the American commands in the high plateaus of Chihuahua. Wind-driven snows beat men and horses so severely that by the next morning all were dropping in their tracks. At least one of the Tenth Cavalry horses dropped dead from fatigue. Nevertheless, the miserable conditions did not stop Pershing's pursuit of Villa.

During the late morning of the following day, April 1, the lead elements of Colonel William C. Brown's Tenth Cavalry, having found no Villistas near Bachíniva, headed south to the Agua Caliente ranch, about twenty miles away. In the vanguard rode Major Charles P. Young, commanding F and G troops.

Charles Young was already a noted figure on the national scene. He was one of the few Negro regular army officers, a West Point graduate (Class of 1889), and a man who had performed important diplomatic assignments in both Haiti and Liberia. His abilities and personality made him universally respected, even in the segregated army of the time.

At about noon, Young's advance guard encountered some 150

Villistas near Agua Caliente and exchanged a few shots. Young managed to maneuver around the Mexicans' left flank and soon routed them. The Villistas left two dead on the field, along with a machine gun and a pack saddle—valuable booty. The Buffalo Soldiers continued to pursue the scattered enemy for a full two hours, until the Mexicans found a strong position in a ravine that Young considered too strong to attack without reinforcements.

Early the next morning, the whole Tenth Cavalry resumed the attack. Drawing his regiment up in a line of skirmishers, Colonel Brown ordered all to open fire. The enemy did not budge. Finally, Brown ordered Young to flank the Mexicans again, in a maneuver similar to the one he had executed the day before. Young pulled back his two troops, mounted up, formed his troopers abreast, in a "line of foragers," and started down a steep hill. On Young's signal, the troopers broke into a pistol charge around the Villistas' right flank, supported by machine-gun fire over their heads.

The combination of the machine-gun fire and the shouting charge was too much for the enemy, who melted away. Young's troopers never had to fire a shot from their pistol chambers, but the Buffalo Soldiers had introduced a new technique: overhead machine-gun fire.

General Pershing mulled over what Frank Tompkins had said by the campfire. He had received credible reports that made Tompkins's proposal seem feasible; Villa had passed Cusihuiriáchic with only forty men, so if his prey was indeed in such a weakened condition, Pershing felt free to push his troopers forward in one final, "superlative" effort. On April 4, he thus decided to follow Tompkins's recommendation: to search for Villa in southern Chihuahua.

So despite the stifled outrage of Major Robert Howze, Pershing ordered twelve mules transferred from the Eleventh Cavalry to Tompkins's squadron of the Thirteenth. Pershing further provided Tompkins with extra rations, grain, and five hundred silver pesos. Tompkins's squadron would lead the next phase of the pursuit to Parral. Tompkins's command would be followed by Brown's Tenth Cavalry, which in turn would be followed by a squadron of the Eleventh under Howze.

Pershing originally intended to send these detachments spread out a day apart, but he soon considered that an excessive risk and sent countermanding orders by way of parachute drops. Brown was to speed southeastward to protect Tompkins's left flank, and Howze was to do the same to support his right (western) flank. Dodd's men, still recovering from their exhausting march, were given a chance to rest, though Dodd himself was to lead a picked squadron into the mountains west of the Continental Divide. Villa could be lurking anywhere, and he must not be allowed to raid Pershing's slender, delicate supply line.

In order to keep in touch with his four columns, Pershing decided to move his own headquarters forward once again, this time all the way to Satevó, about 100 miles south of Chihuahua and fully 350 miles into Mexico. In moving so far into potentially hostile territory—and with so little security—Pershing knew he was taking a personal risk, but the thought of losing contact with his forward units was unbearable to him. And if Funston in San Antonio and Baker in Washington resented his inattentiveness to their questions and directions—well, so be it!

On April 8, after ten days on that sandy, wind-swept ridge, Pershing's party left San Geronimo. No one was sorry to leave.

Frank Tompkins, whose squadron consisted of K and M troops, Thirteenth Cavalry, moved out from the base at Bachíniva in the early afternoon of April 2, even before Pershing had firmly decided to send his small force all the way to Parral. Tompkins passed through Agua Caliente, where Colonel Brown had just dispersed the Villista force, and set off in a direction he thought would lead him to a juncture with the Tenth. He was successful; he found Brown with the Second Squadron and the machine-gun troop of the Tenth at San Antonio, a town on the Mexican Northwestern Railroad. Receiving confirmation that Villa had passed through on the way to Parral, Tompkins decided to leave for San Borja, the anticipated next point of Villa's journey. As Tompkins rode through Cusihuiriáchic, he noted grimly that this was the site of the Cusi Mining Company, where sixteen Americans had been murdered by Villistas less than three months earlier.

Possibly because they were accustomed to Americans, the people of Cusihuiriáchic were friendly. The local Carrancista commander, Major Reyes Castañada, unusually helpful, advised Tompkins that the nearest significant Carrancista force, under General José Cavazos, was camped about forty miles south. Castañada provided Tompkins with three guides, and the next morning, April 5, Tompkins headed south once more.

This part of the trip was agreeable. In the late morning, Tompkins's force reached an arroyo where they found plenty of water. The command traveled at a slow trot, about seven miles per hour, a moderate gait that conserved the strength of the horses and mules, each of which carried a load of 250 pounds. Since the mountainous terrain made it impossible for Tompkins to put out flank security guards, he sent his civilian scouts out about fifty to two hundred yards in front of the main body, which he himself led.

In the middle of the afternoon, the Thirteenth Cavalry troopers reached the outskirts of San Borja. There a party of Mexicans brought a courteous but meaningful note from General Cavazos, who, as Castañada had advised, was commanding that town: "I would esteem it very much if you would suspend your advance. . . . As I do not doubt that you are aware of the reasons which move me to write this, I hope that we can arrive at an agreement. . . ."

Tompkins decided to enter town for a parley. But first he took the precaution of sending his bilingual adjutant, Lieutenant James B. Ord, into town to make his request known. When Ord signaled to come ahead, Tompkins dismounted one of his troops and placed it on the crest of the nearby ridge—just in case.

The conference proceeded with forced civility. Cavazos insisted that Villa was dead and that he, in fact, was headed for Santa Ana to identify the body. He was reluctant to grant Tompkins authority to pass through the town, because, he said, he was very concerned about the prospect of a clash between American and Carrancista troops.

As a gesture of good will, however, Cavazos produced a bottle of brandy, took a swig from it, and handed it to Tompkins, who took a long swig and passed it on to Ord, who did the same. When the empty bottle returned to the Mexican commander, he took a look, threw it in the bush, and uttered something in Spanish that Tompkins took as "strong language." When they parted, the two men shook hands and Cavazos said, in fairly good English, "Be good."

Tompkins was now certain that the Carrancistas were never going to cooperate with the Americans. The best he could hope for was a hands-off policy.

As he continued southward from San Borja, Tompkins had the feeling that the trail was hot. When his squadron arrived at the Rancho Cienégita, he learned firsthand of the atrocities that Villa's men, particularly Villa's brother-in-law, had perpetrated a few days before. The people were still mourning the death of the overseer at the hands of

Corral, and they were furious over Corral's theft of 2,500 pesos. No Villista sentiment existed in that town. Cienégita was hardly typical, however.

At Santa Rosalía, Tompkins found Major Young's squadron of the Tenth Cavalry and camped next to it. Colonel Brown, also present, informed Tompkins that the Tenth, too, was headed for Parral by way of Satevó and Valle de Zaragosa. Tompkins made note of that destination; the information might well come in handy later.

While at Santa Rosalía, Tompkins took time to tally up the Mexican forces around him, any of which could give him trouble:

Villistas	**Location**
Beltrán	Santa María de Cuevas
Hernandez	Santa Ana
Villa	La Gabilana
Total Villistas	320

Carrancistas	
Cavazos	Moving to Santa Ana
Garza	Santa María de Cuevas
Cano	Guerrero
Castañada	Cusihuiriáchic
Total Carrancistas	2,000–3,000

This tabulation made it obvious that the Carrancistas presented a far graver threat to Tompkins's command than did the Villistas, especially since most of the former were located between him and the rest of the Americans, to the north.

Still, Tompkins planned to march to Parral, there to resupply and then march thirty miles even farther south, to Rosario. But he knew that his command comprised fewer than one hundred men, ill fed and low on ammunition. He therefore considered the help he could get if he needed it. Howze was three days' march behind. It would be Brown, going to Parral via Satevó, to whom he would look if he got into trouble.

On April 10, Tompkins arrived at San Zaragosa, a town known familiarly as Concho. There he played Robin Hood; he caught some Villistas looting a factory, dispersed them, and returned the stolen goods to the rightful owners. Having gained much good will, he was able to purchase some canvas trousers, shoes, and socks. The friendly people, however, panicked when Tompkins sent one of his troops into town; they feared that they would be sacked again, this time by the Americans.

Late that night, a Mexican captain named Antonio Mesa, who claimed to come from the Carrancista garrison at Parral, rode into Tompkins's camp. Mesa oozed good will and a spirit of cooperation. He planned to send word ahead by telephone, he said, so that the Americans and their mounts could be met at Parral. There they would be pastured, fed, supplied, and given a place to camp. The next morning, however, Mesa announced that he had encountered a little problem: the telephone did not work. So he promised to carry word of Tompkins's approach in person. He could cover the distance in one day, whereas a cavalry troop, laden with supplies, needed two.

The next morning, well fed and rested, Tompkins and his men began the two-day trip to Parral. That town of twenty thousand promised a longer rest and some recreation—a real luxury. Tompkins's troopers were eager for a break.

The Gunfight at Parral

As Frank Tompkins approached Parral, he kept an eye out for the welcoming committee that he expected to be waiting in the road to greet him. He saw nobody. But Tompkins was still confident, so he led his advance guard to the military guardhouse in the center of town, next to the railway station. There he planned to secure permission for his troops to enter—a mere formality. A Carrancista soldier guided him to the upstairs office of General Ismael Lozano.

General Lozano did not welcome the Americans. When Tompkins attempted to explain the nature of his mission, Lozano brushed off any mention of Villa with the claim that Villa was still in the north. He demanded to know why Tompkins was there. "By your invitation," Tompkins answered somewhat testily, "extended through Captain Mesa."

Lozano shrugged; he had not received any message from Mesa, who he surmised may have been captured by Villistas. Tompkins, Lazano went on ominously, should never have entered the town.

Tompkins looked about Lozano's office. Its French windows permitted a good view of the street below, and through them Tompkins could see his squadron drawn up in the street. But the Mexicans seemed less impressed than annoyed. On hearing a loud noise outside, Tompkins rushed to the window. A mule, hitched to a heavy cart, had been turned loose so as to charge into the American ranks. However, a big trooper stepped out and grabbed the mule by the bit. The incident came to nothing.

This was not, however, a good sign. Tompkins instinctively switched his holster to an accessible place in front of his body. He agreed to camp his squadron outside the town at whatever place Lozano specified. Tompkins's annoyance abated somewhat when a man appeared who claimed to be an American, though he spoke with a strong Spanish accent. Tompkins did not care whether the man was telling the truth, especially since he offered to furnish Tompkins's troopers and horses with provisions and corn fodder.

It took an hour for Lozano to get ready to lead the Americans out of Parral. By the time they left, large crowds had gathered, many of the people shouting "Viva Villa!" and "Viva Mexico!" Lozano may have been a Carrancista, but the people still loved Villa. It was becoming apparent as well that Mexicans directed their antagonism more toward the Americans than toward either Villa or Carranza.

As the troopers rode out of town, the noisy mob continued to follow in their tracks. Tompkins could see that if violence broke out, it would be in the rear. Therefore, as Lozano was leading the long column, Tompkins dropped back to keep an eye on the potential trouble spot. Soon he spotted a rabble-rouser, a small, wiry man with a gray suit and a Vandyke beard, riding a fine pony. Tompkins took special note of this man and resolved to shoot him first in case of trouble. But Tompkins took a moment to have some fun. He drew himself up and shouted "Viva Villa!" The crowd laughed.

Since the road into Parral ran east–west, Lozano was leading the Thirteenth Cavalrymen due east, in the direction they had come from. When the head of the column reached the position that Lozano had selected, Tompkins rode forward. He did not like what he saw. The proposed campsite sat in a cup, surrounded on the north, east, and west by a horseshoe-shaped ridge, open only at the southern end. Two hills on this ridge, one to the east and one to the west, looked right down upon the campsite; a third hill, about a half mile to the south, dominated it from that direction. A camp situated in that bowl would be subject to unrestricted fire from all directions.

Tompkins promptly refused to accept that position. He turned to one of his troop commanders and sent him to occupy the western hill as a precaution while he parleyed. Then, turning on Lozano, Tompkins pointed out that some of the townspeople were firing on his rear.

Lozano denied all responsibility for the firing, and Tompkins gave him the benefit of the doubt; the Carrancista certainly had no control over the populace. Besides, the firing of the mobs was ineffectual. But now a new threat was developing on the south, where a Mexican unit could be seen occupying the hill across the road. Other Mexicans were approaching the closer hills, waving Mexican flags. Tompkins, now furious, was ready to shoot Lozano for leading him into this trap. However, propriety (and doubtless better sense) prevailed: Lozano had also left himself helpless in Tompkins's power, his gun still in its holster. So Tompkins released him.

After Lozano hurriedly left for town, a Mexican officer appeared at Tompkins's position with a message once more urging the Americans to leave. Tompkins was quite willing to depart Parral, but not without the provisions and forage he had contracted for. Tompkins noted, however, that when the "messenger" left, he headed for the Mexican unit on the opposite hill, not for town. The man had obviously come only to scout Tompkins's position.

Still, Tompkins did everything he could to avoid hostilities. When a Carrancista force began moving toward his position, he withheld fire and stood up to wave them back. At the same time, however, he sent out a combat patrol—just in case—and dispatched a troop to the western hill with orders to open fire if the Carrancistas came too close. When Tompkins saw a Mexican flag being raised on the southern hill, he allowed his temper to override his judgment. He borrowed a rifle from his orderly, Sergeant Jay Richley, and stood up, prepared to fire. Then the flag disappeared, and the Mexicans opened fire before Tompkins could squeeze off a round. Sergeant Richley, who was lying prone at Tompkins's feet, was struck in the forehead and died without knowing what hit him.

Soon Tompkins detected a new group of about a hundred Mexicans moving around to flank him on the west. He therefore gave up hope of securing the promised supplies and concentrated on extracting his squadron from the hole that Lozano had placed him in. He marched his command northeast to avoid the fire from the hill to the south and then rejoined the road leading back toward Santa Cruz de Villegas. Santa Cruz, he had noted on his way down, would provide a fortress where his hundred men could put up an effective defense.

On reaching the Parral–Santa Cruz road, Tompkins took stock of his situation. Richley was dead, and his body had of necessity been left behind. Private Hobart Ledford had been shot through the lung. He and another wounded man were in great pain, but Tompkins could not give them a litter; if they were unable to ride, they would have to be left behind.

It was now 1:30 P.M., April 12. Tompkins estimated that Santa Cruz was nearly three hours away. Since the road was good, his troopers could ride two abreast. Tompkins noted with pride that their pace was just what it had been on the way down—a slow trot of seven miles per hour.

But the Americans were not allowed to leave Parral in peace. Some of Lozano's men, not satisfied with merely driving Tompkins from the town, seemed intent on destroying his squadron as well. Mounted Carrancistas attempted to ride along parallel to his column, shooting whenever possible. Tompkins watched with wry amusement as his pursuers tore madly across a field, only to be stopped by a wall, which they could tear down only after dismounting. Finally, the Mexicans gave up trying to stay abreast of Tompkins and instead followed his rear.

The mobs began to get close, so Lieutenant Clarence Lininger, an expert rifleman commanding the eight-man rear guard, fell back to delay behind a stone wall. Tompkins stayed with him. Despite the hot fire, Tompkins stood up to take a look through his binoculars. His soldiers, however, found it hard to fire and to hold their frantic horses at the same time. One soldier, seeing Tompkins standing behind him, handed over his reins with a laconic, "Hold my horse, Major." Another did the same. The normally pompous Tompkins smiled and complied. Accuracy of the men's fire took precedence over a major's dignity.

More difficulties lay ahead. A bullet grazed the head of one of the horses Tompkins was holding, and the mount broke away. As Tompkins ran to catch him, he received a flesh wound through the left shoulder. Lininger had driven the attacking party back, however, and Tompkins ordered the rear guard to mount up.

Major Tompkins's squadron of the Thirteenth Cavalry was still threatened, however. Its peril was eased only by the poor marksmanship of the Mexicans, most of whose shots went wild. At one point, Lieutenant Ord saw the badly wounded Ledford slip from his horse. Though the Mexicans were closing in, the wounded Ord turned back to Ledford, lifted him on his own horse, and led his mount back to the column. By this time, Ledford could no longer ride, and in his agony he begged his fellows to leave him behind. Tompkins gave him a drink from his own canteen and assured him that their destination was near. Ledford held on until another Mexican bullet struck him in the back. He was dead before he hit the ground.

One last action finished the chase. As the men of the Thirteenth dipped temporarily out of sight across a ridge, Tompkins seized a chance for an ambush. Lieutenant Lininger, with twenty men, hid in a position spanning the road. When the Mexicans came within two hundred yards, the Americans opened fire. The Carrancista detachment was reduced to a mass of men and ponies rolling in the dust. Then Lininger's men stood up and poured in "rapid fire." Mexican sources later admitted that their losses in this action alone came to over forty dead.

That fight ended the active pursuit. The Americans stopped at an irrigation ditch to water their horses and covered the short remaining distance to Santa Cruz without further molestation. Tompkins set up a strong defensive position and sent three messengers to summon help from the Tenth Cavalry, eight miles north.

It was a dangerous assignment for those messengers, but Tompkins had no choice. His exhausted men could go no farther. And they had no wish to make Santa Cruz "memorable" as another Alamo!

Captain George Rodney, Tenth Cavalry, was making camp for his weary troop when he heard the thump of hooves. Looking at the hills to his left, he spied three horsemen "riding like John Gilpin." He could get their attention only by firing shots over their heads. Rodney observed that the three men were "scared beyond speech." At first, he mistook them for deserters.

"Sir, we're from Major Tompkins' squadron," one of them gasped. "He's been fighting a heavy rear guard action north from Parral. He's surrounded at a ranch about eight miles away. We're riding for aid."

"Riding for aid, hell!" Rodney roared. "You're running away. Go over and tell your troubles to the Commanding Officer."

But even if the men were deserters, Rodney reasoned, the next command would be "Boots and Saddles." He therefore mounted up his troop to wait. In a moment, the order came: "Pull out at a trot as advance guard. Head southwest to Santa Cruz de la Villegas. It's about eight miles—by guess and by God."

An hour later, the Buffalo Soldiers arrived at Santa Cruz. The two American detachments, both cautious, exchanged bugle calls to identify each other. When Major Charles Young finally entered the Thirteenth Cavalry camp, a bandaged Frank Tompkins, not nearly so cool as his later book implies, hobbled out of a trench and burst out, "I could kiss every one of you!"

Young grinned. "Hello, Tompkins! You can start with me."

Young now assumed command of both forces. Even in the face of this combined strength, the Carrancistas remained in the vicinity until Major Robert L. Howze arrived with his provisional squadron of the Eleventh Cavalry. At that point, the balance of force turned definitely in favor of the Americans.

From that time on, General Ismael Lozano, at Parral, became the very picture of cooperation. When summoned by Colonel Brown, he and his staff arrived promptly. When Brown needed to dispatch a message to General Pershing, a Mexican messenger carried the note to Parral and sent it by commercial wire to the American consul at Chihuahua.

In his book's summation, Frank Tompkins describes the Parral action rather immodestly as a "hot little campaign of less than two weeks . . . well planned and gallantly executed . . . the last appearance of the Old Cavalry."

But the gunfight at Parral was more than a "hot little campaign." It signaled the end of John J. Pershing's pursuit of Pancho Villa.

22

****

To the Brink

It took nearly two full days for General Pershing to get word of the fight at Parral. It came not from Colonel Brown, but from Captain Ben Foulois, who drove hurriedly into his headquarters at Satevó on Friday, April 14, 1916. Foulois carried the message General Lozano had forwarded to the American consul at Chihuahua, and aware of its importance, he lost no time in delivering it. The message was garbled, however. Errors in the translation from English to Spanish and back—plus the primitive telegraphy—produced such confusion that Pershing could not even identify which American unit had been involved. He first surmised it to be the Tenth Cavalry, not the Thirteenth.

But Pershing knew that one or another of his task forces had clashed with Carrancistas. That sufficed to make him realize that the nature of his mission had changed. Now that his force was being threatened by his supposed former friends, his first concern was to ensure the safety of his troops. More immediately, he worried about the vulnerability of his own headquarters. That night Pershing's headquarters dug in to make a defensive position for the first time in the campaign.

The next day, Pershing sent a messenger to Colonel Brown, at

Santa Cruz, to confirm and clarify the situation. The messenger returned that same evening with word that all four of the cavalry units—the Seventh, Tenth, Eleventh, and Thirteenth—had concentrated at Santa Cruz and were preparing to repel any further Carrancista attacks. Fuming over the Carrancista "betrayal," his troopers were itching to strike out at the new enemy. Fortunately, such a foolhardy action was out of the question; the horses were too weak from lack of forage.

Pershing saw that Brown's force could not remain very long at Santa Cruz. The Carrancistas could never muster enough strength to destroy him in a single fight, but Brown's men were too numerous to live off the limited land that the Santa Cruz area offered. Since he could not supply Brown, Pershing therefore decided to withdraw him. As Pershing reported, "to have retained troops [in the vicinity of Parral] would have required an extension of the line of communications 180 miles from San Antonio, and the road was difficult. . . . [The] rapidly moving columns had out run the means of supply, and as there was neither food nor forage obtainable in that district, withdrawal was the best solution to the problem."

Pershing was probably not surprised to learn that his commanders at Santa Cruz objected to the idea of withdrawing in the face of Mexican threats. He therefore sent his chief of staff, Colonel Cabell, to Santa Cruz. Cabell was officially instructed to "investigate the situation, and, if desirable, to direct the retirement of the forces." In fact, Pershing had already decided on their withdrawal.

Pershing's most pressing need, even more urgent than withdrawing Brown, was to communicate with Washington. To make this possible, he had to move his headquarters back to a point close enough to reach the powerful radio station at Casas Grandes. But the timing for relocating his small command group presented a problem. Should he wait for the cavalry units at Santa Cruz to join him and afford him protection on the move? Or should he move his group back from its isolated position alone? Pershing could not wait to consult with Washington, so the next morning he assembled his staff, his cooks, his mechanics, and the correspondents to begin the long trek back to Namiquipa unaccompanied.

Pershing was taking a personal risk. He did not have enough men to put up much of a fight if hostile Carrancistas ambushed him. He and his staff were traveling through desolate territory, so Pershing said little but quietly held his breath until, a few days later, his headquarters met friendly troops, the Sixteenth U.S. Infantry, swinging down the road toward San Geronimo. On arrival at Namiquipa, Pershing was able to establish communications with Dublán. Through relays, he sent a request to Washington for instructions.

For all their bravado, Colonel Brown and his commanders were feeling the pinch of supply shortages at Santa Cruz. The Mexican authorities, though not threatening, were unwilling to give further supplies in exchange for "receipts" to be cashed at the American consulate in Chihuahua. They did, however, allow Brown to send out foraging parties. In one instance, Brown paid a bill of $226 by his own personal check, a considerable sum in those days. And on April 17, the mayor of Parral actually arranged for some resupply. Neither Mexicans nor Americans, in their sensible moments, desired any resumption of the conflict.

On Thursday, April 20, Colonel Brown received a note in which General Luis Herrera offered to come to Santa Cruz for a conference. On that same afternoon, a convoy arrived at Santa Cruz from San Antonio carrying some supplies and a considerable amount of welcome cash. But with the supplies and cash came an unequivocal order from Pershing: ". . . on account of the difficulties of supply in your present locality you [will] move your force . . . by easy marches to Satevó." That order took matters out of Brown's hands, but he decided to go ahead and meet with the Mexicans the next day anyway.

At 10:00 A.M. on April 21, the Mexican generals Luis Herrera and Ismael Lozano arrived at Santa Cruz with a small escort. After the Americans had accorded them a brief welcome, the two sides retired to a nearby hut to confer. Brown had arranged the layout of the meeting room to give the Americans every psychological advantage as they talked. The two sides sat at a long table, the Americans on the north side facing south, with the national colors and those of the Tenth Cavalry arrayed behind them. Brown placed the Mexicans on the south side of the table, facing north.*

Colonel Brown opened the meeting by presenting a detailed let-

---

*Before the meeting began, Frank Tompkins noticed that General Lozano was looking at him uncertainly. Tompkins, with his left arm in a sling, hobbled up to him and called him "Amigo Mio." The two shook hands and both laughed. Frank Tompkins, *Chasing Villa* (Harrisburg, 1934), p. 169.

ter of complaint regarding the Parral affair. Herrera, though denying that Mexico was in any way responsible for the fight, promised to deliver a reply early the next morning. He also promised to transport American wounded from Parral to El Paso by rail.

Herrera still wanted Brown to leave the area, however, and therefore suggested that the Americans withdraw to Valle de Zaragosa, a town about forty miles to the north of Santa Cruz. At first, Herrera seemed reasonable: the Americans, he urged, were too close to Parral, and that fact "was adding to Villa's strength." Since Valle de Zaragosa was forty miles closer to Parral than was Satevó, where Pershing had already ordered Brown to go, Brown did not commit himself.

As the conference progressed, however, Herrera's attitude became more hostile. He declared that the Americans would be permitted to move only north, not "south, east, or west." Brown now became angry at Herrera's tone. He pointed to the U.S. flag behind him and snarled, "That flag does not move one step north until I have orders from my commanding general to move it." With that truculent exchange, the meeting broke up.

The next morning, Brown's Tenth Cavalry, along with the attachments from its sister regiments, moved north toward Satevó in accordance with Pershing's order.

Officials in both Mexico City and Washington received the news of the Parral fight with remarkable calm. It was in the best interests of both countries to do so. Carranza had a double incentive for keeping the hostility of the Mexican people within reasonable limits, because war with the United States would endanger his own political position in Mexico. The First Chief remained convinced that Villa's main purpose in conducting raids across the border was to bring about such a war, and Carranza had no intention of playing into Villa's hands. Carranza could afford to react slowly to each development. His control of the communications within Mexico enabled him to manipulate the news that the people received.

Washington also anticipated something like this development. The hostile attitude behind Carranza's delay in permitting Pershing to use the Mexican railroad, for example, was now recognized for what it really was. In addition, Washington was receiving direct reports of growing Mexican resentment against Pershing's presence. News of the fight at Parral was therefore almost expected.

In that spirit of mutual restraint, Foreign Minister Cándido Aguilar sent Secretary of State Lansing a note on April 12. Its tenor was mild and its careful wording suggested that it was merely triggered, not inspired, by the Parral incident. It expressed Mexico's "desire to keep cordial and unalterable the good relations of friendship which ought to exist between Mexico and the United States." Its arguments for an American withdrawal from Mexican territory were couched in diplomatic language. It reminded Wilson and Lansing that the Mexican offer of mutual rights to pursue across the border was not open-ended but "conditional," reciprocal, and intended to apply to *future* situations. Now that Villa's band had been dispersed, it could be handled adequately by Mexican troops. The time had therefore come to "treat with the Government of the United States upon the subject of the withdrawal of its forces from our territory." The note made no mention of the gunfight at Parral.

The Mexican note came to a President Wilson preoccupied with relations with Germany. Two weeks before the note arrived, a German U-boat had without warning sunk the unarmed French passenger vessel *Sussex* as it was crossing the Channel. Though no American lives were lost, Wilson was unwilling to let the matter drop. He again warned the Germans that "the use of submarines for the destruction of an enemy's commerce is . . . utterly incompatible with the principles of humanity, the . . . rights of neutrals, and the sacred immunities of non-combatants." This European crisis passed, but the furor served to divert Wilson's attention from the skirmish at Parral.

In these crises with Mexico and Germany, the U.S. Congress was decidedly two-faced on the subject of a foreign war. The majority of its members strongly opposed a big war with Germany but were not nearly so averse to a little one with Mexico.* Joseph R. Tumulty, Wilson's appointment secretary, was keenly aware that the Columbus raid and the lack of cooperation by the Carranza government were causing popular opinion to demand more vigorous action on Wilson's part. Even the pacifist Secretary of War Newton D. Baker insisted that

---

*"A poll of 4500 business men in all states of the Union, netting 1710 replies, was completed by a New York investment firm early in May, 1916. It indicated a wide division of opinion on intervention; 696 found the people of their sections 'generally in favor of military intervention' in Mexico, 653 found opinion opposed to intervention." Harris, Winthrop and Co., comp., *American Business as Affected by Peace and Preparedness, The Composite Opinion of Seventeen Hundred American Business Men* (New York, 1916), p. 7, quoted in Harley Notter, *The Origins of the Foreign Policy of Woodrow Wilson* (New York, 1965), p. 507n.

the United States intervene and "put an end to the pusillanimous rule of Carranza and clean up Mexico."

President Wilson stood his ground. One evening, he expressed himself forcefully in private to Tumulty. "You may inform the Cabinet officers who discuss it with you," he said, "that 'there won't be any war with Mexico if I can prevent it,' no matter how loud the gentlemen on the Hill yell for it and demand it."

"The gentlemen who criticize me," he continued, "speak as if America were afraid to fight Mexico. Poor Mexico, with its pitiful men, women, and children, fighting to gain a foothold in their own land! They speak of the valour of America. What is true valour? Valour is self-respecting. Valour is circumspect. Valour strikes only when it is right to strike." The president went on in this vein for some time.

Not all of Wilson's officials agreed. Army Chief of Staff Hugh L. Scott, for one, executed the policies of his civilian superiors only out of a sense of duty, not out of conviction. At this moment, April 1916, Scott's recommendations for a call-up of the National Guard to protect the U.S. border were overridden by the president. Calling up a few thousand men, Scott believed, could at least demonstrate American determination to defend the border. Though Scott had once advised the president that the guardsmen could not operate in deserts, they could at least "wear a uniform, carry a rifle, and occupy towns so as to release the regular troops for mobile purposes." This appearance would discourage the Mexicans from making raids in American territory that might bring on a war unnecessarily.

President Wilson rejected Scott's urgings for a call-up of the National Guard, but he still recognized the general's potential value as a bridge to the Mexican military. Scott had time and again demonstrated a remarkable ability to deal with "natives" of any land, be they Filipinos, American Indians, or Mexicans. For despite his innate belief in Anglo superiority, Scott always dealt with anyone on a "man-to-man basis," demonstrating a sincere appreciation of the other fellow's viewpoint. Wilson hoped that if Carranza refused to deal directly with American diplomats, a meeting between Mexican and American generals might bring about some understanding. Specifically, Wilson decided to promote a conference between Generals Scott and Obregón. It was worth a try.

In the late evening of Friday, April 21, Secretary Lansing sent a message to James L. Rodgers, his "special representative" with Carranza, suggesting that a conference between Scott and Obregón might be held at "some convenient place" near the border. Its objective would be to "prevent misunderstandings and make possible real cooperation" between the military forces of the two governments.

Two days later, Rodgers reported back. Carranza, he advised, was unhappy about the prospect of such a mission for Obregón. Rodgers believed that Carranza was reluctant for personal reasons. After all, Obregón was far more popular than he, and since the general was showing signs of political ambitions, Carranza now saw him as a threat to his own political position. A successful meeting with the Americans would build up Obregón at Carranza's expense. Nevertheless, Carranza could come up with no logical grounds for denying Obregón permission to accept the American invitation.

Carranza, Rodgers went on, resorted to passive resistance; in order to avoid being put on the spot, he refused to meet personally with Rodgers. In the meantime, he tried to placate the United States in private while maintaining a defiant stance in public. To the first end, Carranza released certain long-promised supplies for Pershing's troops; to the second, he continued presenting himself as Mexico's defender against the Yankee intruders. Carranza dissociated himself in public from the resupply being sent to Pershing and encouraged the newspaper El Pueblo, which he controlled, to tout the possibility of war.

Meanwhile, Obregón left Mexico City on his own authority. He headed for El Paso "or some other point" on the border to meet with Scott.

Obregón probably needed to disappear from the public scene for his personal safety, but since he had not formally accepted the invitation to meet with Scott, his absence worried the U.S. State Department. Wilson and Lansing set great store by this meeting, so the diplomatic wires sizzled with messages to all parts of Mexico in an effort to locate Obregón—Mexico City, Chihuahua, and the border town of Piedras Negras. Always the message was the same: Scott and Funston would meet with Obregón in any place Obregón specified.

Finally Obregón appeared. He arrived at Juárez on the morning of Friday, April 28. After the population greeted him with "profuse military and civil official honors," he made contact with the American consulate and specified that his meeting with Scott should be held in Juárez, Mexican territory. That venue would be more prestigious from Obregón's viewpoint than some location across the river in El Paso.

Obregón seemed to be every bit as eager for this conference to bear fruit as were the Americans. On the day that Obregón arrived at Juárez, the U.S. consul in Chihuahua reported that seventeen railroad cars of supplies had been released for shipment to Pershing. That act could well have been arranged by Obregón; at least, the Carranza government made a point of declaring this act to be a "special concession," not to be expected on a regular basis. But whatever the machinations within Mexico, the Americans read the gesture as designed to improve the atmosphere for the pending talks.

General Scott received his formal instructions while en route to El Paso from Washington. He and General Funston were to meet with Obregón and to discuss "the future of military operations of our forces in Mexico." The guidelines were definite and conciliatory:

a. The U.S. government wishes to avoid any appearance of "intervention in the domestic affairs" of Mexico.

b. The pursuit of Villa and his bands is solely for the purpose of "removing a menace to the common security" of the two countries.

c. Villista attacks like that at Columbus can irritate American public opinion "to the point of requiring general intervention."

d. American commanders, respecting Mexican public opinion, will observe all proprieties and proceed in "harmonious cooperation" with Mexican forces.

e. "If deemed better American troops can be detained in the northern part of the State of Chihuahua while the forces of the Mexican Government drive Villa and his associates toward the north, in this way enabling the American troops to aid in his ultimate capture."

f. The U.S. government has "no pride involved" as to who makes Villa's capture. It will "fully and generously" cooperate with Obregón.

Those talking points were completely military in nature. The generals were given no latitude to make political concessions. In the event that Obregón issued anything like a "peremptory command" for U.S. forces to withdraw across the border, Scott and Funston should call such a question a "diplomatic matter," to be worked out through diplomatic channels.

Scott and Funston arrived at El Paso during the morning of April 30. Because Obregón, a minister of war, held a higher governmental position, the two Americans called on him first, in Juárez. Obregón returned the call the next morning, at which time the two sides agreed to meet in Juárez that afternoon. Then the three crossed the river to Juárez for their first official meeting, at the Hotel Aguana.

From the beginning, it was apparent that the Americans and Mexicans had come to discuss different matters. Obregón and General Jacinto Treviño, who accompanied him, were interested only in securing Pershing's immediate withdrawal from Mexico. They claimed that Villa was dead and that the presence of American troops on Mexican soil could therefore no longer be justified to the Mexican people. Obregón made no threats, but he refused to discuss areas of cooperation between their respective national troops. After only two hours, the conference was obviously deadlocked.

Despite the absence of any kind of agreement—or even of any real communication—the first meeting ended amicably. The two delegations ate dinner that evening aboard an American railroad car in the Juárez yards; Scott and Funston then took their leave and returned to El Paso. Obregón and Treviño remained in Juárez.

Scott and Obregón may have been getting along personally, but their countries were on the brink of a war that neither wanted.* One serious danger was that hot-headed Mexican and American commanders in the field would provoke clashes that, by inflaming public opinion in both countries, could force war on the reluctant heads of government.

Another danger was that members of Carranza's government, ignoring the careful policies of the First Chief himself, would for their own ends bring on fighting that Carranza would want to avoid. On May 1, the day after Scott and Obregón first met, someone in the Mexican chain of command alerted Mexican commanders at both Chihuahua and Agua Prieta for action against the American forces in Mexico. One message used the terms "crush" and "annihilate"; the

---

*There was no widespread hostility against the Mexicans in the eastern United States. The New York Times rotogravure section of Sunday, May 7, 1916, shows large crowds cheering Carranza in the streets of Mexico City, without mentioning that the subject of the speech was probably anti-Americanism. The same section, contains not only a photo of the U.S. Sixth Infantry digging in near Las Cruces (very casually, it seems) but also a formal portrait of Obregón with his new bride. It was pointed out demurely that the two "were wedded a few weeks before General Obregón" came to El Paso for the conference.

other mentioned cutting off the Americans in a sudden move "after the Scott-Obregón conference."

The American officers in the field were no cooler. For many, the humiliation of being ordered to retreat from Parral still rankled. Some even advocated starting a war right then.*

When it came to the ultimate choice between war and peace, however, neither the presidents nor the more responsible generals desired to dismiss the Juárez conference as a failure. Another meeting was generally considered inevitable, and on May 3, after waiting two days, Scott received an invitation from Obregón to meet in El Paso, Texas, at the Paso del Norte Hotel. Scott, of course, accepted. They agreed to meet around noon.

In moving the conference to El Paso, Obregón hoped to escape the Mexican press, whose intrusions had helped make the previous conference almost impossible. But the American press in El Paso turned out to be no better than the Mexican. When Scott left his hotel, he discovered that his car was being pursued by a flock of correspondents bent on following him wherever he went. Scott therefore indulged the streak of boyish play in him. He jumped out of his car, commandeered a passing laundry truck, and ordered the bewildered driver to take him into the service entrance of the Paso del Norte Hotel.

The game did not end there. While searching for Obregón's room, Scott took a wrong corridor and ran straight into a Hearst correspondent. "I got you!" the correspondent cried out. Scott dashed for Obregón's room and unceremoniously slammed the door. Thirty newspapermen waited outside as he, Obregón, and a single interpreter remained virtual prisoners for the rest of the day.

Scott was better prepared for argument than he had been two days earlier. He now possessed two confirmed reports that large Mexican

---

*Mr. Wilson's Mexican policy, . . . was a hodge-podge of interference and nonintervention, of patience and petulance, of futile conferences and abortive armed invasion, which has been described as the idealistic policy in the treatment of Mexican affairs . . . thus maintaining a policy of peace with Mexico under any and all forms of humiliating aggravation. . . .

As a matter of fact, war with Mexico in the spring of 1916 would have been a splendid preliminary to our entrance in the World War. Half a million men would have cleaned up Mexico in short order. . . .

TOMPKINS, *Chasing Villa*, p. 184.

forces were being concentrated at Chihuahua and at the Púlpito Pass, in Sonora. Together, these forces constituted a giant vise, an obvious potential threat to Pershing. Scott made the most of this knowledge. "If you want to lose your country," he warned Obregón, "the best way would be to attack Pershing." Instead of one American expedition in Mexico, Obregón could well be facing several—"and who knows then if either will come out of Mexico? Those are matters for you to consider very carefully."

Obregón listened to Scott this time. Nobody knows why, but perhaps "mutual friends" of Scott's and Obregón's had been successful in convincing him of (a) Wilson's friendship for Mexico and of (b) the dire consequences for Mexico in case of war. Perhaps it was easier for him to be reasonable in the absence of a large audience, including the disastrously abrasive Funston. Or perhaps something had happened between Obregón and Carranza. In any event, Obregón was now willing to talk.

The meeting lasted twelve hours, interrupted only by breaks for meals. But the going remained difficult. Scott became exasperated by Obregón's tactic of reopening issues after they were supposedly settled. But eventually they agreed that Pershing should withdraw his advanced elements to Namiquipa (where supply dictated they go anyway) and that he should remain at Casas Grandes and Colonia Dublán. The hard-core issue then became simple: whether Obregón and Scott could set a definite date for Pershing's withdrawal from Mexico. Obregón dearly wished to take home an agreement on that issue, but such a concession lay far out of Scott's purview. So at 12:30 A.M., May 4, the conferees signed a document covering the various points of commonality. They agreed to remain in the vicinity.

President Wilson signed the Scott-Obregón agreement readily. However, President Carranza held off.

On Friday evening, May 6, a band of sixty Mexicans forded the Rio Grande near Glen Springs, Texas, shouting both "Viva Villa!" and "Viva Carranza!" Sweeping some fifteen miles into Texas territory, they raided the small Glen Springs settlement and attacked a nine-man detachment from A Troop of the Fourteenth Cavalry. The American troopers, warned by an alert sentry, took refuge in a small adobe hut and returned fire until the raiders finally managed to set the hut ablaze. The suffocating Americans knocked down the door and charged out into the night. The raiders did not mow them down;

instead, they continued on to nearby Deemer's Store, hauling off the proprietor and a ten-year-old boy.

Eventually, the raiding party was driven back across the river by two troops of the Fourteenth Cavalry, and four troops pursued the presumed Villistas well over a hundred miles into Mexican territory. The final casualty count included three American troopers and one civilian dead. Only two Villistas were killed.

Though the losses at the celebrated Glen Springs raid were not spectacular, the timing was significant in that it represented the last straw for a weary President Woodrow Wilson. On May 10, Wilson accepted the advice of his military leaders and called up 4,500 National Guardsmen from the states of Arizona, New Mexico, and Texas. Over 38,000 others were alerted but not mobilized. Infantry troops were sent to El Paso and other threatened points. Wilson publicly rejected the Mexican demand that U.S. forces be withdrawn from Mexico. The border, now manned by the National Guard, would be less inviting to Mexican depredation.

In Mexico City, President Venustiano Carranza responded to Wilson's acts by categorically denouncing the Scott-Obregón agreement and renewing his demand for the immediate withdrawal of the Punitive Expedition.

The conferences at Juárez and at El Paso might just as well have never happened.

23

****

Carrizal

Lieutenant George S. Patton was savoring a moment of triumph as he drove into General Pershing's headquarters at Namiquipa. To everyone's astonishment, Patton's automobile had stretched across its hood the bodies of three Mexicans, tied like carcasses of deer brought home from a successful hunting expedition. Patton had carried the corpses through miles of Villista-infested territory because, as he claimed, he needed to have their identities confirmed. He had taken a small detail of riflemen to stalk a Villista general named Julio Cárdenas, onetime leader of Villa's *dorados*, and he wanted confirmation that one of his victims was indeed Cárdenas. Like a terrier laying a mouse at the feet of his master, Patton delivered his trophies directly to Pershing.

The identity of Cárdenas was soon verified, and Patton's daring feat was generally applauded in Pershing's headquarters; in the callous atmosphere of the Punitive Expedition, little concern was expressed for the dignity of the dead. Patton, in fact, became an instant celebrity; Frank Elser gave his exploit wide publicity, and Pershing, doubtless much to Patton's satisfaction, thereafter referred to his aide as "my bandit."

Patton had not actually been sent out to ambush Cárdenas; his mission had been simply to purchase corn at the nearby Coyote Ranch, east of Namiquipa. But after he completed his purchase he was free to "mix a little business with pleasure," as he later wrote. He knew that the hacienda of San Miguelito, near Rubio, was Cárdenas's home, and this trip was not his first effort to trap Cárdenas. But on this day in mid-May 1916 Patton succeeded. He surrounded the hacienda with his six men, and when three terrified Mexicans burst out the door, Patton stood in their way to goad them into shooting first. The shots of the running Mexicans went wild, but Patton was set. He fired back, killing two of them. The third man was picked off by other members of the party.

Patton's moment in the spotlight was soon overshadowed, however, by the elimination of an even more important Villista, Candelario Cervantes. Cervantes had been playing cat-and-mouse with Dodd and the Seventh Cavalry for six weeks. He was bold enough to prey on the helpless inhabitants of Namiquipa, right under Pershing's nose.

On May 25, Cervantes's marauding party encountered an American reconnaissance party under Lance Corporal Davis Marksbury. The sides were evenly matched, and Marksbury was killed; three of his men were wounded. But a cool infantry private kept his wits and picked off two of the attackers. One of the Mexican dead turned out to be Cervantes.

In his report, Pershing crowed that Candelario Cervantes was, "next to Villa himself, the most able and the most desperate of Villa's band."

Pershing now began preparing for an indefinite stay in Chihuahua. In the face of Carrancista hostility toward the expedition, he could no longer risk sending far-ranging parties in pursuit of Villa. He could, however, ensure that a certain area would be denied to Villa. Pershing therefore divided up the territory currently occupied by U.S. troops, holding each subordinate commander responsible for a sector to defend and supply. If possible, each sector commander was to continue to search for Villa while the Carrancistas—in theory, at least—continued to scour southern Chihuahua and Durango. On the basis of the various district capitals in the region, Pershing assigned the following regions to his major commanders:

District	Troops	District Commander
Namiquipa	Tenth Cavalry	Major Ellwood W. Evans
Guerrero	Seventh Cavalry	Colonel George A. Dodd
Bustillos	Thirteenth Cavalry	Colonel Herbert J. Slocum
Satevó	Fifth Cavalry	Colonel Wilbur E. Wilder
San Borja	Eleventh Cavalry	Colonel James Lockett

This arrangement made sense from a tactical viewpoint, because it brought some order out of the confusion that had reigned for weeks. However, word of the plan inevitably leaked to the Mexican public, and it appeared that Pershing was preparing to occupy northwestern Chihuahua permanently. The Punitive Expedition was daily becoming more and more of an embarrassment to the United States.

Hindsight indicates that the end of May 1916 would have been the optimal time to withdraw the Punitive Expedition from Chihuahua. At that date, Pershing could point to certain tactical victories to justify a claim of limited success. One of those had occurred on May 4, when the townspeople and the small Carrancista detachment at the town of Cusihuiriáchic sent a plea to Major Robert L. Howze, Eleventh Cavalry, to rescue them from two Villista chiefs leading some 120 men. Howze, in nearby San Antonio, moved his squadron of about 320 men to Cusihuiriáchic and followed the Villistas to Ojos Azules, thirty-six miles away, and Howze descended on them at dawn on the fifth. After a running fight of several miles, Howze completely dispersed the Villistas with heavy losses and, thanks to complete surprise, without casualties to his own command. Such actions and the killings of Cervantes and Cárdenas beclouded the fact that Villa himself had not been captured.

Nevertheless, the advisability of withdrawing the Punitive Expedition was not obvious at the time. Personal tensions between Wilson and Carranza obscured the realities of the situation.

Pershing now set about to establish some sort of working arrangement with General Gabriel Gavira, the cooperative Carrancista commander at Juárez. The prospect of doing so looked good, for Gavira shared Pershing's desire to improve communications between the Americans and the Carrancistas. With Washington's approval, therefore, Pershing invited Gavira to meet him at Colonia Dublán. When Gavira accepted, Pershing drove the eighty miles up from Namiquipa and, on June 1, boarded Gavira's railway car.

The two-hour meeting was tense, but the two generals finally agreed on a plan whereby Gavira would reduce the Carrancista garrisons along the Mexican Northwestern Railroad line that ran through the mountains from Juárez through Colonia Dublán to Guerrero and San Antonio.* Since that section of the railroad was solidly garrisoned by Americans, such a reduction in Carrancista presence would reduce the threat of clashes. The War Department in Washington approved of the arrangement without hesitation; but, as with earlier proposals, nothing was heard from Mexico City.

Venustiano Carranza did not share Gabriel Gavira's conciliatory attitude. The First Chief, possibly as an indirect reply to the Pershing-Gavira agreement, sent a warning to Pershing through the commander of the Mexican force in Chihuahua City, Jacinto B. Treviño. On June 16, Treviño sent Pershing a message that, while couched in stiffly correct language, conveyed a now familiar ultimatum: "I have orders from my government to prevent, by the use of arms . . . the American forces that are in this state from moving to the south, east or west of the places they now occupy. . . . Your forces will be attacked by Mexican forces if these indications are not heeded."

Pershing responded quickly. The U.S. government, he informed Treviño, had placed no restrictions upon the movements of American forces. Pershing would therefore use his "own judgment as to when and in what direction" to move his forces. He added, "If under these circumstances the Mexican forces attack any of my columns the responsibility for the consequences will lie with the Mexican government."

Carranza did not stop with a routine warning to Pershing; he made his ultimatum public, and his threats infuriated many Americans. In the forefront of those angered stood the controversial news-

---

*The Mexican Northwestern Railroad line was the one employed in the unsuccessful attempt to take the Tenth Cavalry behind Villa in the first days of the campaign.

paper magnate William Randoph Hearst, whose fabulous Babícora Ranch now seemed threatened.* Hearst's newspapers carried a series of inflammatory headlines:

BANDITS JOIN CARRANZA TO FIGHT US!

MEXICANS PREPARE FOR WAR WITH U.S.!

On June 19, Hearst's *New York Journal* went so far as to advocate an American invasion of Mexico.

> Is it not time for the soldiers of the U.S. to do something PERMA-NENT? . . . Nothing worthwhile will be accomplished by occa-sional "punitive expeditions." . . . The way to IMPRESS the Mexicans is to REPRESS the Mexicans. . . . The way to begin is to say to them: "We are no longer planning to catch this bandit or that. We are GOING INTO MEXICO. And as far as we GO, we'll stay."

Wilson and Lansing were no admirers of Hearst, but Hearst was verbalizing something very much on many people's minds. Further-more, President Wilson and Secretary Lansing were becoming frus-trated with Carranza's hardening. On June 20, Lansing sent a long, harsh message to the Mexican government that threatened the "grav-est consequences" if Carranza's troops took action against Pershing's forces.

The stage was now set for trouble.

William R. Hearst and others in the United States could rant and rave, but General John J. Pershing, who had moved his headquarters back to Colonia Dublán, was forced to take Carrancista bluster seriously.

---

*Hearst protected Babícora with a private "army" of about a hundred men, well armed and organized. At the time of Pershing's pull-back, this Babícora security detachment was reported to have engaged a group of Mexican bandits and killed more than twenty in one pitched battle. *San Francisco Examiner*, 21 May 1916, quoted in W. A. Swanberg, *Citizen Hearst* (New York, 1961), p. 297.

He was well aware that Carrancista troops were concentrating to the north in Sonora and to the south around Chihuahua City, and since his small fleet of airplanes was of no value, he depended on long-range cavalry patrolling to keep him informed. He would have been remiss had he not taken such measures to secure his command.

At about the time that Pershing was exchanging messages with Treviño, he received reports that a third Carrancista army was assembling a force of ten thousand men at Villa Ahumada, a crossroad about seventy miles east of Dublán, on the direct Juárez–Chihuahua railroad. Carranza had brought these new units into Chihuahua from Coahuila. If those reports were accurate, that single Carrancista force would be about equal in numerical strength to his own.

To determine that army's strength and, if possible, the intentions of its commander, Pershing called on one of the several troops of his old Tenth Cavalry, whose Buffalo Soldiers were located in the vicinity of Dublán. He asked their new commander, Major Ellwood W. Evans, to select which troop should perform the mission. On Saturday, June 17, Captain Charles T. Boyd, commanding Company C, Tenth Cavalry, reported to Pershing to receive his instructions in person.

Pershing was highly satisfied with the choice of Captain Boyd, whom he had known since the days of their service together in the Tenth Cavalry. He considered Boyd the right officer to perform this touchy mission. When they met, Pershing was still smarting at the peremptory message he had received from General Treviño the day before, but he still wanted to avoid a fight between American and Mexican troops. As he later recalled the interview with Boyd, he was cautious indeed:

> Take your troop and reconnoiter in the direction of Ahumada and obtain as much information as you can regarding the forces there. This is a reconnaissance only, and you will not be expected to fight. In fact, I want you to avoid a fight if possible. Do not allow yourself to be surprised by superior numbers. But if wantonly attacked, use your own judgment as to what you shall do, having due regard for your command.

Pershing then brought Boyd up-to-date on the recent exchange of messages with General Treviño. In light of that new situation, he warned Boyd that it would be unwise to go into any place garrisoned by Carrancista troops.

Captain Boyd apparently failed to appreciate the overriding need to avoid a fight with Carrancista troops. Perhaps Pershing's anger at Treviño seemed to belie his words of caution. At any rate, Boyd left Pershing with his fighting spirit up. He assembled his noncommissioned officers and told them, "It is reported that the Mexicans say that they will attack us if we move in any direction except to the north. We are going to test that."

Boyd's Troop C left Colonia Dublán on the day of his meeting with Pershing. For some reason, Boyd was unaware that another troop of the Tenth Cavalry, K Troop, was also leaving from Ojo Federico, a town about halfway between Dublán and Columbus. Troop K, commanded by Captain Lewis S. Morey, was headed for Santo Domingo Ranch, about nine miles short of Carrizal, there to join up with Boyd. The two troops were then to proceed together.

Boyd's and Morey's units were desperately understrength. Boyd's had only one other officer, First Lieutenant Henry Rodney Adair, and forty-one enlisted men. Morey was even worse off. The only officer present in K Troop, he had only thirty-nine enlisted men. Together, the two troops boasted only three officers and eighty men.

After long marches of over fifty miles, the troops joined at Santo Domingo Ranch. Captain Boyd, as the senior officer, assumed command of the combined force,* and that evening Boyd called a meeting to discuss their next move. Besides the three officers, two civilians attended: Boyd's Mormon guide, Lemuel Spillsbury, and the American foreman of the ranch, W. P. McCabe.

Boyd outlined his plan. He intended to ride straight through Carrizal to Villa Ahumada. McCabe urged caution; part of Carrizal featured adobe construction, he said, and the buildings were bulletproof. Going through that portion of town could be hazardous. McCabe therefore advised Boyd to bypass Carrizal to the east. Morey agreed with McCabe and Spillsbury in urging Boyd to proceed with care, but Boyd and Adair, who seemed to hold the Mexicans in contempt, remained adamant. Morey, as he later testified, began to feel that his own bravery was being questioned. He therefore volunteered to go through Carrizal first—even alone—if Boyd so ordered him.

During the evening, a patrol from the Mexican force at Carrizal rode into Santo Domingo Ranch. The patrol leader claimed that he had come to purchase some beef. That claim was either spurious or

*All three officers were West Pointers. Boyd was from the Class of 1896, Morey from that of 1900, and Adair from that of 1904.

ignored in the excitement of the moment. Boyd's conversation with the patrol leader was not overheard, but witnesses observed that the Mexicans left "hurriedly."

At 4:00 A.M., June 21, Captain Boyd's troopers trotted out of Santo Domingo Ranch toward Carrizal, nine miles off. Since combat was possible, they left behind all unnecessary impedimenta, each man taking only a canteen of water and a belt and bandoleer of ammunition. Captain Morey, who anticipated the worst, turned his valuables over to McCabe with instructions for their disposition in case, as he expected, he did not return.

Although it was still early when Boyd's command approached Carrizal, over four hundred Carrancista troops were drawn up in battle formation on a low ridge in front of the town. Since the Mexicans made no move, Boyd sent Lem Spillsbury, his guide, to ask permission for his command to go through Carrizal. Spillsbury was to tell the Mexicans that the Americans "wanted to see about a deserter" who had been reported in Carrizal.

Spillsbury was an independent cowboy, neither a diplomat nor a soldier, but he did his job conscientiously. He crossed the flats and rode into Carrizal, where he met with an officer named Major Genevevo Rivas, who seemed to be in command. Rivas proved to be hostile indeed. "There are no Villistas in this part of the country," he said. "And if there are any enemies of yours over here, we're them."

Spillsbury saw at once that he could not reason with Rivas, so he induced the Mexican to accompany him back to the grass flat where Captain Boyd was waiting. Soon thereafter, General Félix U. Gómez, the Carrancista force commander, joined them.

In contrast to Rivas, Gómez was courteous. But he was equally firm. "I have orders to stop any movement of American troops through this town and am therefore bound to oppose you," he said. "However, if you would like to wait here, I will go back to Villa Ahumada and wire General Treviño, our commanding general. If he gives permission to come through, you will be welcome to do so."

Boyd then turned to Spillsbury for advice. The two agreed that Gomez was playing for time. "What would you do if you were in my shoes?" Boyd asked. Spillsbury's answer was consistent with his attitude all along. The best thing to do, he said, was to leave the field, fortify Santo Domingo Ranch, and prepare to hold the Mexicans off. Boyd could never accede to withdrawing, so he finally answered, "I'm going through the town. Tell the son-of-a-bitch that we're going through."

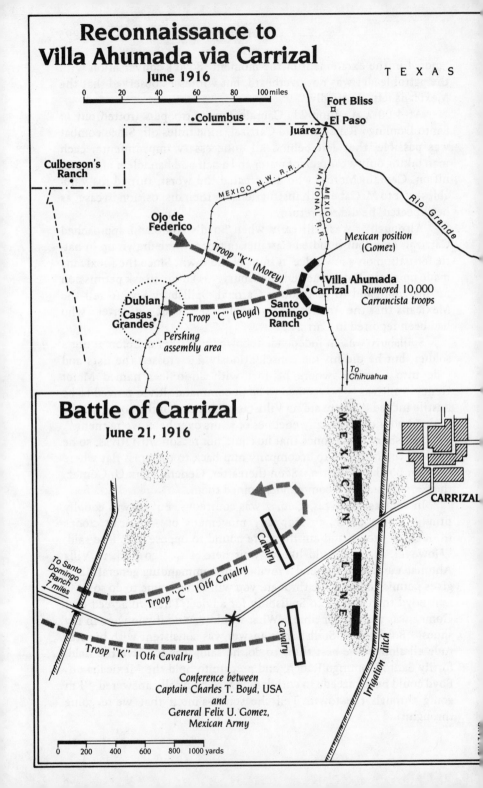

Reconnaissance to Villa Ahumada via Carrizal

June 1916

0 20 40 60 80 100 miles

TEXAS

•Columbus

Fort Bliss
El Paso

Juárez

Culberson's
Ranch

MEXICO N.W. R.R.

MEXICO NATIONAL R.R.

Rio Grande

Ojo de
Federico

Troop "K" (Morey)

Mexican position
(Gomez)

Villa Ahumada
Carrizal

Rumored 10,000
Carrancista troops

Dublan
Casas
Grandes

Troop "C" (Boyd)

Santo
Domingo
Ranch

Pershing
assembly area

To
Chihuahua

Battle of Carrizal

June 21, 1916

MEXICAN LINE

CARRIZAL

Cavalry

Troop "C" 10th Cavalry

To Santo
Domingo
Ranch
7 miles

Cavalry

Troop "K" 10th Cavalry

Irrigation ditch

Conference between
Captain Charles T. Boyd, USA
and
General Felix U. Gomez,
Mexican Army

0 200 400 600 800 1000 yards

Spillsbury did not need to interpret; General Gómez understood. "You might pass through the town," he said in Spanish. "But you'll have to walk over my dead body." Gómez then walked back toward his men, while Boyd and Spillsbury returned to theirs.

Boyd dismounted his troops, deploying C Troop on the left of the road leading into Carrizal and K Troop on the right. At that moment, the Mexicans opened fire. The Buffalo Soldiers moved forward.

The battle was no contest. Boyd's C Troop, on the left, pushed forward aggressively, but the enemy numbers were far too great. Boyd, who remained mounted, was wounded twice. Nevertheless, he continued to press on until a rifle bullet through the forehead toppled him. Lieutenant Adair assumed command of C Troop but was also killed immediately. On the right, Lewis Morey's K Troop lost contact with C Troop and stopped well short of its assigned objective. Captain Morey was badly wounded.

The seventy leaderless Americans now faced overwhelming odds and fell back in confusion. Thirty-three of them stayed on the field, however. Ten were killed outright, and twenty-three were taken prisoner. Still, the Buffalo Soldiers had conducted themselves well; the fact that Gómez lost forty-five officers and men (including himself) attests to American marksmanship.

Foreman W. H. McCabe had remained behind at Santo Domingo Ranch when the troopers rode out that morning; this was not his battle. Sometime between 8:00 and 9:00 A.M., he spied five troopers galloping back from Carrizal, followed by two loose horses and part of the pack train. All of them were still armed with rifles and ammunition. The Mexicans, they said, had fired on Boyd's command and "massacred the bunch." McCabe berated these troopers for leaving their comrades behind but found it advisable to provide the guide they demanded. He watched as they rode off to the west.

Straggling troopers continued to flow through the ranch in the course of the morning, and nearly all of McCabe's ranch hands likewise left. By noon, McCabe was alone at Santo Domingo Ranch with only six workers—three Mexicans and three Chinese. He slept that night in the bushes some distance from the ranch. On the morning of the twenty-third, two days after the fight at Carrizal, he sighted a group of about fifteen Carrancistas in the distance, riding toward the ranch. McCabe, with a couple of men, hastily headed west in search of American troops.

At the Suterano windmill, McCabe found Captain Morey, who had taken refuge with four other wounded men. There they all remained until the next day, when they were picked up by a detachment from the Eleventh Cavalry under Major Robert Howze. By this time, Pershing had heard of the debacle and had sent Howze out to the rescue.

Word of the disaster at Carrizal had been slow in reaching Pershing, because he had lost contact with Boyd and Morey ever since they left Dublán. Pershing's only sources of information were the stragglers from the battle. The Carrancistas, however, telegraphed the news to all points, and General Funston, in San Antonio, received his first word from Mexican reports. Funston, with his customary short fuse, sent Pershing a message on June 22, the strung-out wording of which reflects his exasperation:

> Why in the name of God do I hear nothing from you the whole country has known for ten hours through Mexican sources that a considerable force of your command was apparently defeated yesterday with heavy loss at Carrizal.
>
> Under existing order to you why were they so far from your line being at such distance that I assume that now nearly twenty-four hours after affair news has not reached you who was responsible for what was on its face seems to have been a terrible blunder.

Pershing was already anguished enough on his own, trying to find out what had happened and to assess what had gone wrong. Until he learned the facts, Pershing presumed that the Carrizal fight had been brought on by Mexican, not American, action. In that case, he hoped he might be "turned loose" and allowed to attack and cut the Juárez–Chihuahua railroad line. Perhaps he would even be permitted to take Chihuahua. He did not doubt that he could do so.

As the reports filtered in, though, Pershing began to understand what had actually happened. His first inkling came from reports within his own headquarters, from men who had overheard Captain Boyd's remarks, made right after his conference with Pershing on June 17. Boyd, they revealed, had boasted indiscreetly about his intentions. But Pershing remained confused. "I am very much cut up over the calamity caused by the error in judgment on poor Boyd's part, and which caused such a heavy toll. It is entirely inexplicable to me in view of the fact that I personally gave him instructions, and especially cautioned him against exactly what happened."

Finally, when the wounded Lewis Morey arrived back at Dublán, Pershing accepted the unpleasant truth that Boyd, not the Mexicans, had instigated the fight at Carrizal. That placed the situation in a different light. Pershing's only consolation now was assurance that the Buffalo Soldiers of the Tenth Cavalry, even though leaderless, had fought well—as long as any hope of success remained.

Funston instructed Pershing that his forces were to remain at Colonia Dublán. Carrizal was the last battle the men of the Punitive Expedition would fight against anybody.

In Washington, President Wilson and Secretary Lansing also presumed that the fight at Carrizal had been begun by the Carrancistas. On that assumption, they quickly sent angry messages to Carranza demanding the release of the twenty-three prisoners. At the same time, the War Department ordered General Funston to seize all the international bridges across the Rio Grande as the prelude to a full-scale American invasion of Mexico. On June 22, Wilson wrote to House, "The break seems to have come with Mexico; and all my patience to have gone for nothing. I am infinitely sad about it. . . . Right or wrong, the extremest consequences seem upon us."

Tensions between the United States and Mexico now approached the breaking point. Anti-American demonstrations erupted in all major Mexican cities, largely staged by Carranza himself, who was thereby risking a war he did not want. Carranza's attitude changed, however, when he became conscious of Wilson's ferocious reaction. Alarmed, the First Chief ordered General Treviño to return the twenty-three American prisoners by train to El Paso. The men arrived at Juárez on the afternoon of June 29, stripped of their uniforms—one wore only a blanket—but otherwise in reasonable condition.

On July 4, Carranza suggested "direct and friendly negotiations" to end the causes of Mexican-American tension. Wilson, who did not want war either, accepted the offer quickly.

But many Americans were not enchanted by Wilson's conciliatory attitude. Among them was Major Frank Tompkins, who later wrote:

If one has the gift of humor, many a laugh can be had from a reading of the diplomatic correspondence between the two countries. . . . Just to illustrate: When Carranza notified our government that he intended to resist by force any movement of the Punitive Expedition except in a northerly direction, our Department of State replied that any act of force would bring the "gravest consequences." . . . Then came the fight at Carrizal . . . and the "gravest consequences" consisted in our State Department on July 7th, addressing a note to the Mexican Government dwelling upon the spirit of friendship and solicitude which animates the American government for the *continuation of cordial relationships* between the two governments!!!

24

★★★★★★★★★★

Exit the
United States

The original objective of the Puni-
tive Expedition—to capture Pancho Villa—was now forgotten. The
humiliating American defeat at Carrizal had seen to that. Though
Pershing remained in Mexico for another seven months, the expedition's whole purpose was nullified on June 21, 1916, the day of the
Carrizal fight.

The serious pursuit of Villa had actually been given up after the
skirmish at Parral, two months earlier, but during the time between
Parral and Carrizal the Americans and Carrancistas had maintained at
least some pretense of mutual tolerance. After Carrizal, however,
American attention was focused entirely on protecting Pershing's
force from the Carrancistas. For a short while, as war between the
United States and Mexico seemed imminent, the War Department
was planning for a possible major invasion of Mexico. The planners
estimated that such an invasion would require an army of 200,000
men.

The disaster at Carrizal stirred Pershing's fighting blood, even
though the general realized that the Americans had been the aggres-
sors. In order to reassert American prestige vis-à-vis the Carrancistas,
Pershing even considered requesting permission to take Chihuahua,

which he was confident he could do without much difficulty. But Funston, in San Antonio, for once took a more sensible view than Pershing. Until such time as the government in Washington declared war, Funston concentrated on ensuring that there would be no repetition of the Carrizal incident.

Funston therefore ordered Pershing to cease sending out long-range patrols. Deprived of information regarding the Carrancistas, Pershing was thus forced to concentrate his command in two enclaves, seven thousand men at Colonia Dublán and four thousand at El Valle. Though the Carrancistas could doubtless concentrate a greater number of men to attack him, Pershing was unworried. He had built strong defensive positions, his infantry was reliable, and the Americans enjoyed the advantage of superior artillery.

Pershing's Achilles' heel was therefore the long and tenuous supply line that ran between Dublán and Columbus, New Mexico. The barrenness of the land around both Dublán and El Valle forced him to depend on the quartermasters in the United States for supply of all sorts—bacon, hardtack, and even firewood. Because the railroad from Dublán to Juárez and El Paso traversed Carrancista territory, resupply depended on the carrying capacity of his "truck trains." Security for the main supply route was maintained by the posting of strong garrisons at the critical points. Pershing calculated that he could reinforce any one of these strongholds quickly in case of Carrancista attack.

That need never arose. The Carrancista victory at Carrizal had actually cost more Mexican than American lives, and the First Chief had no intention of resuming hostilities. Besides, political relations between the two countries were bad enough already.

In Washington, too, the war fever subsided as soon as Carranza offered to participate in "joint and friendly discussions." A commission was set up in July 1916 to study the problems between the two countries. American pride was further soothed when Carranza consented to holding the meetings on American soil. And finally, when Captain Lewis Morey's testimony categorically laid the blame for the Carrizal fight on the Americans, domestic public opinion softened. President Wilson was soon convinced that the people favored patience, despite what he considered Carranza's personal provocations.

The easing of tensions with Mexico greatly relieved the beleaguered Wilson, for the removal of the threat from the south allowed him to concentrate more of his energies on the worsening relations with Germany over the *Sussex* issue. The easing also eliminated the Mexican situation as a serious issue in the impending presidential election.

Neither Carranza nor Wilson seemed to be in any hurry for the joint commission to begin its work, however, because the most important thing about it was its very establishment. The lack of urgency notwithstanding, both countries appointed men of stature as members. Wilson's three-man delegation included Secretary of the Interior Franklin K. Lane, the Reverend John R. Mott, and former Judge George Gray. The Mexican members were Luis Cabrera, Ignacio Bonillas, and Alberto J. Pani. Particularly important was Luis Cabrera, one of Carranza's closest advisers.

The commissioners met on September 6, at New London, Connecticut. After the first wave of euphoria, Wilson and Carranza began to argue over the portfolios the commission members would carry. The only subjects to be addressed by the commission, Carranza insisted, were the immediate withdrawal of the Punitive Expedition and measures to be taken on both sides to ensure the protection of the frontier. Wilson, on the other hand, wanted the commission's authority widened to include broader issues. The prospects for success may have been unpromising, but war had been delayed if not averted, and Wilson could claim that his policy in Mexico had been "uncompromised."

At Dublán and El Valle, Pershing's soldiers were unconcerned about the details of the diplomatic activities as they moved from New London to Atlantic City and finally to Philadelphia. The resurgence of Pancho Villa, however, was very real to them, for it made a mockery of their claim of success at the end of weeks of hardship and exhaustion. Up to now, the Americans' humiliation over withdrawal from Namiquipa empty-handed had been eased by the argument that Villa's bands had been eliminated as organized military units. But as Villa recovered from his wounds and even reemerged as a force to be reckoned with, Americans' chagrin became great.

Villa was very much in evidence. In early September 1916, just as the Mexican and American conferees were sitting down in New London, Villa appeared at the head of five hundred men at Satevó. In their attack on that town, the Villistas killed two hundred Carrancistas. Villa repeated the incredible feat a week later, at Santa Isabel, this time seizing a military train.

In mid-September, Villa outdid himself. Exhibiting his old panache, he wrote a note to General Treviño at Chihuahua promising to return to the city to "shake hands with you on the sixteenth." Villa added that he "might be hungry and would like to have something to eat." It was later reported that Villa, in disguise, had personally entered Chihuahua on the fifteenth to reconnoiter.

Villa made good on his threat. At 2:30 A.M. on September 16, Villa left his camp near Chihuahua with a band numbering somewhere between 500 and 1,700. He entered Chihuahua City and headed first for the penitentiary, where he freed 200 prisoners and added them to the ranks of his followers. He then turned down the street to take the governor's palace. He met little resistance: Treviño's personal guards turned out to be nearly all Villista sympathizers, and many deserted their posts and joined the raiders.

Villa was once again in his element. He ran up the steps of the Governor's Palace and appeared on the main balcony. There he made a short speech to the wildly cheering crowd below: "Viva Mexico! You do not have your liberty; I will give you your liberty for I am your brother. I am going to return in a few days." Villa remained in Chihuahua over seven hours—until 10:00 A.M.—and then left practically unmolested. This he accomplished even though the Carrancista garrison at Chihuahua was said to exceed six thousand men.

At Dublán, General Pershing found such developments unbearable. After a couple of weeks, he sent a message to Funston advising that Carranza was "totally unable to put down banditry in the State of Chihuahua." Villa's numbers and prestige were growing every day, he claimed. Furthermore, those people of Chihuahua who opposed Villa were wondering why Carranza refused to send capable officers to cope with this new Villista menace.

Pershing suspected that all the Carrancista generals were either incompetent or engaged in a conspiracy to rob the populace. Those in Chihuahua, he argued, were diligent about collecting taxes but were making only "a flimsy pretext at hunting bandits." The Carrancista troops were poorly paid and provisioned—in contrast with their officers, who were comfortable.

Pershing again asked permission to take Chihuahua. Since the Carrancistas could or would not restore order, he wrote, "the occupation of the city of Chihuahua would be very advantageous and would probably not be difficult, as there would be little opposition on the part of [Carrancista] troops, while the population would doubtless welcome us." Pershing's entreaties were in vain. Funston agreed with him, but Washington did not.

Once Pershing and his men had resigned themselves to the idea that their present camps were destined to be their homes for a while, they set about to make life tolerable. Before long, the camps at Dublán and El Valle took on some of the comforts of garrison posts. Most of Pershing's men were disciplined regulars, prepared to tolerate any necessary deprivation, but they were not automatons. It was essential to show them that everything possible was being done to improve their living conditions.

Colonia Dublán's climate was milder than that of the mountains, but the town was dusty, barren, and windswept. To protect themselves from the elements, therefore, Pershing's men built two-man adobe huts and waterproofed them by spreading their shelter halves on top. One ingenious captain provided comfort for mealtimes by having his men dig holes for their feet as they sat on the ground. Food was adequate.

The most daunting enemy to morale was boredom. Since this expedition had been mounted on short notice—and since such organizations as the United Service Organization and the YMCA had not yet been established—the men were left to their own devices for recreation. Some of the privileged—officers and noncommissioned officers—were able to hunt deer and waterfowl under the guidance of Apache scouts. Occasionally, Pershing's aides were sent back to El Paso to escort a visiting dignitary down to Dublán. And once, though he allowed himself few privileges not accorded his troops, Pershing returned to El Paso for a few days in early September. He took Lieutenant Patton with him, a good move to foster his friendship with Patton's sister Nita.

Most soldiers spent their spare time during the days at the baseball diamonds and boxing rings. In the evening, they tended to be exhausted from the strenuous training conducted during the day. Some prostitutes from El Paso had followed the Punitive Expedition, and Pershing did not fight human nature. He rounded the women up, placed them comfortably in a separate building, and detailed Captain Julien E. Gaujot, Eleventh Cavalry, to supervise them.

Captain Gaujot took good care of his charges. He housed them, paid them, and even scheduled their activities. As a result, the venereal-disease rate among the soldiers of the Punitive Expedition ran far below the average, even for troops in garrison. And the women were socially active in other ways. They prepared an elaborate party for Thanksgiving, making their benefactor, Julien Gaujot, the guest of honor.

Although members of the Punitive Expedition would rather have been somewhere other than Dublán or El Valle, the period in the wilderness provided benefits. The troops received invaluable training for their coming participation in World War I, which the United States entered soon after the expedition's withdrawal. Isolated from the distractions of peacetime domestic life, the various units went through training programs more rigorous than any found in the still-peaceful atmosphere of the United States.

Pershing's command included all of the army's combat elements—infantry, artillery, and cavalry—and he trained each to the highest level possible. He established special courses in rifle and machine-gun fire, making full use of instructors who had been observers in the European war. Staff officers worked on daily maneuver problems. Pershing delegated his routine paperwork to his staff and concentrated on soldiering. Lieutenant George S. Patton, always a military perfectionist, marveled at the thoroughness of Pershing's training, at the fitness of his troops, and at Pershing's personal involvement in the entire process.* The future commander of the American Expeditionary Force in France benefited from this period as much as did his troops.

As the summer of 1916 passed into fall and winter, and as relations with the kaiser's Germany degenerated, President Wilson and his administration grew less and less belligerent toward Mexico, even toward First Chief Venustiano Carranza. The easing of tensions was

---

*Under the personal supervision of the General every unit went through a complete course in range and combat firing, marches, maneuvers, entrenching, and combating exercises with ball ammunition. Every horse and man was fit; weaklings had gone; baggage was still at a minimum, and discipline was perfect. When I speak of supervision I do not mean that nebulous staff control so frequently connected with the work. By constant study General Pershing knew to the minutest detail each of the subjects in which he demanded practice, and by his physical presence and personal example and explanation, insured himself that they were correctly carried out.

The Patton Papers, ed. Martin Blumenson, vol. 1 (Boston, 1972), p. 362.

aided by reports of a new Mexican constitutional congress, which began to meet in Querétaro during September. Few details of the proceedings at Querétaro were known to Wilson or Lansing at the time, but from the outset it was apparent that Carranza would be unable to dictate the results. The fact that representation at Querétaro seemed to be relatively broad-based meant that Carranza would probably not become another Díaz or Huerta. Word of this ongoing development placed the Mexican situation in a much improved light in Washington.

Thus it was of secondary importance that the Joint High Commission accomplished very little in its drawn-out meetings. The document that this body signed on December 24, 1916, was indeed innocuous. Though it called for the withdrawal of the Punitive Expedition within forty days, it added the caveat that conditions in northern Mexico must warrant it. Carranza rejected the agreement three days later, insisting that the expedition evacuate Mexican soil immediately. The commission did nothing more; it broke up on January 17, 1917. No matter: its chief usefulness lay in its having come into being at all.

On January 18, the day after the commission dissolved, Secretary of War Newton D. Baker informed General Funston that the president would soon withdraw the Punitive Expedition. The final order to break camp arrived at Dublán on January 27, by which time Pershing and his homesick troops were more than ready to go.

The withdrawal was orderly, regretted by neither Mexicans nor Americans. On February 5, Pershing's command recrossed the border into Columbus, New Mexico. They were lavishly welcomed by the people at home.

25

****

The Triumph
of Obregón

When Pershing's Punitive Expedition crossed the border from Chihuahua to New Mexico, the U.S. intervention in the Mexican Revolution came to an end. All Mexicans cheered. But the Revolution was not quite resolved; once again, as in 1915, the victors in Mexico's internecine quarrel fell out. First Chief Venustiano Carranza, who fully intended to remain indefinitely as head of the Mexican government, now found himself challenged by his onetime loyalist Alvaro Obregón. This time, fortunately for Mexico, the political battles did not involve military clashes.

Obregón was fully aware of his critical role in Carranza's eventual triumph over Pancho Villa. Others knew it also, even President Woodrow Wilson. Wilson had, in fact, privately called Obregón the "man of the hour," even as he was deciding to recognize Carranza as de facto president, back in October 1915. So Obregón, as Mexico's most popular figure, felt that he deserved to succeed Carranza as president when Carranza's constitutional term ended in 1920.

Obregón was a far more complex man than he allowed the public to perceive. Described as "the happy man with one arm," his wisecracking demeanor disguised his real no-nonsense nature. In private, he was a moody man, given to fits of depression at times—but never immobilized by them. Obregón had his detractors. Martín Luis Guzmán, for example, described him as "a person who was convinced of his own importance, but who pretended not to take himself seriously, [whose] pretense lay at the bottom of every one of his acts." However he appeared to others, the ambitious Obregón intended to use his immense popularity to his own political advantage.

Obregón realized, though, that the glamour and mystique he had acquired on the battlefield would not suffice to convince the people that he was the man to govern Mexico. He therefore set about to stress the civilian side of his makeup, a fairly easy task since Obregón had never thought of himself as a "military man on horseback." His opportunity arrived when Carranza called the Querétaro convention in late 1916 to revise the Mexican constitution. Obregón determined to influence the outcome of the proceedings and to let the public see him in a political role.

Obregón was still Carranza's secretary of war when the constitutional convention opened in December 1916. Nevertheless, Obregón quickly overstepped his military bounds and threw his backing to the "radicals" or "Jacobins," who wanted to liberalize the constitution. The leader of these Jacobin radicals was the young General Francisco J. Múgica, who added to Carranza's original draft detailed articles providing for the rights and privileges of labor. These articles regulated conditions for Mexican labor: working hours, wages, child labor, overtime pay, maternity care, and the right to strike. The Jacobins also introduced provisions that delineated the relations between church and state: for example, they made marriage a civil rather than a religious act, and they placed the clergy in the professional class along with doctors and lawyers, thus subject to civil law.

The new constitution also subordinated the property rights of individuals and corporations to the interests of the state. It gave the Mexican central government authority over the division of land and waters. Minerals—copper and gold—were to be the property of the state. The implications for the foreign-owned mining companies, especially the American firms, were obvious.

Obregón helped push these measures through in two ways. First, he influenced his political followers to support Múgica; second, he enforced the authority of the constitutional convention with the power of the army. Without that strong arm, the remarkable new document would have been next to meaningless.

The delegates signed it on January 31, 1917. Carranza withheld its publication, however, until the day the American Punitive Expedition recrossed the Mexican–U.S. border.

February 5 therefore marked the high point of the career of

Venustiano Carranza. For as the Yankees left, he published the new constitution. Though nearly all its provisions ran counter to Carranza's original desires, the First Chief rightfully received the credit for having called the convention in the first place, and he was the official who signed the final document.

Obregón's reasons for deferring his own presidential candidacy until 1920 were probably idealistic, for the Sonoran general deeply believed in the principles of the Revolution. His decision to wait was made easier by his poor health. Obregón had never completely recovered from the shock of losing his right arm at León in 1915, and he had been functioning under strong pressures ever since. So Obregón agreed to serve as provisional secretary of war until after Carranza's official inauguration as president. After that, Obregón decided to retire to his chick-pea farm in Sonora. But he was also determined to become president in 1920.

The Mexican presidential election, a pro forma affair held on March 11, 1917, saw Carranza virtually unopposed. Two days after the results were announced, President Woodrow Wilson nominated Henry P. Fletcher to be American ambassador to Mexico. The first man to carry that title since the recall of Henry Lane Wilson nearly four years earlier, Fletcher presented his credentials to Carranza at Guadalajara, where the president-elect was staying. On April 24, Carranza moved back to Mexico City for the first time in four months. A week later, on May 1, he took the oath of office as president.

Carranza soon proved that he was still totally inept at governing Mexico. He made his first great diplomatic blunder even before his inauguration. It grew out of his intense desire to aid Germany in its struggle against the hated Allies.

Carranza's admiration for the German kaiser was long known, and as First Chief he had granted liberal privileges to the 4,000-strong German community. Germans living in Mexico were permitted to organize into such fronts as the Union of German Citizens and the Iron Cross Society. German citizens also subsidized a newspaper that distributed German war propaganda. Officially, fifty German "advisers" occupied key positions in Carranza's army, most prominent of whom was Maximilian Kloss, an officer of Mexican-German birth who had helped Obregón apply the lessons of the European war to defeat Villa at Celaya two years earlier. Kloss, though a German citizen, had been appointed Carranza's director of munitions manufacture, with the rank of general in the Mexican army.

Mexico's involvement with Germany did not begin with Carranza. Teutonic influence in Mexico went back at least to 1914, when Admiral Paul von Hintze, the German minister to Mexico, approached President Huerta with an offer. The German government would provide Huerta with military aid for use against the rebels, in exchange for which Huerta would agree to close the Tampico oilfields to the British Royal Navy in case of war between Germany and Britain. Huerta was tempted, but he was ousted from power before the European war actually broke out, in August 1914.

When approached by the German minister to Mexico in 1916, Carranza proved to be even more receptive to the notion of cooperation with the kaiser than Huerta had been. On October 16, Carranza declared himself "disposed, if necessary, to give aid to [German] submarines in Mexican waters." "Germany [is] the only great power with which [Carranza] would like stronger economic and political ties." Carranza was prepared to deny Tampico oil to the Royal Navy. Such news was encouraging, indeed, to the kaiser's foreign office.

Carranza's receptivity, however, caused the German government to overstep itself. On January 16, 1917, the German foreign secretary, Arthur Zimmermann, sent a message over the U.S. State Department's "neutral" cable route to the kaiser's ambassador in Washington, Count Johann von Bernstorff. Zimmermann ordered Bernstorff to notify the envoy in Mexico City that Germany would help Mexico regain territories lost to the United States in 1848 if it and Japan would enter the European war on the German side: "we make Mexico a proposal of alliance: . . . make war together, make peace together. Generous financial support and *understanding on our part that Mexico is to reconquer the lost territory in Kansas, New Mexico, and Arizona. . . .*"

British naval intelligence intercepted the German message and routinely began to decode it—something the senders of the message thought impossible. As the message took form, the British realized they had fallen upon a great prize. The threat to the United States would give tremendous impetus to British efforts to bring the Americans into the European war against Germany. For the moment, however, the British government withheld its contents. The decoding process took time, and an exposure of its contents without some corroborating intelligence source would alert the Germans that their "unbreakable" code had been compromised.

On February 13, Carranza took an overt step to aid Germany

against Britain and France. He called on all neutral countries to "cooperate in placing an embargo on all war materials destined for belligerents." That proposal was far from neutral; it actually singled out the British, whom the United States was supplying with ammunition. The British, fully alarmed, now decided to play their trump card. On March 1, just before the Mexican presidential election, the British Foreign Office found a ruse to make it appear that the contents of the Zimmermann telegram had been leaked through the Mexican Foreign Office.

When the Zimmermann telegram appeared in U.S. newspapers, the American people were shocked. All their ambivalence toward entering the European war melted away. On April 6, only six weeks after the telegram's publication, the United States declared war on Germany. Other factors contributed, but the Zimmermann telegram had proven to be a potent catalyst.

Once again, Carranza was startled by the virulence of the American reaction. Upon the U.S. declaration of war against Germany, he backed off from his transoceanic flirtations. On April 13, when Herr von Eckhardt approached him again, Carranza declared that Mexico would remain neutral. Cultivating friendship with Venustiano Carranza had proven expensive to Kaiser Wilhelm; it had hastened the entry of the United States into the war against him.

Meanwhile, the untamed Pancho Villa continued to raid in northwest Mexico. On May 30, 1917, Villa once more attacked Ojinaga, on the Rio Grande, and drove the Federal garrison, as before, across the river into Texas. He repeated the same raid in November 1917. Villa was less successful in attacking Chihuahua, however. There a general named Francisco Murguía, a man who could match Villa at his own game of cruelty, beat off a Villista attack and forthwith hanged 250 of Villa's men in the city. The street where the executions took place has ever since been known to the townspeople as the Avenue of Hanging Men.

Villa's depredations continued until the night of June 14, 1919, when he again attacked Juárez. Once more, stray bullets killed and wounded American soldiers in Fort Bliss. This time, the Americans had had enough. An American force of infantry and cavalry crossed the river and roundly trounced Villa's twelve hundred men. Villa's army was now truly destroyed for good.

The plight of the Mexican people continued to worsen. The country was "in ruins, industry prostrate, a people in rags, diseased, despairing, dying." Land reform had been neglected. And labor, which had supposedly come into its own with the constitutional convention at Querétaro, was growing more impatient all the time. However, it was his political mistakes, not economic conditions, that eventually brought Carranza down. They involved violence, which he normally eschewed.

First, Carranza plotted the murder of the popular Emiliano Zapata. It had long irritated him that Zapata still remained at large in the state of Morelos, adjacent to Mexico City. Supported by a loyal peasantry, the wily Zapata continued to write insulting public letters to Carranza,* which were so effective that by early 1919 Carranza decided that something drastic had to be done.

Up to 1919, Carranza had left the pursuit of Zapata in the hands of the inept Pablo González—"General Horserace," as he was called. González had taken Cuernavaca and Ayala (from which Zapata's original plan had emanated), but he lacked the imagination to capture or kill Zapata himself. On Carranza's prodding, however, González finally came up with an idea. He enlisted the services of a ruthless young colonel named Jesús María Guajardo, a man known to hate agrarian reformers and therefore eager to eliminate Zapata.

Since Zapata could not be caught in the open, any plot against him would have to be conducted by treachery from within. Guajardo therefore had to gain Zapata's confidence. This he did by planting false information in the ear of a gullible and frightened Zapatista captive named Eusebio Jáuregui. Guajardo had captured General Jáuregui and, instead of shooting him, had allowed him to roam free within the Federal headquarters. Guajardo made audible remarks in which he criticized Carranza and declared his intention of joining Zapata—all for Jáuregui's benefit. Jáuregui, grateful to have his life

---

*Citizen Carranza: From the time you first . . . named yourself chief of a movement which you maliciously called "constitutionalist" . . . you proceeded to turn to the advantage of yourself . . . riches, honors, business, banquets, sumptuous fiestas, bachanals of pleasure, orgies of satiation, of ambition, power and of blood. It never entered your mind that the Revolution was for the benefit of the great masses. . . . You turned against those whom you used; . . . you took justice in your own hands and created a dictatorship which you gave the name of "revolutionary."

WILLIAM WEBER JOHNSON,
Heroic Mexico (New York, 1968), p. 331.

spared, reported Guajardo's remarks to Zapata when Guajardo released him. Zapata, like Jáuregui, was taken in.

Zapata then made discreet contact with Guajardo, but before accepting the young colonel into the rebel movement, he required Guajardo to exhibit some evidence of sincerity. As proof, Zapata designated a small Carrancista town, Jonacatepec, and directed Guajardo to seize it. Guajardo did so, though he used only blank ammunition. When reproached by an unwitting Federal superior named Victoriano Bárcenas, Guajardo summarily captured Bárcenas, plus sixty of his Carrancista troops, and executed all of them. Zapata, who hated Bárcenas, was highly impressed.

From then on, Guajardo's path was easy. Guajardo called on Zapata, bearing elaborate presents. Zapata, now won over, appointed Guajardo a general in his army and accepted an invitation to visit Guajardo's headquarters at San Juan Chinameca.

Zapata took a contingent of only ten men to Chinameca for his visit on April 10, 1919. As he and his escort approached the gate of the hacienda, he gave little thought to the honor guard that was drawn up to meet him. The men snapped to attention as he began to pass between their ranks. Then a bugle sounded three times. On the third blast, the members of the "honor guard" raised their rifles and blasted Zapata and his party to kingdom come.

Zapata's body was carried to the municipal building of Chinameca and placed on display. Jáuregui, the hapless messenger of treachery, was called in to identify Zapata's body. Then he, too, was shot. Carranza made Guajardo a general in the Federal army and awarded him fifty thousand pesos.

The peasants of Morelos were at least allowed to file past their slain leader's body to pay their last respects. Carranza wished to show definite proof that their leader was dead. Zapata was indeed dead, but the treacherous act dealt a fatal blow to Carranza's standing with any fair-minded Mexicans.

As the 1920 election approached, the political ambitions of Carranza and Obregón came more and more into conflict. Carranza was seeking a way to remain in office for a second term, whereas Obregón expected Carranza to accept him as a logical successor. Neither man's hope was realistic. Carranza, who could not abide the idea of turning over his office to a mere soldier, decided that if he could not retain the presi-

dency himself, the next best thing would be to name his own successor, someone he could control. Obregón, of course, would have none
of that.

Early in 1919, Carranza settled tentatively on a successor. He
chose Ignacio Bonillas, currently Mexican ambassador to Washington
and onetime member of the joint Mexican–U.S. commission. Bonillas
could meet many requirements for the presidential office but he totally lacked one: electability in any honest political contest. Nobody
could take him seriously.

Actually, the gentlemanly Bonillas was personally popular. He
was well liked in Washington diplomatic circles but had been there so
long that Mexican humorists derisively referred to him as "*Meester
Bonillas*." When Bonillas was held up in returning from Washington
to Mexico, wags explained the delay: he had stopped off somewhere
in order to study up on his Spanish. Carranza was cagey in his support;
he spent two million pesos in promoting Bonillas's candidacy without
formally announcing his support.

Obregón, meanwhile, had largely recovered his health. He ab-
stained from political activities for nearly two years after Carranza's
inauguration, but during that period he traveled around Mexico on
"business" matters, making political friends and contacts. He went
on an extensive tour of the United States, where he was cordially
received by President Wilson. Because his role in the Querétaro convention had established him as a friend of organized labor, Obregón
readily picked up the political support of the Liberal Constitutionalist
party (PLC) as well as of many of the regional governors, especially in
northwest Mexico.

During the spring of 1919, the relations between Carranza and
Obregón degenerated from political rivalry to outright hostility. Carranza issued a manifesto to the Mexican nation pleading for "unity"
in the troubling times and pointed his finger at Obregón as the troublemaker. Obregón countered by publicly accusing Carranza of seeking to remain illegally in office past 1920. Carranza then canceled
Obregón's telegraph privileges, a perquisite enjoyed by the prominent
veterans of the Revolution.

That insult brought Obregón into open conflict with Carranza.
On June 1, 1919, Obregón formally declared himself a candidate in
the 1920 presidential election. In doing so, he was careful to avoid
affiliating himself exclusively with any particular party, though several endorsed him. Even the Liberal Constitutionalists did not com-

mand a large enough percentage of Mexican voters to elect him—nor did any one of the several other parties. Obregón was showing himself to be a shrewd politician.

In early September, Carranza retaliated against Obregón by officially endorsing Bonillas for president.

Carranza's downfall was triggered by a crisis in Sonora, the state in which he had based his 1914 military campaign against the dictator Huerta. It involved an old, touchy subject: the waters of the Sonora River. Carranza now insisted that the constitution of 1917 made the river the property of the central Mexican government, subject to reallocation by Mexico City. Adolfo de la Huerta, governor of Sonora, saw it otherwise. In late 1919, de la Huerta fired another barb at the Mexican president: he accused Carranza of plotting a campaign to deprive Sonora's Yaqui Indians of their rights. In March 1920, Governor de la Huerta, backed up by the Sonora legislature, withdrew recognition of Carranza as president.

Since Governor de la Huerta was out of Carranza's physical reach, Carranza decided to take vengeance on Sonora's most prominent son, Alvaro Obregón. He invented a pretext on which to order Obregón to appear in Mexico City on April 2, 1920, to testify in the trumped-up treason trial of one Colonel Roberto Cejudo. Obregón was aware of the danger he faced by obeying, but he decided to go anyway. Possibly, he felt it necessary to show the Mexican public that he was not afraid.

Obregón was in the middle of political campaigning in Tamaulipas when he received Carranza's order, and he left for Mexico City immediately. To minimize his personal danger, he announced that while in the capital he would reside at the home of his friend Miguel Alessio Robles, rather than accept accommodations at the hotel where he was expected. He also kept the loyal General Benjamín Hill with him at all times. Moreover, Obregón made use of the enthusiastic crowds that always trailed him. He kept his followers cognizant of his whereabouts, a device to lower the risk of treachery.

Obregón's first appearance at the military court-martial had its comic aspects. As the popular general entered the courtroom, the two armed guards standing beside the judge's bench spontaneously cried out "Viva Obregón!" That outburst made the judge so nervous that he reportedly put the lighted end of the cigar in his mouth. Order restored, the trial proceeded. Obregón truthfully testified that he did not even know the accused Colonel Cejudo. Dismissed as a witness, Obregón was nevertheless ordered to remain in Mexico City for further questioning. No fool, Obregón knew the time had come to make a break.

That evening, Obregón left Robles's home by car, accompanied by Benjamín Hill and another friend—and followed, as usual, by motorcycle police. At an opportune moment, Obregón switched hats with one of his companions. He and Hill then dropped out of the car and hid behind some trees. According to the plan, the two were then picked up by two other friends, who disguised them as railroad workers and placed them aboard a freight train bound for the state of Guerrero. After some frightening scrapes, Obregón and Hill wound up among friends.

Obregón now realized that any election held under the auspices of the Carranza regime would be a farce. While still in Guerrero, he therefore issued a manifesto: ". . . it is indispensable that we once more take up arms and reconquer those things which they are by force trying to take away from us." It was now late April 1920. General Plutarco Elías Calles, in Sonora, seized the occasion to declare war on Carranza and invited other states to do the same. Thirteen Mexican states were soon in rebellion.*

Carranza saw that his situation was hopeless, at least temporarily. He decided to flee Mexico City, but not before he had looted the government as it had never been looted before. On his orders, loyal followers removed coin, currency, gold, silver, even the dies from the mint. Printing presses, cartridge makers, and disassembled airplanes were all crated for removal. Carrancistas—ten thousand men, women, and children—assembled for the departure. The total length of the loaded trains was fifteen miles.

Large-scale, systematic looting took time, however, and Carranza exhibited remarkable aplomb by never losing his composure. While his long train was waiting to pull out of the railway station, Carranza paced up and down the platform encouraging his followers. That day, he had visited his private home in Mexico City and assured his nephew, "I am not fleeing into exile like Díaz, nor resigning like Madero. I will return to my house, either in victory or in death."

When it came time for the trains to leave Mexico City, however,

*Nayarit, Nuevo León, Veracruz, Michoacán, San Luis Potosí, Chihuahua, Hidalgo, Oaxaca, Morelos, Chiapas, Zacatecas, Tabasco, and Mexico. Johnson, *Heroic Mexico*, pp. 347–48.

little happened. Most of the railroad people were partial to Obregón, so they resisted passively. Before Carranza's train could depart, a locomotive filled with dynamite penetrated the cordon of guards and crashed into a troop train. In one moment, Carranza lost most of his artillery and a thousand infantry soldiers, four hundred of whom were members of his personal guard. When the trains finally did pull out, they still carried a respectable security force of three thousand infantry and eleven hundred cavalry.

But it was to no avail. At Rinconada, Puebla, Carranza's train ground to a halt, its path blocked by insurgents. The president left the train and actually took command of a pitched battle to clear the way. At that point, Carranza courageously refused an offer from Obregón promising him safe conduct to Veracruz and exile.

The train trip came to its end on the morning of May 14, at a place called Aljibes. The rail line had been demolished beyond that point, and word arrived that hostile cavalry had cut the railroad tracks. Carranza seemed unperturbed. He ate a hearty breakfast aboard the train and, with "maddening slowness," left the railroad car. He borrowed a horse and sent some aides scurrying back to the train to retrieve certain important papers. His entourage then loaded supplies (including Carranza's portable typewriter) on pack mules. The party headed slowly off to the hills, leaving over four million pesos in gold and silver money behind on the train.

Carranza's party, on horseback, set out under miserable conditions. A rainstorm created torrents in the chasms of the rough terrain of northern Puebla. At Cuautempan, Carranza dismissed much of his security guard, bringing the size of his "Expeditionary Column of Legality" down to a hundred men. Still, despite hunger and abandonment, Carranza did not complain.

On the morning of May 20, Carranza reached La Unión, Puebla. There he encountered a local chieftain named General Rodolfo Herrero, who had recently joined the Carranza group. Herrero ingratiatingly conducted the president to Tlaxcalantongo, a small town perched on a ledge in a steep chasm. As Carranza spread his saddle and blanket on the earthen floor of the largest hut in town, Herrero announced grandly, "This is the best house. For the present it is your National Palace."

Carranza seemed to sense that his end was near. With only a single candle for illumination, he made idle conversation with his few remaining aides until well after dark and then slept. At 4:00 A.M. on May 21, gunfire burst out in Carranza's hut. Shouts of "Viva Obregón!'' and ''Muera Carranza!'' pierced the air. When a bullet hit Carranza in the left thigh, he shouted to his companions to leave him and save themselves. Three bullets then struck him in the chest, and he was gone.

Some members of Carranza's staff, including Ignacio Bonillas, miraculously escaped harm. Bonillas was sleeping in a nearby hut, in which the assassins had no interest. The previous evening a spy had marked Carranza's location accurately.

Carranza's body was transported the next day to Villa Juárez, where it was embalmed and ceremoniously placed on a train to Mexico City. The late president was buried on May 24, in a modest grave in Mexico City.

Rodolfo Herrero, who had orchestrated the assassination, was never punished; he was subjected to the formality of a trial, but the prosecutor, Benjamín Hill, pushed his case without conviction. General Hill then died unexpectedly, and Herrero's trial for murder ground to a halt. The thirty Carrancista prisoners Herrero had taken at Tlaxcalantongo were released from custody—but only after they signed a document testifying that Carranza had committed suicide.

As soon as Carranza's funeral rites were completed, the Mexican legislature met to select an interim president to serve out the remainder of Carranza's term. Since the constitution forbade even an interim president from succeeding himself, Obregón threw his support behind Adolfo de la Huerta. With Obregón's backing, de la Huerta was elected unopposed.

Adolfo de la Huerta, then thirty-nine, was inaugurated interim president at the Chamber of Deputies in Mexico City on June 1. The next day, he stood on the balcony of the National Palace reviewing a parade of 25,000 troops. He was a good choice. Though he carried the label of a political ''radical,'' de la Huerta became an enlightened and constructive healer of wounds. He was a practical man, previously a bank official, a member of the Sonora state legislature, Carranza's home secretary, the Mexican consul general in New York, and most recently governor of Sonora. De la Huerta's frank and informal ways appealed to a country sick of civil war, and people were happy when he freed political prisoners and permitted Mexican exiles to return home.

De la Huerta was not Obregón's puppet, however, and his best-remembered act was done over Obregón's objections. He ended Pancho Villa's depredations by an act of out-and-out bribery; he granted Villa a great ranch and provided for its maintenance at government expense. Obregón, who hated Villa, was furious.

It took Mexico some time to settle down after the turmoil that accompanied the overthrow of Carranza, and the presidential election was therefore postponed from June to September 1920. On September 5, Obregón was elected president over insignificant opposition.

At midnight of November 30, Alvaro Obregón, standing on a dais in the Chamber of Deputies, raised his one arm and was inaugurated president of Mexico.

****

Epilogue

Like most of the great upheavals of history, the Mexican Revolution simply wound down; it did not end in a single, dramatic moment. Students of the Revolution, in fact, differ among themselves as to when it could be called "complete." Most place the end at the inauguration of Obregón in 1920, but some put it at the nationalization of the Mexican oil industry by President Lázaro Cárdenas in 1938. A few go so far as to say the Revolution is still not completed. This narrative has ended with Obregón's inauguration.

When Alvaro Obregón assumed the Mexican presidency in late November 1920, many of the leading revolutionaries had already died, a good number of them violently. Francisco Madero, Gustavo Madero, Venustiano Carranza, Emiliano Zapata, and Abraham González had all been assassinated. Felipe Angeles had been apprehended by the Carrancistas in 1919 and formally executed. On the other hand, the dictators against whom the Revolution had been directed, Porfirio Díaz and Victoriano Huerta, had died peacefully in exile. Of the major figures, Obregón, Pancho Villa, Elías Calles, Lucio Blanco, Félix Díaz, and Pablo González had survived.

But even Obregón and Villa were destined to die violently, and no story of the Mexican Revolution would be complete without a word about the circumstances.

Pancho Villa accepted Interim President Adolfo de la Huerta's offer for "peace terms" on July 28, 1920, while he was encamped at San Juan de Sabinas, a pretty town in Coahuila. He had begun negotiating with de la Huerta some time earlier, but in order to do so in relative peace, he had made the long trip to San Juan to escape harassment by Federal troops. When de la Huerta's terms arrived, Villa found them irresistible. The Mexican government contracted to deed Villa a 25,000-acre hacienda located in Durango, just across the border from Chihuahua and about fifty miles from Parral. The Mexican government also accorded Villa an annual retirement income of 500,000 pesos in gold. Villa's seven hundred remaining followers were each granted a full year's pay, and some were given land. Villa was permitted to retain fifty of his *dorados* at government expense. Those of his troops who so desired were accepted into the Federal army at the ranks they had held in Villa's service.

Villa accepted those generous terms at once—he had grown tired of fighting by now anyway—and within a day of his acceptance the Federal commander in Coahuila arrived at Sabinas to escort Villa's party back to Parral by way of Chihuahua.

As a matter of pride, Villa refused to make this final journey by train. Instead, he led his contingent on horseback, though unarmed. At every town along the way, the villagers greeted Villa's party with uproarious enthusiasm. Local telegraph offices delivered congratulatory messages from such prominent politicians as Adolfo de la Huerta, Plutarco Elías Calles (Villa's foe at the Battle of Agua Prieta), and General Benjamín Hill. Notably missing was any message from Alvaro Obregón, who could never stomach this deal with his former foe.

Villa's hacienda of Canutillo, as it was named, had once been a magnificent building, but it was now badly run-down. Villa was not surprised; he had occupied it as his temporary headquarters when fighting against the Federal forces under Murguía the year before. The thick adobe walls were intact, but the windows had been shot out and the doors and furniture removed.

Villa relished the task of repairing the dilapidated hacienda, for it gave him an outlet for his energy and would employ his five hundred workmen, many of whom came from the ranks of his former troops. Villa wired to El Paso and Chicago to buy tractors, plows, disks, and harrows, and he bought a secondhand Dodge touring car in Parral. As befitted his new life, Villa dismissed his current mistress and sent for his "official" wife, Luz Corral, who had taken refuge from the Federals in El Paso. Villa's life would now be "rooted, respected, and orderly." Canutillo would become a "model farm."

As a man who had not learned to sign his own name until he reached the age of twenty-five, Villa was determined to further his own education and that of his men and their families. He converted a former storehouse into a school and encouraged everyone—his own children, the children of his farmhands and neighbors, and a number of the farmhands themselves—to come and learn. He hired a qualified teacher and visited the school often, though he studied by himself at night in his hacienda. To one American journalist, he expressed his ambition as follows:

> Poor, ignorant Mexico. Until she has education nothing much can be done for her. I know . . . what it is to try to help people who can't understand what you are trying to do for them. I fought . . . so that poor men could live like human beings, have their own land, send their children to school and have human freedom. But it wasn't much use. So I stopped. . . . Nothing much can be done at all until the common people are educated.

A bit self-serving, perhaps, but a clear indication of how Villa wished to be perceived.

Embarking on a new, peaceful life was not easy, however, because Villa had a great deal to answer for in his past. The nearby town of Parral was the home of many Carrancistas thirsting to avenge Villa's former acts of brutality. Prominent among these enemies were members of the Herrera family. In his seizure of Parral the year before, Villa had gone on an orgy of revenge, hanging the Carrancista mayor as well as the relatives of his onetime friend Maclovio Herrera, who had left Villa to join Obregón. Herrera was dead, but Villa hanged his father and two of his brothers anyway. Strong anti-Villa sentiment at Parral was further inflamed by Villa's habit of purchasing goods and machinery from outside areas, principally from the United States, while local merchants suffered.

More of a problem than the resentment in Parral was the continuing hostility of President Alvaro Obregón in Mexico City. Villa's continuing popularity across all of Mexico was constantly being reported, much to Obregón's annoyance. Soon after retiring to Canutillo, Villa visited Mexico City in hopes of making peace with Obregón. When Villa arrived, mobs thronged the streets shouting "Viva Villa!" but Obregón refused to receive him. In fact, Villa's enthusiastic reception increased Obregón's animosity. At the National Palace, Obregón complained, "This man only has to raise his flag and the whole country, even my capital, will follow him." Instead of making a reconciliation with Villa, he sent a detachment of hand-picked troops to garrison Parral. They were placed there for the sole purpose of watching Villa.

The arrival of the Federal garrison at Parral alerted Villa to Obregón's enmity, and for a while Villa increased the normal precautions he followed for his personal safety. But as 1920 faded into 1921, 1922, and 1923, his vigilance gradually relaxed.

Early in the morning of July 20, 1923, Pancho Villa left Parral in a Dodge touring car, accompanied by his lawyer, his driver, and four bodyguards. On the preceding afternoon, they had attended the christening of the son of one of Villa's old soldiers and stayed overnight in the town. Villa usually took a large security force when he went into Parral, but on this occasion he knew that the soldier he was honoring, a poor man, could not host a large group.

Villa was in high spirits; he had spent a happy night with a favorite lady friend. As he and his henchmen headed back to Canutillo, Villa insisted on driving himself; his usual driver rode on the running board. Villa had been warned of danger but had brushed the warning off. "The man hasn't been born," he boasted, "who can lay a hand on Pancho Villa."

A little after 7:00 A.M., Villa's car drove down the Calle Juárez and prepared to make a turn at the corner of the Plaza Juárez. At that moment, a vendor by the side of the street raised his hand, shouted "Viva Villa!," took a bandana from his pocket, and wiped his face. On these signals, a group of gunmen in a nearby house fired their rifles again and again.

Villa's car swerved and crashed into a tree. Villa, though badly wounded in the head, pulled his pistol and succeeded in killing one of the attackers before he succumbed. Five of Villa's men were killed almost instantly; the sixth, though wounded in the stomach, managed to escape to the Parral River bottom and eventually made his way back to Canutillo, the only survivor.

The eight assassins who gunned Villa down made no effort to conceal their identities. Their leader was one Melitón Lozoya, a local cattle dealer. Lozoya had set up ambushes in order to kill Villa twice before, but had been thwarted both times. In the first instance, Lozoya was blinded by the glare of sunlight reflected off the windshield and was not able to aim. In the other, he held his fire when a group of schoolchildren suddenly appeared in his line of fire.

Lozoya's motivation has never been completely clarified. The ambush may have been an act of self-preservation, for Villa had threatened to have Lozoya killed only shortly before. On the other hand, Obregón himself may have been behind the plot. Obregón had taken no action against Villa so long as Villa had stayed out of public life, but in 1923 Villa openly supported his friend Adolfo de la Huerta in the upcoming 1924 presidential election despite Obregón's publicly expressed preference for Elías Calles. Obregón was furious at this reminder that Villa still had influence.

Melitón Lozoya and his men fired the weapons that killed Villa and his companions, but they were officially relieved of responsibility. One Jesús Salas Barraza appeared on the scene and assumed responsibility, apparently anxious to receive credit as the "intellectual author" of Villa's demise. Lozoya, Salas Barraza insisted, had served only as his own hired gun. The Mexican government accepted Salas Barraza's claim of responsibility, and he was sentenced to prison. He served less than a year and upon release was immediately commissioned in the Federal army. Salas Barraza later sat in the Mexican National Congress and to the end of his days, in 1951, always insisted, "I'm not a murderer. I rid humanity of a monster."

The assassination of Alvaro Obregón, in 1928, was less spectacular. It was the result not of any act of venality or cruelty on his part but of an all-too-common failing, inability to give up power.

Obregón, only forty years of age when he was sworn in as president, was no radical. His administration between 1920 and 1924 was a model of pragmatism, moderation, and good sense. He placed his first priority on rebuilding the tottering economy of Mexico, which objective ruled out instant and total implementation of land reform. Obregón did manage to redistribute three million acres among some six hundred villages during his term in office—seven times more land than Carranza distributed—but that figure admittedly fell short of "revolutionary" promises.

When the time came for Obregón to step down as president, as the constitution required, he had to choose between two obvious candidates to succeed him, Calles and de la Huerta. It was a difficult decision. Both men were his friends, both from Sonora. But Calles had been Obregón's closer associate during his administration, so Obregón chose Calles.*

De la Huerta, however, still enjoyed a strong following among the people, and he was not prepared to step aside. He fled Mexico City for Veracruz and there began organizing an armed rebellion. The revolt was soon crushed, but de la Huerta managed to escape to California. Calles was elected president in 1924.

At the end of Calles's term, however, Obregón yearned once more for a return to power. It was fairly easy for his supporters, who controlled the Congress, to amend the constitution to legalize an exception, so on July 1, 1928, Obregón was elected president for a second time.

But the one faction that Obregón had offended most during his term in office was also the most determined: the country's religious fanatics. That group would have left Obregón alone had he remained as a businessman in Sonora, but in 1928 they were resolved that he should not return to power. So while Obregón was awaiting his inauguration, a rightist cabal recruited an assassin, a young artist named José de León Toral, who wanted to "give his life for Christ" in his own way. Toral accepted the assignment and began tailing Obregón from place to place.

In spite of warnings that plots against his life were being hatched, Obregón accepted an invitation to a dinner held in his honor on July 16, 1928, two weeks after the election. Toral closed in on his prey, claiming that he needed to get close in order to make a sketch of the guest of honor. As Obregón turned and smiled from the speakers' dais, Toral shot him five times in the face. Obregón died instantly.

Three of the American participants in this story went on to greater fame during World War I: President Woodrow Wilson, Admiral Henry T. Mayo, and General John J. Pershing. Foremost among them, of

---

*Obregón got de la Huerta to agree that Calles should succeed him, while the three men were taking a ride through Chapultepec Park: "You and I, Plutarco [Calles], cannot leave politics because we would die of hunger; on the other hand Adolfo [de la Huerta] knows how to sing and give classes in voice and music. Under these circumstances who do you feel should follow me in the presidency?" Calles said nothing; eventually de la Huerta managed to force out "Well, after you should come Plutarco."

RONALD ATKIN, *Revolution!* (New York, 1969), p. 326.

course, was President Woodrow Wilson, whose life story has been the subject of many volumes that cannot be discussed here. However, an absorbing study could be made of the similarities between Wilson's performance as president during World War I and his performance during the Mexican Revolution.

Wilson's later role in drawing up the Treaty of Versailles in 1919 very much resembles his role in Mexico. Always the professor, he has deservedly received accolades for his ideals, expressed in his famous Fourteen Points, which include the concept of "self-determination of peoples." But when it came to persuading the U.S. Senate to ratify the treaty, Wilson proved himself inept. His performance in directing U.S. intervention in Mexico pointed the way to his later role on the larger stage.

Admiral Henry T. Mayo and General John J. Pershing both reached the highest command positions of their respective branches of service during the First World War. Mayo, in contrast to Admiral Frank Fletcher, found his reputation enhanced by the incidents at Tampico and Veracruz; he was promoted to the rank of vice admiral soon thereafter. On June 19, 1916, the day before the fight at Carrizal, Mayo was appointed commander in chief, Atlantic Fleet, with the rank of admiral. Thus Mayo became the senior U.S. naval officer at sea during World War I.

John J. Pershing went on to glory as commander of the American Expeditionary Force in France during the First World War. In an age of extravagant hero worship, he was rewarded in 1919 with promotion to the artificial rank of six-star "general of the armies," a grade reserved for himself (and later bestowed posthumously on George Washington). He became chief of staff, U.S. Army, in 1921 and survived another quarter century as an austere and lonely figure on the American scene. During the Second World War, Pershing provided useful advice to both Chief of Staff George C. Marshall and President Franklin D. Roosevelt. He died at Walter Reed Army Hospital in 1948.

Two other American officers were not so fortunate. Admiral Frank Fletcher, possibly because of his age—he was sixty-two in 1917—was not given a major command in World War I, although he continued to serve in secondary positions until 1919. General Frederick Funston, who remained the U.S. Army's favorite general even while Pershing garnered the headlines in Mexico, suffered a fatal heart attack on February 19, 1917, only two weeks after Pershing's men recrossed the border from Chihuahua into Columbus, New Mexico. It is generally conceded that Funston, had he lived, would have been accorded the command of the American Expeditionary Force in France.

Two points regarding the Mexican Revolution bear repeating. First, its magnitude. The Revolution was a tremendous upheaval, whose costs cannot even be guessed. Second, one must keep in mind that the issues were not always clear; semi-independent warlords fought among themselves, changing sides often, and seizing the opportunity the chaos afforded in order to enrich themselves. Once Díaz and Huerta were removed in 1914, the Revolution lacked any national goal. Peace came with Obregón's election to the presidency in 1920 primarily because Mexico was exhausted; its people were seeking peace at any price.

Finally, it is obvious that U.S. efforts to influence the Mexican Revolution were largely ineffectual. The occupation of Veracruz in 1914 may have helped the Constitutionalists topple Victoriano Huerta from the presidency, but his presidency was doomed anyway. The Punitive Expedition was even less effective, despite the miracles of endurance that Pershing's troops demonstrated in the wastelands of Chihuahua.

U.S. efforts to interfere notwithstanding, the Revolution was started by Mexicans, conducted by Mexicans, and resolved in a wholly Mexican fashion.

APPENDIX A

****

Sequence of Events, Mexican Revolution 1910–1917

1910

July 8

Porfirio Díaz is reelected president of Mexico, a post he has held almost continuously since 1876. His main political rival, Francisco I. Madero, is in jail, along with 60,000 other supporters. Madero, released on bail eleven days later, flees to San Antonio, Texas.

Nov. 20

Francisco Madero returns to Mexico from Texas, an event still commemorated in Mexico.

1911

May 5

Francisco I. Madero, leader of the rebellion against President Porfirio Díaz, holds a meeting at Bustillos.

May 10

City of Juárez falls to Madero's forces, thanks largely to the aggressiveness (and insubordination) of Francisco ("Pancho") Villa and Pascual Orozco.

May 13–15 Villa and Orozco break with Madero over his clemency to General Navarro, whom they took prisoner at Juárez. Villa returns to his wife at San Andrés, Chihuahua.

May 25 Porfirio Díaz resigns as president, is escorted to Veracruz, departs for exile in Paris. Madero refuses to take office until elected. Vice President Francisco de la Barra is installed as interim president.

Oct. Madero is elected president, inaugurated in November.

1912

March 3 Threatened by Orozco, Villa flees from Chihuahua after refusing to join in rebellion against Madero. Villa sets about raising his own force.

March 24 Villa takes the city of Parral from the Orozco rebels.

April 3 Orozco retakes Parral from Villa, who melts into the mountains and joins Victoriano Huerta, Madero's field commander, at Torreón.

June 3 Villa, sentenced to be shot for insubordination by Huerta, is spared by Madero's order at the last moment and sent to Santiago Tlatelolco prison, in Mexico City.

Nov. Woodrow Wilson elected president of the United States.

Dec. 26 Villa escapes prison, where he has learned of plots hatched by Generals Bernardo Reyes and Félix Díaz, but has refused to join them. Villa crosses Rio Grande into El Paso on January 3, 1913.

1913

Feb. 9–18 "Ten Tragic Days." Rebellion of Bernardo Reyes, Félix Díaz, and Victoriano Huerta.

Huerta arrests Madero on February 18 and assumes power.

Feb. 22   President Madero and Vice President Pino Suárez are murdered outside Lecumberri prison, Mexico City.

March 4   Inauguration of Woodrow Wilson as president of the United States.

March 23 Villa returns to Mexico after learning of Madero's assassination; gathers army on way to San Andrés; sends message of defiance to governor of Chihuahua.

March 28 Venustiano Carranza draws up Plan of Guadalupe, in which he declares himself "First Chief of the Constitutionalist Army," claiming to be the rightful successor to Madero.

June 1   President Wilson sends William Bayard Hale to Mexico on a fact-finding mission. Hale sends reports throughout June.

Aug. 9   President Wilson sends Governor John Lind to Mexico as an unofficial agent. Lind, rebuffed by Huerta, spends some months in Veracruz.

Aug. 26   Villa's new army routs forces under Félix Terrazas at San Andrés, taking three trains and other booty.

Aug. 27   Woodrow Wilson declares policy of "watchful waiting" before a joint session of Congress. Start of the "honeymoon" between Mexico and the United States.

Oct. 2   Villa's Division of the North captures Torreón. Villa becomes a civil governor for the first time.

Oct. 10   Huerta's second coup. Arrest and imprisonment of eighty-five Mexican congressmen. Huerta is elected president in an election so obviously rigged as to be nullified and deferred for nine months.

Oct. 17   Carranza establishes a provisional government at Hermosillo, in Sonora.

Nov. 7   Wilson's "Circular Note," which includes an obvious implied threat to remove Huerta.

Nov. 15   Villa captures Juárez, taking 3,000 prisoners.
Mid-Nov. Wilson sends William Hale to Nogales, Mexico,

for a conference with Carranza, which turns out disastrously. Hale returns to the U.S. side on November 19. Wilson levies an arms embargo against Carranza.

Nov. 19   Villa defeats General José Inés Salvador at Tierra Blanca.

Dec. 8   Chihuahua City falls to Villa's Division of the North.

1914

Jan. 11   Villa defeats Salvador Mercado at Ojinaga, across from Presidio, Texas, on the Rio Grande. Mercado and his army escape to the Texas side of the river. John J. Pershing comes to the Mexican side to call on Villa.

Feb. 3   President Wilson lifts the embargo of arms against Carranza.

Feb.   The Benton affair, in which Villa murders the British subject William H. Benton. Villa claims "self-defense," but nobody believes him.

March   Villa and Carranza fall out over plans for the future. Villa gives in and attacks Saltillo, at Carranza's insistence. Villa then learns that Carranza has sent another general to take Zacatecas, Villa's own objective.

April 10   A Huertista general at Tampico arrests crewmen from the USS *Dolphin*. U.S. demands for a public display of contrition create an international crisis.

April 20   Wilson asks Congress for extraordinary military powers as a result of the Tampico incident.

April 21   The German ship *Ypiranga* arrives off Veracruz. Admiral Frank Fletcher lands sailors and marines at Veracruz the next day.

April 24   Meeting between Wilson and his cabinet. Secretary of War Lindley M. Garrison urges that the U.S. Army push on to Mexico City. Argentina, Brazil, and Chile offer to mediate between the United States and Mexico the next day.

April 30	Fifth Infantry Brigade, under Brigadier General Frederick Funston, relieves marine garrison at Veracruz.
May 20–July 2	U.S. and Mexican diplomats meet at Niagara Falls, Canada, under ABC sponsorship. As a result, Wilson asks Carranza to hold up the march on Mexico City. Carranza refuses on June 16.
June 23	Villa takes Zacatecas, though without Carranza's approval. Carranza responds by withholding supplies of ammunition and coal from Villa.
July 8	Alvaro Obregón, military commander under Carranza, captures Guadalajara.
July 15	Huerta resigns as provisional president and flees to Spain.
Aug. 15	Obregón occupies Mexico City on behalf of the Constitutionalists. Carranza soon follows.
Aug. 16	Woodrow Wilson sends Paul Fuller to visit Villa at Santa Rosalía and urges him to establish a government and then retire. Villa agrees.
Sept. 5	Fuller confers with Carranza in Mexico City. Carranza promises to cooperate.
Sept.	Obregón, now minister of war in Mexico City, visits Villa in Chihuahua. Together they visit Pershing in Fort Bliss, Texas, and Maytorena in Nogales.
Sept. 23	Villa declares war on Carranza.
Oct. 12–Nov. 12	Convention at Aguascaliente. General Eulalio Gutiérrez is elected president.
Nov. 23	U.S. Fifth Infantry Brigade debarks at Veracruz.
Dec.	Generals Alvaro Obregón and Pablo González join the deposed Carranza, who occupies Veracruz as his capital. Villa and Emiliano Zapata occupy Mexico City.

1915

Jan. 6	Carranza issues a decree revising the Plan of Guadalupe to include land reform, electoral reform, workers' rights.

Jan.	Villa meets with U.S. General Hugh S. Scott and sells out Governor Maytorena in the Sonora civil war.
Jan. 15	Obregón begins a campaign against Villa's forces.
April 6–15	Obregón defeats Villa in two battles at Celaya, near Querétaro.
June 2	Wilson warns Mexico, threatening intervention.
June–Sept.	Villa is defeated at León and takes refuge in Chihuahua.
Oct. 19	The United States and six Latin American nations recognize the Carranza government.
Nov. 1	Villa's army is decimated by Carrancista forces under Plutarco Elías Calles in a two-day battle at Agua Prieta, opposite Douglas, Arizona. Later word that the U.S. had assisted Calles infuriates Villa. Agua Prieta is soon followed by a similar defeat at Hermosillo, Sonora.
Dec.	Pascual Orozco, jumping bail in El Paso, is killed by Texas Rangers near Presidio, Texas. Huerta dies in El Paso.

1916

Jan. 11	Villa raids a train, running from Chihuahua City to the Cusi mines, at Santa Isabel, Chihuahua. Villa's men kill sixteen of the seventeen Americans aboard.
March 9	Villista raid on Columbus, New Mexico, killing nineteen Americans.
March 15	Brigadier General John J. Pershing, on President Wilson's order, crosses the Mexican border at Columbus and Culberson's Ranch, pursuing Villa.
March 24	Protocol signed between Washington and Carranza, interpreted by Wilson as allowing the Punitive Expedition into Mexico.
April 8	Pershing's Punitive Expedition, now 6,675 men strong, reaches over three hundred miles into Mexico.

April 12	Skirmish between U.S. cavalry and Carrancistas at Parral, over five hundred road miles into Mexican territory. End of Pershing's pursuit of Villa.
May 22	Long and bitter note from Carranza to Wilson.
June 18	Wilson calls up the National Guard, eventually 100,000 men.
June 21	Battle of Carrizal, in which Captain Charles T. Boyd, Lieutenant Henry R. Adair, and Mexican General Félix G. Gómez are killed. Heavy losses on both sides. Twenty-three Americans are taken prisoner by the Carrancistas.
July 4	Carranza proposes Mexican–U.S. talks.
Sept. 16	U.S.–Mexican meetings begin in New London. Later shifted to Philadelphia and Atlantic City. A protocol is signed November 24.
Oct.	Constitutional convention meets at Querétaro.
Dec. 17	Carranza rejects protocol of November 24 between the United States and Mexico.

1917

Jan. 27	Beginning of the withdrawal of the Punitive Expedition.
Jan. 31	Completion of the radical new Mexican constitution.
Feb. 5	Last of the Punitive Expedition crosses the Rio Grande into the United States.
March 11	Venustiano Carranza is elected president.
March 13	President Woodrow Wilson establishes full diplomatic relations with the new Carranza government by sending Henry P. Fletcher as ambassador to Mexico.
April 6	The United States declares war on imperial Germany.
May 1	Carranza is inaugurated as president of Mexico.

1919

April 10	Emiliano Zapata is assassinated at Chinameca on orders of Carranza.

June 1   Alvaro Obregón declares himself a candidate for
                    the presidency in the election to be held in
                    1920. Carranza, in early September, endorses
                    his own candidate, Ignacio Bonillas.

1920

April 2   Carranza summons Obregón to Mexico City to
                    face trumped-up charges. Obregón escapes with
                    his life through the aid of friends.

April 20   Obregón manifesto declaring rebellion against
                    Carranza.

May 7   Carranza flees Mexico City. Abandons train on
                    May 14.

May 21   Carranza is assassinated in the village of Tlax-
                    calantongo, Puebla.

June 1   Adolfo de la Huerta is inaugurated provisional
                    president.

Sept. 5   Obregón is elected president, inaugurated on
                    November 30.

1923

July 20   Assassination of Pancho Villa and his body-
                    guards in Parral. His executioners are never pun-
                    ished.

APPENDIX B

****

Visiting Points of Interest

The Mexican Revolution ended over seventy-two years ago, and Mexico is now a very different place. Still, some of the backdrop remains. I shall describe only a few high points of my efforts to see these places.

Mexico City

Mexico City is barely recognizable in terms of its 1920 self. The population of the city now approaches, or exceeds, twenty million people. The resultant smog and pollution are known worldwide. Remedial measures are being taken, but even if planned restrictions—on autos, for example—are observed, it will require time for them to have an impact.

As for specific historic sites, the *Zócalo* and the *National Palace* are essential to any visit. One is most struck by their size. The palace stretches over blocks in both directions, and within its walls lie so many courtyards that one cannot be sure which one was actually the courtyard of the old "intendancy," where President Francisco Madero and his vice president were held in February 1913. But it makes little difference; the gloomy atmosphere that pervades one courtyard pervades the others. The Zócalo, outside the palace, is a vast concrete area. It is not difficult to imagine a pitched battle outside the palace gates, in which machine guns took a terrible toll among advancing troops and passers-by on the other side.

The *Citadel*, about a mile from the Zócalo, still exists, although converted now into Mexico's National Library. Outside its main portal, the imposing statue of Morelos, at the base of which Gustavo Madero fell, continues to dominate the pleasant little park. The *Lecumberri prison* still stands. Like the Citadel, it has been put to more congenial use, as Mexico's National Archives. Built with a spoked-wheel configuration, its vast halls conveniently house the stacks of the archives. A bust of the murdered Francisco Madero stands a couple of hundred yards from the main entrance to the National Archives, at the place where it is claimed he fell. (Its location does not look quite right to me, from the accounts I have read.)

Other places and streets—Chapultepec Castle, the Avenida de la Reforma, the Palace of Fine Arts—have changed little since early this century. Tours are available to *Xochimilco*, just south of Mexico City. Though the town has grown, one can appreciate why this spot, with its gondolas and waterways, appealed to Emiliano Zapata.

Cuernavaca

An hour south of Mexico City is Cuernavaca, Morelos—Zapata country and the place where Francisco Madero fled after the first morning's fighting in Mexico City on Sunday, February 9, 1913. Here Rosa King's Hotel Bella Vista still stands, well marked. Surprisingly, the hotel is right downtown, on one of the squares. In 1913, when Cuernavaca was still small, the hotel was probably just a bit away from town. In any case, it is only half a mile from the Palace of Cortés, the main edifice.

Chinameca

Chinameca, Morelos, is Zapata country, as tourists who approach it are often reminded. The spot where Zapata fell is marked by a large gold statue, showing him on his horse. The bullet holes in the whitewashed gateway remain. Chinameca is not easy to reach, incidentally. Even my Mexican friends who made the visit possible had to stop for directions every five miles or so. Zapata's birthplace is Anene-cuilco, about twenty miles from Chinameca. Here every street, every plaza, every drugstore, for that matter, is named after the local hero. Zapata's alleged birthplace is partially preserved, along with elaborate murals. All the hoopla and the new buildings and paved roads make it difficult, however, to imagine the Morelos of 1911–19.

Veracruz

Veracruz, "three-times heroic," is a rewarding spot for anyone interested in the Mexican Revolution. Although the city has grown a great deal since 1914, the important buildings, now much enlarged, still stand in the same places.

The first structure any visitor wants to see is Pier Four, where Admiral Fletcher's bluejackets and marines landed on April 21, 1914. It remains the predominant pier in that part of the harbor. To the northeast of Pier Four lies a great new shipping area, but the port of 1914 is relatively intact. The telegraph office and the customhouse are also still located in their old places, though the buildings are now large, almost oppressive.

Perhaps it is because the buildings are now larger (or because photographs of the area are inadequate), but my wife and I were struck by how small the harbor is—and how expansive the great empty square is between the Sanitary Wharf and the Naval Academy. The maps show the dimensions accurately, but they cannot reproduce the ambiance. After all, the distance from Pier Four to Fort San Juan d'Ulloa is only four hundred yards across the water, and that from the Sanitary Wharf to the fort is only about six hundred yards. These are the equivalent of golf course holes.

Two features of that scene are new and striking. One is the monument to Lieutenant José Azueta, of the Mexican navy, the most noted victim of the Veracruz invasion. The prophecy of Consul William Canada that Azueta would be immortalized has indeed come true. His monument, located on the corner of the Sanitary Wharf, is impressive. It makes a Yankee a bit uncomfortable to know that it was American guns that killed him.

That great concrete square also contains a large monument to Venustiano Carranza, a man not much celebrated in other parts of Mexico. Veracruz remembers Carranza because he spent some months there during 1914. In its Fort San Juan d'Ulloa, Carranza issued revisions to his Plan of Guadalupe. Veracruz has truly embraced Carranza as one of its own.

Fort San Juan d'Ulloa differs little from other Spanish structures in the Caribbean. Even the large rooms that were used as dungeons in earlier years are now open to visitors. Those dungeons are still frightening. It is easy to imagine how horrible they were when the fort was a prison. Several of Carranza's proclamations are inscribed on bronze plaques on the walls of San Juan.

We made our visit to Veracruz in April, the month of the landings in 1914. The weather was warm and humid, but not overly so. The climate (except for the "northers," which we were spared) was not a factor in the landings at Veracruz.

Chihuahua

Chihuahua is difficult to reach unless one is willing to drive in Mexico. The railway from Juárez no longer carries pasengers. That leaves the bus, which is adequate, though a bit primitive by American standards. On the five-hour trip, the bus makes one stop, at a small restaurant at Villa Ahumada. We were curious about that location, for there the Constitutionalists were massing in June 1916 according to the report that caused General Pershing to send Captain Boyd and Captain Morey to nearby Carrizal. Unfortunately, one can see nothing of significance from the main road; Villa Ahumada was evidently a road and railroad junction and little else.

Chihuahua is a pretty town, with an excellent hotel, which boasts potable water. Guides abound. The Plaza Hidalgo is a pleasant park, which the Governor's Palace and the cathedral face. Pancho Villa's house stands nearby, and for some time it has been a museum. Villa's wife, Luz Corral, survived Pancho by many years and ran the museum herself until she died, in the 1980s. Inside the courtyard, one can see the touring car in which Villa was assassinated in Parral. It is remarkably free of bullet holes; the assassins were good marksmen.

The territories to the west of Chihuahua, where Pershing's Punitive Expedition searched vainly for Pancho Villa, is still not developed enough for a quick visit. We were advised that the roads are narrow and dusty and the towns very small. We did not have time to risk a visit to that territory.

Columbus

Columbus, New Mexico, has not changed much over the years. It is still the dilapidated little place that John Lucas described in 1916. Its houses are fragile, and the land is arid. Its appeal is mainly to the historian, who finds it rewarding because everything remains in place except the railroad, which no longer runs through Columbus. Perhaps in a few years the old town of Columbus also will be a memory. Cootes Hill, in the southwest corner, is now named after Pancho Villa, much to the annoyance of many of the local people. The site of Lieutenant John Lucas's tiny adobe hut is properly marked. Columbus has two good museums—one run by the state of New Mexico and the other private, in the old train station.

As of March 1992, the best way to reach Columbus was to drive to Deming, New Mexico, from El Paso or Las Cruces, on Interstate 10. Columbus is then about thirty-five miles south on Highway 11. However, the direct road between El Paso and Columbus that was then being improved may well be the easier route in the future.

APPENDIX C

****

The Plan of Guadalupe

We, the undersigned, chiefs and officers in command of the Constitutionalist Army, have agreed on and shall sustain by force of arms the following:

I. Gen. Victoriano Huerta is hereby repudiated in his character as President of the Republic.

II. The legislative and judicial powers of the Federation are hereby also repudiated.

III. The Governments of such States as shall continue to recognize the Federal powers forming the present Administration, thirty days after the publication of this plan, are hereby also repudiated.

IV. In order to organize the army entrusted with the accomplishment of of our purposes, we hereby appoint the First Chief of the army, which shall be named "Constitutionalist," Venustiano Carranza, Governor of the State of Coahuila.

V. When the Constitutionalist Army occupies Mexico City, Venustiano Carranza, as First Chief of the Constitutionalist Army, or whoever may succeed him in command of the army, will be appointed ad interim head of the Executive power.

VI. The ad interim President of the Republic shall call a general election as soon as peace is established, delivering the power to the man who shall be elected.

VII. Such citizens as act as First Chiefs of the Constitutionalist Army in those States where the Governments have recognized Huerta shall assume the character of provisional Governors there and hold local elections after those citizens elected to the high national office, according to the aforesaid provisions, have already taken possession of their posts to fulfill their duties.

Signed in the Hacienda of Guadalupe, Coahuila, on the 26th day of March 1913.

New York Times, 1 July 1914, p. 2.

NOTES

****

ABBREVIATIONS

Fletcher Report   Frank F. Fletcher, "Seizure and Occupation of Vera Cruz, April 21–30, 1914" (report to Charles J. Badger, 13 May 1914)

Foulois Report   Benjamin D. Foulois, "Report of the Operations of the First Aero Squadron, Signal Corps, with the Mexican Punitive Expedition, for period March 15 to August 15, 1916"

FRUS   *Papers relating to the Foreign Relations of the United States*, 1913–16 (Washington, D.C.: U.S. Government Printing Office, 1920–25)

NARA   National Archives and Records Administration, Washington, D.C.

NYT   *New York Times*

Pershing Report   John J. Pershing, "Report of the Punitive Expedition to June 30, 1916" and "Report of the Punitive Expedition, July 1916–February 1917"

INTRODUCTION

p. xvii *"strike out at us"*: Martín Luis Guzmán, *The Eagle and the Serpent* (New York, 1930), p. 44.

1: Assassination

p. 8 *Cecilio Ocón:* This fanatic admirer of Porfirio Díaz was one of a handful of conspirators who had instigated the Félix Díaz rebellion.

p. 8 *ignored the boys:* Neither Romero nor Hernández was harmed. Both boys were, however, later forced to sign documents without being allowed to read them.

p. 9 *Madero's body:* Robert H. Murray, in his serialized article "Huerta and the Two Wilsons," in *Harper's Weekly*, wrote three years after the event: "I have seen this: A dead man, shrouded in coarse, filthy prison sheets, who in life had been President of Mexico, his face and skull mutilated where bullets had entered . . . the corpse mocked obscenely by laughing, foul-mouthed men." It is highly doubtful, however, that Murray actually saw Madero's body. The corpses were kept hidden.

p. 9 *"lost their lives":* FRUS, 1913, p. 732.

p. 9 *murder of Madero:* William Weber Johnson, *Heroic Mexico*, rev. ed. (San Diego, 1984), pp. 119–22, provides the backbone of this account. Other sources on which Johnson draws heavily, are Edward I. Bell, *The Political Shame of Mexico* (New York, 1914), Robert H. Murray, "Huerta," March 25, April 1, 8, 15, 22, 29, 1916, and FRUS 1913.

p. 9 *Francisco Cárdenas:* Cárdenas turned out to be an unsuccessful general. Defeated in battle, he soon defected to Guatemala, where he was captured and confessed to Madero's murder. Cárdenas claimed that he had acted upon direct order from Victoriano Huerta himself. He later apparently committed suicide, though it was reported that the corpse had two bullets in its head. Johnson, *Heroic Mexico*, pp. 122–24.

2: Uprising

p. 11 *"against General Díaz":* Francisco I. Madero, *La sucesión presidencial en 1910*, quoted in Jonathan Kandell, *La Capital* (New York, 1988), p. 393.

p. 12 *"fool was President":* William Weber Johnson, *Heroic Mexico*, rev. ed. (San Diego, 1984), p. 38.

p. 14 *young cadets:* The military school from which these cadets came was fifteen miles south of the city. They traveled partway on foot and partway on commandeered tram cars.

p. 14 *fighting at the National Palace:* Johnson, *Heroic Mexico*, p. 98; Alan Knight, *The Mexican Revolution* (New York, 1986),: 482; Edward I. Bell, *The Political Shame of Mexico* (New York, 1914), pp. 276–78.

p. 16 *loyal cadets:* These were the cadets from the Chapultepec Military Academy, Mexico's West Point. They remained loyal to Madero, while those from Tlalpan joined the rebels, at least temporarily.

p. 16 *"shot [Villar's wounding]":* Bell, *Political Shame*, p. 278. On p. 280, Bell indicates that Huerta was not appointed until that Sunday evening. This account stems from Johnson, *Heroic Mexico*, p. 98, written seventy years later with the advantage of many sources, including Bell's 1914 account.

p. 17 *Ruiz's execution:* Bell, *Political Shame*, p. 280, says that Ruiz's execution was ordered by Madero at a cabinet meeting, whereas Johnson, *Heroic Mexico*, p. 99, implies that Huerta acted on his own. Johnson seems the more reliable, for the reasons given above.

p. 18 *the fighting in the streets:* Knight, *Mexican Revolution,* 1:483–84; Johnson, *Heroic Mexico,* p. 101; Bell, *Political Shame,* pp. 283–84.

p. 18 *Huerta's duplicity:* The cited works by Knight, Johnson, and Bell, plus William D. Lansford, *Pancho Villa* (Los Angeles, 1965), p. 158. Gustavo Madero noticed this tactic, as he had also gotten word of Huerta's meeting with Díaz. As always, though, Gustavo could not persuade his brother.

3: "I HAVE OVERTHROWN THIS GOVERNMENT"

p. 19 *foreign investment in Mexico:* Jonathan Kandell, *La Capital* (New York, 1988), p. 392, estimates that two-thirds of all capital investment in Mexico was under the control of foreigners, particularly Americans.

p. 20 *Society of Friends:* Ernest Gruening, *Mexico and Its Heritage* (New York, 1928), p. 561.

p. 20 *Lane's antipathy toward Madero:* President Woodrow Wilson was always sure that Lane Wilson had "actively abetted" the "handful of military plotters." Roy Stannard Baker, *Woodrow Wilson: Life and Letters* (Garden City, N.Y., 1931), 4:239. It is also noteworthy that Wilson's friends the Guggenheims were active commercial competitors of the Madero family. However, that must be presumed to be a minor element of Wilson's antipathy. Madero was also alleged to have refused to follow Porfirio Díaz's policy of providing a "reasonable subsidy" to help the American ambassador maintain the embassy. William Weber Johnson, *Heroic Mexico,* rev. ed. (San Diego, 1984), p. 111.

p. 20 *"disorganized brain":* Johnson, *Heroic Mexico,* p. 11.

p. 20 *what Wilson's report suggested:* Wilson to State, 9 and 10 Feb. 1913, FRUS, 1913, pp. 700–702. See also Cole Blasier, "The United States and Madero," *Journal of Latin American Studies* 4 (Nov. 1972): 207–31; Kandell, *La Capital,* p. 411; Robert H. Murray, "Huerta and the Two Wilsons," *Harper's Weekly,* 25 March 1916.

p. 21 *Wilson's messages to State Department:* One of three messages of 10 Feb. 1913 was not given a time, one was at noon, and the last was at 4 P.M. FRUS, 1913, pp. 700–702. The fear of Zapatista invasion seems far-fetched, but it was always present in Mexico City.

p. 21 *supervision of Ambassador Wilson:* Wilson to State Department, 10 Feb. 1913, FRUS, 1913, p. 702.

p. 22 *effect his words had on Madero:* Wilson to Knox, 14 Feb. 1913, cited in Blasier, "United States," p. 212.

p. 22 *"if the ambassador thinks":* Wilson to Knox, 12 Feb. 1913, quoted in Blasier, "United States," p. 218 (italics added).

p. 22 *Lascuráin, not himself:* Wilson to Knox, 15 Feb. 1913, FRUS, 1913, pp. 712–13.

p. 22 *Wilson's meeting with Huerta representative;* Blasier, "United States," p. 218.

p. 24 *"in the arms of General Huerta":* Johnson, *Heroic Mexico,* p. 102

p. 24 *"an affair of skirts":* Ibid.

p. 25 *administration had gone wrong:* Alan Knight, *The Mexican Revolution* (New York, 1986), 1:487; Johnson, *Heroic Mexico,* p. 104.

p. 26 *for his own purposes:* Stanley R. Ross, "The Arrest of Francisco Madero," in James W. Wilkie and Albert L. Michaels, eds., *Revolution in Mexico* (New York, 1969), pp. 50–51.

p. 27 *Gustavo Madero's death:* Johnson, *Heroic Mexico*, p. 105; Bell, *Political Shame*, p. 304; Ross, "Arrest," pp. 50–51.

p. 28 *"peace of the country":* Wilson to Knox, 19 Feb. 1913, *FRUS, 1913*, p. 724. Wilson also accepted Huerta's explanation for Gustavo Madero's death. Gustavo had been killed by "soldiers, without orders."

p. 28 *suffer no bodily harm:* Interview, Señora Sara Madero and Robert Hammond Murray, of the *New York World*, 15 Aug. 1916, quoted in Ernest Gruening, "Mrs. Madero's Attempt to Save the Life of Her Husband," in Wilkie and Michaels, *Revolution*, pp. 55–57.

p. 28 *"consistent with peace and humanity":* Knox to Wilson, 20 Feb. 1913, *FRUS, 1913,* p. 725–26.

p. 28 *conversations inside the intendancy:* Lansford, *Villa*, pp. 167–68; Gruening, "Mrs. Madero's Attempt," p. 58.

4: WATCHFUL WAITING

p. 30 *Knox was "disposed":* Knox to Wilson, 21 Feb. 1913, *FRUS, 1913*, p. 728.

p. 30 *murder a "closed incident":* Wilson to Knox, 24 Feb. 1913, *FRUS, 1913*, p. 736.

p. 31 *Edward's, Hanna's, and Wilson's reports:* Ernest Gruening, *Mexico and Its Heritage* (New York, 1928), p. 575.

p. 31 *"submission to the federal authorities":* Ibid., p. 576.

p. 32 *"irony of fate":* Samuel Flagg Bemis, "Woodrow Wilson and Latin America," in Edward Henry Buehrig, ed., *Wilson's Foreign Policy in Perspective* (Bloomington, 1957), p. 117.

p. 32 *"leaders of those countries themselves":* Arthur S. Link, *Woodrow Wilson and the Progressive Era* (New York, 1954), p. 81.

p. 32 *"to elect good men":* Walter H. Page, *Life and Letters* (Garden City, N.Y., 1925), 1:205.

p. 33 *"Declaration of Policy":* Quoted in Bemis, "Wilson," p. 120.

p. 33 *executed before a firing squad:* William Weber Johnson, *Heroic Mexico*, rev. ed. (San Diego, 1984), p. 131.

p. 34 *volley of curses at Díaz:* Alan Knight, *The Mexican Revolution* (New York, 1986), 2:65.

p. 35 *"going into the cannon's mouth":* Edith O'Shaughnessy, *A Diplomat's Wife in Mexico* (New York, 1916), pp. 66–67. Also see Michael C. Meyer, *Huerta* (Lincoln 1972), pp. 99–100.

p. 35 *Porfirio Díaz, Blanquet, and himself:* Johnson, *Heroic Mexico*, p. 132.

p. 35 *rurales, or constabulary:* "The rurales, established in the 1860s as the Juárez government's answer to endemic banditry, had by the 1900s become a symbol of the Porfirian regime's machismo and efficiency." They were sometimes said to be ex-bandits with dashing outfits and the congenial job of hunting down robbers and malcontents. Actually, their activities were less glamorous: escorting paymasters, keeping order in the streets on fiesta days, policing local elections, conveying prisoners, and quelling revolts against unpopular authorities. See Knight, *Mexican Revolution*, 1:33.

p. 35 *"unprecedented in the nation's history":* Jonathan Kandell, *La Capital* (New York, 1988), pp. 422–23.

p. 35 *"a traitor and assassin":* Johnson, *Heroic Mexico*, p. 135.

p. 36 *grew thoroughly alarmed:* Knight, *Mexican Revolution*, 2:66–67.

p. 36 *true state of affairs in Mexico:* Leonard Wood Diary, 12, 13 Jan. 1914, quoted in Knight, *Mexican Revolution*, 2:69.

p. 37 *a friend of Bryan's:* Hale has been described in this fashion:

Even more than his predecessor Hale, Lind carried the prejudices of Progressive North America into revolutionary Mexico. Physically, he was tall, blond, blue-eyed and gaunt, as befitted a Swedish immigrant; philosophically, he adhered to a stern Protestantism; politically, he was a loyal member of Bryan's mid-Western, populist clientele. Honourable and idealistic, . . . he was hardly at home among the Mexicans, he regarded the Catholic Church as the whore of Babylon and, like many of his kind, he superimposed North American, Protestant values on disordered, dirty, revolutionary Mexico. . . . KNIGHT, *Mexican Revolution*, 2:72.

5: FIRST CHIEF

p. 40 *"compromises commits suicide":* Carranza to Madero, quoted in William Weber Johnson, *Heroic Mexico*, rev. ed. (San Diego, 1984), p. 146.

p. 40 *"of no political significance":* Ibid., p. 144.

p. 41 *"conform to the new administration":* U.S. Consul Philip E. Holland, Saltillo, quoted ibid., 148–49. See also Michael C. Meyer, *Huerta* (Lincoln, 1972), p. 68, and Kenneth J. Grieb, *The United States and Huerta*, p. 32, quoted in Alan Knight, *The Mexican Revolution* (New York, 1986), 2:14–15.

p. 41 *curry Huerta's favor:* Carranza's backing and filling were consistent with his way of conducting business. As one authority puts it, "Carranza was no revolutionary firebrand; he was a shrewd, experienced politician; he was aware of his isolation both within Coahuila and the Federation as a whole. . . . Thus his preparedness to negotiate was hardly surprising. . . ." Knight, *Mexican Revolution*, 2:15.

p. 41 *"attempting to establish":* Carranza to Taft, 26 Feb. 1913, quoted in Ronald Atkin, *Revolution!* (New York, 1970), p. 129.

p. 43 *"the respectable bourgeois":* Knight, *Mexican Revolution*, 2:23.

p. 44 *Spanish descent:* Obregón claimed descent not only from the Spanish but also from the Irish—from one Michael O'Brien, whose name somewhat resembled his. O'Brien was an Irishman assimilated into Mexican society.

p. 44 *"the panderers":* This and other quotations relating to Carranza and his entourage come from Martín Luis Guzmán, *The Eagle and the Serpent* (New York, 1930), p. 149.

6: THE RETURN OF PANCHO VILLA

p. 47 *"thirst for revenge intensified":* William Lansford is vivid on this subject: Don Abraham González, who had dwelt next to Madero in the *querrilo's* heart, was ordered taken to Mexico City from Cihuahua by President Huerta, to be confined in the penitentiary. Like so many others who had embarked on this now fateful journey, he never arrived.

As the prison detail reached the Mapula Station, *don* Abraham was taken off, shot, and his body thrown under the wheels of the train to make his death appear an accident. His severed corpse was then buried along the railroad bed. . . . LANSFORD, *Pancho Villa* (Los Angeles, 1965), p. 174.

p. 48 *about eight hundred men:* Martín Luis Guzmán, *The Memoirs of Pancho Villa* (Austin, 1965), p. 96.

p. 48 *"make war on you":* Ibid., p. 95.

p. 48 *the people to see:* Lansford, *Villa*, pp. 178–79.

p. 50 *at the edge of town:* Guzmán, *Villa*, pp. 96–97.

p. 50 *purchase arms and ammunition:* William Weber Johnson, rev. ed. *Heroic Mexico* (San Diego, 1984), p. 165.

p. 51 *"appoint them myself":* Lansford, *Villa*, p. 98.

p. 51 *and 20,000 cartridges:* Johnson, *Heroic Mexico*, p. 167.

p. 52 *ants and the buzzards:* Lansford, *Villa*, p. 184.

p. 53 *how impressive his titles:* Clifford Irving, *Tom Mix and Pancho Villa*, (New York, 1982), p. 26.

p. 53 *"their 'avenging angel' ":* Sylvestre Terrazas, cited in Ramón Eduardo Ruiz, *The Great Rebellion* (New York, 1980), p. 193.

p. 54 *"that is euthanasia:* Bertha Pope, ed., *The Letters of Ambrose Bierce* (San Francisco, 1922), pp. 196–97.

p. 54 *one of Villa's great favorites:* Elias Torres, *Twenty Episodes in the Life of Pancho Villa* (Austin, 1973), pp. 35–36.

p. 55 *the six semi-independent brigades:* The other brigades were commanded by Tomás Urbina, Maclovio Herrera, Calixto Contreras, Aguirre Benavides, and Juan E. García. See Guzmán, *Villa*, p. 102.

p. 56 *"defeated and dispersed":* Accounts differ as to whether Mercado or Orozco was in command at Chihuahua. Mercado was the senior Federal commander, and probably had overall command. Three-fourths of the troops, however, were Orozquistas. See Alan Knight, *The Mexican Revolution* (New York, 1986), 2:115.

p. 57 *disaffection in Villa's army:* Guzmán, *Villa*, pp. 116–17.

p. 57 *"undecided little man":* John Reed, *Insurgent Mexico* (1914; reprint, New York, 1969), p. 3.

p. 58 *the regular Federals:* For convenience, the term "Federal" will be used here in connection with Salazar's troops, as they were under overall Federal command.

p. 58 *many small arms:* Knight, *Mexican Revolution*, 2:116–17, says that Villa seized "four locomotives, eight field guns, seven machine-guns, horses, rifles, and 400,000 rounds of small arms ammunition."

p. 59 *Mercado's five thousand refugees:* Johnson, *Heroic Mexico*, p. 171.

7: HUERTA AGONISTES

p. 61 *Twenty-ninth Battalion:* Blanquet kept command of his battalion, even though he held the post of minister of war.

p. 61 *Huerta's "second coup":* Alan Knight, *The Mexican Revolution* (New York, 1986), 2:74–76.

p. 62 *Blanco's land distribution:* Frank Samponaro and Paul J. Vanderwood, *War Scare on the Rio Grande* (Austin, 1992), pp. 43–51.

p. 63 *"without foreign assistance":* NYT, 19 Nov. 1913.

p. 64 *regardless of the outcome":* Bryan to American embassy, 13 Oct. 1913, State Department papers, quoted in Arthur S. Link, *Woodrow Wilson and the Progressive Era* (New York, 1954), p. 117.

p. 64 *for Huerta's "rehabilitation":* Memo, State Department Papers, quoted ibid.

p. 64 *particularly Mexican oil:* State Department Papers, quoted ibid., p. 118. The target of this remark was the British Lord Cowdray, upon whose great oil interests in Mexico Britain was counting to fuel its navy in the anticipated world war.

p. 64 *recognition of an American government:* Ibid.

p. 64 *Wilson's conversation with Colonel House:* House Diary, 10 Oct. 1913, quoted ibid., p. 120n.

p. 66 *their friends from helping them:* NYT, 21 Nov. 1913. See also NYT, 20 Nov. 1913.

p. 66 *Elim, to run around in:* Edith O'Shaughnessy, *A Diplomat's Wife in Mexico* (New York, 1916), pp. 4–5.

p. 68 *red carnation for his buttonhole:* Ibid., p. 192. See this work for details of this period.

8: The Benton Affair

p. 70 *"under your orders":* Martín Luis Guzmán, *The Memoirs of Pancho Villa* (Austin, 1965), p. 135. This relationship was totally baffling to Rosa King, who tended to see everyone in black and white. Her affection for Angeles was balanced by her horror of Villa. See King, *Tempest over Mexico* (Boston, 1935), pp. 115–19, 140.

p. 71 *Villa's decoration ceremony:* John Reed, *Insurgent Mexico* (1914; reprint, New York, 1969), pp. 113–16.

p. 72 *William Benton:* Elias L. Torres, *Twenty Episodes in the Life of Pancho Villa* (Austin, 1973), pp. 18–19. See also the interview with William P. Pettit, in NYT, 22 Feb. 1914.

p. 73 *trespassed on Benton's property:* Alan Knight, *The Mexican Revolution* (New York, 1986), 1:119.

p. 73 *in local political matters":* Torres, *Twenty Episodes,* p. 19.

p. 73 *with unusual courtesy":* Knight, *Mexican Revolution,* 1:120.

p. 73 *"stay out of Mexico":* Guzmán, *Villa,* p. 133. The rest of this account comes from this book, which makes no effort to exonerate Villa from any crimes and which may have exaggerated some crimes in order to be sensational.

p. 74 *Benton remained cool:* Ibid., pp. 133–34; Torres, *Twenty Episodes,* p. 23.

p. 74 *to be on the lookout:* Torres, *Twenty Episodes,* p. 26.

p. 75 *"on account of their nationality":* NYT, 20 Feb. 1914.

p. 75 *tried by the revolutionary army:* Guzmán, *Villa,* p. 134.

p. 75 *First Chief of the Revolution":* Reed, *Insurgent Mexico,* p. 268.

p. 76 *Reed's interview with Carranza:* Ibid., pp. 270–76.

p. 78 *confirm the first one:* Guzmán, *Villa,* pp. 136–37.

9: The Tampico Incident

p. 80 *positions in the hills*": Robert E. Quirk, *An Affair of Honor* (Lexington, Ky., 1962), pp. 6–7.

p. 81 *wishes American civilians:* Mayo to Fletcher, 28 March 1914, quoted in Quirk, *Affair*, p. 12.

p. 99 *Tampico incident:* The most thorough account of this often written-up incident is given in Jack Sweetman, *The Landing at Veracruz, 1914* (Annapolis, 1968), pp. 30–33, from which this has been taken.

p. 99 *Mayo was one:* Admiral Ernest King, chief of naval operations during World War II, described Mayo as "restrained and judicious . . . well-endowed with the unobtrusive common sense." Surprisingly, King attributes Mayo's later advancement partly to the action Mayo took at Tampico. King, *Fleet Admiral King* (New York, 1952), pp. 100–101.

p. 99 *"returned by this ship"*: Mayo to Morelos Zaragoza, 9 April 1914, *FRUS, 1914*, p. 448.

p. 100 *O'Shaughnessy learned:* O'Shaughnessy to Bryan, 10 April 1914, *FRUS, 1914*, p. 449.

p. 100 *defuse the situation had failed:* Edith O'Shaughnessy, *A Diplomat's Wife in Mexico* (New York, 1916), pp. 258–59.

p. 101 *"on the part of Colonel Hinojosa"*: *NYT*, 11 April 1914.

p. 101 *an excuse to start trouble:* Ibid.

p. 101 *"have done otherwise"*: Bryan to Wilson, 10 april 1914, *FRUS, 1914*, p. 449.

p. 101 *"apology as sufficient"*: *NYT*, 12 April 1914.

p. 102 *"lives of many young men"*: Josephus Daniels, *The Wilson Era*, (Chapel Hill, 1946), p. 189.

p. 102 *discuss any official business: NYT*, 14 April 1914.

p. 102 *"humiliating terms of the United States"*: O'Shaughnessy to State Department, 12 April 1914, *FRUS, 1914*, p. 455.

p. 102 *orders of a Mexican soldier.* Canada to Bryan, 12 April 1914, *FRUS, 1914*, p. 455.

p. 102 *regiment of marines:* Bryan to O'Shaughnessy, 14 April 1914, 10 P.M., *FRUS, 1914*, p. 459.

p. 103 *"to the Panama Canal": NYT*, 15 April 1914.

p. 103 *"our next meeting"*: David F. Houston, *Eight Years with Wilson's Cabinet*, 1:116, quoted in Ray Stannard Baker, *Woodrow Wilson*, vol. 4 (Garden City, N.Y., 1931), p. 324.

p. 104 *four influential members of Congress:* Senator Benjamin F. Shively, acting chairman of the Foreign Relations Committee, Senator Henry Cabot Lodge, its ranking Republican, and Congressmen Henry D. Flood and Henry A. Cooper.

p. 104 *taking action against Mexico:* Henry Cabot Lodge, *The Senate and the League of Nations* (New York, 1925), p. 13.

p. 104 *Lodge insisted:* Ibid., p. 14.

p. 104 *the German freighter Ypiranga:* The cargo, reputedly the largest arms shipment ever to enter a Mexican port, was said to include 200 guns and 15 million rounds of small-arms ammunition.

p. 105 *in only a few minutes:* Lodge also wrote, "The reason for the extraordinary proposition . . . was the mere excuse. General Huerta had declined to obey Mr. Wilson, and he had interfered with Mr. Wilson's plans. . . . [Wilson's] egotism, so little comprehended then, was so vast that he did not hesitate to say to the world that Huerta's resistance to him must be punished." Lodge, *Senate*, pp. 15–16. Lodge wrote this after he had publicly broken with Wilson.

p. 105 *"promptly, firmly, and wisely":* FRUS, 1914, pp. 474–76.

p. 105 *message in Mexico City:* Fletcher to Secretary of the Navy, 16 April 1914, NARA.

p. 105 *into the next day:* Lodge, *Senate*, pp. 14–15, 17.

p. 106 *The small booklet:* "Squadron Instructions for Naval Vessels in Mexican Gulf Waters," signed by F. F. Fletcher, Rear Admiral, Commander of Detached Squadron, Atlantic Fleet," NARA, RG 45, Box 776.

p. 106 *"confer with* Ypiranga": Fletcher to Daniels, 11:00 P.M., 20 April 1914, NARA, RG 45, Box 776.

p. 107 *"act Tuesday evening":* Daniels to Fletcher, 12:00 midnight, 20 April 1914, NARA, RG 45, Box 776.

p. 107 *"city and vicinity":* Daniels to Fletcher, 1:00 A.M., Tuesday, 21 April 1914, NARA, RG 45, Box 776.

p. 107 *received any such orders:* Fletcher, Report, p. 5. The command arrangement was odd. Fletcher's and Mayo's commands were theoretically coequal in status. Fletcher, however, had the only radios that could communicate with Washington. Fletcher appears to have acted as "first among equals."

p. 108 *orders for departure:* Clarence Miller, "Political Considerations at Tampico including the attacks of the Constitutionalists in April, the Tampico flag incident, the capture of Tampico, and the exodus of the Americans," Tampico, Mexico, 21 May 1914, NARA, 812.00/12436.

p. 108 *"no alternative but to land":* Josephus Daniels, *The Life of Woodrow Wilson* (Philadelphia, 1924), pp. 182–83. This version has been rounded out by Sweetman and Quirk. An elaborate reconstruction appears in Barbara W. Tuchman, *The Zimmermann Telegram* (New York, 1966), pp. 49–50.

p. 108 *"or any other party":* Florida log, 21 April 1914, quoted in Quirk, *Affair*, p. 85.

10: The Landing at Veracruz

p. 110 *was completely unknown:* Fletcher Report.

p. 110 *Old sea dog:* Fletcher used proper federal prose, however: "It was decided to land." Ibid., p. 11.

p. 111 *any action that might occur:* Ibid., pp. 11, 12.

p. 113 *no resistance would be offered:* William W. Canada, "Occupation of the Port of Veracruz by the American Forces, April 21st and 22d, 1914;" 11 Aug. 1914, Naval Records Collection, NARA.

p. 113 *disappeared like the others:* Ibid., pp. 3–4.

p. 113 *going according to plan:* Ibid., pp. 5–7.

p. 114 *ran roughly north–south:* The waterfront actually runs a little northwest–southeast, but it is easier to visualize as north–south.

p. 114 *mustaches and plumed helmets:* On meeting Maass, Edith O'Shaughnessy wrote, "He will not prove efficient—a blue-eyed Mexican, wearing his sandy-gray hair in a brush effect, *can't* be!" O'Shaughnessy, *A Diplomat's Wife in Mexico* (New York, 1916), pp. 135, 305–6.

p. 114 *Fletcher had anticipated:* Robert E. Quirk, *An Affair of Honor* (Lexington, Ky., 1962), p. 69. These regiments were actually the size of small battalions, but each was commanded by a general. Generals were in ample supply in the Mexican army.

p. 114 *the day before the American landing:* Jack Sweetman, *The Landing at Vera Cruz* (Annapolis, 1968), pp. 59–60.

p. 114 *These unfortunate wretches:* Quirk, *Affair*, p. 90.

p. 114 *up the Avenida Cinco de Mayo:* Sweetman, *Landing*, pp. 59–60.

p. 114 *"officer of the Nineteenth Regiment":* Lieutenant Colonel Albino Rodríguez Cerrillo.

p. 115 *what had happened:* Quirk, *Affair*, p. 91.

p. 115 *await further developments:* Quirk, *Affair*, p. 92. This railroad line is different from the one served by the terminal at the northern end of town.

p. 115 *at first remaining quiet:* Canada, "Occupation," p. 8.

p. 116 *in self-defense as necessary:* Ibid.; Fletcher Report.

p. 116 *first American casualties:* Fletcher Report, p. 15. Rush's message did not specify the number of casualties at that moment. The *Utah* had been under orders to prepare to follow the *Ypiranga* to Puerto México, an alternative port where her cargo of arms might be unloaded.

p. 116 *were never interrupted:* Ibid., p. 18.

p. 117 *and one of his men was killed:* Ibid., p. 17.

p. 117 *the night of April 21–22:* Ibid.; Canada to Bryan, 21 April 1914, NARA 800/11595.

p. 118 *to the American Consulate:* Canada, "Occupation," pp. 12–14; *NYT*, 23 April 1914. One wonders about Franco's creativity in telling of his alleged exploits. In any case, Canada did not mention Franco's name in his official report.

p. 118 *"four dead twenty wounded":* Fletcher Report, p. 21.

p. 118 *with his big naval guns:* Canada to Bryan, 21 April 1914, *FRUS*, 1914, p. 479.

p. 118 *simply a "gesture":* Ray Stannard Baker, *Woodrow Wilson*, vol. 4 (Garden City, N.Y., 1931), p. 330.

p. 119 *"was positively shaken":* J. H. Forman, quoted ibid. Fletcher's entire message is contained in the Fletcher Report.

p. 119 *occasional shots at each other:* *NYT*, 23 April 1914.

p. 119 *earning Fletcher's gratitude:* Fletcher Report, p. 22.

p. 119 *preassigned sectors of the city:* *NYT*, 23 April 1914; Fletcher Report.

p. 120 *shelled by the American warships:* Fletcher Report, p. 24.

p. 120 *rest of the city":* Fletcher and Badger had organized Captain Rush's Seaman Brigade into four regiments, two of seamen and two of marines. The First and Second Seaman Regiments each comprised about 1,200 officers and men, organized into battalions of 300 men each, according to the ships they came from. The First and Third Provisional Marine Regiments numbered about 700 officers and men each. This organization and scheme of maneuver all come from Sweetman's excellent *Landing*, pp. 97–89, 174–81.

p. 121 *a few of his men men around him:* Ibid., pp. 104–5.

p. 121 *Some fifteen naval cadets:* NYT, 24 April 1914.

p. 121 *"against the Americans in 1847":* Canada, "Occupation," p. 24.

p. 121 *the wounded at 195:* Sweetman, *Landing,* p. 123. Sweetman considers the Mexican estimate low. As of the evening of twenty-second, only twelve Americans had been reported dead and forty wounded. NYT, 23 April 1914.

p. 122 *"young men to their deaths":* Arthur S. Walsworth, *Woodrow Wilson: American Prophet,* 1:373, quoted in Sweetman, *Landing,* p. 91.

p. 122 *apologize to the ship's captain:* Quirk, *Affair,* pp. 98–99. I have found no evidence that Fletcher ever apologized. The *Ypiranga* was probably gone before Fletcher received any such instructions.

p. 122 *required a larger ground force:* NYT, 24 April 1914.

p. 122 *as many as 400,000 reservists:* Ibid.

p. 123 *"I'm off for Mexico":* Sheet music, "I'm Off to Mexico," by J. Will Callahan and F. Henri Klickman. Provided courtesy of Daniel Holt, director, Eisenhower Library, Abilene, Kan.

p. 123 *was on the high seas:* Clarence C. Clendenen, *Blood on the Border* (New York, 1969), pp. 161–63. The NYT, 24 April 1914, reported that the 5th Brigade consisted of four infantry regiments (the 4th, 7th, 19th, and 28th), one mountain artillery regiment (the 4th), and one cavalry regiment (the 6th), for a total of 3,200 infantry, 1,000 artillery, and 1,000 cavalry.

p. 123 *bury all the corpses:* Canada, "Occupation," pp. 28–30, which shows photos of bodies being burned.

p. 124 *"Star-Spangled Banner":* Ibid., pp. 31–34.

p. 124 *"upon our country":* John A. Lejeune, *Reminiscences of a Marine* (Philadelphia, 1930), p. 211.

11: THE CLOUDS OF WAR

p. 125 *breakwaters at Veracruz:* Before the National Defense Act of 1947, the army maintained its own set of military transports, all named after Civil War generals.

p. 126 *Philippine insurgents:* Funston's daring action was described by the War Department as "the most important single event of the year in the Philippines." Secretary of War, Annual Report, 1901, NARA.

p. 126 *Robert J. Kerr:* This lawyer had helped Fletcher deal with local Mexican officials. Jack Sweetman, *The Landing at Vera Cruz* (annapolis, 1968), p. 151.

p. 126 *U.S. Forces Ashore:* Funston to AGWAR, 30 April 1914, NARA, AG Records, RG 94, #2149991, Box 7480.

p. 126 *reported to Fletcher:* Sweetman, *Landing,* p. 151.

p. 127 *auspicious beginning:* Washington Post, 2 May 1914. The laughter and cries of "Mi dulce corazón" nearly drowned out the band music. Admiral Carlton H. Wright to Sweetman, quoted in Sweetman, *Landing,* p. 153.

p. 127 *"an unequal war":* Carranza to Wilson (through Carothers), in NYT, 23 April 1914.

p. 127 *"justice and conciliation":* Carranza to Wilson, 22 April 1914, ibid.

p. 127 *"traitor, and assassin":* Ibid.

p. 128 *"into a tangle at last":* Villa had taken Torreón for the second time on April 3. Carranza had moved from Sonora to Chihuahua. NYT, 24 April 1914.

p. 128 *"our neighbors to the north":* Ibid.

p. 128 *The reaction of nearly all:* The only exception was Brazil.

p. 128 *"greatly to his credit":* NYT, 24 April 1914.

p. 128 *"having a seaport":* Arthur S. Link, *Woodrow Wilson and the Progressive Era* (New York, 1954), pp. 124–25.

p. 129 *"bad day for civilization":* Economist, 18 April 1914, quoted in Link, *Wilson,* p. 124.

p. 129 *"with vanity and cowardice":* Independiente, 22 April 1914, quoted in Edith O'Shaughnessy, *A Diplomat's Wife in Mexico* (New York, 1916), p. 291.

p. 129 *"the place each merits":* Ibid., p. 292.

p. 130 *"Besides the chargé":* NYT, 24 April 1914.

p. 130 *"He has not understood":* O'Shaughnessy, *Diplomat's Wife,* pp. 292–97.

p. 131 *"longing for an exit":* Wilson to Dr. M. W. Jacobus, 29 April 1914, quoted in Ray Stannard Baker, *Woodrow Wilson,* vol. 4 (Garden City, N.Y., 1931), p. 335.

p. 131 *spelled trouble ahead:* Lodge later wrote that the mediation was "in itself a good thing, [which] shows our readiness for a peaceful solution but also, which is infinitely more important, improves our relations with the three most important South American states and unites them with us." Henry Cabot Lodge, *The Senate and the League of Nations* (New York, 1925), p. 19. The others present were Stone, Shively, Flood, and Cooper.

p. 131 *"pieces a moment before":* The Life of Joseph Rucker Lamar, pp. 246–47, quoted in Baker, *Wilson,* p. 337.

p. 131 *pressure from the British minister:* Alan Knight, *The Mexican Revolution* (New York, 1986), 2:165.

p. 132 *between the United States and Huerta:* Baker, *Wilson,* 337.

p. 132 *acceptable to all parties:* Memo, undated, from Wilson to the mediators, quoted in Link, *Wilson,* p. 126.

p. 133 *"rights, shall prevail":* Samuel G. Blythe, "A Conversation with the President," in *The Public Papers of Woodrow Wilson,* 3 vols. (New York, 1925), 2:111–12.

p. 133 *with minimum bloodshed:* Bryan to the Special Commissioners, 27, May 1914, FRUS, 1914, p. 510.

p. 133 *"it was Carranza himself":* U.S. Representatives to Bryan, 12 and 16 June 1914, FRUS, 1914, pp. 528, 538.

p. 134 *"as soon as constituted":* Secretary (to the Commissioners) Dodge to Bryan, 25 June 1914, FRUS, 1914, p. 548.

p. 134 *at Puebla on April 30:* Funston to AGWAR, 3 May 1914, NARA, AG Records, RG 94, #214991, Box 7480.

p. 134 *"recent humiliation here":* Ibid.

p. 135 *"the rest to us":* Funston to AGWAR, 7 May 1914, ibid.

p. 135 *Benton killing was still fresh:* Robert E. Quirk, *An Affair of Honor* (Lexington, Ky., 1962), p. 123.

p. 135 *Letter from J. O. Jack:* NARA, AG Records, RG 94, #2149991, Box 7480.

p. 135 *"harbor to Mexico City":* Washington Post, 1 May 1914, quoted in Quirk, *Affair,* p. 127.

p. 136 *Funston was not amused:* Medill McCormick, "Just Out of Jail,"

Harper's Weekly, 30 May 1914, cited in Clarence C. Clendenen *Blood on the Border* (New York, 1969), p. 170.

p. 136 *civil positions in Veracruz:* Funston to AGWAR, 1 May 1914, NARA, AG Records, RG 94, #2149991, Box 7480.

p. 136 *"Military Governor of Vera Cruz":* Garrison to Funston, 1 May 1914, and Funston to AGWAR, 30 April, 1, 2 May, 1914, all ibid.

p. 137 *"to remain in the vicinity":* Paul A. Wolf, "History of the Department of Public Works," AGO file, NARA; Charles Jenkinson, "Vera Cruz: What American Occupation Has Meant to a Mexican Community," *Survey* 30, no. 2 (Feb. 1960).

p. 137 *before it was too late:* Jenkinson, "Vera Cruz."

p. 137 *season was just beginning:* Quirk, *Affair*, p. 138.

p. 138 *with a rifle and ammunition:* Funston to AGWAR, 10 May, 23 June 1914, NARA, AG Records, RG 94, #2149991, Box 7480.

p. 138 *Mexican commander at Tejería:* Funston to AGWAR, 8 May 1914, ibid.

p. 138 *Parks had been cremated:* Funston to AGWAR, 28, 30, July, 1 Nov. 1914, ibid.

p. 138 *"close at hand":* Funston to AGWAR, 6 May 1914, ibid.

12: THE FALL OF VICTORIANO HUERTA

p. 140 *one thousand troops surrendered:* Alan Knight, *The Mexican Revolution* (New York, 1986), 2:146.

p. 140 *as provisional governor:* William Weber Johnson, *Heroic Mexico*, rev. ed. (San Diego, 1984), p. 197.

p. 141 *soon rebel against him:* Carranza interview with Heriberto Barrón, quoted ibid., p. 198.

p. 141 *as well as Villa himself:* Martín Luis Guzmán, *The Memoirs of Pancho Villa* (Austin, 1965), p. 207.

p. 141 *"leave at once":* Ibid., p. 211.

p. 142 *"to whom to deliver it":* Ibid., pp. 213–14.

p. 142 *a general to replace Villa:* Villa claims, in his memoirs, that the action was spontaneous on their part. Without a doubt it was, especially after he had explained the details of his contretemps with Carranza over the prospect of sending a 3,000-man reinforcement to Natera.

p. 142 *"rights of the people":* Angeles to Carranza, quoted in Guzmán, *Villa*, p. 220.

p. 144 *"your cannon to win the battle":* Ibid., pp. 223–24.

p. 144 *those two, were secondary:* Johnson, *Heroic Mexico* p. 204; Guzmán, *Villa*, p. 225.

p. 144 *20,000 men in the assault:* Guzmán, *Villa*, p. 229.

p. 145 *back to their pieces:* Ibid., p. 235.

p. 145 *another twenty-five hundred wounded:* Johnson, *Heroic Mexico*, p. 208.

p. 146 *"triumph at Aguascalientes":* Guzmán, *Villa*, p. 243.

p. 146 *"unworthy revolutionary":* The message had reached Angeles during the battle, but he did not even bother to tell Villa until later.

p. 147 *declaring himself First Chief:* Johnson, *Heroic Mexico*, p. 227.

p. 147 *"South on your side":* Ibid. (italics added).

p. 147 *Alvaro Obregón:* Knight, *Mexican Revolution,* 2:24.

p. 148 *Federals two thousand dead:* Johnson, *Heroic Mexico,* p. 223.

p. 149 *"to an unjust power":* NYT, 16 July 1914.

p. 150 *bound for Spain:* NYT, 18 July 1914.

13: THE CONVENTION AT AGUASCALIENTES

p. 153 *followed Huerta into exile:* Lyle C. Brown, "The Politics of Armed Struggle in the Mexican Revolution, 1913–1915," in James W. Wilkie and Albert L. Michaels, eds., *Revolution in Mexico* (New York, 1969), p. 63.

p. 153 *"General Velasco . . . August 13":* For an amusing and instructive description of the mutually deferent parley between Angeles and Velasco just prior to the second taking of Torreón, see William Weber Johnson, *Heroic Mexico,* rev. ed. (San Diego, 1984), p. 190.

p. 153 *services eulogizing Madero:* Ibid., p. 232.

p. 154 *in the Morelos mountains:* Brown, "Politics," p. 63.

p. 154 *implement the Plan of Ayala:* Ibid., pp. 63–64. The Plan de Ayala, in itself, did not provide for governmental structure. It was totally philosophical:

> The land, woods, and water which have been usurped . . . will be restored immediately to the villages or citizens who have the corresponding titles to them. . . . The usurpers who think they have a right to such property may present their claims before special courts to be established after the triumph of the Revolution. . . . The properties of those who may oppose this Plan . . . shall be seized. Johnson, *Heroic Mexico,* p. 85. For a reference to Xochimilco, see ibid., p. 265.

p. 154 *a term of instant familiarity:* At thirty-four, Obregón was only two years younger than Villa.

p. 155 *Colonel Plutarco Elías Calles:* He has been described as "the most adroit, successful politician" of "the many leaders thrown up by the Revolution." Alan Knight, *The Mexican Revolution* (New York, 1986), 2:218.

p. 155 *entertained them at a banquet:* The NYT carried the story on 27 Aug., on p. 7, without photos. In the same column was a report that Paul Fuller, expected to become the next U.S. ambassador to Mexico, had reported to the president that "there was little danger of a conflict between Villa and Carranza, and that prospects for continued peace in Mexico were bright." The *Times* editorial of 25 Aug. was equally optimistic about the prospects of peace between Villa and Carranza.

p. 156 *"and the President":* NYT, 2 Sept. 14.

p. 156 *the two men approved it:* Martín Luis Guzmán, *The Memoirs of Pancho Villa* (Austin, 1965), pp. 302–3. One wonders how sincere Obregón was when he agreed to a petition asking Carranza to step down. He was, after all, in Villa's hands when he signed it.

p. 156 *pesos of Constitutionalist currency:* Johnson, *Heroic Mexico,* pp. 233–34.

p. 157 *remained in Villa's hands:* Ibid., p. 239.

p. 157 *as a traitor by Pancho Villa:* Brown, "Politics," p. 66; Johnson, *Heroic Mexico,* pp. 243–44.

p. 158 *to be invited to attend:* Brown, "Politics," pp. 66–67.

p. 158 *rank of "general":* Supposedly, a delegate had to have commanded a force of a thousand men and to have been in uniform before the Battle of Zacatecas, the previous June. However, records were nonexistent, so an individual's credentials were always negotiable.

p. 159 *pistols into the air:* Johnson, *Heroic Mexico,* p. 247.

p. 160 *"law and knowledge":* Guzmán, *Villa,* p. 338.

p. 160 *"great culture and knowledge":* John Womack, Jr., *Zapata and the Mexican Revolution* (New York, 1969), p. 215.

p. 161 *"forthright and rousing":* Knight, *Mexican Revolution,* 2:259.

p. 161 *"ill-defined anarchy":* Ibid.

p. 161 *"articulate militancy":* Womack, *Zapata,* p. 193, cited ibid., p. 260.

p. 162 *"I'll go on":* Guzmán, *Eagle,* pp. 271–73.

p. 162 *formalized at that moment:* Johnson, *Heroic Mexico,* pp. 249–51.

p. 163 *not even the Convention itself:* Guzmán, *Eagle,* pp. 288–91.

p. 164 *he would support Gutiérrez:* Brown, "Politics," p. 67.

14: VILLA'S AND ZAPATA'S REIGN OF TERROR

p. 166 *features visible underneath:* William Weber Johnson, rev. ed. *Heroic Mexico* (San Diego, 1984), p. 266.

p. 167 *doomed Paulino Martínez:* Ibid., pp. 267–68.

p. 169 *"I have a heart too":* Martín Luis Guzmán, *The Eagle and the Serpent* (New York, 1930), pp. 343–48.

p. 170 *the recent assassinations:* Johnson, *Heroic Mexico,* p. 273.

p. 170 *José Isabel Robles:*

Robles was as brave as a lion in the hour of danger, and austere as a hermit afterward, and thus he seemed to Villa twice perfect. This made him immune to all criticism and entitled to every privilege.

Robles was permitted by his chief to counsel, advise, reprove, and even protest in situations where others had to keep quiet. That "fluky" pistol of Villa's, so ready to punish on the least suspicion, for the most trifling mistake, would have pardoned real disloyalty in Robles. GUZMÁN, *Eagle,* pp. 314–15.

p. 171 *the president's "safety":* Martín Luis Guzmán, *The Memoirs of Pancho Villa* (Austin, 1965), p. 409.

p. 171 *a great humiliation:* Ronald Atkin, *Revolution* (New York, 1970), p. 239.

p. 172 *"grateful to you, Señor":* Guzmán, *Villa,* p. 414.

p. 172 *"like a bandit":*

Señor, my ministers and I believe that honor and patriotism force us to carry forward our present intention to fight and annihilate Francisco Villa and Emiliano Zapata, who are bandits and criminals. . . . We ask you, Señor, to stop your attacks on the . . . forces of the Convention government and give us time to prepare the plan of campaign we will pursue. . . . We are conducting talks with Obregón. . . . Ibid., p. 417.

p. 172 *money in the treasury:* Atkin, *Revolution,* p. 237.

p. 173 *Zapata in the south:* Guzmán, *Villa,* pp. 432–34.

p. 173 *shipped to Veracruz:* Atkin, *Revolution,* p. 241.

p. 173 *"sooner than the latter":* Obregón, *Memoirs,* quoted ibid., p. 245.

p. 174 *"jingle of my spurs":* Guzmán, *Villa,* p. 446.

p. 174 *Villa's decision to attack Obregón at Celaya:* ibid., pp. 448–52.

15: CARRANZA BY DEFAULT

p. 175 *as many as twelve thousand:* Martín Luis Guzmán, *The Memoirs of Pancho Villa* (Austin, 1965), p. 453.

p. 176 *"Villa's supplies were running low":* Through his brother Hipólito in Juárez, Villa had ordered and paid for huge quantities of ammunition from across the border, but Hipólito now reported that the U.S. authorities in El Paso were "not so favorable as before." He was able to send only 200,000 rounds of ammunition. Ibid.

p. 176 *arrived on the scene:* Robert E. Quirk, *The Mexican Revolution* (Bloomington, 1960), p. 221.

p. 177 *to remaining in place:* Alan Knight, *The Mexican Revolution* (New York, 1986), 2:323.

p. 177 *dead on the field:* Guzmán, *Villa,* pp. 454–59; Ronald Atkin, *Revolution* (New York, 1970), pp. 250–51.

p. 177 *"myself be conquered":* Guzmán, *Villa,* p. 465.

p. 179 *broke into flight:* Knight, *Mexican Revolution,* 2:324; Atkin, *Revolution,* p. 252. Atkin places Villa's strength at 25,000.

p. 179 *including 5,000 prisoners:* J. R. Ambrosins, who was in the area just after the battle, estimated that Villa had lost 5,000 prisoners and at least 4,000 killed. Quirk, *Revolution,* p. 225.

p. 179 *thirty-four cannon:* Atkin, *Revolution,* p. 252; Obregón report to Carranza, quoted in *NYT,* 17 April 1915.

p. 179 *both dead and wounded:* Obregón report to Carranza, quoted in toto in *NYT,* 17 April 1915.

p. 181 *perhaps Villa was finished:* See *NYT,* 20 April 1915.

p. 182 *to Fierro for execution:* Atkin, *Revolution,* pp. 254–55; Johnson, *Heroic Mexico,* p. 296.

p. 182 *"this man Carranza":* Wilson to Lansing, 2 June 1915, quoted in Arthur S. Link, *Woodrow Wilson and the Progressive Era* (New York, 1954), p. 133n.

p. 182 *His friends Carothers and Scott:*
George C. Carothers, Consul accredited to Villa's headquarters, and General Hugh A. Scott, Chief of Staff, [had] pleaded Villa's cause and played upon the President's prejudices against Carranza. Villa had enjoyed a friendly press in the United States and had been depicted as a natural leader of the downtrodden Mexican masses. It was assumed that Villa would effect land reform more quickly than Carranza. Ibid., p. 129n.

p. 182 *distribute land to peasants:* Johnson, *Heroic Mexico,* p. 304.

p. 182 *included John Lind:* The agents were Jorge Orozco, Carrancista consul in El Paso, Rafael Múzquiz, a nephew, and Roberto V. Pesqueira, a former agent. The Americans were Richard H. Cole, of Pasadena, and Richard Lee Metcalf, of Washington, D.C., a friend of Bryan's. Ibid., p. 305.

p. 183 *"help Mexico save herself":* Wilson statement, 2 June 1915, in Roy Stannard Baker and William E. Dodd, eds., *The Public Papers of Woodrow Wilson,* vol. 2 (New York, 1925), pp. 339–40.

p. 184 *uprising in southern Mexico:* Atkin, *Revolution,* pp. 259–60.

p. 184 *even mowed the lawn:* Johnson, *Heroic Mexico,* p. 300.

p. 185 *his family in El Paso:* Atkin, *Revolution,* pp. 259–61; Johnson, *Heroic Mexico,* pp. 300–301.

p. 185 *activities of Captain Rintelen: NYT,* 8 Dec. 1915, estimated that Germany spent between $27 million and $30 million for sabotage and conspiracy. Of this, $12 million was allegedly allocated to Huerta's efforts. This word, however, came out after the United States had extended de facto recognition to Carranza.

p. 185 *"call to general elections":* American Journal of International Law, vol. 10. pp. 364–65, quoted in Baker and Dodd, eds., *Public Papers,* pp. 359–60.

p. 185 *"chiefs of the rebel party":* Johnson, *Heroic Mexico,* p. 294.

p. 185 *"as dominant in Mexico":* In late June 1915, Lansing wrote to himself as follows:

> Germany desires to keep up the turmoil in Mexico until the United States is forced to intervene; *therefore we must not intervene.*
>
> Germany does not wish to have any one faction dominant in Mexico; *therefore we must recognize one faction as dominant in Mexico.* . . .
>
> It comes down to this: Our possible relations with Germany must be our first consideration; and all our intercourse with Mexico must be regulated accordingly.
>
> BARBARA W. TUCHMAN, *The Zimmermann Telegram*
(New York, 1966), p. 89.

p. 185 *other than Carranza's:* Baker and Dodd, eds., *Public Papers,* p. 282.

p. 185 *"who had helped us":* Hugh Lenox Scott, *Some Memories of a Soldier* (New York, 1928), p. 517.

CHAPTER 16: BLOOD ON THE BORDER

p. 188 *one fleeting chance:* I. Thord-Gray, *Gringo Rebel* (Coral Gables, 1960), p. 463.

p. 188 *his whole division:* Haldeen Braddy, *Cock of the Walk* (Albuquerque, 1955), p. 111.

p. 188 *the death of Fierro:* Ronald Atkin, *Revolution* (New York, 1970), p. 267; William Weber Johnson, *Heroic Mexico,* rev. ed. (San Diego, 1984), p. 297.

p. 189 *"against any man":* Braddy, *Cock,* pp. 113–14.

p. 191 *field fortifications:* Interview with George Ruiz, Douglas, Ariz., 8 Dec. 1992; Braddy, *Cock,* p. 115; Johnson, *Heroic Mexico,* p. 297.

p. 191 *the American garrison:* Clarence CL Clendenen *Blood on the Border* (New York, 1969), p. 187.

p. 191 *fight against Carranza:* Carothers to Secretary of State, 31 Oct. 1915, quoted in Harley Notter, *The Origins of the Foreign Policy of Woodrow Wilson* (New York, 1965), p. 453; interview with Cindy Hayostek, Douglas, Ariz., 10 Dec. 1992. Clendenen, *Blood,* p. 187, asserts that Villa exhibited none of the mad behavior later attributed to him.

p. 192 *Agua Prieta battle:* Braddy, *Cock,* pp. 115–21. Villa always believed that the searchlights, crucial in repelling his night attack, had come from American territory. That was not true, though they were powered by electricity from the American part of the town. The important thing, however, was the way Villa perceived the U.S. role. See Atkin, *Revolution,* p. 266.

p. 192 *story of Winifred Paul:* Interview with Mayor Elizabeth Ames, Douglas, Dec. 1992.

p. 209 *Yaqui attack on the barbed wire:* Braddy, *Cock,* p. 120, which claims that the Indians were so frenzied that some succeeded in breaking the barbed wire with their hands.

p. 210 *of the ordeal:* Braddy, *Cock,* pp. 121–22.

p. 210 *Footnote:* Johnson, *Heroic Mexico,* p. 297. Atkin, *Revolution,* p. 267, attributes Maytorena's departure only to greed: Maytorena fled with the money that Villa had sent to him. The two versions are not necessarily incompatible.

p. 210 *destruction in their path:* Clendenen, *Blood,* p. 189.

p. 210 *eleven thousand men:* Johnson, *Heroic Mexico,* p. 298.

p. 211 *"demanded as a forfeit":* Coerver and Hall, *Texas and the Mexican Revolution,* p. 58, quoted in Frank N. Samponaro and Paul J. Vanderwood, *War Scare on the Rio Grande* (Austin, 1992), p. 44.

p. 211 *Texas state authorities:* Charles C. Cumberland, "Border Raids in the Lower Rio Grande Valley," *Southwestern Historical Quarterly* 57 (1954): 287, quoted in Clendenen, *Blood,* p. 181.

p. 211 *larger number of Mexicans:* Annual Report for the fiscal year 1916 (1 July 1915–30 June 1916) of Major General Frederick Funston, U.S. Army, Commanding Southern Department, pp. 15–19.

p. 211 *Carranza government in Mexico:* Ibid., p. 15.

p. 212 *sixteen were to be killed:* Clendenen, *Blood,* p. 181. See Samponaro and Vanderwood, *War Scare,* appendix B, for the entire plan. Funston included another version in his 1916 report.

p. 212 *"tried for lunacy":* Clendenen, *Blood,* p. 181.

p. 212 *as a warning to others:* Samponaro, and Vanderwood, *War Scare,* p. 77.

p. 213 *buried it the next morning:* Ibid., pp. 77–78.

p. 214 *crying "Viva Carranza!":* Ibid., pp. 79–80; Funston Report, p. 18.

p. 215 *to resume operations:* The attitude of the Villistas in Sonora should have been a warning. They robbed the Asarco Mining Company and stated that "in accordance with policy . . . all Americans were to be killed." Another band, in Coahuila, attacked ranches on Villa's order, which specified that all Chinese, Arabs, and Americans were to be killed. Alan Knight, *The Mexican Revolution* (New York, 1986), 2:344; *FRUS,* 1915, p. 954.

p. 216 *they mutilated the bodies:* Interview with José María Sánchez, quoted in Clarence C. Clendenen, *The United States and Pancho Villa* (Ithaca, 1961), pp. 218–19, 223.

p. 216 *Holmes's escape:* Atkin, *Revolution,* pp. 269–70.

17: Villa Raids Columbus

p. 218 *seven rifle troops:* On the average, a troop had three officers and seventy-five men.

p. 218 *were at Columbus:* Frank Tompkins, *Chasing Villa* (Harrisburg, 1934), p. 44.

p. 218 *"cactus, mesquite, and rattlesnakes":* Ibid., 50.

p. 219 *"had come off unscathed":* Haldeen Braddy, *Pancho Villa at Columbus* (El Paso, 1965), pp. 9–10.

p. 219 *drop the scheme:* Tompkins, *Chasing Villa,* p. 41.

p. 219 *moving toward Columbus:* FRUS, 1916, p. 478.

p. 219 *in that area:* FRUS, 1916, p. 478; Tompkins, *Chasing Villa,* p. 39.

p. 219 *Slocum could only shrug:* Slocum testimony at the later investigation, quoted in Tompkins, *Chasing Villa,* p. 46.

p. 219 *the American cowboy with Favela:* H. H. Marshall to his father, E. J. Marshall, owner of the Paloma Land and Cattle Company, *NYT,* March 19, 1916, quoted ibid., pp. 60–61.

p. 221 *the scout in Columbus:* Braddy, *Columbus,* pp. 14–15.

p. 221 *reserve behind Cootes Hill:* ibid., p. 16, paraphrased from Pershing Papers, Box 372, Library of Congress. In this document, Villa supposedly designated his own position, and it has been cited as proof of Villa's presence at Columbus, a contention that many writers, Hugh Scott among them, have contested.

p. 222 *were attacking Columbus:* Although none of the available sources say so, the attackers must have been carrying flares with which to torch the town. The sun does not rise in that region in early March until after 6:00 A.M., and total blackness is not consistent with picking out the color of sombreros or with other feats later claimed by the Americans. The official Lucas report is reproduced in Tompkins, *Chasing Villa.*

p. 223 *troop of soldiers into town:* "It developed that Lieutenant Castleman had turned out his troop . . . and had marched it over to town, where he took station in front of his residence." Tompkins added, "And opposite the bank." Lucas report, ibid.

p. 223 *soles of his feet:* Lucas report, ibid., pp. 50–52.

p. 224 *being gunned down:* Herbert Molloy Mason, Jr., *The Great Pursuit* (New York, 1969), p. 17.

p. 225 *The man released her:* Tompkins, *Chasing Villa,* pp. 58–59.

p. 225 *to take care of her:* Braddy, *Columbus,* pp. 28–29. Mrs. Wright's husband, she later learned, had been murdered, but her baby had been spared. One witness, Colonel Charles W. Hoffman (USAR), insisted later that Mrs. Moore had been raped and her baby murdered. (See Clendenen, *Blood,* p. 209.) This allegation has not been substantiated by more-responsible accounts, and Clendenen himself does not subscribe to it.

p. 226 *on that foray alone:* Tompkins, *Chasing Villa,* p. 57. Modesty was not one of Tompkins's traits, but since his force was pursuing, that body count seems possible.

p. 227 *accused of brutality:* Slocum was later accused of having been drunk when the attack fell. This accusation was later refuted, or at least shouted down, by the members of Slocum's garrison.

p. 227 *off to be cremated:* Mr. Jack Zimmatore, then a private in the army, quoted in Braddy, *Columbus,* p. 74.

p. 227 *objective was attain booty:* See Braddy, *Columbus,* p. 36.

p. 227 *dead behind him:* Ibid., p. 33.

18: "YOU WILL PROMPTLY ORGANIZE . . ."

p. 228 *the border into Mexico:* Roy E. Stivison and Della M. McDonnell, "When Villa Raided Columbus," *New Mexico Magazine,* Dec. 1950, pp. 41, 43, quoted in Clarence C. Clendenen *Blood on the Border* (New York, 1969), p. 213.

p. 230 *"and leaves at daylight":* George B. Rodney, *As a Cavalryman Remembers* (Caldwell, Idaho, 1944), pp. 249–50.

p. 231 *"morning of the ninth instant":* Hugh Lenox Scott, *Some Memories of a Soldier* (New York, 1928), pp. 519–20 (italics added).

p. 231 *"for sovereignty of Mexico"*: Secretary of War to Funston, 10 March 1916, quoted in Frank Tompkins, *Chasing Villa* (Harrisburg, 1934), p. 70 (italics added).

p. 232 *"from the Mexican side"*: Consul Marion H. Letcher to the Secretary of State, 9 March 1916, 3 P.M., *FRUS*, 1916, p. 480.

p. 232 *"to capture Villa"*: Ibid., p. 482.

p. 232 *"westward from Columbus"*: Lansing to special agents John R. Silliman and John W. Belt, 9 March 1916, 4 P.M., *FRUS*, 1916, p. 481.

p. 233 *questions up with Carranza:* Belt to Lansing, Irapuato, 10 March 1916, *FRUS*, 1916, pp. 483–84.

p. 233 *"any other point on the border"*: Silliman to Lansing, Irapuata, 10 March 1916, 11 P.M., *FRUS*, 1916, p. 486.

p. 233 *"invasion of national territory"*: Carranza to Lansing, 11 March 1916, 11:00 P.M., from Querétaro, *FRUS*, 1916, p. 486.

p. 234 *"a single electoral vote"*: House Diary, 17 March 1916, quoted in Alan Knight, *The Mexican Revolution* (New York, 1986), p. 347.

p. 234 *"of the Republic outraged"*: La Opinión (Querétaro), 12 March 1916, cited in *FRUS*, 1916, p. 487.

p. 234 *"Villa and his band"*: *FRUS*, 1916, p. 490.

p. 235 *"any recommendations to make"*: Pershing Report (30 June 1916).

p. 235 *"subject to your orders"*: Ibid., p. 606.

p. 235 *"to help corral Villa"*: On 12 March, Pershing himself said that he "had sufficient faith in the good sense of the Mexican people" that he expected their help. *NYT*, 12 March 1916.

p. 236 *George A. Dodd:* In 1887, while stationed at Fort McIntosh, Texas, Dodd developed a modern system of training cavalry and cavalry mounts, which was afterward incorporated into the Cavalry Drill Regulations. His Troop F, Third Cavalry, was known for many years as "the best-trained troop of cavalry in the United States Army." West Point Annual Report, 8 June 1928.

p. 237 *the Buffalo Soldiers:* In the army of 1916, an officer was assigned to a regiment, supposedly for the duration of his career. In practice, other assignments usually kept him from his regiment most of the time. Since 1906, however, Pershing, as a general officer, had not belonged to any regiment.

p. 238 *"You are appointed aide"*: The Patton Papers, ed. Martin Blumenson, vol. 1 (Boston, 1972), p. 320.

p. 239 *the lead cavalry troops:* Pershing Report, pp. 37–43.

p. 239 *transportation for the expedition:* The squadron had assembled the rest of the planes by the next day. Clendenen, *Blood*, p. 223.

p. 240 *6:00 A.M. on the fifteenth:* Frank E. Vandiver, *Black Jack* (College Station, Tex., 1977), 2:610.

p. 240 *the Columbus column:* It was led by the K Troop, Thirteenth Cavalry, followed by the L, M, and machine-gun troops and then the Second Squadron. Major Frank Tompkins, by his own account, was given command of the advance guard "as a mark of appreciation for the part taken by [him] in pursuit of Villa on the morning of March 9th." Tompkins, *Chasing Villa*, p. 74.

p. 240 *Border Gate had disappeared:* Funston later reported that Pershing had bribed the commander of the detachment by hiring him as a guide. Funston to AG (telegram), 15 March 1916, cited in Vandiver, *Black Jack*, 2:610.

p. 240 *on March 16:* There are many versions as to the exact time that this column crossed the border, none of them important.

p. 240 *"is hereby approved":* Joint Resolution No. 17, 64th Cong., 1st sess. 17 March 1916.

19: Pancho Villa's Narrow Escape

p. 241 *border in the north:* Edgcumb Pinchon, *Viva Villa!* (New York, 1933), p. 340.

p. 242 *complex at 8:00 P.M.:* Frank Tompkins, *Chasing Villa* (Harrisburg, 1934), p. 77.

p. 243 *plans to his staff:* A photograph in the *San Francisco Chronicle,* 12 April 1916, shows Pershing with Cabell, Hines, and six others, in varying uniforms, standing in front of a row of tents. *The Patton Papers,* ed. Martin Blumenson, vol. 1 (Boston, 1972), p. 322.

p. 244 *"country of no answers":* Gledon Swarthout, *They Came to Cordura* (New York, 1958), p. 3.

p. 245 *that line of fencing:* George B. Rodney, *As a Cavalryman Remembers* (Caldwell, Idaho, 1944), p. 257.

p. 246 *ran out of water:* Tompkins, *Chasing Villa,* p. 89.

p. 246 *to Madera only the casualties:* Ibid., p. 95.

p. 247 *for needed refitting:* Ibid., pp. 79–81.

p. 248 *"until fresh troops arrive":* Ibid., p. 83.

p. 248 *Agua Prieta, and Hermosillo:* Herbert Molloy Mason, Jr., *The Great Pursuit* (New York, 1970), pp. 94–95.

p. 249 *approached from the south:* Ibid., 96–97. The Mexican captive who supplied most of this account was one Modesto Nevares, of El Valle.

p. 250 *too worn out to go farther:* Tompkins, *Chasing Villa,* pp. 85–87.

20: Colonia Dublán

p. 252 *sent by this means:* QM, Columbus Base Report, p. 18, National Archives.

p. 253 *The trucks were sent:* Hugh Lenox Scott, *Some Memories of a Soldier* (New York, 1928), p. 531.

p. 254 *"attained in our service":* Pershing Report, p. 34.

p. 254 *his campaign in Mexico:* Herbert Molloy Mason, Jr., *The Great Pursuit* (New York, 1970), p. 103.

p. 255 *Germany spent $28 million:* Ibid., p. 104.

p. 255 *Foulois's squadron":* The pilots were Captains Benjamin D. Foulois and T. F. Dodd and Lieutenants C. G. Chapman, J. E. Carberry, Herbert A. Dargue, Thomas S. Bowen, R. H. Willis, Walter G. Kilner, Edgar S. Gorell, Arthur R. Christie, and Ira A. Rader. See Foulois Report.

p. 255 *found no adverse effects:* They were aloft less than an hour. Their purpose, primarily, was to test the effect of the high altitude on the performance of the aircraft. They found no adverse effects; however, the surface is only 4,000 feet above sea level at Columbus and 8,000 to 10,000 feet at Casas Grandes. Mason, *Great Pursuit*, pp. 108–9.

p. 255 *The eighth crashed at Pearson:* Foulois sent a small detachment to salvage the plane at Pearson on March 22, but it was turned back by Mexican fire. A larger detachment reached the site the next day and retrieved what equipment was deemed serviceable. See Foulois Report.

p. 256 *over a hundred miles:* Carrol Y. Glines, *The Compact History of the United States Air Force* (New York, 1963), p. 68.

p. 256 *to find Erwin:* Foulois Report.

p. 256 *"present military needs":* Glines, *Compact History*, p. 69.

p. 256 *it was turned down:* Foulois Report; also Mason, *Great Pursuit*, p. 116.

p. 257 *and the frontline troops:* Foulois Report.

p. 257 *account of that period:* "General Pershing's Mexican Campaign," *Century Magazine*, Feb. 1920, pp. 433–47.

p. 258 *"general was, it ended":* Ibid., p. 438.

p. 258 *in good humor:*

Throughout the campaign there was censorship, military and—I know of no better terms—political and diplomatic. . . . by the latter I mean, of course, as with reference to the relations between the United States and Mexico. . . . [A]s befitted a delicate situation, we emphasized the "cooperation" we were getting. It was part of the game, and, as we realized with wry smiles, "military necessity." Ibid., p. 436.

p. 258 *"value to Villa":* Memoir of General Hines, Carlisle Barracks, Penn., quoted in Frank E. Vandiver, *Black Jack* (College Station, Tex., 1977), 2:618.

p. 258 *"communiqué to an end":* Elser, "Campaign," p. 438.

p. 259 *"The command group that Pershing":* The other correspondents were W. H. Blakelee, of the Associated Press, and Robert Dunne, of the *New York Tribune*. Elser, "Campaign," pp. 438–39.

p. 259 *it was something new":* Vandiver, *Black Jack*, 2:625.

21: GUNFIGHT AT PARRAL

p. 261 *home to El Valle:* Herbert Molloy Mason, Jr., *The Great Pursuit* (New York, 1970), pp. 126–27. Some of Nevares's information was obviously hearsay. However, there is no reason to doubt his general reliability.

p. 261 *with a stubble of beard: The Patton Papers*, ed. Martin Blumenson, vol. 1 (Boston, 1972), p. 325.

p. 261 *"we've got Villa":* Frank B. Elser, "General Pershing's Mexican Campaign," *Century Magazine*, Feb. 1920, p. 439.

p. 262 *like cattle before a blizzard:* Ibid., p. 440.

p. 262 *"rat in a cornfield":* Ibid., p. 441.

p. 263 *knife cuts and cigarette burns:* Mason, *Great Pursuit*, pp. 117–18.

p. 263 *telling the truth: NYT*, 28 March 1916.

p. 264 *the parley and rode away:* Elser, "Campaign," pp. 442–43.

p. 264 *"should capture Villa":* Pershing Report, p. 11.

p. 265 *had made an impression:* Tompkins, *Chasing Villa*, pp. 117–18.

p. 265 *segregated army of the time:* Clarence C. Clendenen *Blood on the Border* (New York, 1969), p. 267n.

p. 266 *considered too strong:* Colonel Brown has been criticized for his personal lack of aggressiveness. See Mason, *Great Pursuit,* p. 125.

p. 266 *"line of foragers":* The cavalry equivalent of the infantry "line of skirmishers." Essentially, it means a formation in which all files advance abreast, with space enough between them that a single bullet cannot reasonably be expected to hit more than one.

p. 266 *overhead machine-gun fire":* Tompkins, *Chasing Villa,* pp. 145–46.

p. 266 *one final, "superlative" effort:* Elser, "Campaign," pp. 443–44.

p. 266 *five hundred silver pesos:* Mason, *Great Pursuit,* p. 128.

p. 267 *delicate supply line:* Tompkins, *Chasing Villa,* p. 120.

p. 268 *arrive at an agreement:* Ibid., p. 131.

p. 269 *tally of Mexican forces:* Ibid., p. 133.

p. 273 *rear guard to mount up:* Ibid., p. 140. Tompkins mentions another soldier whom Lininger rescued after his horse had been killed. Tompkins recommended Lininger for the Congressional Medal of Honor for this action. The award was downgraded to a Distinguished Service Cross.

p. 274 *before he hit the ground:* Tompkins recommended the CMH for Ord, as he had for Lininger; again, the award was the Distinguished Service Cross.

p. 274 *"memorable" as another Alamo:* Soon after his messengers had left, Tompkins received a note from Lozano urging him to evacuate Santa Cruz. Tompkins did not bite. He would remain where he was. Tompkins, *Chasing Villa,* pp. 142–43. The entire account of the battle of Parral comes from this book.

p. 275 *"You can start with me":* George B. Rodney, *As a Cavalryman Remembers* (Caldwell, Idaho, 1944), pp. 261–63.

p. 275 *in favor of the Americans:* Clendenen, *Blood,* p. 266.

p. 275 *consul at Chihuahua:* Ibid., p. 264.

22: TO THE BRINK

p. 277 *"solution to the problem":* Pershing Report, p. 23.

p. 278 *resumption of the conflict:* Frank Tompkins, *Chasing Villa* (Harrisburg, 1934), p. 168.

p. 278 *"easy marches to Satevó":* J. A. Ryan, acting chief of staff, to Brown, 15 April 1916, quoted ibid.

p. 279 *the meeting broke up:* Allen diary, quoted ibid, pp. 170–71.

p. 280 *"forces from our territory":* Note, Aguilar to Lansing, 12 April 1916, *FRUS,* 1916, pp. 515, 517.

p. 280 *"immunities of non-combatants":* Wilson note, signed by Lansing, 18 April, 1916, cited in Harley Notter, *The Origins of the Foreign Policy of Woodrow Wilson* (New York, 1965), p. 501.

p. 281 *"clean up Mexico":* Joseph R. Tumulty, *Woodrow Wilson as I Knew Him* (Garden City, N.Y., 1921), p. 154.

p. 281 *"it is right to strike":* Ibid., pp. 157–59.

p. 281 *"forces of the two governments":* Lansing to Rodgers, 22 April 1916, *FRUS,* 1916, pp. 527–28.

p. 282 *the possibility of war:* Rodgers to Lansing, 24 April 1916, *FRUS,* 1916, p. 528.

p. 282 *to meet with Scott:* Rodgers learned of Obregón's departure from another official. Ibid., pp. 528–29.

p. 282 *any place Obregón specified:* Ibid.

p. 282 *river in El Paso:* Edwards to Lansing, 28 April 1916, *FRUS*, 1916, p. 532.

p. 283 *atmosphere for the pending talks:* Letcher to Lansing, 28 April 1916, *FRUS*, 1916, p. 532.

p. 283 *cooperate with Obregón:* TAG, the War Department, to General Scott and General Funston, 26 April 1916, *FRUS*, 1916, pp. 530–32.

p. 283 *through diplomatic channels:* Ibid.

p. 284 *was obviously deadlocked:* Scott to War Department, 30 April 1916, *FRUS*, 1916, 534; Hugh Lenox Scott, *Some Memories of a Soldier* (New York, 1928), p. 525.

p. 285 *"the Scott-Obregón conference":* Scott to War Department, 1 May 1916, *FRUS*, 1916, p. 536; Funston to War Department, 1 May 1916, ibid., p. 537.

p. 285 *"When Scott left his hotel":* Scott, *Memories*, pp. 525–26.

p. 286 *"consider very carefully":* Scott was further aware of a force being assembled to the east in Tamaulipas, under General Nafarrete, which Scott presumed would be used for raids across the border into Laredo and Brownsville. Scott, *Memories*, pp. 527–28.

p. 286 *Mexico in case of war:* Scott and Funston to War Department, 3 May 1916, *FRUS*, 1916, p. 537.

p. 286 *they were supposedly settled:* Scott likened the situation to Penelope's web, which she wove during the day only to tear it out at night.

p. 287 *other threatened points:* Frederick Funston, "Annual Report for the Southern Department, 1916," NARA, AGO Records, RG 94, p. 21; *NYT*, 8 May 1916.

p. 287 *withdrawn from Mexico: NYT*, 10 May 1916.

23: CARRIZAL

p. 289 *Patton's ambush of Cárdenas:* For a highly detailed account, see *The Patton Papers*, ed. Martin Blumenson, vol. 1 (Boston, 1972), pp. 330–37.

p. 289 *cool infantry private:* George D. Hulett, Seventeenth Infantry.

p. 289 *most desperate of Villa's band:* Pershing Report, p. 28.

p. 290 *Assignments chart:* Ibid., p. 26.

p. 291 *two Villista chiefs:* Julio Acosta and Cruz Domínguez.

p. 291 *to his own command:* Howze to Pershing, 5 May 1916, cited in Pershing Report, p. 27.

p. 291 *heard from Mexico City:* Clarence C. Clendenen *Blood on the Border* (New York, 1969), p. 300; Frank E. Vandiver, *Black Jack* (College Station, Tex., 1977), 2:646–47.

p. 291 *"indications are not heeded":* Treviño to Pershing, 16 June 1916, cited in Pershing Report, p. 29. The identical words, incidentally, were used by Luis Herrera when conferring with Colonel Brown at Santa Cruz a month earlier.

p. 291 *"lie with the Mexican government":* Pershing to Treviño, cited in Pershing Report, p. 30.

p. 292 *"we'll stay"*: Ibid.

p. 293 *action against Pershing's forces*: Harley Notter, *The Origins of the Foreign Policy of Woodrow Wilson* (New York, 1965), p. 333; *FRUS*, 1916, pp. 581–90.

p. 293 *"regard for your command"*: "Memorandum from General Pershing for the Inspector General, Headquarters, Punitive Expedition, Camp Dublan, Mexico, June 30, 1916," quoted in Clendenen, *Blood*, pp. 303–4.

p. 294 *"going to test that"*: Clendenen, *Blood*, p. 305, quoting the Reverend John Jeter, a veteran.

p. 294 *estimates of American troop strengths*: Ibid.

p. 294 *if Boyd so ordered him*: Boyd mumbled something about "making history," but McCabe could not understand the rest. McCabe testimony, cited in Frank Tompkins, *Chasing Villa* (Harrisburg, 1934), p. 211. See also Spillsbury report, in *NYT*, 25 June 1916.

p. 295 *bandoleer of ammunition*: Clendenen, *Blood*, p. 306.

p. 295 *he did not return*: Statement of Captain Lewis Morey, quoted in Tompkins, *Chasing Villa*, p. 210.

p. 297 *attests to American marksmanship*: Tompkins' *Chasing Villa*, p. 209, is critical of Morey's K Troop, asserting that if it had shown the C Troop's dash, the Americans would have won the day. This assertion seems doubtful, given the loss of all the American officers. Also the Pershing Report, p. 31, claims that C Troops "carried" the position. If the Americans ever reached the ridge line, they did not hold it for more than a few moments.

p. 298 *"a terrible blunder"*: Funston to Pershing, 22 June 1916, NARA, quoted in Vandiver *Black Jack*, 2:652.

p. 298 *about his intentions*: Ibid., 654.

p. 298 *"exactly what happened"*: Pershing, quoted ibid.

p. 299 *"consequences seem upon us"*: Wilson to House, quoted in Notter, *Origins*, p. 533.

p. 299 *war he did not want*:

> The tension which preceded Carrizal was partly illusory. It was screwed up by the Carranza government with the understandable objective of pressuring the Americans out of Mexico; it did not represent wanton belligerence; still less did it derive from a powerful, popular hatred of Americans. The [Anti-American] demonstrations . . . were tame affairs. The Monterrey demonstration seemed "very mild"; that held in Mexico City "did not amount to much"; at Veracruz the US consul knew many of the 150 demonstrators and "they smiled as they passed."
>
> ALAN KNIGHT, The Mexican Revolution
(New York, 1986), 2:351–52,
which also offers examples from Saltillo and Durango.

p. 299 *in reasonable condition*: Herbert Molloy Mason, Jr., *The Great Pursuit* (New York, 1970), p. 217.

p. 299 *did not want war either*: The aforementioned June 22 letter to House ended, "But *Intervention* (that is, the arrangement and control of Mexico's domestic affairs by the U.S.) there shall not be either now or at any other time if I can prevent it." Arthur S. Link, *Woodrow Wilson and the Progressive Era* (New York, 1954), p. 143.

p. 300 *"the two governments"*: Tompkins, *Chasing Villa*, pp. 214–15.

24: Exit the United States

p. 301 *army of 200,000 men:* Frank E. Vandiver, *Black Jack* (College Station, Tex., 1977), 2:649. See also Clarence C. Clendenen *Blood on the Border* (New York, 1969), for this period.

p. 302 *Carranza's personal provocations:* Harley Notter, *The Origins of the Foreign Policy of Woodrow Wilson* (New York, 1965), p. 534.

p. 303 *Wilson's three-man delegation:* FRUS, 1916, pp. 607–8. See also Rodgers to Secretary of State, 29 July 1916, ibid., p. 605.

p. 303 *had been "uncompromised":* Notter, *Origins*, p. 535.

p. 303 *seizing a military train:* Herbert Molloy Mason, Jr., *The Great Pursuit* (New York, 1970), p. 223. The losses in these Mexican battles seem staggering, considering the sizes of the forces involved. However, a wound too often led to a kill in that wasted land, and neither side gave any quarter in battle.

p. 303 *on the fifteenth to reconnoiter:* Funston to Secretary of War, 20 Sept. 1916, NARA.

p. 304 *exceeded six thousand men:* Frank Tompkins, *Chasing Villa* (Harrisburg, 1934), p. 216.

p. 304 *"would doubtless welcome us":* Pershing to Funston, 2 Nov. 1916, quoted ibid., p. 217.

p. 305 *Food was adequate:* Clendenen, *Blood*, p. 334. Clendenen makes the point that the term "pup tent" was a pet of the newspapers at this time. However, it was certainly a common term among soldiers later on as well.

p. 305 *Patton's sister Nita:* See *The Patton Papers*, ed. Martin Blumenson, vol. 1 (Boston, 1972), p. 349, for a sketchy account of this trip.

p. 306 *guest of honor:* Clendenen, *Blood*, pp. 334–35.

p. 306 *daily maneuver problems:* Vandiver, *Black Jack*, 2:655–56.

p. 307 *came into being at all:* Link, *Progressive Era*, p. 143.

25: The Triumph of Obregón

p. 308 *Wilson's high opinion of Obregón:*

September 23, 1915: We breakfasted at eight. . . . The President . . . laughingly said that when the A. B. C. Conference resumed on the 8th of October, we would perhaps have to recognize Carranza. We were both of the opinion that General Obregón was responsible for the accelerated fortunes of Carranza and that he would perhaps finally turn out to be the "man of the hour" in Mexico.

The Intimate Papers of Colonel House,
ed. Charles Seymour (Boston, 1926), pp. 223–24.

p. 308 *real no-nonsense nature:* Hudson Strode, *Timeless Mexico* (New York, 1944), p. 265.

p. 309 *"every one of his acts":* Martín Luis Guzmán, *The Eagle and the Serpent* (New York, 1930), p. 70.

p. 309 *property of the state:* For the provisions of the constitution of 1917, see Linda B. Hall, *Alvaro Obregón* (College Station, Tex., 1981), p. 180, and William Weber Johnson, *Heroic Mexico*, rev. ed. (San Diego, 1984), p. 223.

p. 310 *principles of the Revolution:* De la Huerta, in his memoirs, assumes a good deal of credit for Obregón's decision not to run. According to him, he saw Obregón, at Carranza's behest, and sat for a full four hours on a park bench in Querétaro discussing the matter, and on the next day Obregón resigned as secretary of war. See Johnson, *Heroic Mexico*, p. 323.

p. 310 *become president in 1920:* Hall, *Obregón*, p. 162.

p. 311 *in the Mexican army:* Ronald Atkin, *Revolution* (New York, 1970), p. 293.

p. 311 *"economic and political ties":* Johnson, *Heroic Mexico*, p. 325. Carranza liked that word "disposed"; he had used it in promising the conferees at Aguascalientes that he would resign in late 1914.

p. 311 *oil to the Royal Navy:* Atkin, *Revolution*, p. 293.

p. 311 *"New Mexico, and Arizona":* Zimmermann to Bernstorff, 16 Jan. 1917, slightly condensed (italics added).

p. 311 *had been compromised:* On 5 Feb., the day Pershing left Mexico and Carranza published the new constitution, the German government sent another telegram to Mexico City urging Eckhardt to push the alliance.

p. 312 *truly destroyed for good:* Villa's grief was also deep when General Felipe Angeles, trying to rejoin Villa after years in the United States, was in late 1918 captured by Federal troops, tried, and executed.

p. 313 *"diseased, despairing, dying":* Ernest Gruening, *Mexico and Its Heritage,* quoted in Atkin, *Revolution*, p. 308.

p. 314 *their leader was dead:* Johnson, *Heroic Mexico*, 329–37. Actually, Zapata took more than just the ten men with him to Chinameca, but he had left most of them to guard against a false Carrancista attack, trumped up as part of Guajardo's plot.

p. 315 *well liked in diplomatic circles:* "Obregón had known Bonillas since childhood—Bonillas was also from Sonora—and conceded that he was 'a nice fellow . . . reliable, conscientious, and hard-working. The world has lost a first-class bookkeeper.' " Johnson, *Heroic Mexico*, p. 343.

p. 315 *"He went on an extensive tour":* Hall, *Obregón*, p. 189.

p. 315 *in northwest Mexico:* Ibid., p. 187. Interestingly, Obregón did not completely control his home state of Sonora despite his national prominence, since de la Huerta and Calles were rivals, albeit friendly ones.

p. 316 *a shrewd politician:* Atkin, *Revolution*, p. 312; Hall, *Obregón*, pp. 203–10.

p. 316 *risk of treachery:* Atkin, *Revolution*, 313, Hall, *Obregón*, pp. 237–39.

p. 317 *"victory or in death":* Johnson, *Heroic Mexico*, p. 350.

p. 318 *members of his personal guard:* Herbert Ingram Priestly, *The Mexican Nation* (New York, 1969), p. 449.

p. 318 *to Veracruz and exile:* Johnson, *Heroic Mexico*, pp. 350–51.

p. 318 *"your National Palace":* Ibid., p. 353.

p. 319 *he was gone:* Atkin, *Revolution*, p. 317; John W. F. Dulles, *Yesterday in Mexico* (Austin, 1961), pp. 38–46.

EPILOGUE

p. 322 *harassment by Federal troops:* Edgcumb Pinchon, *Viva Villa!* (New York, 1933), p. 356.

372 NOTES

p. 322 *500,000 pesos in gold:* Ibid., p. 357.

p. 322 *deal with his former foe:* William Weber Johnson, *Heroic Mexico*, rev. ed. (San Diego, 1984), p. 362.

p. 323 *his current mistress:* Austreberta Rentería.

p. 323 *"respected and orderly":* Pinchon, *Viva Villa*, p. 361.

p. 323 *"common people are educated":* Johnson, *Heroic Mexico*, p. 364.

p. 324 *to garrison Parral:* Pinchon, *Viva Villa*, p. 364.

p. 324 *vigilance gradually relaxed:* Ibid., p. 365.

p. 324 *"hand on Pancho Villa":* Johnson, *Heroic Mexico*, pp. 374–75.

p. 324 *the only survivor:*

p. 325 *"rid humanity of a monster":* Ronald Atkin, *Revolution* (New York, 1970), p. 324. The weapons used were new government rifles, recently supplied to Barraza, according to a story by a Mexico City journalist, Justino Palomares. See Johnson, *Heroic Mexico*, p. 377.

p. 325 *"revolutionary" promises:* Atkin, *Revolution*, p. 326.

BIBLIOGRAPHY

****

BOOKS

Atkin, Ronald. *Revolution! Mexico, 1910–1920*. New York: John Day, 1970.

Baker, Ray Stannard. *Woodrow Wilson: Life and Letters*. Vols. 3–4. Garden City, N.Y.: Doubleday, Doran, 1931.

Bell, Edward I. *The Political Shame of Mexico*. New York: McBride, Mast, 1914.

Bell, Sidney. *Righteous Conquest: The World War and the Evolution of the New Diplomacy*. Port Washington, N.Y.: Kennikat Press, 1972.

Braddy, Haldeen. *Cock of the Walk: The Legend of Pancho Villa*. Albuquerque: University of New Mexico Press, 1955.

———. *Pancho Villa at Columbus: The Raid of 1916*. El Paso: Texas Western College Press, 1965.

———. *The Paradox of Pancho Villa*. El Paso: University of Texas at El Paso Press, 1978.

Buehrig, Edward Henry, ed. *Wilson's Foreign Policy in Perspective*. Bloomington: Indiana University Press, 1957.

Butler, Smedley D., and Arthur J. Burks. *Walter Garvin in Mexico*. Philadelphia: Dorrance, 1927.

Clendenen, Clarence C. *Blood on the Border: The United States Army and the Mexican Irregulars*. New York: Macmillan, 1969.

Cumberland, Charles C. *The Mexican Revolution: The Constitutionalist Years*. Austin: University of Texas Press, 1972.

Daniels, Josephus. *The Life of Woodrow Wilson*. Philadelphia: John C. Winston, 1924.

———. *The Wilson Era, 1917–1923*. Chapel Hill: University of North Carolina Press, 1946.

Dulles, John W. F. *Yesterday in Mexico: A Chronicle of the Revolution, 1919–1936*. Austin: University of Texas Press, 1961.

Foreign Relations of the United States, Papers Relating to 1913–16. Washington, D.C.: U.S. Government Printing Office, 1920–25.

Foulois, Benjamin. *From the Wright Brothers to the Astronauts*. New York: McGraw-Hill, 1968.

Freudenthal, Samuel J. *El Paso Merchant and Civic Leader*, ed. Floyd S. Fierman. El Paso: Texas Western College Press, 1965.

Glass, E.L.N., ed. and compiler. *The History of the Tenth Cavalry, 1866–1921*. Fort Collins, Colorado: The Old Army Press, 1972.

Glines, Carroll V. *The Compact History of the United States Air Force*. New York: Hawthorn Books, 1963.

Goltz, Horst von der. *My Adventures as a German Secret Agent*. New York: Robert M. McBride, 1917.

Grattan, C. Hartley. *Bitter Bierce: A Mystery of American Letters*. Garden City, N.Y.: Doubleday, Doran, 1929.

Greene, Robert Ewell. *Colonel Charles Young*. Washington, D.C.: privately printed, 1985.

Gruening, Ernest. *Mexico and Its Heritage*. New York: Century, 1928.

Guzmán, Martín Luis. *The Eagle and the Serpent*. New York: Knopf, 1930.

———. *The Memoirs of Pancho Villa*. Austin: University of Texas Press, 1965.

Haley, P. Edward. *Revolution and Intervention: The Diplomacy of Taft and Wilson with Mexico, 1910–1917*. Cambridge: MIT Press, 1970.

Hall, Linda B. *Alvaro Obregón: Power and Revolution in Mexico, 1911–20*. College Station: Texas A&M University Press, 1981.

Hansen, Roger D. *The Politics of Mexican Development*. Baltimore: Johns Hopkins University Press, 1971.

Hodges, C. B., W. P. Edeman, R. M. Kelley, W. E. Selbie, and L. H. Drennan. *American Occupation: Vera Cruz, 1914*. Washington, D.C.: National Capital Press, 1914.

Horgan, Paul. *Great River: The Rio Grande in North American History*. New York: Reinhart, 1954; reprint, Austin: Texas Monthly Press, 1984.

House, Edwin M. *The Intimate Papers of Colonel House*, ed. Charles Seymour. 4 vols. Boston: Houghton Mifflin, 1926.

Irving, Clifford. *Tom Mix and Pancho Villa*. New York: St. Martin's Press, 1982.

Islas, Martha Eva Rocha. *Las defensas sociales en Chihuahua*. Mexico City: Instituto Nacional de Antropología e Historia, 1988.

Johnson, William Weber. *Heroic Mexico: The Narrative History of the Twentieth Century Revolution*. Rev. ed. San Diego: Harcourt Brace Jovanovich, 1968.

Kandell, Jonathan. *La Capital: The Biography of Mexico City*. New York: Random House, 1988.

Katz, Friedrich. *The Secret War in Mexico: Europe, the United States, and the Mexican Revolution*. Chicago: University of Chicago Press, 1981.

King, Ernest J., and Walter M. Whitehill. *Fleet Admiral King: A Naval Record.* New York: W. W. Norton, 1952.

King, Rosa E. *Tempest Over Mexico.* Boston: Little, Brown, 1935.

Knight, Alan. *The Mexican Revolution.* 2 vols. New York: Cambridge University Press, 1986.

Lansford, William Douglas. *Pancho Villa.* Los Angeles: Sherburn Press, 1965.

Lansing, Robert. *War Memoirs.* New York: Bobbs Merrill, 1935.

LeJeune, John A. *The Reminiscences of a Marine.* Philadelphia: Dorrance, 1930.

Link, Arthur S. *Woodrow Wilson and the Progressive Era, 1910–1917.* New York: Harper and Row, Harper Torchbooks, 1954.

Lodge, Henry Cabot. *The Senate and the League of Nations.* New York: Charles Scribner's Sons. 1925

Machado, Manuel A., Jr. *Centaur of the North.* Austin: Eakin Press, 1988.

Mason, Herbert Molloy, Jr. *The Great Pursuit.* New York: Random House, 1970.

May, Henry F. *The End of American Innocence: A Study of the First Years of Our Own Time, 1912–1917.* New York: Alfred A. Knopf, 1969.

Meyer, Michael C. *Huerta: A Political Portrait.* Lincoln: University of Nebraska Press, 1972.

Meyer, Michael C., and William L. Sherman, *The Course of Mexican History.* New York: Oxford University Press, 1979.

Mix, Olive Stokes. *The Fabulous Tom Mix.* Englewood Cliffs, N.J.: Prentice-Hall, 1957.

Moats, Leone B. *Thunder in Their Veins.* New York: Century, 1933.

Notter, Harley. *The Origins of the Foreign Policy of Woodrow Wilson.* New York: Russell and Russell, 1965.

O'Connor, Richard. *Black Jack Pershing.* Garden City, N.Y.: Doubleday, 1961.

O'Shaughnessy, Edith. *A Diplomat's Wife in Mexico.* New York: Harper and Brothers, 1916.

Page, Walter H. *Life and Letters.* 3 vols. Garden City, N.Y.: Doubleday, Page, 1925.

Palafox, Ricardo Avila. *¡Revolución en el estado de México!* Mexico City: Instituto Nacional de Antropología e Historia, 1988.

Patton, George S., Jr. *The Patton Papers.* Edited by Martin Blumenson. Vol. 1, *1885–1940*, Boston: Houghton Mifflin, 1972.

Peterson, Jessie, and Thelma Cox Knoles, eds. *Pancho Villa: Intimate Recollections by People Who Knew Him.* New York: Hastings House, 1977.

Pinchon, Edgcumb. *Viva Villa!* New York: Grosset & Dunlap, 1933.

Pope, Bertha Clark, ed. *The Letters of Ambrose Bierce.* San Francisco: Book Club of California, 1922.

Priestly, Herbert Ingram. *The Mexican Nation: A History.* New York: Cooper Square, 1969.

Quirk, Robert E. *An Affair of Honor: Woodrow Wilson and the Occupation of Veracruz.* [Lexington:] University of Kentucky Press, 1962.

———. *The Mexican Revolution, 1914–1915.* Bloomington: Indiana University Press, 1960.

Raat, W. Dirk, and William H. Beezley, eds. *Twentieth-Century Mexico.* Lincoln: University of Nebraska Press, 1986.

Rakocy, Bill. *Villa Raids Columbus, NM, March 9, 1916.* El Paso: Bravo Press, 1981.

Reed, John. *Insurgent Mexico.* 1914; reprint, New York: International Publishers, 1969.

Rodney, George Brydges. *As a Cavalryman Remembers.* Caldwell, Idaho, Caxton Printers, 1944.

Ross, Stanley R. *Francisco I. Madero, Apostle of Mexican Democracy.* New York: Columbia University Press, 1955.

———. *Is the Mexican Revolution Dead?* Philadelphia. Temple University Press, 1966.

Ruiz, Ramón Eduardo. *The Great Rebellion: Mexico 1905–1924.* New York, W. W. Norton, 1980.

Russell, Thomas H. *Mexico in Peace and War.* Chicago. Reilly and Britton, 1914.

Samponaro, Frank N., and Paul J. Vanderwood, *War Scare on the Rio Grande: Robert Runyon's Photographs of the Border Conflict, 1913–1916.* Austin: Texas State Historical Association, 1992.

Scott, Hugh Lenox. *Some Memories of a Soldier.* New York: Century, 1928.

Smythe, Donald. *Guerrilla Warrior: The Early Life of John J. Pershing.* New York: Charles Scribner's Sons, 1973.

Strode, Hudson. *Timeless Mexico.* New York: Harcourt, Brace, 1944.

Swanberg, W. A. *Citizen Hearst: A Biography of William Randolph Hearst.* New York: Charles Scribner's Sons. 1961.

Swarthout, Gledon. *They Came to Cordura.* New York: Random House, 1958.

Sweetman, Jack. *The Landing at Vera Cruz, 1914.* Annapolis, U.S. Naval Institute, 1968.

Tenth Cavalry. *History.*

Thomas, Lowell. *Old Gimlet Eye: Adventures of Smedley D. Butler.* New York: Farrar and Reinhart, 1933.

Thord-Gray, I. *Gringo Rebel: Mexico, 1913–1914.* Coral Gables: University of Miami Press, 1960.

Timmons, W. H. *El Paso: A Borderlands History.* El Paso: University of Texas at El Paso Press, 1990.

Tompkins, Frank. *Chasing Villa.* Harrisburg: Military Service Publishing Company, 1934.

Torres, Elias L. *Twenty Episodes in the Life of Pancho Villa.* Austin: Encino Press, 1973.

Tuchman, Barbara W. *The Zimmermann Telegram.* New York: Macmillan, 1966.

Tuck, Jim. *Pancho Villa and John Reed.* Tucson: University of Arizona Press, 1984.

Tumulty, Joseph R. *Woodrow Wilson as I Know Him.* Garden City, N.Y.: Doubleday, Page, 1921.

Vandiver, Frank E. *Black Jack: The Life and Times of John J. Pershing.* 2 vols. College Station: Texas A&M University Press, 1977.

War Department Annual Reports, 1916. Washington, D.C.: U.S. Government Printing Office, 1916.

Wharfield, H. B. *The 10th Cavalry and Border Fights.* El Cajon, Calif., 1964.

Weinstein, Edwin A. *Woodrow Wilson: A Medical and Psychological Biography.* Princeton: Princeton University Press, 1980.

Wilkie, James W., and Albert L. Michaels, eds. *Revolution in Mexico: Years of Upheaval, 1910–1940.* New York: Alfred A. Knopf, 1969.

Wilson, Henry Lane. *Diplomatic Episodes in Mexico, Belgium, and Chile.* Garden

City, N.Y.: Doubleday, 1927; reprint, Port Washington, N.Y. Kennikat Press, 1971.

Wilson, Woodrow. *The Papers of Woodrow Wilson*, ed. Arthur S. Link. Vol. 29. Princeton: Princeton University Press, 1979.

———. *The Public Papers of Woodrow Wilson*. Edited by Roy Stannard Baker and William E. Dodd. 3 vols. New York: Harper and Brothers, 1925.

Witcover, Jules. *Sabotage at Black Tom: Imperial Germany's Secret War in America.* Chapel Hill: Algonquin Books, 1989.

Womack, John, Jr. *Zapata and the Mexican Revolution.* New York: Alfred A. Knopf, 1968.

MANUSCRIPTS AND DOCUMENTS

Bisher, Jamie Furman. "A Bullet Silenced Madero's Alleged Assassin." Unpublished MS, 1 April 1992.

Canada, W. W. "Report of the Occupation of Vera Cruz by the American Forces, April 21st and 22d, 1914." 11 Aug. 1914. NARA. Naval Records Collection.

Fletcher, Frank F. "Seizure and Occupation of Vera Cruz, April 21–30, 1914." NARA. Naval Records Collection.

Foulois, Benjamin D. "Report of the Operations of the First Aero Squadron, Signal Corps, With the Mexican Punitive Expedition, for period March 15 to August 15, 1916." NARA. (Published as appendix B, in Tompkins, *Chasing Villa.*)

Funston, Frederick. Correspondence with AGO (AGWAR), April–Nov. 1914. NARA. Mil Reference. RG 94, AG Document File #2149991, Boxes 7473–80.

———. "Annual Report for the Southern Department, 1916." NARA. AGO Records, RG 94.

Miller, Clarence. "Political Considerations at Tampico including Repulsed Attack of Constitutionalistas in April, the Tampico Flag Incident, Capture of Tampico, Exodus of Americans, etc." Tampico, Mexico, 21 May 1914. NARA. State Department Papers, Post Records (Tampico).

Pershing, John J. "Report of the Punitive Expedition to June 30, 1916," and "Report of the Punitive Expedition, July 1916–February, 1917." NARA. AGO Records, RG 94.

Semus, Thomas T. "Report of Operations of Quartermaster Corps, in Connection with Base and Line of Communications, Punitive Expedition, Columbus, N.M." Office, Base Quartermaster, 17 Feb. 1917. NARA. RG 94, AGO Document File #2480591.

"War Diary, United States Expeditionary Forces, Vera Cruz, 1914." 9 May 1914. Library of Congress. Records of the War Department, Records of the Adjutant General, RG 94.

NEWSPAPERS, PERIODICALS, ARTICLES

Bemis, Samuel Flagg. "Woodrow Wilson and Latin America." In *Wilson's Foreign Policy in Perspective*, ed. Edward Henry Buehris. Bloomington: Indiana University Press. 1957.

Bisher, Jamie Furman. "Charles Young." *Military Illustrated Past and Present* (London: Windrow and Greene Ltd.) Aug./Sept. 1989, pp. 54–56.

———. "Welcome to Dallas, Mexico." *CEO International Strategies*, July–Aug. 1991, p. 48.

Blasier, Cole. "The United States and Madero." *Journal of Latin American Studies* (London: Cambridge University Press) 4 (November 1972): 207–31.

Brown, Lyle C. "The Politics of Armed Struggle in the Mexican Revolution, 1913–1915." *Revolution in Mexico*, ed. Wilkie and Michaels.

Callahan, J. Will, and F. Henri Klickman. "I'm Off to Mexico." Chicago and New York: Frank H. Root, 1914. (Sheet Music.)

Carranza, Venustiano. "Note to President Wilson concerning the United States Occupation of Veracruz." In *Revolution in Mexico*, ed. Wilkie and Michaels.

Cline, Howard F. "Moral Imperialism and United States Intervention." In *Revolution in Mexico*, Wilkie and Michaels.

Cochran, Robert T. "Smedley Butler: A Pintsize Marine for All Seasons." *Smithsonian*, June 1984, pp. 137–56.

Elser, Frank B. "General Pershing's Mexican Campaign." *Century Magazine*, Feb. 1920, pp. 433–47.

———. "Pershing's Lost Cause." *American Legion Monthly*, July 1932.

Hamill, Pete. "Zapata Remembered." *Travel-Holiday*, Oct. 1990, p. 52.

Harris, Charles H., and Louis R. Sadler. "Pancho Villa and the Columbus Raid: The Missing Documents." *New Mexico Historical Review* 50 (Oct. 1975): 335–46.

Hinckley, T. C. "Wilson, Huerta, and the Twenty-One Gun Salute," *The Historian: A Journal of History* 22 (February 1960): 197–206.

Katz, Friedrich. "Pancho Villa and the Attack on Columbus." *American Historical Review* 83 (1978): 101–30.

Murray, Robert H. "Huerta and the Two Wilsons." *Harper's Weekly*, 25 March, 1, 8, 15, 22, 29 April, 1916.

Reed, John. "Pancho Villa and the Rules of War." In *Revolution in Mexico*, ed. Wilkie and Michaels.

Ruhl, Arthur S. "Vera Cruz: The Unfinished Drama." *Collier's Magazine* 52 (May 30, 1914).

Sandos, James A. "German Involvement in Northern Mexico, 1915–1916: A New Look at the Columbus Raid." *Hispanic American Historical Review* 50 (Feb. 1970): 70–88.

Stivison, Roy E., and Della M. McDonnell. "When Villa Raided Columbus." *New Mexico Magazine*, Dec. 1950, pp. 41–43.

Troxel, O. C. "The Tenth Cavalry in Mexico." *Cavalry Journal*, Oct. 1917, pp. 199–208.

Wharfield, H. B. "The Affair at Carrizal." *Montana: The Magazine of Western History*, Oct. 1968, pp. 24–39.

Young, Karl. "A Fight That Could Have Meant War." *American West*, Spring 1966, pp. 17–23.

ACKNOWLEDGMENTS

****

To an unusual degree, I am indebted to my wife, Joanne Thompson Eisenhower, for her efforts in behalf of this book. It would be trite to try to describe her role, which far transcended the usual family support. Joanne was practically a coauthor. She reviewed every chapter of the book before its submission and researched many topics. Most important, she arranged trips to Mexico to ensure that I saw firsthand the terrain I was writing about.

I am also highly indebted to Mrs. Jerome ("Dodie") Yentz for her untiring efforts. Dodie's patience, willingness, and mastery of modern electronic equipment saved me untold time and aggravation. In addition, she was a fine in-house copy editor, able to catch many errors.

I am also indebted to Gerard F. McCauley, literary agent, who, out of friendship, performed services far beyond those normally expected from an agent.

Other individuals took a special interest in this work, for which I am grateful. They include Colonel Bruce Aiken and Robert Vezzetti, from Brownsville, Texas; Professor Louis D. Rubin, Jr., Chapel Hill, N.C.; Jamie Furman Bisher (referred by General Colin Powell, chairman of the Joint Chiefs of Staff); Daniel and Marilyn Holt, Abilene, Kansas; Major General John W. Huston USAF (ret.) and Dr. Jack

Sweetman, of the History Department, U.S. Naval Academy; Ms. Louise Arnold-Friend, U.S. Army Military History Institute, Carlisle Barracks, Pennsylvania; Mrs. Lydia F. Roberts, Saint Davids, Pennsylvania; and Herbert Molloy Mason, Jr., author of the fine book *The Great Pursuit.*

Mexican friends were of tremendous help. Dr. Modesto Suárez and his wife, Dr. Guadalupe Jiménez, of San Luis Potosí, not only supplied materials but also took me to Chinameca, Morelos, the site of Emiliano Zapata's murder in 1919. Chinameca is a place that few Americans visit.

Enriqueta de la Garza, of Mexico City, was our guide on a trip to Veracruz, and she arranged for us to see places we would never have reached without her. Enriqueta later acted as my agent for obtaining certain critical photographs in Mexico City, something difficult to do from Maryland.

Thanks also to Elizabeth W. Ames, mayor of Douglas, Arizona, who supplied the information on her mother-in-law, Mrs. Winifred Paul Ames. As a child, Mrs. Ames, Sr., was wounded while watching the Battle of Ague Prieta, on November 1, 1915. Mayor Ames also introduced me to Mrs. Cindy Hayostek, a walking encyclopedia on the subject of Douglas–Agua Prieta history. Thanks also to Mr. John H. Davis, Jr., George Ruiz, and Linda Martinez, all of Douglas.

Various libraries also performed invaluable services. They include (alphabetically):

El Paso Public Library (Ramiro S. Salazar, director): Wayne Daniel, Marta Estarada, and their staff.

Fort Bliss Museum: Paul Martin, and Floyd ("Twister") Geery.

Fort Huachuca Museum: Tim Phillips.

Library of Congress: Dr. John R. Hébert, George Hobart, Barbara Natanson, Mary Ison, and Thomas G. deClaire.

National Archives: Richard Von Doenhoff (Navy), Sally Marks (State Department), Michael Knapp (Army), Judy Edelhoff, and Douglas Thurman and his assistant, Mary Finch.

Naval Institute, Annapolis: Dot Sappington.

United States Military Academy, West Point: Monica Sullivan and Lois Pucino (Association of Graduates). Judy Sibley (Special Collections).

University of Texas, Austin: John Slate, Photographic Collections.

Washington College, Chestertown, Maryland, Miller Library: William J. Tubbs and Lavinia Slagle.

INDEX

****

Acuña, Jesús, 140, 232–33
Adair, Henry Rodney, 294, 297
"Adobe Wall," 94
Agrarian Decree, 182
Aguascalientes, 145–46
Aguascalientes Convention, 158–64, 185
Aguilar, Cándido, 279–80
Aguinaldo, Emilio, 126
Aguirre Benavides, Eugenio, 55, 157n, 180
American Expeditionary Force, xviii, 306, 327–28
Anderson, E. A., 120–21
Angeles, Felipe, 17, 25, 28, 69–71, 90, 142–46, 160, 166, 174, 175, 179, 180, 321
Apache Indians, 202, 212, 233, 305
Aragón, Guillermo García, 167, 168
Argentina, 131–34
Arizona, 212, 311
Arkansas, 119
Army War College, U.S., 37n
Arrieta, Domingo, xivn, 38, 43, 141, 142
Arrieta, Mariano, xivn, 38, 43, 141, 142
Associated Press, 138, 219
Atkin, Ronald, 326n
Avila, Fidel, 48, 50

Azveta, José, 121, 339
Azveta, Manuel, 121

Babícora Ranch, 292
Bachíniva, 248, 262, 265, 267
Badger, Charles J., 102, 109, 119
Baker, Newton D., 230, 231, 253, 256, 280–81, 307
barbed wire, 176, 209
Bárcenas, Victoriano, 314
Barker, J. B., 249
Barrón, Luis Medina, 144, 145
Bassó, Adolfo, 12, 14, 26, 27, 153
Battle of Agua Caliente, 265–66, 267
Battle of Agua Prieta, 187, 188–210, 322, 361
Battle of Carrizal, 293–300, 302, 369
Battle of Hermosillo, 190, 210, 214
Battle of Juárez, 56–57, 58, 62
Battle of León, 179–80, 310
Battle of Orendáin, 148
Battle of San Andrés, 51
Battle of Tierra Blanca, 57–58, 70
Battle of Torreón, 55–56, 60, 62, 127
Battle of Verdun, 257
Battle of Wounded Knee, 235
Battle of Zacatecas, 139, 140, 141, 142, 143–45, 146, 147, 358–59

Beacon, John H., 237n
Becerril, Luis, 115
Belt, John, 232–33
Benton, Maxima, 74
Benton, William S., 72–78, 135
Berlanga, David, 168–70, 171
Bernstorff, Johann H. von, 122, 311
Bierce, Ambrose, 54, 181
Bitter Bierce (Grattan), 181n
Blanco, Lucio, 5n, 62–63, 85, 162–63, 166,
    321
Blanquet, Aureliano, 24, 25, 34, 35, 60–61,
    115, 148, 149, 150
Blumenson, Martin, 306n
Blythe, Samuel G., 132
Bonillas, Ignacio, 303, 315, 316, 319
Booker, Johnnie, 259, 263
Borah, William, 103
Bowie, Hamilton, 223
Boyd, Charles T., 207, 293–99
Braddy, Haldeen, 189, 218–19
Brazil, 131–34
Bristol, 150
Brown, William C., 246, 247, 262, 265, 266,
    267, 269, 275, 277–79
Brownsville, Tex., 187, 210–14
Bryan, William Jennings, 88
    Mexican policy of, xiv; 32, 61, 63, 64, 66,
        75, 173, 182, 183, 211
    Tampico incident and, 101, 103
    Veracruz landing and, 107, 108, 118, 122,
        127, 128, 131, 132
    Villa and, 156
Bustillos meeting, 3–6
Butler, Smedley, 37n, 121n

Cabell, De Rosey C., 200, 204, 237, 251,
    259, 277
Cabell, Martha Otis, 237
Cabrera, Luis, 303
California, 212
Calles, Plutarco Elías, 155, 189–92, 317,
    321, 322, 325–26
Camp Furlong, 218, 220, 221–24, 228–29,
    252
Canada, William W., 102, 104, 108, 110–13,
    117–18, 120, 121, 123, 339
Canova, Leon, 167
Carden, Lionel, 61, 64
Cárdenas, Francisco, 8–9, 29
Cárdenas, Julio, 288–89, 290
Cárdenas, Lázaro, 321
Carlos V, 111, 119
Carothers, George C., 74, 127, 128, 179,
    182, 360

Carranza, Venustiano:
    ABC mediators and, 131–32
    Aguascalientes Convention and, 158–59,
        162–64
    assassination of, 318–19, 321
    Benton affair and, 75–78
    border disputes and, 213–14, 216, 227
    at Bustillos meeting, 3n, 4, 5
    character of, xvii–xviii, 40, 44–45, 76–78
    downfall of, 316–19
    Federalist threat to, 41–42
    as First Chief of Constitutionalists, xvii, 4,
        42–43, 50, 63, 140, 147, 151–52, 157,
        163–64, 165, 310
    Germany supported by, 310–12
    as governor of Coahuila, 3n, 4, 31, 36, 39,
        40, 41–42
    Huerta opposed by, 31, 39, 41, 42, 133,
        316
    land reform and, 182, 325
    Madero and, 40, 44, 57, 65, 77, 141
    military forces of, 42, 44, 62–63, 70,
        139–40, 172, 187
    Obregón's opposition to, xvii, 308–12,
        314–17
    Obregón's support for, 44, 147–48, 151,
        164, 173, 282
    photographs of, 84, 90, 163, 193
    political leadership of, 43, 156, 163–64,
        182–83, 282, 284n
    as president, xix, 156, 163–64, 182–83,
        232, 307, 308, 309–16
    press coverage of, 53, 66, 76–78
    Punitive Expedition and, 231–34, 236,
        239, 245, 252, 279, 280–82, 286, 287,
        291–93, 299–300, 303, 307
    Querétaro convention and, 307, 309–10
    Reed's interview with, 76–78
    resignation of, 163–64, 165
    as revolutionary, xiv, 3n, 4, 5, 39–40,
        41–42, 65, 149
    Scott-Obregón meeting and, 281–82, 286,
        287
    territory controlled by, 183, 214
    Torreón conference and, 151–52
    U.S. recognition of, xix, 182–83, 185–86,
        187, 188, 191, 214
    U.S. relations of, 65–66, 67–68, 75
    in Veracruz, 166, 173
    Veracruz landing and, 127, 128, 131–32,
        140, 156
    Villa's opposition to, xv, xvii, xix, 57, 69,
        133, 140–42, 145, 146, 147, 151–52,
        156–57, 158, 164, 173, 181, 182–83,
        210, 218, 227, 308

Villa's support for, 50–51, 53
Wilson and, 65, 67–68, 182, 183, 185–86, 188, 190, 191, 216, 231–34, 302, 303, 306, 307
Zapata and, 63, 147, 153–54, 164, 313–14
Carvajal, Francisco, 148, 149, 152–53
Casa Moneda, 143
Castañada, Reyes, 267
Castleman, James C., 222, 223
Cavazos, José, 267, 268
Cejudo, Roberto, 316–17
Celaya, 174, 175–76
  First Battle of, 176–77, 179, 183, 310
  map of, 178
  Second Battle of, 177–79, 183, 310
Cepeda, Enrique, 34
Cervantes, Candelario, 289, 290
Chao, Manuel, xivn, 38, 71, 72
Chasing Villa (Tompkins), xx, 219n, 237n, 254n, 264, 275, 278n, 285n
Chester, 111, 121
Cheyenne, 128
Chihuahua, 39, 42, 214
  Punitive Expedition in, xix, 201, 234, 241, 252, 263, 283, 289–90, 293, 298, 301–2, 304–5, 340
  Villa in, 46–47, 48, 55, 59, 62, 69–78, 188, 210, 243, 304, 312
Chihuahua City, 54, 56, 58–59, 62, 69–78, 293, 304, 312
Chile, 131–34
Chinameca, 338–39
cientificos, xii, 11
Citizen Hearst (Swanberg), 292n
Coahuila, 3, 4, 31, 36, 39, 40, 41–42
Cobb, Zach, 184–85
Collins, James L., 204
colorados, 52–53, 57, 193
Colquitt, Oscar B., 211
Columbus, N. Mex. raid, 217–27, 341, 363
  Camp Furlong in, 218, 220, 221–24, 228–29, 252
  death toll in, 222, 224, 226–27
  map of, 220
  military response to, 217–18, 221–24, 228–34
  photograph of, 199
  public opinion on, xv, 217, 227, 228, 234, 280, 283
  Punitive Expedition and, 227, 228–34, 283
  Villa's command of, xv, 218–19, 221, 223, 227, 228, 248, 264
  Wilson and, 228
Cone, H. I., 111, 117
Connecticut, 81, 111, 118

Consolidated Copper Mine, 209
Constitutionalist party:
  arms embargo against, 67–68
  Carranza as First Chief of, xvii, 4, 42–43, 50, 63, 140, 147, 151–52, 157, 163–64, 165, 310
  founding of, 42–43
  press coverage of, 63
  Tampico incident and, 79–81
  Torreón conference for, 151–52
  U.S. support for, 65–66, 67–68, 75
  victory of, 149
  Villa and, 50
Contreras, Calixto, xivn
Copp, Charles C., 82, 99
Corbett, William, 219n
Corral, Manuel, 260–61, 268–69
Corral, María ("Luz"), 47, 56, 69, 323, 340
Cradock, C.G.F.M., 111
"Cucaracha, La," 52
Cuernavaca, 338
Culberson's Ranch, 234, 236, 237
Curtiss, Glenn, 255
Cusi Mining Company, 55, 187, 214–16, 267
Custer, George A., 237
Cyclops, 111, 118

da Gama, D., 132n
Daniels, Josephus, 101, 102, 106–7, 108, 109, 110, 111, 118, 127
Dargue, Herbert A., 248, 262
Davis, William Harding, 135–36
"Declaration of Policy in Regard to Latin America," 33
de la Barra, Francisco Léon, 10, 11
de la Huerta, Adolfo, 188, 319–20, 322, 325–6
de la Rosa, Luis, 211–14
de la Rosa group, 211–14
Democratica, 213
Democratic party, 103, 104
Des Moines, 111, 118
Díaz, Félix, 8, 61, 62, 86, 184, 321
  rebellion led by, 12–29, 33–34, 40
Díaz, José de la Cruz Porfirio:
  death of, 321
  as dictator, xii–xiii, 18, 19, 20, 321
  downfall of, xiii, xiv, xxi, 3, 5, 317, 328
  Huerta and, 16–29, 34, 35
  Madero's opposition to, xiii, xvii, 3, 4, 5–6, 11, 39, 40
  photograph of, 83
  U.S. support for, 33
  Zapata's opposition to, 146

Díaz Soto y Gama, Antonio, 161–62
Division of the North:
  ammunition of, 50, 51, 55, 58, 68, 151,
    176–77, 188
  artillery of, 48, 50–51, 55, 58, 69, 143,
    144–45
  campaign maps for, 49, 190
  cavalry of, 48, 51, 57, 58, 177, 179, 180
  Chihuahua City captured by, 54, 56,
    58–59, 62
  defeat of, xv, 174, 175–80, 188–210, 248
  Federalists attacked by, 48, 50, 51, 55, 56,
    57–59, 60, 70, 140, 143, 145
  infantry of, 48
  Juárez victory of, 56–57, 58, 62
  Mexico City as goal of, 54
  morale of, 51–52, 144, 189
  name of, 55
  organization of, 48, 51, 69–71, 157, 158,
    166
  railroad used by, 54–55, 94, 146, 173
  recruitment for, 48, 50, 55, 59, 249, 260
  reinforcements for, 57, 141
  San Andrés victory of, 51
  Tierra Blanca victory of, 57–58, 70
  Torreón victory of, 55–56, 60, 62, 127
  victories of, xvii, 51–59, 60, 145–46, 163
  Villa as commander of, xx, 46, 62, 69–71,
    97, 140, 142, 149, 151–52, 163, 164,
    172–73, 174, 180–81, 312
  Yaqui Indians in, 97, 209
  Zacatecas victory of, 139, 140, 141, 142,
    143–45, 146, 147, 358–59
Dodd, George A., 205, 237, 240, 245,
  247–50, 261, 262, 267, 290, 364
Dodd, T. F., 255, 256, 261
Dolphin, 81, 82, 99, 106, 107, 111, 118
Domínguez, Belisario, 35–36, 60, 61, 153
dorados, 177, 189, 192, 248, 288, 322
Douglas, Ariz., 191, 192
Dresden, 81, 150
Durango, 38

Eagle and the Serpent, The (Guzmán), xx, 44,
  70n, 162
Eckhardt, Herr von, 311, 312
Economist, 129
Eighth Cavalry, U.S., 238
Eisenhower, Dwight D., xvi
Eleventh Cavalry, U.S., 248, 262, 266, 277,
  290, 298
El Paso, Tex., 31n, 47–48, 58, 73, 74,
  184–85, 216, 285–86, 287, 305
El Paso & Southwestern Railroad, 245
El Paso Times, 219
Elser, Frank B., 257, 259, 262, 263, 264, 288

El Valle, 247, 302, 303, 305, 306
Erwin, James B., 245, 256
Espagne, 66
Esperanza, 111
Essex, 111
Evans, Ellwood W., 229–30, 246, 290, 293

Fabela, Isidro, 76–78
Favela, Juan, 219–21, 224
Federalist army:
  anti-Huertista sentiment in, 47
  artillery of, 92
  Division of the North vs., 48, 50, 51, 55,
    56, 57–59, 60, 70, 140, 143, 145
  loyalty of, xiii
  officers of, 96
  recruitment for, 35, 93
  Tampico incident and, 80, 81, 82, 99,
    100–101
Fierro, Rodolfo, 53, 58, 73, 74, 89, 168–70,
  174, 175, 176, 181, 188–89, 195
Fifth Cavalry, U.S., 290
First Aero Squadron, U.S., 239, 254–57
First Cavalry, U.S., 237n, 240
First Infantry, U.S., 237n
Fletcher, Frank F., 81, 95, 99, 100, 102
  in Veracruz landing, 106, 107, 109–11,
    116, 117, 118, 119–22, 123, 126, 134,
    136, 327
Fletcher, Henry P., 310
Florida, 106, 108, 110, 111, 113, 116, 118,
  119
Fort Bliss, Texas, 59, 155–56, 194, 235, 236,
  312
Fort Huachuca, 229, 230
Fort San Juan d'Ulloa, 109–10, 111
Fort Sill, Oklahoma, 255
Foulois, Benjamin D., 239, 254–57, 262–63,
  276
Fourteenth Cavalry, U.S., 287
Franco, Julio, 117–18
Fuentes, Alberto, 3n, 84
Fuller, Paul, 358
Funston, Frederick, 95, 191, 192, 206, 211, 214
  capture of Aguinaldo, 126
  Pershing and, 228, 230–31, 234–35,
    239–40, 259, 282, 298, 299, 302,
    304–5, 327–28
  Punitive Expedition and, 234–35, 236,
    239–40, 255, 256, 304–5, 307
  Scott-Obregón meeting and, 282, 283, 286
  Veracruz landing and, 123, 125–27,
    134–38, 153, 156, 166

Garibaldi, Giuseppe, 4, 85
Garner, Jolly, 224

Garrison, Lindley M., 108, 118, 127, 135, 136, 211
Garza, Encarnación, 212–13
Garza Aldape, Manuel, 60–61
Gaujot, Julien E., 305–6
Gavira, Gabriel, 219, 290–91
Gibbons, Floyd, 257, 259
Gibson's Line Ranch, 218
Glen Springs, Tex. raid, 286–87
Gómez, Félix U., 295–97
Gómez, Vazquez, 3n, 84
González, Abraham, 3n, 4, 5n, 39, 41, 47, 69, 84, 321, 349–50
González, Pablo, 43, 63, 80, 81, 139, 140, 146, 147, 151–52, 313, 321
González Garza, Roque, 162, 172
Grattan, C. Hartley, 181n
Gray, George, 303
Great Pursuit, The (Mason), xx
Griffin, Fred, 222
Guadalajara, 148, 174
Guajardo, Jesús María, 313–14
Guardia Rural, 92, 348–49
Guerrero, Mexico, 248–50, 261, 262, 290
Gutiérrez, Eulalio, 164, 165, 166, 167, 168, 170–71, 172, 173, 195, 232
Guzmán, Martín Luis, xx, 44–45, 70n, 142n, 147, 161, 162–63, 168–70, 180, 308–9

Hale, William Bayard, 36–37, 65–66, 67, 349
Hancock, 102
Hart, H. M., 224
Hearst, William Randolph, 243, 247, 248, 292
Hermione, 81
Hernández, Gabriel, 34
Hernández, Ricardo, 8–9, 29
Hernández, Rosalío, xivn
Heroic Mexico (Johnson), xivn, xxi, 313n, 317n
Herrera, Luis, 263–64, 278–79
Herrera, Maclovio, 55, 323
Herrera brothers, xivn, 43
Herrero, Rodolfo, 318, 319
Hidalgo y Costilla, Father, xiin
Hill, Benjamín, 176, 180, 316, 317, 319, 322
Hines, John L., 200, 251, 258
Hinojosa, Ramón, 82, 99, 100–101
Hintze, Paul von, 22, 129, 311
Holmes, Thomas B., 216
House, Edward, 36, 64, 65
Howze, Robert L., 248, 262, 266, 269, 275, 290, 298
Huerta, Victor, son of Victoriano, 130

Huerta, Victoriano:
  British recognition of, 61, 63, 64, 75, 78
  Carranza's opposition to, 31, 39, 41, 42, 133, 316
  death of, 321
  Díaz and, 16–29, 34, 35
  Díaz-Reyes rebellion and, 16–29
  as dictator, 60–62, 321
  downfall of, xiii–xv, xix, 138, 139–50, 151, 153, 328
  elections held by, 34, 36, 37, 61–62, 63–64, 65, 133
  Madero opposed by, 11, 16–18, 23–28
  Madero's assassination and, xiii, 27–29, 41, 184
  military support for, 35, 62, 143, 145, 146
  photographs of, 87, 184
  popular opposition to, 31, 34, 35–36, 38–39
  as president, 25–26, 27, 30, 33–35, 60–62
  resignation of, 148–50
  return to Mexico attempted by, xvii, 183–85
  Tampico incident and, 100, 102, 103, 104
  U.S.-Mexican relations and, 31, 36–37
  U.S. recognition of, 26, 28, 30–33, 36–37, 41, 61, 63–64, 66, 67
  Veracruz landing and, 104, 105, 108, 117, 124, 127, 129–34, 138
  Villa's opposition to, 47, 52, 128, 149
  Wilson's opposition to, xix, 32–33, 36–37, 61, 63–68, 75, 104, 105, 129–34, 149
  Zapata's opposition to, 33, 63, 146
Huse, H. M., 117

Independiente, 129
Insurgent Mexico (Reed), 54, 59n
Iron Cross Society, 310

Jack, J. O., 108
Jáuregui, Eusebio, 313–14
JN-3 biplanes ("Jennies"), 239, 255–57
Johnson, William Weber, xivn, xxi, 313n, 317n
Joint High Commission, 302–3, 307
Jonacatepec, 314
Juárez, Mexico, 31n, 56–57, 58, 62, 216, 282–85, 287, 312
Juárez, Benito, xii

Kansas, 311
Kennedy-King Ranch, 214
Kerr, Robert J., 126, 136
Kilpatrick, 125
King, Rosa E., 16n, 17
Kingdon, George, 209
Kloss, Maximilian, 176, 310–11

Knox, Philander, 21, 28, 30, 32
Kohler, Captain, 150

Lamar, Joseph Rucker, 132n
Lane, Franklin K., 303
Lansford, William, 349–50
Lansing, Robert:
  Mexican policy of, 183, 185–86, 191, 307, 361
  photograph of, 197
  Punitive Expedition and, 231, 233, 280, 282, 292, 299
Lascuráin, Pedro, 20–21, 22, 26
Law and Order League, 212
Lea, Tom, 185
Ledford, Hobart, 273–74
Lehmann, Frederick W., 132n
Lejeune, John A., 124, 126
Liberal Constitutionalist Party (PLC), 315–16
Lind, John, 37, 67, 118, 182
Lininger, Clarence, 273, 274
Lockett, James, 237n, 240, 290
Lodge, Henry Cabot, 104–5, 128, 352–53, 356
London, Jack, 80n, 135
López, Pablo, 215–16, 219
Los Borregos, 62
Los Remedios ranch, 72
Lozano, Ismael, 270–72, 273, 275, 276, 278–79
Lozoya, Melitón, 324–25
Lucas, John P., 220, 221–22, 341

Maass, Gustavo, 109–10, 113, 114–15, 118, 136, 138, 353–54
Maass, Joaquín, 43
McCabe, W. P., 294, 295, 297
McCain, Mrs. William A., 225–26
McClellan, 125
McCloy, John, Chief Boatswain, 116–17
machine guns, 176, 177, 210, 266
McKinney, Arthur, 219n
Madero, Francisco I., Jr.:
  assassination of, xiii, xiv, 7–9, 10, 27–29, 30, 38, 41, 70, 77, 184, 321, 337–38
  at Bustillos meeting, 3–5
  Carranza and, 40, 44, 57, 65, 77, 141
  character of, 11–12, 16
  Díaz opposed by, xiii, xvii, 3, 4, 5–6, 11, 39, 40
  downfall of, 10–29, 40–41
  enemies of, 10, 11, 40
  grave of, 153
  Huerta's opposition to, 11, 16–18, 23–28
  Mexico City occupied by, 5, 10
  military support for, 11, 23, 24–25
  photographs of, 84, 86
  as president, xiii, 5–6, 10, 11–29
  resignation of, 22, 26, 317
  as revolutionary, 3–5, 10–11
  Villa's support for, xiv, 46, 47, 52, 57, 69, 147
  Zapata's opposition to, 11, 38, 39, 147, 167
Madero, Francisco I., Sr., 5, 85
Madero, Gustavo, 5, 11–12, 14, 15, 23–24, 25, 26–27, 28, 40, 85, 321
Madero, Sara, 28
"Manifesto to the Mexican People," 182–83
Marksbury, Davis, 289
Marshall, George C., 327
Martin, Glenn, 255
Martínez, Paulino, 161, 167, 168
Mason, Herbert Molloy, xx
Matamoros, Mexico, 187, 210–14
Maximilian, Emperor of Mexico, 123
Mayo, Henry Thomas, 111, 118, 326, 327
  in Tampico incident, 81, 82, 95, 99, 100, 101, 102, 103, 106, 107, 108
Maytorena, José María, 3n, 31, 39, 41, 42, 51, 62, 84, 154–55, 171–72, 188, 189, 210
Meade, 125
Medal of Honor, 121n
Medina, Juan, 89
Memoirs of Pancho Villa, The (Guzmán), xx, 142n
Mercado, Salvador, 56, 57, 58, 59
Mesa, Antonio, 270
Metropolitan, 76
Mexican National Railroad, 54–55, 252
Mexican Northwest Railroad, 55, 236, 245, 291
Mexican Revolution:
  Aguascalientes Convention and, 158–64
  Bustillos meeting and, 3–6
  chronology of, 329–36
  Díaz-Reyes rebellion in, 12–29, 40
  ending of, 320, 321, 328
  factions in, 151, 158–64, 308–10
  intellectuals in, 160
  literature on, xix–xx, 373–78
  Mexican states involved in, 38–39, 42, 328
  Nogales conference and, 154–56
  personalities in, xvi–xvii, 3–6
  press coverage of, xix–xx
  Torreón conference and, 151–52
  U.S. arms supplies and, 67–68, 79, 185
  U.S. intervention in, xii, xv, xvii, xix, 6, 21, 22, 23, 37, 77, 104–8, 183, 308, 328

violent nature of, xi, 5, 321–22
World War I and, xv, 152, 175–76, 327
see also individual revolutionaries
Mexico:
anti-U.S. sentiment in, 37, 102, 107, 129,
231–32, 270–71, 284n
British relations with, 61, 63, 64, 75, 78,
152
Catholic Church in, 34, 44, 309, 326
city-states in, xiii–xiv, 38
Congress of, 35–36, 60–61, 103, 156
constitution of, xi, xv, 26, 31, 41, 61, 307,
309–10, 313, 319, 326
currency of, 156
dictatorship in, xii–xiii
economy of, xi, 325
education in, 11, 323
flag of, 161–62, 272
foreign interests in, xi–xii, 65, 79, 80, 309
German relations with, 22, 34, 105, 152,
310–12, 361
independence of, xii, xiii
Indian population of, xviii, 97, 162, 182,
209, 316
land reform in, xviii, 11, 62, 146–47, 153,
160, 182, 313, 325
local warlords in, xiv, 38, 41
mining in, xi, 55, 143, 309
newspapers of, 11, 35, 213, 279, 282
oil reserves of, 64, 80, 311, 321
people of, xx–xxi, 36, 37, 328
points of interest in, 337–41
poverty in, xii, xx–xxi
railroads of, 54–55, 80, 94, 143, 146, 157,
173, 236, 245, 252, 291, 317–18
roads of, 253, 277
sovereignty of, 78, 102, 127, 232, 233
upper class in, xi, 34, 132–33
U.S. border with, xi, 187, 198, 210–16,
234–35, 286–87
U.S. corporate interests in, 36, 55
see also United States-Mexican relations;
individual cities and states
Mexico, 111–13
Mexico City:
Citadel in, 15, 17–18, 21, 23–24, 25, 27,
338
Díaz-Reyes rebellion in, 12–29, 33–34,
40
foreigners in, 18, 20–22, 80, 134–35, 152,
153
Madero's occupation of, 5, 10
map of, 13
martial law in, 153
National Palace in, 7–8, 12, 14–15, 17–18,
25, 337–38

Obregón's occupations of, xv, 147, 148,
149, 152–53, 173
reign of terror in, 165–71
U.S. embassy in, 19–28, 30–31, 66–68,
129–30
U.S. proposed occupation of, 37n, 134–35,
153
Villa as threat to, 54, 138, 140, 146,
165–71
Zapata as threat to, 135, 138, 146, 165–71
Zócalo of, 14–15, 337, 338
Michigan, 119
Miller, Charles D., 224
Miller, Clarence, 107–8
Miller, Dr., 209–10
Minnesota, 102
Mix, Tom, 54
Moats, Alice, 92
Monclova, Mexico, 42
Mondragón, Manuel, 12, 14, 16, 27, 34
Moore, John Bassett, 64
Moore, Mrs. J. J., 224
Morelos, José María, 27
Morelos Zaragoza, Ignacio, 80, 99, 100–101
Morey, Lewis S., 294, 295, 296, 297, 298,
299, 302
Morse, Thomas, 255
Mott, John R., 303
Múgica, Francisco J., 309
Muñoz, Antonio, 219–21
Murguía, Francisco, 312

Naco, 171–72, 229
Nafarrete, Emiliano P., 214
Namiquipa, 247, 248, 250, 257, 258, 261,
277, 286, 288, 290, 303
Naón, Ramón S., 132n
Natera, Pánfilo, 141, 142, 143, 144
National Archives, U.S., 237
National Guard, U.S., 281, 287
Navy, British Royal, 311
Navy, U.S.:
Atlantic Fleet of, xiv, 102, 106, 109, 327
Mexican ports blockaded by, 21, 65
Tampico incident and, 81, 82, 99–103
in Veracruz landing, 106–8, 111, 116, 117,
118, 119, 121, 126–27
Neuvo León, 40
Nevares, Modesto, 260–61
Neville, W. C. ("Buck"), 111, 115
New Hampshire, 119, 120
New Jersey, 119
New Mexico, 212, 311
New York Journal, 292
New York Times, 63, 75, 101, 122, 127,
152, 179, 257, 284n

Nogales, Mexico, 43–44, 65–66, 198, 229
Nogales conference, 154–56
Notter, Harley, 280n

Obregón, Alvaro:
  Aguascalientes Convention and, 159, 166
  assassination of, 321–22, 325–26
  Carranza opposed by, xvii, 308–12, 314–17
  Carranza supported by, 44, 147–48, 151, 164, 173, 282
  character of, 308–9
  defensive strategy of, 176, 177, 179
  Funston's meeting with, 206
  Gutiérrez and, 170
  land reform and, 325
  Mexico City occupied by, xv, 147, 148, 149, 152–53, 173
  as military commander, 44, 62, 97, 139, 146, 147–48, 149, 152, 158, 172, 214–15, 309
  as military strategist, 175–76, 177, 179, 310
  photographs of, 163, 194, 197, 206
  as political leader, 154–58, 282, 308–12, 314–17
  as president, 310, 315–20, 325–26, 328
  press coverage of, 157
  public support for, 307, 309, 316
  as revolutionary, 5, 310
  right arm lost by, 180, 310
  Scott's meeting with, 281–86
  Torreón conference and, 152
  Villa defeated by, xv, 174, 175–80, 182, 188
  Villa opposed by, xvii, 148, 151, 154–58, 160, 322, 323–24, 325
  as war minister, 154, 156, 164, 173
  Wilson and, 308, 315
  Zapata and, 153, 172
Ocón, Cecilio, 8, 12
Ojinaga, Mexico, 59
Old gimlet Eye (Thomas), 121n
Ord, James B., 268, 273
Origins of the Foreign Policy of Woodrow Wilson, The (Notter), 280n
Orozco, Pascual, 4, 5, 11, 16, 24, 38, 39, 44, 52–53, 57, 59, 69, 84, 184–85, 193
Ortega, Toribio, 89
O'Shaughnessy, Edith Coues, 66–68, 129–30, 353–54
O'Shaughnessy, Elim, 66
O'Shaughnessy, Nelson, 66, 100, 101, 102, 103, 129, 130
"Our Adventures at Tampico" (London), 80n

"Pact of the Embassy," 25–26, 34
Pani, Alberto J., 303
Parks, Samuel, 138
Parral, 260, 261, 265, 267, 269, 323, 324
  gunfight at, 270–75, 276–77, 279–80, 285, 301
Patton, George S., Jr., 200, 288–89
  Pershing and, xviii, 238, 259, 261, 305, 306
Patton, Anne, ("Nita"), 305
Patton Papers, The (Blumenson, ed.), 306n
Paul, Mabel, 192
Paul, Winifred, 192
Pereyra, Orestes, xivn
Pershing, Frances Warren, 235
Pershing, John J.:
  background of, 235–37
  Battle of Carrizal and, 293–94, 298–99, 301, 302
  character of, xviii–xix
  Colonia Dublán headquarters of, 208, 242–43, 247, 251–59, 261, 286, 291, 292–93, 299, 302, 304, 305–6, 307
  Columbus, N.Mex raid and, 228
  family lost by, xix, 235–36
  at Fort Bliss, 59, 155–56, 194, 235, 236
  Funston and, 228, 230–31, 234–35, 239–40, 259, 282, 298, 299, 302, 304–5, 327–28
  Gavira's meeting with, 290–91
  as military commander, xv–xvi, xviii–xix, 230–31, 234–47, 251–59, 261–62, 263, 264, 266, 275, 276–78, 279, 286, 290–94, 301–2, 304–6, 326, 327–28
  as military strategist, 241–48, 264–65, 266, 289–90
  nickname of, 251
  Parral gunfight and, 275, 276–77
  Patton and, xviii, 238, 259, 261, 305, 306
  photographs of, 194, 200, 204
  at San Geronimo Ranch, 259, 261–62, 263–64, 265, 267
  at Satevó, 267, 276
  staff of, 251, 259, 277
  Villa's meeting with, 155–56, 194
  in World War I, xviii–xix, 306, 326, 327–28
Pershing, Warren, 235
Pesqueira, Ignacio, 42
Philippine Insurrection, 125–26, 235, 237, 251
Piedras Negras, 42, 43
Pino Juárez, José María, 8–9, 10, 25, 26, 27–29, 30, 70, 141
Plan of Ayala, 154, 162, 163, 358

Plan of Guadelupe, 42–43, 50, 63, 156, 182, 339–40, 343–44
Plan of San Diego, 211–14
Polk, James K., xvi
Prairie, 106, 110, 111, 113, 116, 117, 118, 119, 121
prostitution, 126–27, 137, 305–6
Providencia, 262
Puebla, 172
Pueblo, 282
Puerto México, 148, 149, 150
Punitive Expedition, 228–307
  African-Americans in, 229, 265
  aircraft used by, 203, 234, 242, 248, 254–57, 259, 262–63, 293
  anti-U.S. sentiment as result of, 231–32, 270–71
  Apache scouts for, 202, 305
  artillery of, 254, 302
  border raids as reason for, 187, 210–14, 227, 228–34, 281
  Carrancista forces and, 232, 240, 247, 249, 263–64, 267–75, 276, 277, 278–79, 284–86, 289, 290–300, 301–2
  Carranza and, 231–34, 236, 239, 245, 252, 279, 280–82, 286, 287, 291–93, 299–300, 303, 307
  in Casas Grandes, 236, 241–45, 251–59, 277
  cavalry of, 237, 257–58, 293
  in Chihuahua, xix, 201, 234, 241, 252, 263, 283, 289–90, 293, 298, 301–2, 304–5, 340
  Columbus, N.Mex. raid and, 227, 228–34, 283
  communications of, 239, 248, 251, 255–56, 257–58, 259, 262, 275, 276, 277
  congressional support for, 240, 253, 280
  field telegraph used by, 239, 258, 259, 276
  Funston and, 234–35, 236, 239–40, 255, 256, 304–5, 307
  ineffectiveness of, xv, 236, 328
  infantry of, 236, 237n, 240, 242, 277–78, 284n
  as intervention, xix, 231, 233, 263, 283, 289–90, 304–5
  joint commission, 302–3, 307
  Lansing and, 231, 233, 280, 282, 292, 299
  maps for, 244
  Mexican public reaction to, 231–32, 236, 241, 262–63, 270–71, 273, 279, 284, 290
  morale of, 305
  organization of, 234–35, 236–40
  Pershing as commander of, xv–xvi, xviii, xix, 230–31, 234–47, 251–59, 261–62,
    263, 264, 266, 275, 276–78, 279, 286, 290–94, 301–2, 304–6
  press coverage of, xx, 257–58, 259, 262, 279, 282, 284n, 285, 288, 291–92, 327
  railroads used by, 245, 246, 252
  Scott and, 230, 231, 235, 252–53, 281–86
  Scott-Obregón meeting on, 281–86
  sectors established by, 289–90
  supplies of, 203, 238–39, 252–54, 256–57, 267, 277, 278, 282, 283, 302
  surprise used by, 241
  timing of, 39–40, 252
  truck transport for, 252–54, 302
  U.S. businesses and, 280n
  U.S.-Mexican relations and, 231–34, 239–40, 279–80, 299–300, 302–3, 306–7, 366
  U.S. public reaction to, 232, 234, 257, 283, 284, 292, 302
  Villa pursued by, xv, xvi, xix, 4, 201, 230–31, 236, 241–50, 257–58, 262, 264, 265, 267, 268, 275, 279, 283, 284, 301, 303
  Villistas vs., 249–50, 265–66, 267, 268–69, 288–89, 290
  war as result of, 231, 280–81, 284, 285n, 286, 292, 299, 301, 303, 369
  Wilson and, 185, 231–34, 236, 239, 280, 281, 282, 286, 292, 299
  withdrawal of, 208, 275, 280, 284, 287, 290, 300, 301–7, 308, 309, 327
  World War I and, 254, 257, 280, 285n, 302–3, 306
  see also individual cavalry and infantry units

Querétaro convention, 307, 309–10, 313, 315

Rancho Casa Colorado, 261
Rancho Cienégita, 268–69
Ravel, Arthur, 225
Ravel, Louis, 225
Ravel, Samuel, 50, 225
Reed, John, 54, 57, 59n, 71, 76–78
Remington Company, 117
Rendón, Cecilia Almaguer, 212–13
Republican party, 103, 104
Revolution! (Atkin), 326n
Reyes, Bernardo, 12–18, 33–34, 40, 47
Richley, Jay, 272–73
Rintelen, Franz von, 184, 185
Ritchie, William T., 224
Rivas, Genevevo, 295
Riveroll, Jiménez, 24, 25
Robles, José Isabel, 157n, 170, 359

Robles, Miguel Alessio, 316, 317
Rodgers, James L., 281–82
Rodney, George B., 229–30, 274
Rodriguez, José, 216, 219
Romero, Ricardo, 7–9, 29
Roosevelt, Franklin D., 327
Roosevelt, Theodore, 32, 126, 235
Ruiz, Gregorio, 14, 15
Rush, W. R., 111, 115, 116, 121n
Ryan, James A., 251, 259
Ryan, Mrs. Thomas, 225

Salas, Colonel, 247
Salas Barraza, Jesús, 325
Salazar, José Inés, 57–58
Saltillo, 41, 42, 139, 140, 172
San Borja, 290
Sánchez, José María, 215
San Francisco, 107
San Geronimo Ranch, 259, 261–62, 263–64, 265, 267
San Isidro, 249
San Miguel Babícora, 243–46, 247, 248
Santa Anna, Antonio López de, 139
Santa Cruz de Villegas, 272, 273, 274, 276–77
Santa Isabel massacre, 214–16, 218, 219, 267
Santo Domingo Ranch, 294, 295, 297
San Zaragosa, 269–70
Satevó, 267, 276, 290, 303
Sayre, Francis B., 101
Scott, Hugh L.:
  Obregón's meeting with, 281–86
  Punitive Expedition and, 230, 231, 235, 252–53, 281–86
  Villa and, 127–28, 139, 171–72, 182, 185–86, 196, 360
Scott, Winfield, 120, 136
Second Cavalry, U.S., 237, 245
Seese, George L., 219, 228
Seventh Cavalry, U.S. ("Garryowens"), 237, 245, 246, 247–50, 256, 262, 277, 290
Shallenberger, Martin C., 238
Sixth Infantry, U.S., 284n
Slaughter, "Texas John," 189, 191
Slocum, Herbert J., 218, 219–21, 226, 227, 228, 290
Society of Friends of the American Ambassador, 20
Solace, 111, 118
soldaderas, 52, 98
Sonora, 31, 39, 42, 43–44, 62, 154–55, 188, 214, 293, 316, 317
South Carolina, 119
Spanish-American War, 125, 235

Spillsbury, Lemuel, 294, 295, 297
Standard Oil Corporation, 80
State Department, U.S., 31, 36, 100, 101, 231, 300
Suárez Mujica, Eduardo, 132n
Sulzberger, Cyrus L., 128
Sumner, 125
Sussex sinking, 280, 303
Swanberg, W. A., 292n

Taft, William Howard, 87
  Mexican policy of, xiv, 6, 19, 22, 23, 31, 32, 41
Tampico, 139, 311
Tampico incident, 79–108
  Bryan and, 101, 103
  Constitutionalist forces and, 79–81
  Dolphin seized in, 82, 99
  Federalist forces and, 80, 81, 82, 99, 100–101
  Huerta and, 100, 102, 103, 104
  Mayo's role in, 81, 82, 95, 99, 100, 101, 102, 103, 106, 107, 108
  Mexican reaction to, 100, 102, 104, 107
  political impact of, 99–108
  press coverage of, 80n, 101, 103–4
  U.S. congressional reaction to, 103, 104
  U.S. intervention based on, 104–8
  U.S. Navy and, 81, 82, 99–103
  U.S. residents and, 79, 80, 81, 104
  Veracruz landing and, 104–8, 127, 129, 131, 134
  Wilson and, 79, 101–6
Taylor, Zachary, 120
Tempest Over Mexico (King), 16n
Tenth Cavalry, U.S. ("Buffalo Soldiers"), 207, 229–30, 237, 245–46, 247, 256, 262, 263, 265–66, 267, 269, 274–79, 290, 291, 293–99
Ten Tragic Days, 12–29, 33, 40, 79, 106
Terrazas, Félix, 51
Terrazas, Silvestre, 51n, 71
Terrazas family, 51n, 72, 73
Texas, 211–14
Texas Rangers, 212–13
Thigpen, Dr., 209–10
Thirteenth Cavalry, U.S., 199, 217–27, 262, 267–75, 276, 277, 290
Thomas, Lowell, 121n
Tompkins, Frank, 226, 262, 299–300
  historical account by, xx, 219n, 237n, 254n, 264, 275, 278n, 285n
  in Parral gunfight, 270–75
  squadron commanded by, 264–75
Toral, José de León, 326
Torreón, 55–56, 60, 62, 127

Torreón conference, 151–52
Torrés, Elias L., 55, 181
Torres, Juana, 56
Treaty of Teoloyucan, 153
Treaty of Versailles, 327
Treviño, Jacinto, 241, 284, 293, 294, 295, 299, 304
Tumulty, Joseph, 122, 280, 281
Twenty Episodes in the Life of Pancho Villa (Torres), 181*n*

Union of German Citizens, 310
United States:
  arms embargoes by, 67–68, 79, 185
  Carranza recognized by, xix, 182–83, 185–86, 187, 188, 191, 214
  Carranza's relations with, 65–66, 67–68, 75
  Constitutionalists supported by, 65–66, 67–68, 75
  Díaz supported by, 33
  German relations with, 122, 184, 280, 302–3, 306, 311–12
  Huerta and recognition by, 26, 28, 30–33, 36–37, 41, 61, 63–64, 66, 67
  Mexican embassy of, 19–28, 30–31, 66–68, 129–30
  public opinion in, xiv, xv, 30
  Villa's relations with, 58, 66, 68, 74–75, 79, 127–28, 171–72, 182–83, 185–86, 187, 190, 191, 209, 361
  in World War I, xv, xviii, 311–12
  Zapata's relations with, 185
United States-Mexican relations:
  Benton affair and, 75–78
  border raids and, 210–16
  foreign investment and, xi–xii
  historical importance of, xvi
  Huerta regime and, 31, 36–37
  improvement of, xxi, 60, 302–3, 306–7, 310
  Lansing's policies and, 183
  Tampico incident and, 79–108
  Punitive Expedition and, 231–34, 239–40, 279–80, 299–300, 302–3, 306–7, 366
  Veracruz landing and, 104–8, 129–34
  war and, xii, 64–65, 104–5, 280–81
United States-Mexican War, xvi, 120, 121, 139
Urbina, Tomás, xiv*n*, 38, 55, 143, 144, 168, 170, 180–81, 195
Utah, 106, 110, 111, 113, 116, 117, 118, 119

Valle de Zaragosa, 279
Velasco, José Refugio, 152–53

venereal disease, 137, 305–6
Veracruz, 80, 166, 173, 328
Veracruz, 80
Veracruz landing, 109–38
  ABC mediators for, 131–34
  Bryan and, 107, 108, 118, 122, 127, 128, 131, 132
  Carranza and, 127, 128, 131–32, 140, 156
  casualties in, 119, 121
  cease-fire in, 117–18
  customhouse seized in, 107, 111, 118
  Fletcher's role in, 106, 107, 109–11, 116, 117, 118, 119–22, 123, 126, 134, 136, 327
  Funston and, 123, 125–27, 134–38, 153, 156, 166
  Huerta and, 104, 105, 108, 117, 124, 127, 129–34, 138
  Latin American reaction to, 128, 131–34
  map for, 112
  martial law in, 123–24
  Mexican opposition in, 109–10, 114–22, 134
  Mexican residents in, 123, 156, 166
  military government in, 126, 134–38
  morale in, 137–38
  photograph of, 96
  points of interest in, 339–40
  political impact of, 127–34
  press coverage of, 119, 122, 127, 128, 135–36, 138
  sanitation implemented in, 136–37
  signalmen in, 116
  sniper fire in, 116–17, 119–20
  Tampico incident and, 104–8, 127, 129, 131, 134
  U.S. congressional support for, 104–5, 106, 128, 131
  U.S. consulate in, 110–13
  U.S. land forces in, 106, 108, 113–23, 126–27
  U.S.-Mexican relations and, 104–8, 129–34
  U.S. naval forces in, 106–8, 111, 116, 117, 118, 119, 121, 126–27
  U.S. occupation in, xiv, xvi, 113–38, 148
  U.S. residents in, 111, 113, 115, 120, 121, 136
  Villa and, 127–28
  war as result of, 104–5, 127, 134
  Wilson and, 104–8, 118–19, 122, 127–34
  withdrawal of forces in, 156, 166
  Ypiranga shipment and, 104, 105, 106, 107, 108, 109, 110, 113, 117, 118, 122
Villa, Francisco ("Pancho"):
  as administrator, 59, 69, 73

Villa, Francisco (*continued*)
Aguascalientes Convention and, 158–60,
161, 162, 163, 164, 166, 172
Ascensión as base of, 50
assassination of, 321–22, 340
as bandit, 46–47, 53, 218–19, 265, 303–4,
312, 320
Benton affair and, 72–78
bribery of, 320, 322
Bryan and, 156
at Bustillos meeting, 4, 5
Carranza opposed by, xv, xvii, xix, 57, 69,
133, 140–42, 145, 146, 147, 151–52,
156–57, 158, 164, 173, 181, 182–83,
210, 218, 227, 308
Carranza's telegraphic conference with,
141–42, 164
Carranza supported by, 50–51, 53
cattle stolen by, 51*n*, 72, 73
character of, xvii, xx, 71–72
in Chihuahua, 46–47, 48, 55, 59, 62,
69–78, 188, 210, 243, 304, 312
Columbus raid commanded by, xv,
218–19, 221, 223, 227, 228, 248, 264
Constitutionalists and, 50
death sentence for, 47
downfall of, 180–83, 209–10
in El Paso, Tex., 47–48
Gutiérrez and, 166, 168, 170–71
hacienda of, 322–23
Huerta opposed by, 47, 52, 128, 149
as Indian, xviii
Madero supported by, xiv, 46, 47, 52, 57,
69, 147
manifesto of, 172–73
"marriages" of, 47*n*, 56
Mexico City threatened by, 54, 138, 140,
146, 165–71
military ceremony for, 71–72
as military chief of Mexico, 166, 170,
172–74
as military commander, xx, 46, 62, 69–71,
97, 140, 142, 149, 151–52, 163, 164,
172–73, 174, 180–81, 312
as military strategist, 48, 55, 56–57,
69–70, 143–44, 188, 221
narrow escape of, 241–50
Obregón's defeat of, xv, 174, 175–80, 182,
188
Obregón's opposition to, xvii, 148, 151,
154–58, 160, 322, 323–24, 325
Pershing's meeting with, 155–56, 194
photographs of, 85, 89, 163, 168, 194,
195, 196
popular support for, 47, 53, 180–83, 236,
264, 271

press coverage of, 53–54, 75, 78, 128, 179
prisoners executed by, 51, 53, 55
Punitive Expedition as directed against,
xv, xvi, xix, 4, 201, 230–31, 236,
241–50, 257–58, 262, 264, 265, 267,
268, 275, 279, 283, 284, 301, 303
reign of terror by, 165–71
reputation of, 46–47, 53, 54, 69, 72–78
resignation submitted by, 142, 164
retirement of, 322–24
in return to Mexico, 46–50
revenge sought by, 47, 52–53
as revolutionary, xiv, xviii, 4, 5, 45, 69
Scott and, 127–28, 139, 171–72, 182,
185–86, 196, 360
Torreón conference and, 151–52
U.S. relations with, 58, 66, 68, 74–75, 79,
127–28, 171–72, 182–83, 185–86, 187,
190, 191, 209, 361
Veracruz landing and, 127–28
violent acts of, 51, 53, 55, 72–78, 157–58,
165–71, 180–81, 209–10, 219
Wilson and, 171
wounding of, 249, 250, 260–61, 264, 303
Zapata and, xviii, 63, 147, 165–70, 195
Villa Ahumada, 293, 294, 295, 296, 340
Villar, Lauro ("Remington"), 14, 15, 16, 17
Villarreal, Antonio I., 154, 159, 164, 172

Walker, Walton R., 225
"War of the Winners," xix
Warren, Francis E., 235
Washington, George, 28, 327
Watson, Charles, 215, 216
Wellington, Arthur Wellesley, Duke of, 250
Wilder, Wilbur E., 290
Wilhelm II, Emperor of Germany, 34, 311,
312
Williams, George, 225–26
Wilson, Ellen Axson, 101
Wilson, Henry Lane, 18, 19–28, 30–31, 36,
37, 41, 66, 79, 88, 106, 310, 347
Wilson, Jessie, 101
Wilson, John Lockwood, 19
Wilson, Margaret, 101
Wilson, Woodrow:
Carranza and, 65, 67–68, 182, 183,
185–86, 188, 190, 191, 216, 231–34,
302, 303, 306, 307
character of, xvi, 327
Columbus, N.Mex. raid and, 228
Huerta opposed by, xix, 32–33, 36–37, 61,
63–68, 75, 104, 105, 129–34, 149
Mexican policy of, xii, xiv, xv, 32, 60,
63–68, 75, 131–32, 173, 185–86, 211,
281, 286, 327

Obregón and, 308, 315
photograph of, 87
Punitive Expedition and, 185, 231–34,
236, 239, 280, 281, 282, 286, 292, 299
reelection of, 234, 303
Tampico incident and, 79, 101–6
Veracruz landing and, 104–8, 118–19,
122, 127–34
Villa and, 171
"watchful waiting" by, 60, 75, 103
World War I and, 280, 320–21, 326–27
World War I:
aircraft used in, 254
Mexican Revolution and, xv, 152, 175–76,
327
Pershing as commander in, xviii–xix, 306,
326, 327–28
Punitive Expedition and, 254, 257, 280,
285n, 302–3, 306
U.S. entry into, xv, xviii, 311–12
Wilson's role in, 280, 320–21, 326–27
World War II, 327
Wright, Maud, 225
Wright, Orville, 254
Wyoming, 212

Xochimilco, Mexico, 154, 338

Yaqui Indians, 97, 162, 209, 316
yellow fever, 136–37

Ypiranga, 104, 105, 106, 107, 108, 109, 110,
113, 117, 118, 122

Zapata, Emiliano:
Aguascalientes Convention and, 159,
160–62, 163
assassination of, 313–14, 321
Carranza and, 63, 147, 153–54, 164,
313–14
Díaz opposed by, 146
Huerta opposed by, 33, 63, 146
as Indian, xviii
land reform supported by, xviii, 11,
146–47, 153, 160
Madero opposed by, 11, 38, 39, 147, 167
Mexico City threatened by, 135, 138, 146,
165–71
as military commander, 164
Morelos controlled by, xviii, 39, 146, 313,
314, 338–39
Obregón and, 153, 172
as "peasant general," 91
photographs of, 91, 168, 195
reign of terror by, 165–71
as revolutionary, xiv, xviii, 5, 146–47
U.S. relations with, 185
Villa and, xviii, 63, 147, 165–70, 195
Zapata, Eufemio, 167
Zimmermann, Arthur, 311
Zimmermann telegram, 311–12

H. C. C.
LIBRARY